CONTENTS

THE PRESIDENT WAS HERE!

Facts and artifacts from more than 200 years on the Lehigh Valley campaign trail

THE MORNING CALL
A TRIBUNE PUBLISHING COMPANY

WRITER: Daniel Patrick Sheehan
EDITOR: William Scheihing
PHOTO EDITOR: Harry Fisher
DESIGN: Jessica DeLorenzo, Craig Larimer, and Martha Miller
PROJECT MANAGER: Dave Dawson

Printed in the United States of America.

ISBN: 978-0-9829422-2-2
Library of Congress Control Number: 2012943796
First edition

ACKNOWLEDGMENTS

The Morning Call extends deep gratitude to the many individuals and institutions that have made it possible to pull together the photographs and artifacts at the heart of this book. "The President Was Here!" would not have come to life without their support and cooperation.

Special thanks go to Kurt Zwikl, a collector of presidential memorabilia for decades, for his guidance and for opening his collection of photographs and memorabilia to us.

Joseph Garrera, executive director, and Jill Youngken, assistant director of the Lehigh Valley Heritage Museum, Allentown, dug deep into their archives to provide a variety of material and made valuable suggestions. Lanie Graf, assistant archivist, Moravian Archives, Bethlehem, provided valuable assistance to the project, and Megan van Ravenswaay, director of the Moravian Historical Society, Nazareth, brought some unexpected and remarkable artifacts to our attention.

Thanks also to Diane Shaw, archivist at Lafayette College's Skillman Library, Easton; Amy Frey, curator, Historic Bethlehem Partnership, Bethlehem; Diane Koch, special collections librarian, Trexler Library, Muhlenberg College, Allentown; presidential memorabilia collectors Stephen Cunningham of Nazareth, William Albert of Catasauqua and Les Barley of Allentown; Ronald Demkee, director of the Allentown Band; Alexandra Lane, rights and reproductions coordinator, the White House Historical Association, Washington, D.C.; Anne Evenhaugen, reference librarian, Smithsonian Institution, Washington, D.C.; and John Zolomij, Whitehall, former curator of the Ray Holland Collection.

INTRODUCTION

When Bill Clinton visited the Charcoal Drive-In near Allentown, left his coffee cup (dregs and all) and the diner permanently encased it in glass, it was as quirky as it gets.

Or was it? It turns out, when The Morning Call began digging into the history of Lehigh Valley presidential visits, we found no end to quirky.

The deeper we scratched, the more amused we became. And the more we felt we had to share this history beyond our newsroom.

The result is "The President Was Here! Facts and artifacts from more than 200 years on the Lehigh Valley campaign trail."

But this is no textbook history.

You'll read about Bill Clinton's dirty coffee cup and also find that George Washington left something behind, too – a lock of hair. We'll tell you why. You'll learn about a private shrine to Eleanor Roosevelt in the Lehigh Valley. You'll find pearls left behind by others. Like Harry Truman. In a Bethlehem speech, Truman condemned "the awful do-nothing 80th Congress," a body that rejected universal health care. (As this book goes to press in the heat of the 2012 presidential election, thank goodness that kind of politics is behind us!) Or, John Adams who visited the Lehigh Valley three times and described Bethlehem as "curious and remarkable ... agreeably diversified with prospects of Orchards and Fields, Groves and Meadows, Hills and Valleys ..." Or Franklin D. Roosevelt, perhaps less taken with the Lehigh Valley, who spent only six minutes at one stop and blew by the rest on a train.

There was Johnson, Nixon and Kennedy. (That was in the day when 85,000 people once gathered to see a president here. You'll marvel at photographs from that era and others carefully selected by the project's photo editor, Harry Fisher, who combed through archives of hundreds of images.) There was Ford, Carter and Reagan. Bush, Dole and Hart. Obama, McCain and Palin.

In all, 24 chief executives visited, not counting vice presidents, surrogates and candidates.

They came on horseback, by train and by Air Force One.

"Maybe people have one chance to see a president drive through in a motorcade but this book will give a historical look over the years ... something the average person has no idea of and can't experience on his own," said Kurt D. Zwikl, a local expert on presidential history who advised The Morning Call on the project. "This book puts it into one place, will be something people can look at every presidential year and is a great way to tell a community story," said Zwikl, a former chairman of the Pennsylvania Historical and Museum Commission.

This project is part of an ongoing effort by The Morning Call to bring the area's rich history to life in a way that is accessible to many. Staff writer Daniel Patrick Sheehan continues this tradition by bringing a light touch to this history as well. (Visit morningcallstore.com to access other projects – "Forging America," an original 158-page story that chronicles how Bethlehem Steel changed the face of America, and "War Stories," a collection of stories as told by Pennsylvanians who served in the armed forces during the major U.S. wars of the 20th century.)

Drawing from the archives of the newspaper and with the generous help of area collectors, museums and libraries, this work offers a unique look back at presidential events, illustrated with dozens of newspaper pages, campaign buttons and ribbons, photos and other memorabilia. From the likely – an "I Like Ike" button – to the unlikely – a tassel from the cover on the catafalque that carried Lincoln's casket – the reader will find history seen from a very intimate and local perspective.

As a bonus, you'll get more than 100 years of history as told through the front pages of The Morning Call.

Enjoy our story of presidents as the Lehigh Valley knew them.

David M. Erdman
Editor and Vice President
The Morning Call

PART I

Horses and Trains

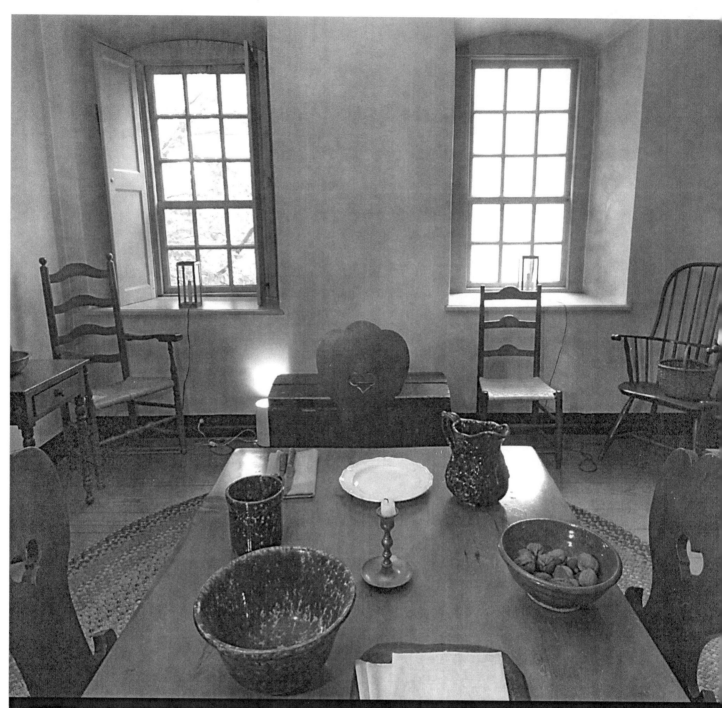

ABOVE: Travel on horseback and dining by candlelight were the norm when politicians traveled in the nation's early days. The dining hall at the Sun Inn is maintained today as it was when John Adams visited Bethlehem in 1777. (Harry Fisher, The Morning Call)

BELOW: Bethlehem in 1784. The Moravians' substantial buildings and well-managed farmland always impressed visitors. (Courtesy of the Moravian Archives)

THE LEHIGH VALLEY

A stop along the way

We begin with a small but gratifying boast, one made by many towns and cities in this part of the country: "George Washington slept here."

Not only can the people of the Lehigh Valley make that claim — they can show you the inn where Washington slept and took meals, because it still stands. And the story gets better. John Adams dined and slept in the same place, the Sun Inn on Main Street in Bethlehem, where he marveled at the hospitality and industry of the city's Moravian founders.

Both men visited many years before their presidencies, but they were the first in a long line of chief executives, 24 in all, to spend time in the Valley before, during or after serving in the nation's highest office.

In the latter half of the 20th century, Pennsylvania would become a significant player in national elections and the Valley a common stopping point for presidential candidates. But in earlier times, the presidents who visited the area usually did so on the way to or from some other engagement in some more significant place — New York or Washington, D.C., Philadelphia or Baltimore.

There was, after all, little here to retain a traveler. The Valley was a densely forested place interspersed with small settlements and roads that were hardly more than Indian trails.

Still, its natural beauty left an impression. In the early 1780s, Englishman George Grieve translated the recollections of the Marquis de Chastellux, a major-general in the French army allied with Washington during the Revolutionary War. In a section on Bethlehem, Grieve, who had lived in America for a time, felt compelled to record his first sighting of the Moravians' stone buildings on the north bank of the Lehigh River:

The first time I visited Bethlehem ... [when] issuing out of the woods at the close of the evening in the month of May, [I] found myself on a beautiful extensive plain, with the vast eastern branch of the Delaware on the right [the name for the Lehigh at the time], richly interspersed with wooded islands, and at the distance of a mile in front the town of Bethlehem, rearing its large stone edifices out of a forest, situated on a majestic, but gradually rising eminence, the background formed the setting sun. So novel and unexpected a transition filled the mind with a thousand singular and sublime ideas and made an impression on me never to be effaced.

Soon enough, that idyllic landscape would begin to disappear under the advance of modernity. Over two centuries, trees were supplanted by smokestacks, farms by factories, Indian trails by interstates.

The modern visitor, swooping in from above on the approach to Lehigh Valley International Airport, sees edifices far different from those that greeted George Grieve: the PPL Building, Martin Tower, Coca-Cola Park, the Lehigh Valley Mall.

Think of it another way: John Adams arrived in the Valley on horseback, Teddy Roosevelt on a train, Barack Obama on Air Force One.

Though the area may have been something of a presidential afterthought for much of its history, the people didn't hold that against the presidents. From the days of Martin Van Buren on, they were feted grandly, with cannon roar and musical serenades and cheerleaders and confetti.

Some came to campaign. Some came to attend college commencements or to give speeches to civic groups or to dedicate buildings. Some (James Buchanan, Benjamin Harrison) visited once and never again. Others (Teddy Roosevelt, William Howard Taft) came a number of times.

In the beginning, though, the first distinguished visitors — Mr. Adams and Gen. Washington — were greeted quietly by the Moravians.

That's where our story starts.

LEFT TOP: An order of protection from the Continental Congress delegates assembled at the Sun Inn in Bethlehem, including John Adams, Samuel Adams and John Hancock. The text, dated Sept. 22, 1777, reads:

Having here observed a humane and diligent attention to the sick and wounded, and a benevolent desire to make the necessary provision for the relief of the distressed, as far as the powers of the Brethren enable them. We desire that all Continental Officers may refrain from disturbing the persons or property of the Moravians in Bethlehem, and particularly that they do not disturb or molest the Houses where the women are assembled. Given under our hands at the time and place above mentioned.

RIGHT TOP: A portrait of John Adams by John Trumbull. (Courtesy of the White House Historical Association)

RIGHT BOTTOM: The traditional Moravian women's white head covering, Haube in German, is displayed on a mannequin at the Kemerer Museum in Bethlehem. The women sat together in church, and the sight brought a cabbage patch to the mind of the visiting John Adams.

LEFT BOTTOM: A German-language Moravian diary entry from Jan. 25, 1777, notes the passage through Bethlehem of John Adams. The entry says Adams and his traveling companions, James Lovell and Lyman Hall, delegates to the Continental Congress, spent the night at the Sun Inn. (Courtesy of the Moravian Archives)

PAGE 12: The Moravian Sisters' House. John Adams found the atmosphere here oppressive and unhealthful for the Moravian women. (Harry Fisher, The Morning Call)

PAGE 13: The sign outside the Sun Inn. This was a common stop for members of the Continental Congress. John Adams stayed here in 1777, George Washington in 1782. (Morning Call Archives)

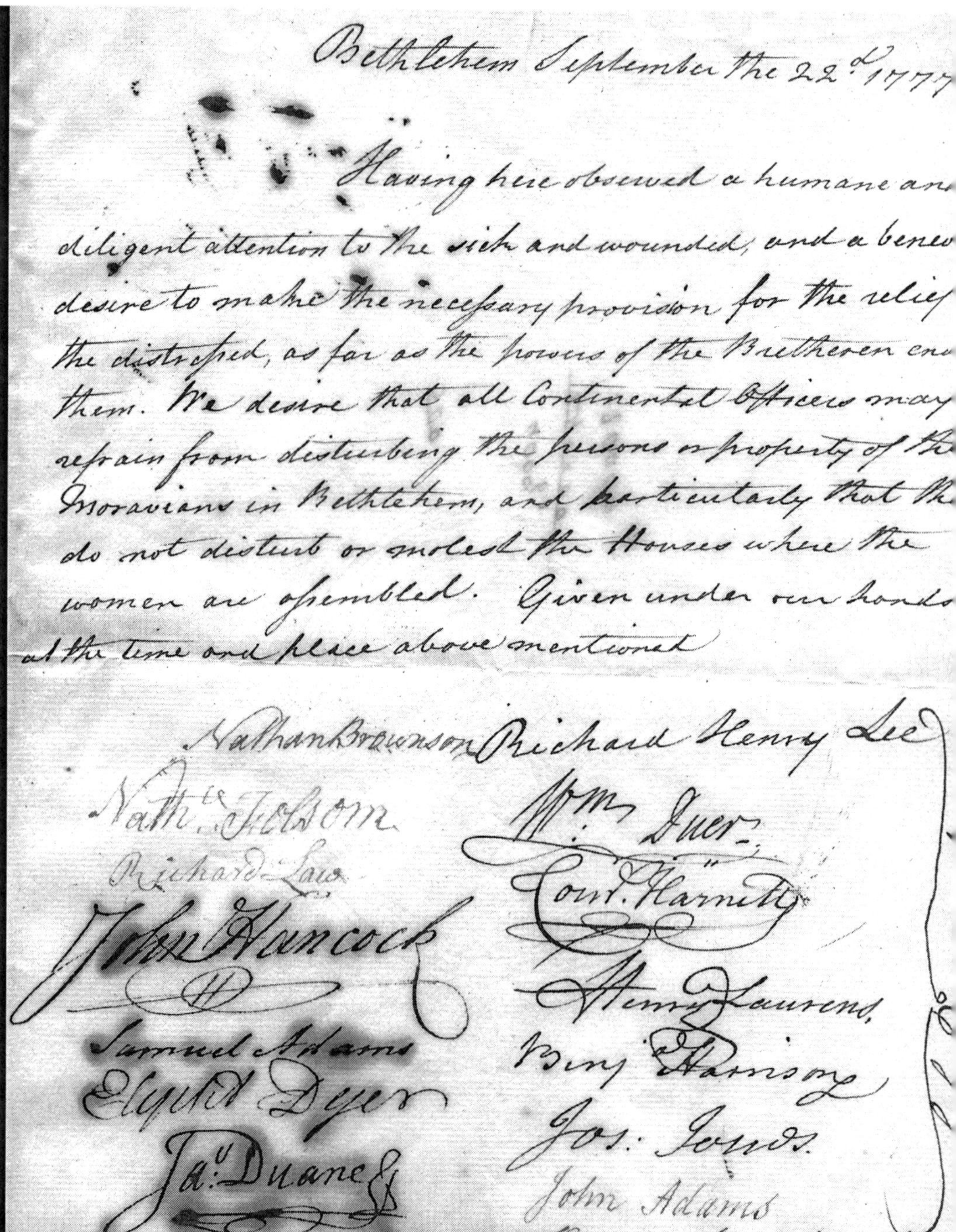

Bethlehem September the 22d 1777

Having here observed a humane an[d] diligent attention to the sick and wounded, and a benev[olent] desire to make the necessary provision for the relie[f of] the distressed, as far as the powers of the Brethren ena[ble] them. We desire that all Continental Officers may refrain from disturbing the persons or property of the Moravians in Bethlehem, and particularly that the[y] do not disturb or molest the Houses where the women are assembled. Given under our hands at the time and place above mentioned

Nathan Brownson Richard Henry Lee
Nath. Folsom Wm. Duer
Richard Law Cornl. Harnett
John Hancock Henry Laurens
Samuel Adams Benj Harrison
Eliphd Dyer Jos. Jones
Jas. Duane John Adams

den 25ten Jan.

Von Boston kamen 3 Congreß Herren J. Ada[ms], Lovel und - - - Hall auf ihrer Reise nach Baltimore ... Bethlehem. Sie versprachen Br. Klose ihm zu dem ... Von Newyork erhielten wir Brie[fe] von Br. Schaukirch durch Br. Abraham v. Vleck vom 13ten dieses.

den 26ten Jan.

ADAMS

John Adams in the cabbage patch: 1777

John Adams was the second president of the United States, but he was the first future holder of the office to visit the Lehigh Valley, beating George Washington here by five years.

Adams came three times in 1777, the third year of the Revolutionary War. At that time, the Valley was a sparsely settled area of farms and woodlands, at least a two-day ride from Philadelphia. Its most important community was the Moravian religious settlement of Bethlehem, which had been founded in 1741 on a 500-acre tract where the Monocacy Creek flows into the Lehigh River. By the time of Adams' visits, Bethlehem consisted of about 60 properties.

The meticulous German-language diaries kept by the Moravians note the future president's first visit on Jan. 25, 1777. Adams, James Lovell and Lyman Hall — delegates to the Continental Congress that would be convening in Baltimore after fleeing the British advance on Philadelphia — "arrived here ... and lodged at the [Sun] Inn. They were shown objects of interest. (They left the next day.)"

Adams was beguiled by his first sight of Bethlehem. Writing later from Baltimore to his wife, Abigail, he described it as "curious and remarkable ... agreeably diversified with prospects of Orchards and Fields, Groves and Meadows, Hills and Valleys ..."

He loved the Sun Inn, "which I think was the best Inn I ever saw."

Congress adjourned in February and delegates left Baltimore to return to Philadelphia. But in September, Adams and the other delegates again fled the British, who were advancing on the city once more after defeating Washington at the Battle of Brandywine.

The fugitives, who would have been hanged for treason had they fallen into British hands, made their way through the Lehigh Valley and west to York, which became the temporary capital.

Adams' diary shows that on his second visit to the Lehigh Valley, he stopped and ate in Quakertown and Easton before arriving in Bethlehem, where he and 13 other delegates convened at the Sun Inn.

Among other matters, they composed a letter commending the Moravians for their care of casualties from the battles around Philadelphia, and ordering the Continental Army to refrain from disturbing their "persons or property ... And particularly that they do not disturb or molest the Houses where the women are assembled."

Besides Adams, the signers included John Hancock, with his familiar bold flourish, and Samuel Adams, whose signature is immediately recognizable to a generation of beer lovers.

John Adams wasn't entirely complimentary of Moravian ways. He complained, for example, that the heat and stale air in the Sisters' House "must I think destroy their Health. Their Countenances were languid and pale."

But by and large he found the place and its people engaging. After church services on Sept. 24, he whimsically noted in his diary that the heads of the bonnet-wearing Moravian women looked like "a Garden of White Cabbage Heads."

In November, Adams visited the Lehigh Valley for the third time, passing through on his way from York to his home in Massachusetts. He paused in Allentown and met with James Allen, son of city founder William Allen, who noted in his diary that Adams declared independence "unalterably settled." That was unhappy news for Allen, a loyalist Tory.

Adams moved on to Bethlehem, dined at the Sun Inn and spent the night at a private home in Easton. That was his last visit to the region, though not his last dealings with its people.

As president in 1799, he would order the quelling of Fries's Rebellion, an anti-tax revolt by Pennsylvania Dutch farmers in Northampton, Bucks and Montgomery counties led by Quakertown auctioneer John Fries.

Fries and his followers harassed and intimidated tax assessors. The rebels were arrested after marching on the Sun Inn in an effort to free several tax protesters being held there.

Fries and two other rebels were convicted of treason and sentenced to be hanged. Adams, however, who regarded the whole episode as a contrivance by political enemies to embarrass him, pardoned the men. He later issued a general amnesty to everyone involved.

1758
SUN
INN

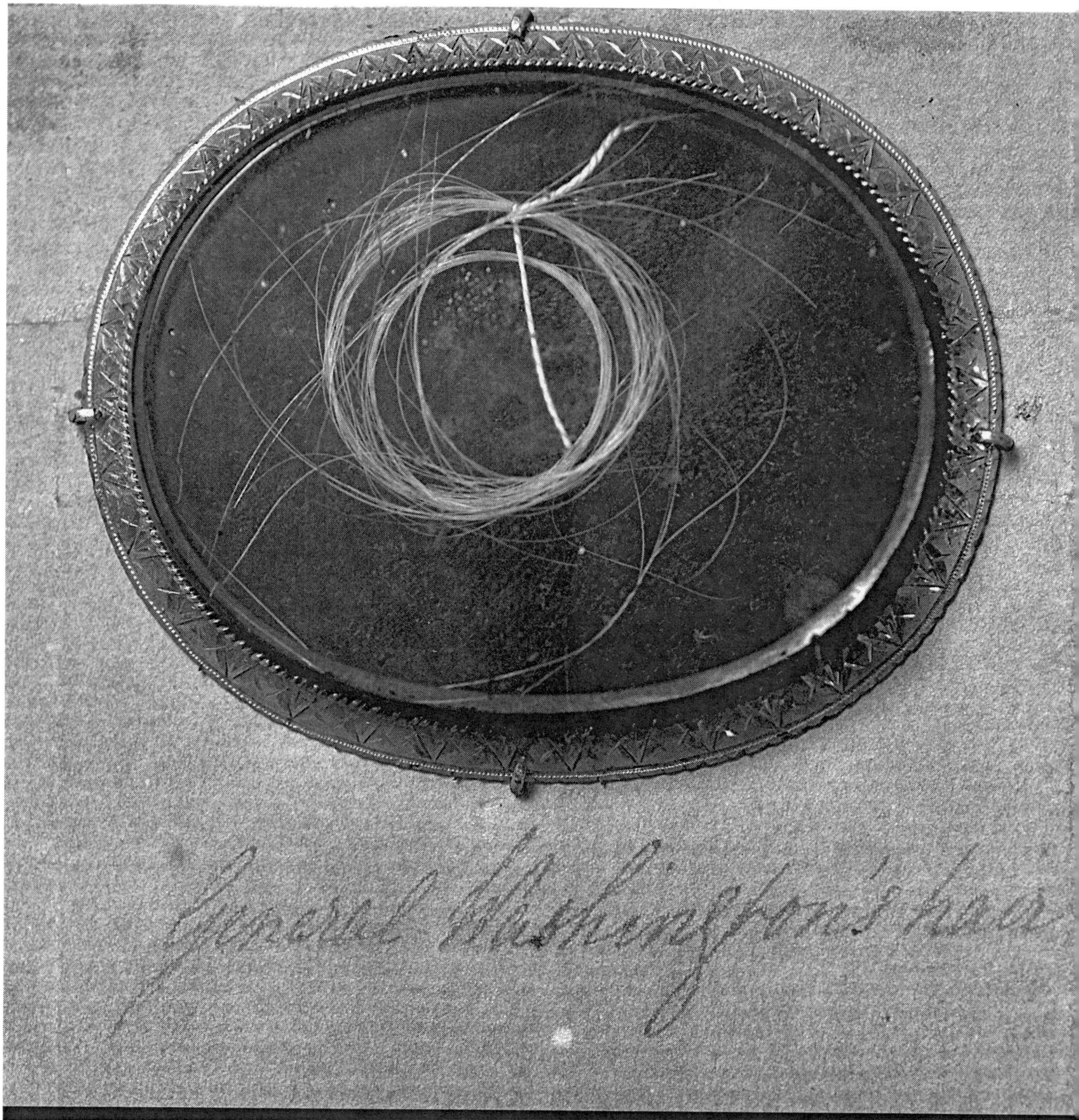

ABOVE: A lock of Gen. George Washington's hair, snipped as a souvenir by a Moravian woman during the future president's stop in Bethlehem in July 1782. The lock is kept at the Moravian Historical Society's Whitefield House in Nazareth.

LEFT: This brass clothing button inscribed "GW Long Live the President" is one of many varieties of buttons produced to commemorate the first president's inauguration in 1789. Produced by New York and Connecticut button makers, the pieces were worn as functional buttons. They are considered by some historians to be forerunners of modern political buttons.

RIGHT TOP: A stipple engraving of Washington from an etching by Joseph Wright. Originally published in Ladies Magazine of London in June 1795. (Courtesy of Kurt Zwikl of Allentown)

RIGHT BOTTOM: The English translation of a German-language Moravian diary noting the arrival of Gen. Washington to Bethlehem in July 1782. (Courtesy of Moravian Historical Society)

WASHINGTON

Hair's to you, George Washington: 1782

Long before his presidency, George Washington was the most famous man in the fledgling United States. So when the great general dined at Bethlehem's Sun Inn in July 1782, it occurred to Anna Gambold, a young Moravian woman, to ask for a lock of his hair as a keepsake.

Such requests were not unheard of. As people today seek autographs, the starstruck of the time sought hair. "Everyone could relate to it," says Megan van Ravenswaay, director of the Moravian Historical Society's Whitefield House in Nazareth, where the lock is kept today. "Though it was more common to clip hair off corpses."

Washington, with two aides, had arrived unexpectedly in Bethlehem on July 25 as he traveled from a conference in Philadelphia to Continental Army headquarters at Newburgh, N.Y.

The German-language diary of the community notes the future president's visit, indicating he was serenaded by trombone music, toured the village with several brethren and attended an evening worship service at the Old Chapel.

He spent the night at the Sun Inn — a popular stopover for members of the military and the Continental Congress — before departing early the next morning for New York.

Bethlehem had been founded as a Moravian religious community in 1741. Men and women lived a communal life, segregated into living arrangements according to their circumstances.

It's tempting to imagine the encounter between Gambold, the 20-year-old wife of a missionary, and the imposing Washington, who was held in such esteem that some wanted him named king of the new nation. "She must have been a firecracker," van Ravenswaay said.

Washington surrendered more than one snippet of hair in his day. The Maine Historical Society owns one. So does Arlington House, the memorial to Confederate Gen. Robert E. Lee in Virginia. In early 2012, an antiques show in New York City included a lock priced at $40,000. And a Virginia man paid $17,000 at auction in 2008 for four strands of hair taken from the president in 1837, when his body was briefly disinterred to be buried in a new marble tomb at Mount Vernon, his Virginia plantation.

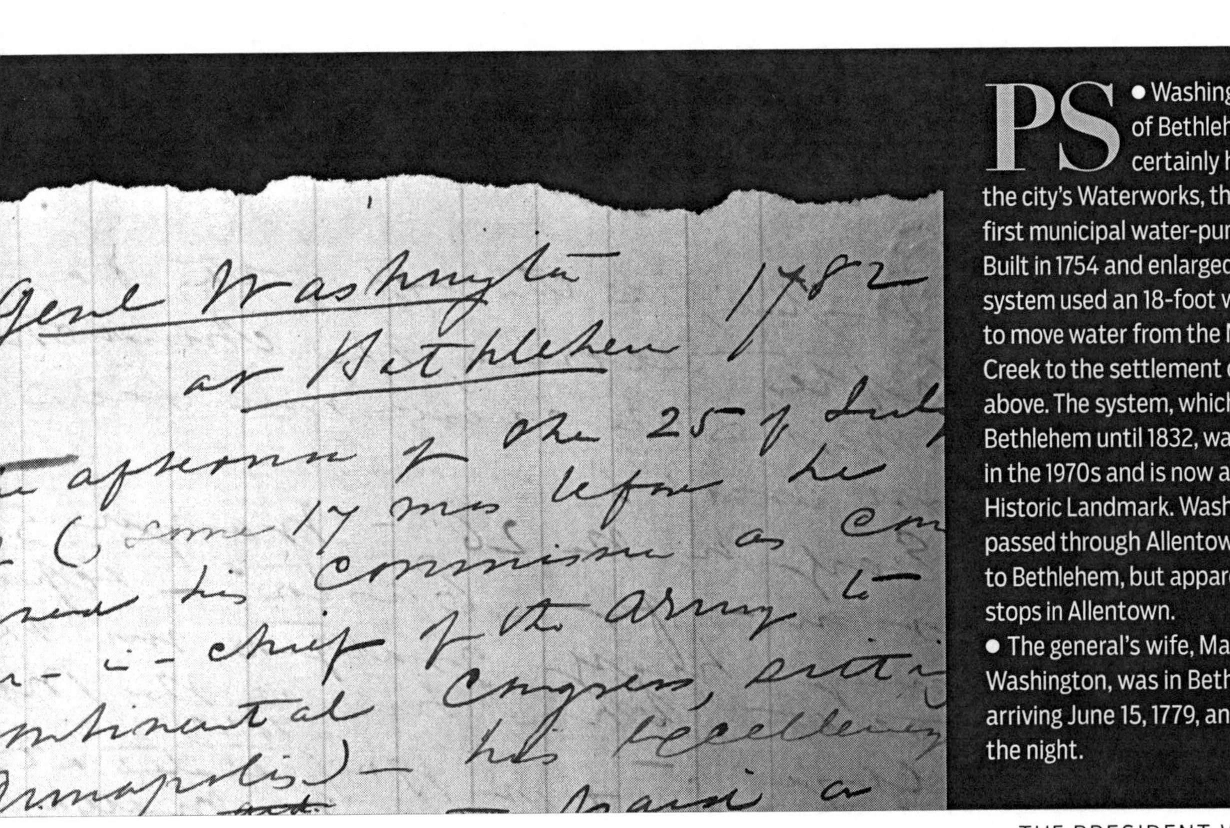

Genl Washington 1782
at Bethlehem
afternoon of the 25 of July
(some 17 mos before he
his commission as Com
Chief of the Army to
Congress, sitti
his Excellency

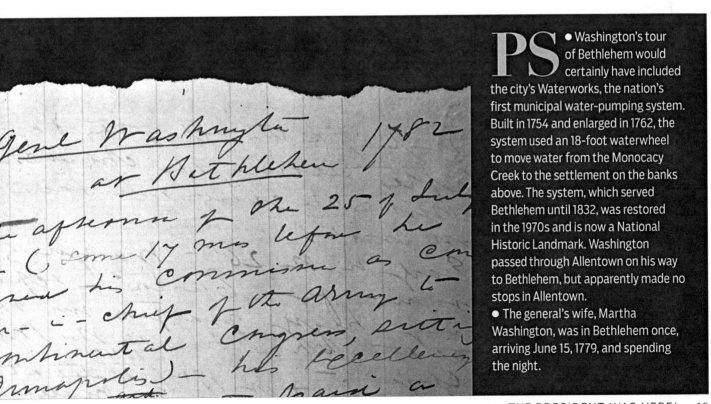

PS • Washington's tour of Bethlehem would certainly have included the city's Waterworks, the nation's first municipal water-pumping system. Built in 1754 and enlarged in 1762, the system used an 18-foot waterwheel to move water from the Monocacy Creek to the settlement on the banks above. The system, which served Bethlehem until 1832, was restored in the 1970s and is now a National Historic Landmark. Washington passed through Allentown on his way to Bethlehem, but apparently made no stops in Allentown.

• The general's wife, Martha Washington, was in Bethlehem once, arriving June 15, 1779, and spending the night.

Der Republikaner.

"Für's Vaterland."

Northampton, den 5ten October, 1836.

Demokratischer = Republikanischer

Wahl=Zettel,

: Lecha Caunty für das Jahr 1836.

Für Congreß:

Edward B. Hubley.

Assembly:

acob Erdman, Ober=Sacona,
eorge Friedrich, Wheithall.

Commißioner:

ohn Scherer, Nord=Wheithall.

Auditor:

harles S. Busch, für 3 Jahr.
acob Hart, für 1 Jahr.

Coroners:

acob Marks, Nied. Macungy.
jarles Foster, Ober=Milford.

Trustees:

ohn Wilson, St. Northampt.
athony Gangwer, do.

An meine Subscribenten.

lit dieser Nummer tretet der "Unabhängige
publikaner" seinen 27sten Jahrgang an.—
fortdauernde Vermehrung meiner Subscrip=
sliste, welche sich auf fast 2,500 erstreckt, liefert
zugleich den sichersten und angenehmsten Beweiß
allgemeinen Zufriedenheit des Publikums mit der
rung desselben.—Es würde daher ungerecht und
nkbar gehandelt seyn, wenn ich bei dieser Gelegen=
nicht den vielfältigen Gönnern und Freunden des
epublikaners" meinen aufrichtigen Dank
atten sollte, vorzüglich aber denjenigen, welche sich
er durch pünktliche Bezahlung als wirkliche
erstützer dieser Zeitung bewiesen haben.

Hubley! Freyheit! Gleichhe
Republikanismus
Freyheits Brüder!—tretet he
Der große Tag ist d

Wollt Ihr Eure theuersten und heili
an eine aristokratische Bank=Anstalt freyn
tragen und das Joch einer übermüthigen G
tie auf Euch nehmen—dann stimmt für
Reichard und Stöhr—denn diese sind alle
terstützer der Brittischen Bank und gehen
Hand für jene gefährliche Anstalt.

Wollt Ihr Euch als Unterstützer der
Inquisition beweisen, die Thaddeus Steve
Anhänger letzten Winter in Harrisburg
—dann stimmet für Audenried, Reichard
—denn diese Herren waren alle dafür, Ge
George M. Dallas und andere graugewor
ner in dem Gefängniß einzukerkern, weil
weigerten, ihre Rechte an dem Fußstuhl d
aufzuopfern.

Wollt Ihr Euch als Unterstützer des
Kopftaxes beweißen, der den armen Tag
im Schweiß seines Angesichts sein Brod ver
zwingt, so viel zu bezahlen, als der reiche
in Kutschen fährt und seine Millionen ei
stimmt für Audenried, Reichard, und S
diese sind alle Freunde des Kopftaxes und bi
was unter Ritner's verdorbenen Adminis
schieht.

Seyd Ihr zu Gunsten von Extra=Si
Assembly, wodurch dem Staat 50,000 Th
rechter Weise entzogen werden, bloß um g
litiker zu bereichern—dann stimmt für
Reichard und Stöhr—denn diese sind eifr
stützer von Extra=Sitzungen und dergleiche
gereyen.

Seyd Ihr aber allen diesen Uebelthat
—gegen die Bank—gegen die Spanische
—gegen den Kopftax—und gegen Extra=S
dann könnt Ihr mit Zuversicht für Hubley
und Friedrich stimmen—denn diese stehen
sowohl als mündlich verpflichtet, sich diese
lichen Handlungen aufs äußerste zu wider

Die Inspectors Wahlen

Die Demokraten von Lecha haben am let
tage bey den Inspectors=Wahlen einen
Anfang gemacht.—In fast jedem Taunsch
Kopftax=Männer Opposition machten,
Republikaner siegreich.

Süd Wheithall.—Jacob Henni
spector—John Troxel, Assessor.—Standha
kraten und Gegner des Kopftaxes.

Ober=Macungy.—Jesse Breinig,
—Jacob Schäffer Assessor.—Hier machte
tax=Leute keine Opposition.

Weisenburg.—Das Demokrati
siegreich.—John Geringer, ist Inspector—

VAN BUREN & THE HARRISONS

Martin Van Buren slept here: 1839

Many Americans know little more about Martin Van Buren than what they learned from that "Seinfeld" sitcom episode when Kramer saves himself from attack by accidentally flashing a gang sign.

Kramer holds up eight fingers and the imaginary gang the Van Buren Boys, named for the eighth president, backs off.

So there you have it. Martin Van Buren was the eighth president. Thanks, Kramer.

Dig a little deeper and you will discover that Van Buren was the first president born as an American citizen and not a British subject (though he grew up speaking Dutch at home); created the modern Democratic Party; and, most importantly for our purposes, was the first and thus far only sitting president to spend the night in Allentown.

That was June 26, 1839, two years after the Panic of 1837 — an economic calamity that marked his White House tenure and earned him the mocking nickname "Martin Van Ruin."

On his way to his home in New York after visits to Harrisburg, Reading and Kutztown, the president stayed at George Haberacker's inn at the northeast corner of Seventh and Hamilton streets.

But Allentown, at the time a modest borough of fewer than 2,500 people, was eager to welcome a sitting president, so borough leaders did not wait for Van Buren to come to them. A greeting party — including members of the Allentown Band, then in its 11th year — went to Kutztown to meet the presidential carriages and escort them back to town.

As the procession approached Allentown around 7 p.m., a welcoming volley of cannon fire roared from an area called Greisemer's Hill, at what is now 21st and Hamilton streets. Church bells rang out and citizens gathered along the road to cheer Van Buren as he passed.

The president passed the evening greeting residents and party members at the inn. He retired and recommenced his journey the next day, reaching Bethlehem by lunchtime to the strains of "Hail to the Chief" played by the municipal band.

Van Buren's arrival later that day in Easton was marked the same way as his arrival in Allentown, with a cannonade. The president spent the night at the American Hotel, greeting, among many others, students from Lafayette College and a few gray-whiskered veterans of the Revolutionary War.

The next morning, having traversed an adoring Lehigh Valley end to end, he passed into New Jersey.

In his successful 1836 campaign, Van Buren's opponent had been Whig Party candidate William Henry Harrison, who visited the Lehigh Valley on Oct. 2-3 and gave speeches in Allentown, Bethlehem and Easton.

Harrison had gained fame as a military officer, earning the moniker "Old Tippecanoe" for his victory in an 1811 battle against a confederacy of Indians opposing American expansion.

One newspaper described his Allentown remarks as "fluent" and "manly," but that didn't do him any good — Harrison lost the state by about 5,000 votes.

Four years later, Harrison ran again and this time beat Van Buren. But the tough old general — at age 68, he was the oldest man elected president to that point — caught pneumonia and died on the 32nd day of his term.

That wasn't the end of Harrisons in the White House. The president's grandson, Benjamin Harrison, was the nation's 23rd president. A Republican, he won the 1888 election and holds the trivial distinction of being the man who served between Democrat Grover Cleveland's nonconsecutive terms.

Eleven years before winning the White House, the younger Harrison had come to Lafayette College in Easton to watch his son, Russell, graduate with the Class of 1877. It was Benjamin Harrison's only known visit to the Valley.

FAR LEFT TOP: Two columns from the Oct. 5, 1836, edition of Der Republikaner, a German-language Lehigh County newspaper. The paper makes reference to the presidential contest between William Henry Harrison, the Whig candidate, and Democrat Martin Van Buren. Van Buren would win handily.
(Courtesy of Lehigh County Historical Society)

FAR LEFT BOTTOM: Benjamin Harrison is pictured on a lapel stud distributed during the 1888 campaign. Harrison, grandson of President William Henry Harrison, visited the Lehigh Valley only once, attending his son's graduation at Lafayette College. A medal minted to commemorate the 1889 inauguration of President Benjamin Harrison. (Courtesy of Kurt Zwikl of Allentown)

LEFT: A campaign ribbon from Whig candidate Harrison's successful 1840 campaign against incumbent Democrat Van Buren. (Courtesy of Kurt Zwikl)

ABOVE: The young Van Buren, an engraving that probably dates from his 1836 campaign for president or his time as Andrew Jackson's vice president. (Courtesy of Kurt Zwikl)

DEMOCRATIC TICKET

Our Principles

The Constitution.
The Sovereignty and equality of the States;
The Repeal of the Missouri Restriction;
The people of the Territories in forming State Governments to adopt their own institutions

Lith of Ritchie & Dunnavant *Richmond, Va*

FOR PRESIDENT

JAMES BUCHANAN

of Pennsylvania

FOR VICE PRESIDENT

JOHN C. BRECKINRIDGE

of Kentucky

ELECTORS

1st *District*.... E. W. MASSENBURG............of. Portsmouth.
2d.... *do*........ THOMAS. H. CAMPBELL..........of. Nottoway.
3d..... *do*....... A. HUGHES DILLARD...........of. Henry.

ABOVE: A paper ballot from the 1856 presidential election, featuring James Buchanan and running mate John Breckinridge. (Courtesy of Kurt Zwikl of Allentown)

RIGHT: President Buchanan.

BUCHANAN

James Buchanan makes a quiet visit: 1856

James Buchanan, though a native of Lancaster and the only Pennsylvanian elected president so far, apparently made just one visit of note to the Lehigh Valley.

According to a Lehigh County Historical Society chronicle nearly six decades later, the Democrat in 1856 "spent a night at Allentown before he was nominated for president, and was introduced to citizens in the southwest room of the Allen House by Hon. Samuel A. Bridges."

It was a quiet visit for Buchanan, who was by any measure a prominent man. By that year, he had already been a Pennsylvania state representative, U.S. senator, minister to Russia and secretary of state under President James K. Polk. But it seems the poor fellow, soon to be elected the 15th president, didn't even get a serenade from the Allentown Band, and his remarks were not recorded.

Perhaps Allentonians had a premonition about Buchanan. He is commonly judged to be one of the worst presidents. He presided ineffectually over a nation coming apart at the seams over the slavery question and watched helplessly as Southern states moved toward secession and ultimately the Civil War, believing the federal government had no authority to stop them. His successor, Abraham Lincoln, believed otherwise.

Buchanan may have spent scant time in the Lehigh Valley, but he was never too far away after leaving the White House in 1861. He retired to his Lancaster County estate, Wheatland, where he died seven years later.

It seems strange that Pennsylvania, which played such a central role in the founding of the nation, has sent only one of its own to the White House.

History provides at least one explanation. For the last half of the 19th century and first half of the 20th, Pennsylvania was a Republican stronghold, so neither party stood to gain much by nominating candidates from the state.

The most recent presidential hopeful was Rick Santorum, the conservative who made a heated but unsuccessful run for the Republican nomination in the 2012 primaries. Santorum was born in Virginia, but grew up in western Pennsylvania and represented the state in the U.S. Senate from 1995 to 2007.

Two of his primary opponents were Pennsylvania born – Newt Gingrich in Harrisburg and Ron Paul in Pittsburgh.

Other candidates with Pennsylvania ties, many quite prominent historical figures, have made White House bids over the years. Winfield Scott Hancock, a Civil War general from Montgomeryville renowned for his leadership of Union soldiers at the Battle of Gettysburg, was the Democratic nominee in 1880, but lost to James Garfield. It was a tight race and Hancock might have emerged the winner had he won his home state, but he didn't.

The 1884 election pitted James Blaine, a Republican born in West Brownsville, Washington County, against Democrat Grover Cleveland. Blaine, who had moved to Maine and started his political life there, lost a close race.

Philander Knox, from Brownsville, Fayette County, represented Pennsylvania in the U.S. Senate and served two terms as U.S. attorney general before losing the Republican nomination to William Howard Taft in 1908. Taft named him secretary of state.

Pennsylvania Gov. William Scranton was considered presidential material by no less a figure than President Dwight Eisenhower, but that wasn't enough to propel the moderate Scranton past arch-conservative Barry Goldwater in the 1964 Republican primaries.

Democratic Pennsylvania Gov. Milton Shapp ran a short-lived campaign of three months in 1976, dropping out of the race that would ultimately put Jimmy Carter in the White House.

Republican U.S. Sen. John Heinz of Pittsburgh was regarded as a contender, but he died in a 1991 plane crash. Former U.S. Sen. Arlen Specter of Philadelphia flirted with a 1996 Republican candidacy. He campaigned for a few months but dropped out before the primaries and endorsed Bob Dole, who lost to Democratic incumbent Bill Clinton.

The 2008 election put a Pennsylvanian a heartbeat from the presidency — Vice President Joe Biden, a Scranton-born Democrat.

THE PRESIDENT AND THE JAPANESE EMBASSY.

Washington City 17 July 1857

Dear Sir/

Your favor of the 13th instant announcing my election as an "Honorary Member of the Moravian Historical Society" has been duly received.

I accept with sincere pleasure this mark of esteem & beg you to present to the members of your Society my cordial thanks for the honor they have conferred upon me.

Yours very respectfully

James Buchanan

LEFT: President Buchanan, the only Pennsylvanian to hold the office, is depicted in this circa 1856 engraving greeting a delegation from Japan. (Courtesy of Kurt Zwikl of Allentown)

TOP: A July 17, 1857, letter from President Buchanan to the Moravian Historical Society, thanking them for making him an honorary member. The honor was extended to all new presidents. (Courtesy of The Moravian Historical Society, Bethlehem)

ABOVE: These tassels were taken from a covering on the table on which rested Abraham Lincoln's casket. (Courtesy of The Moravian Historical Society)

Honest Abe and the 'little giant'

Though he had relatives as close as Berks County, Abraham Lincoln never visited the Lehigh Valley. The most this area can claim of the Great Emancipator is a few pieces of cloth.

After Lincoln's assassination in 1865, his body lay in state in the Capitol Rotunda from April 19-21 on a table called a catafalque. The president's remains were then taken by train to Springfield, Ill., for burial. The journey, punctuated by stops for memorials in various cities, took three weeks.

At the time, the assistant superintendent of the Pennsylvania Railroad was Edward Higginson Williams Sr., who was charged with overseeing the train procession. He came away from that duty with a few souvenirs, including tassels from the catafalque cover and trimmings from the railroad car that carried the casket.

Those items stayed in Willliams' family until 1896, when his son, Lehigh University professor Edward Williams Jr., donated them to a Civil War veterans group in Bethlehem, the Grand Army of the Republic's J.K. Taylor Post 182.

The post later gave the relics to the Moravian Historical Society, which keeps them at the Whitefield House in Nazareth.

While Lincoln never visited, his opponent in the 1860 campaign, Stephen A. Douglas, did. He earned the moniker "little giant" because, though small in stature, he was a spellbinding orator. Douglas passed through in the fall of 1860, and the following translations from German-language newspapers tell the story:

Unabhängiger Republikaner — Wed., September 5, 1860, pg. 2

"[Stephen] Douglas to Come

Judge Douglas will come this week on his trip to Virginia and North Carolina to Pennsylvania and be on Friday, September 7th in Harrisburg, on Saturday in Reading and on Monday in Easton. One also makes an attempt to get him in Allentown. Should this matter be so, then a broadside with the news will be distributed in different regions of the county and one will flock here in a large crowd, in order to see and hear the 'little giant,' who can so brilliantly throw his opponent in Illinois, the 'large dwarf, to the ground. Judge Douglas is a great orator and must have a firm nature, while every day and wherever he goes, he speaks several times and often for an hour long. He goes from here toward New York and then to the western states."

Der Friedens Bote — Wed., September 5, 1860, pg. 3

"[Stephen] Douglas to Come on Saturday. We received news that Senator Douglas, current Presidential candidate, comes directly toward Pennsylvania on his trip in the South and will deliver speeches at the following places: to Harrisburg on Friday, the 7th of September; to Reading on Saturday, the 8th of September; in Philadelphia, the evening of the same day; in Easton on the 10th of September and likely days after that in Allentown, about but more reliable news exists. A Committee should meanwhile depart from here to invite him and it will through handbills and other ways make known on which day the talented orator will be in Allentown."

Unabhängiger Republikaner — Wed., September 12, 1860

"Judge [Stephen] Douglas' Trip

On Monday, Judge Douglas came through here [Allentown] on a trip from Reading to Easton and was welcomed at the train station with cheers from an enormous crowd of people. He gave an address of about ten minutes long. He was already expected here at 9 o'clock, but was, in fact, thwarted by something, and so he had to go on. In the afternoon, he spoke in Easton and on Tuesday, his trip continued on to New York, where today he is to deliver a great speech."

LADIES' TICKET.

RE-OPENING OF PARDEE HALL.

This ticket will admit one to the gallery of the Auditorium and of Geological Hall.

College Marsh

Nov. 30, '80.

Rutherford B. Hayes visits Lafayette landmark: 1880

The most infamous laboratory mishap at a Lehigh Valley college brought the 18th president to Easton on Nov. 30, 1880.

Pardee Hall — a massive, handsome structure and one of the largest collegiate buildings of the time — had burned to cinders 18 months earlier in a fire caused by a chemistry experiment gone bad.

The college built a new Pardee Hall, identical to the 1873 original, and President Rutherford B. Hayes came to rededicate it.

The visit was Hayes' third and final to the Lehigh Valley. He had come through on a campaign visit in 1876. Before that, he had stumped in the area on behalf of John F. Hartranft, who was governor of Pennsylvania from 1873-79.

Hayes brought much of his Cabinet to Lafayette, including prominent alumni of the school: Secretary of War Alexander Ramsey, Class of 1836; Pennsylvania Gov. Henry M. Hoyt, Class of 1849; U.S. Rep. Horatio Gates Fisher, Class of 1855; and U.S. Assistant Postmaster General Abraham D. Hazen, Class of 1863.

The president took the podium to prolonged applause, according to an account in Frank Leslie's Illustrated Newspaper, and offered brief remarks about the essential nature of education in the American experiment.

"The government of this country is in the citizens," he said. "And it will be a good government just in proportion as the citizens have a good education ... Ignorant voters are powder and ball for the demagogue."

Hayes also praised the wealthy citizens who endowed colleges and universities — notably the hall's namesake, Ario Pardee of Hazleton, a coal and iron entrepreneur whose initial gift of $20,000 to Lafayette in 1864 was the largest individual donation to a school in Pennsylvania at the time.

He would give about $500,000 more.

Pardee, said President Hayes, "has set the example, and what an example it is! He does not wait until his last will and testament. He does it while he is alive."

Pardee did not speak. Lafayette's president, the Rev. William C. Cattell, said he had asked him to, "but it always has been easier to get $100,000 from Mr. Pardee than a speech."

LEFT TOP: Pardee Hall at Lafayette College in Easton is shown burning in 1879 after a chemistry lab accident. The rededication of the building would bring President Rutherford B. Hayes to the campus the following year. (Courtesy of Special Collections & College Archives, Skillman Library, Lafayette College)

LEFT BOTTOM: A ticket to the rededication of Pardee Hall at Lafayette College, where President Hayes was the guest of honor. (Courtesy of Special Collections & College Archives, Skillman Library, Lafayette College)

TOP: A portrait of President Hayes. (Courtesy of the White House Historical Association)

BOTTOM: A drawing from Frank Leslie's Illustrated Weekly shows the ceremony in which President Hayes rededicated Pardee Hall in 1880. (Courtesy of Special Collections & College Archives, Skillman Library, Lafayette College)

PS Pardee Hall, which is still in use, had to be restored once again in 1897, when it was badly damaged in a fire set by 31-year-old George H. Stephens. The mentally unstable Princeton graduate had been dismissed from his job as an ethics and logic professor at Lafayette, but returned to campus as a graduate student. He set the fire and committed many other acts of vandalism as revenge for his firing.

ABOVE: President Hayes is visible slightly to the left of center in this Nov. 30, 1880, photo of the rededication of Pardee Hall at Lafayette College. This may be the first photograph of a president ever taken in the Lehigh Valley. (Courtesy of Special Collections & College Archives, Skillman Library, Lafayette College)

RIGHT: A silk ribbon depicting candidate Hayes and his running mate, William Wheeler, from the 1876 campaign. (Courtesy of Kurt Zwikl of Allentown)

B.B. TILT & SON, N.Y. & PATERSON, N.J.

REPUBLICAN
CANDIDATES.

FOR PRESIDENT
R. B. HAYES.
OF Ohio.

FOR VICE PRESIDENT
W. A. WHEELER.
OF New York.

See if there is not a money saving advertisement in the Morning Call which should be answered NOW.

THE ALLENTOWN MORNING CALL

VOL. XLIV, NO. 33. ALLENTOWN, PA., THURSDAY MORNING, FEBRUARY 8, 1912.

A ROYAL WELCOME FOR DR. WOODROW WILSON

Notable Outpouring of Leading Citizens to Hear Aspirant for Presidential Honors

URGES DEMOCRATS TO UNITE FOR SUCCESS

Guest of Honor at Lehigh Democratic Club's Celebration of Jackson Day is Greeted by a Monster Audience.

Whatever Governor Woodrow Wilson, of New Jersey, thought about Allentown before his visit here last evening he certainly will leave to-day impressed with the cordiality of the reception accorded to him, impressed with the underlying sincerity of his welcome; impressed with the immense outpouring of citizens to hear his message and impressed with the fact that there is a live hustling city called Allentown which with Reading shares the honor of being located in a Democratic oasis in a state noted for its Republican strength.

When Governor Wilson rose in the Lyric Theatre last evening as the speaker at the annual Jackson Day celebration, he addressed by far the largest audience that ever congregated in this city for a similar occasion. Not only was the theatre packed to the very roof, but enough people were turned away to fill another theatre comfortably.

Not only was the audience the largest that ever listened to a political address in this city, but the old timers, those who attended meetings of this nature for years, agreed that it was the finest and most intelligent audience that has ever assembled in this city.

The balcony and gallery were open to the public and these were jammed before those for whom seats had been reserved arrived. The Lehigh Democratic club was escorted by the Allentown Band and the Young Men's Democratic Club of the Sixth ward was escorted by the First ward drum corps.

While the band played "The Star Spangled Banner," the curtain rose and the audience rose like one man and every one waved an inspiring American flag. When District Attorney Rupp introduced Governor Wilson, the audience tendered him an ovation such as is seldom tendered, even to a president of the United States. It was several minutes before the applause subsided.

Cheers From Students.

Just before the speaker was introduced two bodies of college students who were seated in the wings gave their college cheers and cheers for Wilson. First of all fifty Muhlenberg men cheered led by Herbert Frederick and then followed the Lehigh crowd, under the direction of cheer leader George Shurts adding three lusty "Wilsons" on the end.

Governor Wilson hit the nail on the head, when in his opening remarks he said that audiences no longer go to political meetings to be entertained. Last night's audience was an example of the point which the speaker made. The audience was not composed of men who came only to make a lot of noise but it was a thinking audience, alert to everything which left the governor's lips and keen to appreciate his words.

Dr. Wilson's very appearance denotes the scholar. He has the feature and the lines of the thinker.

Off to Meet Governor Wilson.

The Allentonians who met Governor Wilson at Wayne Junction and escorted him to this city, left on the 10.14 a. m. train yesterday morning. In the party were: Martin Klingler, candidate for National delegate, Jonathan E. Frederick, county chairman, Rich-

bers of the committee and talked freely on the questions of the day. He gave a graphic description of the La Follette incident at the Publishers' banquet in Philadelphia last week and expressed the opinion that the great insurgent leader was suffering from what seemed to be a nervous breakdown. It was a most tragic event, he said, and additional pathos is presented in the unseemly haste with which the leader is being deserted by the followers he had, most of whom held to be supporters of the great principles represented by LaFollette rather than mere followers of the man.

Roosevelt's Position.

Speaking of Col. Roosevelt in response to a query, Governor Wilson marvelled at the apparent midway position being maintained by the former president on the question of his candidacy and when one of the members of the party ventured the guess that he would be the strongest candidate the Republicans could name, there was no answering conjecture as to the possibility of the outcome on the part of the guest of the day.

(Continued on page 5.)

DOROTHY ARNOLD CLUE FALSE; PARENTS' HOPES DASHED

PHILADELPHIA, Feb. 7.—Convinced that the young nurse in the New Philadelphia General Hospital, who was believed by some attaches of that institution to be Dorothy Arnold, is not the missing heiress, John S. Keith, of New York, attorney for the Arnold family, and a private detective who accompanied him here returned to-night to New York. During their stay in this city today they visited the hospital accompanied by a local detective who had already reported that the missing girl was not at the institution.

Mrs. Hillegas Bean, the nurse who was believed to be the missing heiress came to this city last December and with her husband and seven months old baby took rooms near Fifteenth and Vine streets. Four days after their arrival the baby was stricken with scarlet fever and had to be removed to the hospital. The mother accompanied it and when it died remained as assistant nurse. She told some of the other nurses that she had pawned jewelry in New York and some of them, thinking she was the missing Dorothy Arnold, notified the parents who have searched two continents for their daughter. Mrs. Bean said her maiden name was Florence Myers.

M'GOWAN DENIES PERJURY CHARGES IN LORIMER PROBE

WASHINGTON, Feb. 7.—Charles McGowan, the young Canadian witness, denied before the senate Lorimer committee of investigation that he had admitted receiving money for "perjuring" himself before the committee last July. Instead of receiving $1,500 for "perjuring" himself as private detectives said he told them, McGowan testified that he was paid only $300 by a check signed "Edward Hines Lumber Co., by C. E. Wiehe secretary" to reimburse him for unexpected loss incident to his presence in Washington to testify for Wiehe.

McGowan admitted that he was in a hotel room in Toronto, January 6, with Detective Bailey, of whom he said he "never had a suspicion that he was anything but what he pretended to be, "a claims agent." It was then that Bailey swore the $1,500 statement was made and J. E. Sheridan swore he recorded such statement as coming over a telephone apparatus from the room in which McGowan was alleged to

NAGEL SLATED FOR THE SUPREME COURT BENCH

Hook Eliminated Because of "Jim Crow" Decision.

WASHINGTON, Feb. 7.—The existing vacancy on the supreme court bench, the fifth that has occurred in the present administration, probably will be filled by the appointment of Secretary of Commerce and Labor Charles Nagel, of St. Louis. President Taft is expected to send the nomination of Mr. Nagel to the senate within a few days. United States William C. Hook, of Kansas, who, until last night, was most prominently mentioned for the vacancy, is said to have been eliminated from further consideration at an hour's session of the cabinet today. All of the lawyers in the cabinet, except Mr. Nagel, were present and afterward it was learned that the president had made clear his intention of appointing his secretary of commerce and labor. This report was so generally credited to-night that rumor was busy with a possible successor to Mr. Nagel in the cabinet. Louis Marshall, of New York, and Oscar Rosenwald, of Chicago, were mentioned among those who had been considered by President Taft. Judge Hook's name was scratched from the president's list to-day almost at the eleventh hour. This action was said to be due to his concurrence in a "Jim Crow" law decision in an Oklahoma railroad case. Both the president and Attorney General Wickersham are understood to hold the opinion that Judge Hook "went too far" in this case and Secretary of State Knox, Secretary of War Stimson and Secretary of the Interior Fisher the other lawyers present at the cabinet meeting evidently agreed.

DUKE RESIGNS AS HEAD OF AMERICAN TOBACCO CO.

NEW YORK, Feb. 7.—James B. Duke very shortly will resign from the presidency of the American Tobacco Company to become chairman of the British-American Tobacco Company, Limited, with its chief office in London. It was announced late today at the American Tobacco Company offices. With this announcement was coupled the statement that he will be succeeded as president of the American Tobacco Company by Percival S. Hill, long a vice president.

EX-BANKER MORSE LEAVES ATLANTA FOR NEW YORK.

ATLANTA, Ga., Feb. 7.—Charles W. Morse the New York banker recently pardoned by President Taft, left for New York late this afternoon. Morse was accompanied by his wife. His plans for departure were not known until a few minutes before his train left, when he was recognized at the terminal station.

DEFENSE FAILS TO PROVE THAT BISHIE IS INSANE

SCRANTON, Feb. 7.—The trial of William Peter Bishie, the 15-year-old Kingston youth, charged with the murder of express messenger Irvan G. Borger, on the Lackawanna road, November 17, last, reached a climax to-day when three alienists summoned by the defense declined to say that the defendant is insane. "Mentally deficient" is as far as any of them went in the way of helping to establish the theory

THE REAL THING.

DICKENSON TELLS STORY OF N. Y. BOMB MYSTERY

Statement Describes Explosion Which Caused Death of Helen Taylor

NEW YORK, Feb. 7.—Through his counsel, Charles N. Dickinson, today gave out the first statement he has made describing the explosion that caused Mrs. Taylor's death by a bomb.

After frankly detailing the history of his acquaintance with the woman, which included reference to several quarrels, Dickinson said he went to the Taylor flat above twenty-five minutes before the explosion took place.

"While we were talking the door bell rang," his statement continues, "and she went to the rear hall door. She opened the door. I heard no conversation whatever, the door was closed and she immediately came back into the room with a package in her handes. She walked towards the small table in the parlor and started to open the package and the next thing that occurred was the explosion. The noise was frightful. I thought I was blinded. I put my hands up to my eyes. There was a terrific noise in my ears. I didn't know what was the cause of the explosion for the instant. My first impulse was to get out and get her out. I called 'Grace' but there was no response. I opened the door and somebody was standing there. I think I yelled for a doctor. Some one asked me what was the trouble. I said I did not know, but there had been an awful accident."

Part of Dickinson's statement seems to indicate that another man left the apartment with Edna Le Marre, the young woman who lived with Mrs. Taylor, shortly before the tragedy occurred. He declared that he heard the voices of the La Marre girl and man as they talked in the rear room and that Mrs. Taylor went to the door and said good bye to the pair as they left. The story told by the La Marre girl is that when she went out shortly before the explosion occurred she pretended to be talking to a man in order to deceive Dickinson. If another man was in the apartment at the time as Dickinson says, the police have failed to find any clue to his identity.

Upon a motion made by Assistant District Attorney Srong in he hearing before Coroner Feinberg to-day, the coroner dismissed the charge of homicide against Dickinson. Upon another motion Dickinson was held in $100 bail as a material witness. Bail was furnished.

THOROUGH INVESTIGATION OF AGRICULTURAL DEPT. ORDERED

By House Committee After Hearing Charges Involving Florida Everglade Lands

DOCUMENTARY EVIDENCE INTRODUCED IN SNEED TRIAL.

FORT WORTH, Texas, Feb. 7.—Documentary evidence was presented by the defense this afternoon in the trial of J. B. Sneed, accused of having murdered Captain A. G. Boyce, Sr., in support of the contention that a conspiracy existed among members of the Boyce family to bring about a separation between Sneed and his wife. Joseph T. Sneed, father of the defendant, followed Captain Snyder, father of Mrs. Sneed on the witness stand this morning. His testimony was in support of the theory of the defense that Sneed believed his wife insane and for that reason would not be separated from her.

STEEL TRUST HEAD EXPLAINS DESTRUCTION OF EVIDENCE

NEW YORK, Feb. 7.—Judge Elbert H. Gary, chairman of the United States Steel Corporation, gave out a statement to-night in explanation of the charge made by the government that certain evidence, used in the prosecution of the so-called Jackson Wire pools and needed to support the government's suit to disolve the corporation, had been destroyed.

Judge Gary says that the evidence, a trunk full of "old papers" that had been before the federal grand jury in New York and returned after the indictments in the wire pool investigation "had been disposed of" were ordered destroyed by Frank Baackes, vice president of the American Steel and Wire Company "who supposed that all the prosecutions growing out of the wire pools were at an end and that the papers were no longer needed for any purpose."

BRIDEGROOM OF 76 CLIPPED 6 YEARS OFF HIS AGE

NEW YORK, Feb. 7.—Even if an aged man deceives a young woman

HOUSE DEMOCR[ATS ...] "MONEY TRUS[T ...]

Rep. Henry's Plan for [...] Defeated by a Vot[e ...]

HAYMARKET, NOTORIOUS N. Y. DANCE HALL, NO MORE.

NEW YORK, Feb. 7.—The Haymarket, a notorious dance hall in the Tenderloin, is no more. After a large crusade by vice exterminators by the suppression of the place the commissioner of the bureau of licenses today revoked its dance license. The Haymarket probably was the best known of New York's seven hundred dance halls, and one of the remaining reminders of the Tenderloin district as it was years ago. Slumming parties frequently included the Haymarket in their itinerary of "interesting" places to be visited.

CAPIASES COMPLETED FOR DYNAMITE ARRESTS

Expect to Serve 32 Warrants Almost Simultaneously.

INDIANAPOLIS, Feb. 7.—Capiases for the simultaneous arrest of all the men named in the thirty-two indictments returned by the federal grand jury in the dynamite cases, with certified copies of the indictments, were completed to-day in the expectation that the arrests might be effected within five days—possibly on Saturday, but more probably next Monday.

Although the men, most of them labor union officials and agents are scattered from Boston to the Pacific coast, the papers for their apprehension have been so arranged that they are to be arrested and afforded an opportunity to give bond on the same day as near as possible within a few hours.

Frank M. Ryan, president of the International Association of Bridge and Structural Iron Workers at the headquarters where J. J. McNamara formerly had his offices, said to-day he had made no plans for the defense of any of the men. "There will be time enough to think of that when we learn who have been indicted," said Mr. Ryan.

CHARGES THAT WITNESS IS SHIELDING PACKERS.

CHICAGO, Feb. 7.—A threat made by District Attorney Wilkerson in the packers' trial to-day to use the stenographic report of the proceedings of the federal grand jury to show that John M. Chaplin, a witness, was attempting to shield Charles H. Swift, vice president of Swift and Company and one of the defendants, additional answers were brought from the witness. Chaplin, who has been on the stand two days, declared that all the instructions made for allowance for by-products in 1902, were issued on his own responsibility as head of the plant accounting department of Swift and Company.

MADERO'S FIRST FOLLOWERS ARE NOW OPPOSING HIM

MEXICO CITY, Feb. 7.—"For no reason will I change any of my ministers. The members of my cabinet are honorable men. They are patriots. I shall not permit any of them to be slandered as you are slandering them."

In these words President Madero today brought to a termination an interview sought by a committee from the anti re-electionist party which was attempting to persuade him to dismiss from his cabinet the ministers of war and interior.

The conference had proceeded calmly up to the moment when the spokesman of the committee, in reply to a statement of the president that evil minded Mexicans were aiding the rebels, declared that this was true and

Woodrow Wilson's royal welcome: 1912

When he came to the Lehigh Valley to deliver a one-hour campaign speech in the winter of 1912, New Jersey Gov. Woodrow Wilson was closing in on a presidency that would be marked indelibly by America's entry into World War I.

At the time, however, Wilson's concerns were mainly domestic. Vying against Republican incumbent William Howard Taft and former President Teddy Roosevelt of the Progressive Party, Wilson told a crowd at Allentown's Lyric Theater to look beyond party loyalty and pick the best candidate for the job.

Besides, he added, "that is the greatest party which serves the public most effectively."

That party, of course, happened to be Wilson's beloved Democratic Party.

"I was born a Democrat," he said, "and when I became old enough to think, I became a convinced Democrat."

How many Republicans and Progressives were on hand to hear this message on Feb. 7 is unclear. Allentown, wrote an unidentified Morning Call reporter who covered the visit, was a "Democratic oasis in a state noted for its Republican strength."

According to the Allentown Chronicle and News, Wilson got the traditional welcome extended to dignitaries: an escort into the city by civic leaders and a patriotic serenade by the Allentown Band at the Hotel Allen at Seventh and Hamilton, where the governor rested before his speech.

A first-class ticket to the Lyric event cost $10, which guaranteed six seats and a handshake from Wilson. "For half that price three parlor chairs can be secured," the Chronicle and News had reported. "The balcony and gallery will be thrown open to the public, first come first served."

The Lyric — now Symphony Hall — was "packed to the very roof," The Allentown Morning Call said in its story, headlined "A Royal Welcome for Dr. Woodrow Wilson." Enough people were turned away at the door to fill another theater.

Wilson, a respected academic and former president of Princeton University, had the "features and lines" of a thinker, wrote the Call's unidentified — and clearly impressed — correspondent. He was greeted by a thundering ovation "such as is seldom tendered, even to a president of the United States."

Wilson, who made two other trips to the Lehigh Valley that year, went on to win the White House. He spent much of his first term trying to keep America from being drawn into the European war. Indeed, his 1916 re-election campaign carried the slogan "He kept us out of war."

But many factors — including anti-German sentiment after the 1915 sinking of the British liner Lusitania, with many American lives lost — would finally compel Wilson to decide for war.

America entered the conflict in April 1917. Nearly 117,000 Americans would die of combat and other causes before the armistice of November 1918.

LEFT TOP: The front page of The Allentown Morning Call detailing Democratic presidential candidate Woodrow Wilson's visit to Allentown in February 1912. He spoke at the Lyric Theater, now Allentown Symphony Hall.

LEFT BOTTOM: (Left to right) The message on this button, "Safety First," refers to President Wilson's ultimately futile efforts to keep the United States out of World War I. (Courtesy Kurt Zwikl of Allentown)

A Wilson campaign button bearing a slogan wouldn't hold true in the end, with Wilson finally committing the United States to the war in Europe in April 1917. (Courtesy of Kurt Zwikl)

A third Wilson button. (Courtesy of Stephen Cunningham of Nazareth)

ABOVE: A photogravure of Woodrow Wilson circa 1912. (Courtesy of Kurt Zwikl)

PS • When Wilson arrived at the Hotel Allen, he asked to be taken to a room to rest. The Morning Call described what happened next: "There were quite a number of citizens of all parties in the corridors of the hotel. By some mistake, Building Inspector Frank Minner was introduced as Governor Wilson while the Governor was resting. Mr. Minner made no objection to the mistake and kept up the handshaking ..."

• Also in the news that day, Muhlenberg College celebrated the centenary of Charles Dickens' birth with a lecture by Henry Marx, an Easton librarian recognized as an expert on the British author. And Allentown, home to various minor league teams over the years, was negotiating for a spot in the New York State Baseball League.

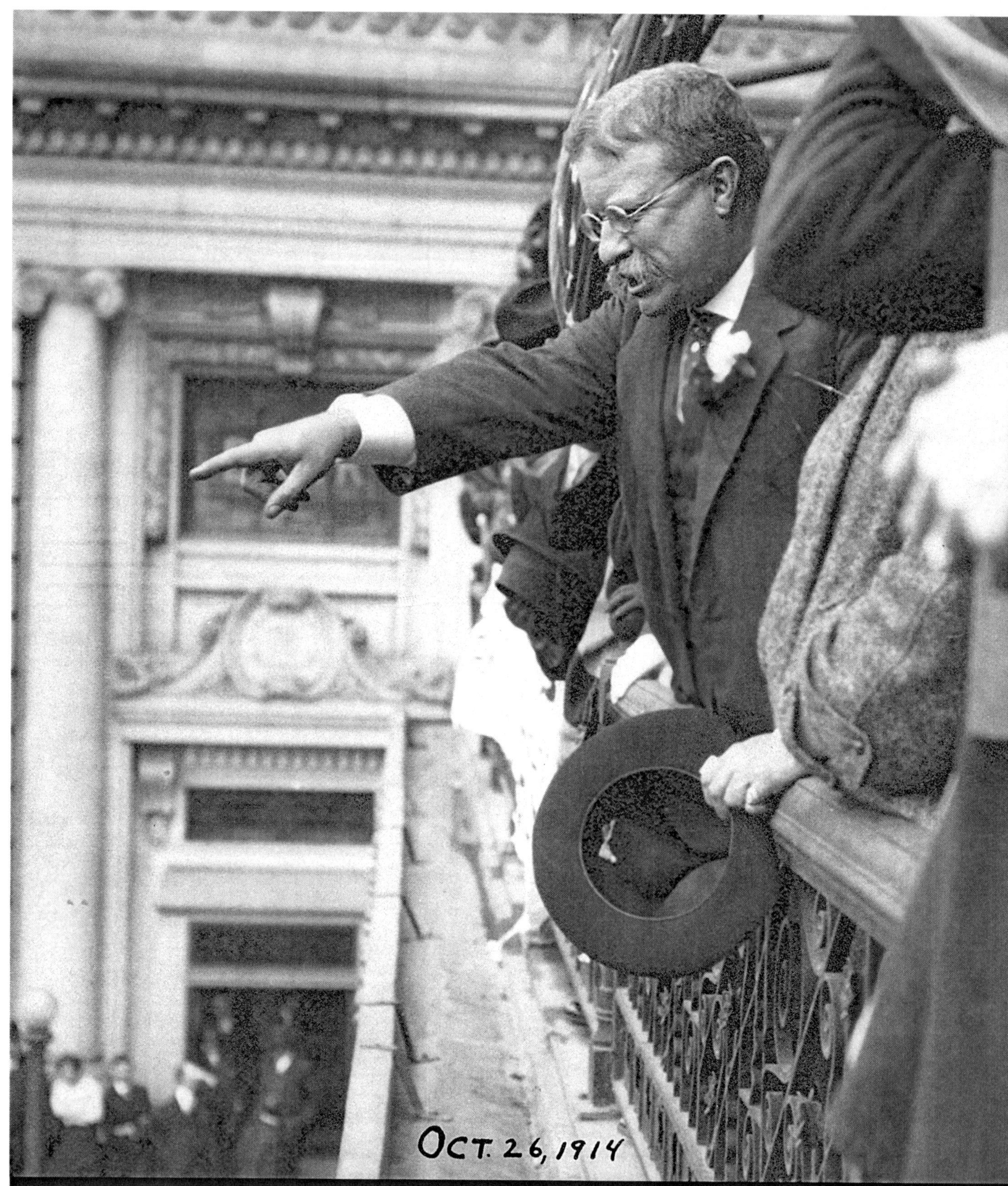

ABOVE: On Oct. 26, 1914, President Teddy Roosevelt, vigorous as always, makes a point to the crowd from a balcony at the Hotel Allen on the northeast corner of Seventh and Hamilton streets in Allentown. The Rough Rider was stumping for U.S. Senate candidate Gifford Pinchot and former Allentown Mayor Fred Lewis, who was running for state secretary of internal affairs. (Courtesy of the Lehigh County Historical Society)

RIGHT TOP: President Roosevelt. (Courtesy of the Theodore Roosevelt Center at Dickinson State University, Dickinson, N.D.)

RIGHT BOTTOM: A campaign ribbon promoting Roosevelt's Progressive Party candidacy of 1912. (Courtesy of Kurt Zwikl of Allentown)

TEDDY ROOSEVELT

The Rough Rider: 1901-14

Who was more charismatic than Teddy Roosevelt? Whenever the famed Rough Rider came to the Lehigh Valley — and he did so at least five times before, during and after his presidency — he was welcomed by roaring throngs and brass bands.

This, after all, was far more than the 26th president. This was the hero of the Spanish-American War, quite literally a self-made man who overcame a sickly, asthmatic youth by virtue of what he called "the strenuous life."

He had been a cowboy, a soldier, a New York City police commissioner and was just 42 in 1901 when the assassination of President William McKinley elevated him to the White House. He remains the youngest person ever to assume the office.

Roosevelt visited Easton on a whistle-stop train tour while running as vice president with McKinley. In 1905, as president, his train made brief stops in Bethlehem and Allentown en route to Wilkes-Barre. Steelworkers cheered him at Bethlehem Steel. A children's choir serenaded him in Allentown's Lehigh Valley Railroad station on lower Hamilton Street.

His April 1912 visit was by far the biggest and grandest. Roosevelt was running again. Four years earlier he had supported Republican William Howard Taft to succeed him, but had come to believe Taft was embracing defective economic policies and decided to challenge him in the primary.

Roosevelt arrived by train and made his way along Hamilton Street to the Lyric Theater (today's Symphony Hall), where he was to speak. He entered the theater to the strains of "My Country 'Tis of Thee" by the Allentown Band and flashed his famously toothy smile to a crowd, prompting a tumult of cheers. A 6-year-old girl, Dorothy Braden, presented the candidate with pink carnations.

Roosevelt spoke for about 10 minutes, condemning the power of political party bosses — a favorite theme — and exhorting the crowd to vote.

Roosevelt lost the Republican nomination to Taft and went on to run as the Progressive Party candidate. He beat both Taft and Democrat Woodrow Wilson in Pennsylvania, but Wilson would win the White House.

Roosevelt returned to Allentown on Oct. 26, 1914, to stump for U.S. Senate candidate Gifford Pinchot and former Allentown Mayor Fred Lewis, who was running for state secretary of internal affairs.

Roosevelt was a day shy of 58 when he arrived in Allentown by train and made his way downtown in an open car, jauntily waving his hat.

It is hard to judge by the quality of the photos of the day, but he seems little the worse for wear given that he nearly died earlier in the year from the malarial fevers that assailed him on a months-long trek through the Brazilian jungle.

The Morning Call said his voice was audible to everyone in Center Square as he spoke from the balcony of the Hotel Allen. Once again, he bemoaned the corrupting influence of party bosses and the power of corporate monopolies.

It would be Roosevelt's last visit. The great adventurer himself had reckoned his Brazilian journey took 10 years off his life. The loss of a son, Quentin, in World War I brought on a depression that probably hastened the end. He died in January 1919.

ABOVE: President Roosevelt travels west on Hamilton Street from the Lehigh Valley Railroad station during his Allentown visit in October 1914. (Courtesy of the Lehigh County Historical Society)

RIGHT: A button from the 1904 presidential campaign depicting Roosevelt and running mate Charles Fairbanks. (Courtesy of Kurt Zwikl)

RIGHT TOP: A cartoon from the Allentown Chronicle and News of Roosevelt, who ran as a Progressive Party candidate in 1912. The cartoonist depicts Roosevelt's run on the Progressive ticket as nothing more than a devastating attack on the Democratic Party. On the right, oxygen is pumped into the withering Progressive Party tree.

RIGHT BOTTOM: A 1904 Roosevelt campaign button. (Courtesy of Kurt Zwikl)

FAR RIGHT: The Allentown Chronicle and News of April 11, 1912, carried news of Roosevelt's visit to Allentown — and the death of Pope Pius X.

ALLENTOWN CHRONICLE AND NEWS, TUESDAY, OCTOBER 27, 1914

THE SPLITTER.

In the early days of Teddy's youth
He was a splitter bold;
He aimed to follow Lincoln,
The way the tale is told;
At splitting he is "bully,"
But not at splitting wood;
His game is splitting parties,
Just now he's making good;

He tried to split the G. O. P.,
But found the axe too dull;
He's busy now with Democrats,
And soon their game he'll [illegible];
The chips they fly at every blow,
His teeth reveal his glee;
You cannot blame the Splitter;
It's the Democratic Tree.

by American Press Association.

THEODORE ROOSEVELT

Born New York City, Oct. 27, 1858.
Graduated Harvard, 1880.
Member New York Legislature, 1882-4. Minority leader.
Delegate at Large Republican National Convention, 1884.
Lived on a North Dakota ranch, 1884-6.
Candidate Mayor of New York, 1886.
United States Civil Service Commissioner, 1889-95.
President New York Police Board, 1895-7.
Assistant Secretary of the Navy, 1897-8.
Colonel Rough Riders, 1898.
Governor of New York, 1899-1900.
Vice President, United States, March 4-Sept. 14, 1901.
President, Sept. 14, 1901-March 4, 1909.
Hunted in Africa and lectured in Europe, 1909-10.

ALLENTOWN'S GREAT OVATION FOR TEDDY

Former President of the United States Greeted by Thousands of People Upon His Visit to Allentown—Made Only a Brief Stop Here—Spoke Ten Minutes in the Lyric Theatre Before a Crowd That Packed the House—Flayed the Political Bosses, and Commended the Veterans.

Balmy weather and sunny skies sent out a big part of Allentown's population into the streets to get a glimpse of Col. Theodore Roosevelt on his whirlwind visit here this afternoon. It was "a case of on again, off again, gone again" with the Colonel, for he hardly appeared "in our midst" until he was speeding away. Many in the big audience in the Lyric Theatre which greeted him barely caught the sound of his voice when the announcement was made that the train was ready to depart and the meeting concluded.

Col. Roosevelt arrived in Reading at 12.15 P. M. He was conveyed through lines of people to the Mansion House where he spoke from the balcony to a large crowd. He appeared immensely pleased when the Allentown delegation was presented to him. His address at Reading was principally a reference to a circular sent out by Postmaster A. M. High, "telling you," addressing the people "how to vote. This is not a Federal office-holding job, this is a people's job and I ask you to rebuke the efforts of these bread and butter politicians. Let that postmaster attend to his job. In this contest when the people have a chance to express themselves they are clearly and unmistakably for the right side. We have lost only when there has been cheating, lying thefts and deeds of violence in which a community is boss-ridden and has been defrauded of its rights."

The special train of diner and three coaches with the Colonel's party left Reading at [illegible] P. M. The Colonel immediately went into the diner where he partook of lunch. Mingling again with the party he spoke about the weather and the country through which the train passed, but couldn't be drawn out to talk on politics. At the approach of the various stations along the route the train slowed down and he was alert to jump to his feet and stride to the rear where he waved to the crowds and shouted a wish for good luck. In response to a telegram he stepped to the platform at Topton and greeted the orphans of the Lutheran Home, who were lined up on the station platform. The tots waved him a greeting. There was very little slowing of the train after that, until it pulled into the Terminal station at quarter to two. Hon. Fred E. Lewis, who was in the party that went to Reading, alighted and assisted Colonel Roosevelt to the platform. The ex-President looked stouter than when he passed through here in [illegible]. He wore a broad-brimmed soft hat and brown suit. He good-naturedly pushed his way through the crowd, jumped into Dr. A. H. Balliet's auto which awaited him and was off up Hamilton street with a squad of mounted officers in the lead. The members of his party and Allentonians who accompanied him to this city followed in the dozen autos which were lined up on Hamilton street. The crowds which lined the street from the station to Sixth street were enthusiastic with an occasional burst of cheers. It was evident that many were attracted by curiosity to see the best advertised man in America. His appearance at the Lyric Theatre, was again the signal for a big demonstration. In the street crowds were hundreds of school children who were permitted a view of the ex-President from the sidewalks. A number of industries deferred blowing the whistles for work until after the distinguished visitor's arrival. Chief Bernhard had 35 officers in uniform and plain clothes mingling with the crowds. Railroad detectives and police officials from Bethlehem and Easton assisted the local force.

In Colonel Roosevelt's party were Henry G. Walton, Pittsburg; E. A. Van Valkenburg, of the North American; Truman D. Carmar, the Colonel's secretary; Walter Darlington, of the North American; E. T. Moore, J. J. Crouth and Col. Fred Wilson, Secretary of the Philadelphia Roosevelt Committee; B. Frank Ruth, Reading; J. W. Slipp, Birdsboro; Thomas H.

PS Teddy Roosevelt was one of the many famous folk who spent time at the Hotel Allen, an ornate Victorian edifice with a mansard roof that stood from 1886 to 1949 at the northeast corner of Seventh and Hamilton streets in Allentown.

The Nations Choice

For President
Hon. William Howard Taft
OF OHIO

COPYRIGHT 1908 BY H. M. ROSE

For Vice President
Hon. James S. Sherma

OF NEW YORK

THE WEATHER.

Washington, D. C., March 14—Eastern Pennsylvania: Rain to-night and warmer; Friday colder and generally fair, increasing winds, shifting to northwest.

Chronicle  and News.

LARGEST CI
CIRCULATI

VOL. XCVI, 19,973. ALLENTOWN, PA., THURSDAY, MARCH 14, 1918. TEN CENTS

EX-PRESIDENT TAFT GUEST AT ARMY CAMP; RAINBOW DIVISION WALLOPS THE GERMAN

DEATH OF MRS. WEBSTER.

Former Resident of Allentown Passed Away in New York City.

Mrs. Caroline Webster, wife of Henry Webster, formerly of Allentown, died yesterday in New York city of a complication of diseases, aged 68 years and 12 days. She was the daughter of the late Mr. and Mrs. David Gilbert, of East Texas. There survives her husband, a granddaughter and two sisters: Mrs. Frank Dorney, of Dorney Park; Mrs. Amanda Knauss, of Allentown. J. B. Shgrer, of No. 1821 Walnut street, is a brother-in-law of the deceased. The body will be brought to Allentown on Saturday and taken at 2 P. M. to Fairview Cemetery for burial. Rev. J. T. White will officiate.

U-BOAT FIRES AT HOSPITAL SHIP

By United Press Leased Wire.

London, March 14.—The hospital ship Guildford Castle, returning to its home port with Red Cross signs showing, was unsuccessfully attacked by a submarine in Bristol Channel Sunday, the Admiralty announced to-day.

Two torpedoes were fired at the Guildford Castle. The second one badly damaged her bow. The vessel carried many sick and wounded.

The Guildford Castle is owned by the Union-Castle Company, which also owned the Glenart Castle, torpedoed and sunk in Bristol Channel February 27 with the loss of [illegible] lives. The Guildford Castle was built in [illegible] and has a displacement of 8036 tons which is somewhat larger than the Glenart Castle.

BRUMBAUGH IN ANANIAS CLUB

Senator Sproul Says Governor Is All Wrong About Anti-Option Remarks.

GERMAN LOOT QUEST SPURS ALLIES TO WIN

Fighting Spirit of America Stirred by Teutons' Plunder of Near East.

OPEN NEW SUPPLY ROUTE

Capture of Odessa Will Open Way of Communication to the Orient in Opinion of Military Experts.

By United Press Leased Wire.

Washington, D. C., March 14.—Germany's plunder quest in the Near East is doing more to spur America and the Allies to a rousing war spirit than anything she has undertaken, not barring U-boat warfare, according to the view of officials to-day.

Capture of Odessa, golden key to a rich wheat country and stopping point on Germany's new route to the East—far from causing gloom here—only served to stir the war spirit.

Game little Rumania has aroused the admiration of officials and her fate has stirred their ire.

Long extracts from Teuton papers just reaching here show that the Germans doubt the wisdom of militarist tactics toward Rumania and Russia.

That Germany has dreams of a new route to the East in place of the Berlin-Bagdad scheme is the thought of military men generally. Odessa—the Black Sea—Persia, Afghanistan, India, is the route she now dreams of.

Germany's talk of peace by negotiation compared to her Russian and Rumanian peace by conquest make her promises idle, say the German papers.

Every nation shall remember German terms as a "decree of terror"

MILLIONS IN TURKEY MAY BE MASSACRED

Germany Believed to Be Inciting Natives to Slaughter of Christians.

MISSIONARIES ARE THERE

Seventeen Americans Among Those Who May Be Forced to Sacrifice Their Lives.

By United Press Leased Wire.

Boston, Mass., March 14.—More than 2,000,000 Christian Armenians, Georgians and others, among whom are seventeen American missionaries, are in imminent peril of being massacred by the Turks and Tartars in Northeastern Turkey and Trans-Caucasia.

This information was contained in private cables to the American Board of Missions here and was announced through the Congregationalist to-day.

The advices, which came from agents of the board now in the line of the Teuton drive in the east, said the Turks and Tartars under German direction, are being incited to wipe out the foreigners. "The details of the Teuton plans would strike terror to the civilized world," according to the report. An international authority whose name, for diplomatic reasons, cannot be given, said Germany would welcome a declaration of war on Turkey by the United States.

Germany is making every effort, and with tangible results, to incite the Tartars and Turks to unite in an attack on the Armenians and Georgians, for the reason that Germany wishes to eliminate the Armenians and Georgians from the political is-

EVERY MAN'S PLEDGE.

America shall win this war! Therefore, I will work, I will save, I will sacrifice, I will endure. I will fight—cheerfully, and to my utmost—as if the whole outcome of the struggle depended upon me alone.—Advertising Club of Allentown.

TROTSKY TO RESUME WAR ON GERMANY

Former Russian Prime Minister Reported to Be Organizing Army.

REPORT FROM FRANCIS

American Ambassador, Now at Vologda, Sends State Department Significant Message.

By United Press Leased Wire.

Washington, D. C., March 14.—Leon Trotsky, former Bolshevik Prime Minister, is talking of organizing an army "under iron discipline" to fight the Germans, evidently believing renewal of war on the Germans is unavoidable.

This was the report Ambassador Francis at Vologda sent the State Department overnight. He said Trotsky was reported to be very curious about the Siberian situation and very sensitive over the report that any of the Allies contemplated entering Siberia.

The authorities regard the message as significant in view of Trotsky's split with Lenine who is trying to head off opposition to the Germans. Francis' message did not indicate with whom

PENNA. TROOPS WIN HIGH PR

First American Troops in Franc Big Victory Over Teuton Receive the Commendati French Army Officers.

By United Press Leased Wire.

Washington, D. C., March 14.—Americans of the crack Rainbow Division walloped the Germans when they tried out strong sorties on the night of March 4th—and received official commendation from French General Gerard, General Pershing cabled the War Department to-day.

Pershing's summary of the action was:

"Enemy attempted trench raids morning of the fifth. Raid repulsed with losses to the enemy. Our losses slight, no missing or prisoners. General Gerard, commanding Eighth French army, congratulated division commander on the way with which troops repulsed raids."

The Rainbow Division—first big American unit to leave for France—was made up of picked guard troops from almost every state, including National Guard troops from Lancaster, Bethlehem, Easton and Reading, Pa.

By FRED S. FERGUSON
(United Press Staff Correspondent)

With the American Army in France, March 13.—The American troops are "ready to attack anything."

The officer commanding the American forces in the Luneville region, including Ohio troops, so stated in a message to the home folks, sent through the United Press to-day.

The last 24 hours in tor have been the quiete taken over by the Am

Five engineers repa tanglements in No Ma countered ten German this front. They killed Boches and the others

By WILLIAM PHIL
(United Press Staff Co

With the British Arm March 14.—Battle plan along the west front, has become more and nounced especially in t Passchendaele and St. C sage balloons are up with observation officers neath, minutely watchi ing lines.

Wherever one goes, t is gained of a full head the huge war machin every joint. The entire state of feverishness, ful, springlike weather the work in all departm

Signs are not lacking tivity by the enemy, wh constantly growing.

The airmen on both s night and day—the Br military works along lines; the latter hoveri and open towns, murd and children.

William Howard Taft at the fairgrounds: 1918

William Howard Taft looked jovial, with his ample mustache and his Santa-like girth. By all accounts, he was. He had the common touch, too, which showed in a March 14, 1918, visit to Camp Crane in Allentown.

Camp Crane was an Army ambulance corps training ground established at the Allentown Fairgrounds as America entered World War I. When Taft dropped by to survey the troops – he was president of the American Red Cross at the time – he bypassed the officers' mess and settled down to eat with the privates.

They dined (heartily, one presumes, given Taft's famously big frame) on corned beef, baked beans, fried potatoes, blackberry jelly, bread and butter.

Taft spent 10 hours in town being serenaded by The Nurses' Chorus and watching boxing matches before addressing the assembled "USAACs" – short for U.S. Army Ambulance Corps.

The Ohio Republican was the 27th president, serving from 1909 to 1913. He was defeated in his re-election bid by Democrat Woodrow Wilson, who tried in vain to keep America out of the European war.

Now, there was a distinct impatience simmering among the soldiers, who wanted to get overseas and wallop "the Hun" – Germany.

"Don't be impatient, boys," Taft told them in an address that condemned both the German war machine and homegrown pacifism. "The war will last until you get there."

Taft had come to Allentown twice before, once in December 1913 to address the Jordan Masonic Lodge, and again in 1915 for the dedication of Allentown Hospital's nursing school.

The 1913 visit was made at the behest of Allentown Treasurer A.L. Reichenbach and businessman Harry W. Kress, both Masons who thought an address from a former president would be just the way to draw attention to their newly minted lodge.

Taft at the time was a professor of constitutional law at Yale University – he would go on to serve as chief justice of the United States – and had no particular reason beyond graciousness to accept the invitation. But he agreed to come. Perhaps it was out of deference to his old friend Harry Trexler, the industrialist who was the city's most prominent son.

On the evening of Dec. 16, Taft arrived to find enthusiastic crowds at the Lehigh Valley Railroad station. Trexler was there to greet him on the platform.

The president's first stop was Zion Reformed United Church of Christ at 620 Hamilton St., where he addressed high school and college students. He told the boys that the world would not hand them what they wanted but make them fight for it. And he told the girls that they could find fulfillment outside of marriage.

"Understand," he said, "I am not speaking against matrimony. It is the happiest state in life but only happy when voluntary."

After a pause for handshaking at the Hotel Allen at Seventh and Hamilton streets, Taft and his entourage made their way to Mealy's Auditorium, a vast ballroom on the site of the present-day City Hall.

After the traditional serenade offered to distinguished city guests by the Allentown Band, Taft spoke of his admiration for the Masons, a fraternal order devoted to charitable work whose top officers are called "worshipful masters."

"I have filled many offices," he said. "When they were passed around my plate was right side up. I have been a district attorney, several kinds of judges, a governor of the Philippines and president of the United States. So far I have got through without getting into the penitentiary. But I never had an office like that of your worshipful master and how they manage to keep all those things in their heads I'd like to know. I never had a task to equal it in all my office holding."

LEFT TOP: A 1908 postcard supporting William Howard Taft and his running mate, James Sherman. Taft, a Republican, would be elected the nation's 27th president. (Courtesy of Kurt Zwikl of Allentown)

LEFT BOTTOM: The Chronicle and News front page from March 14, 1918, headliines Taft's visit to Allentown and news of the war.

ABOVE: A portrait of President Taft. (Courtesy of William Howard Taft National Historic Site, Cincinnati)

THE ALLENTOWN MORNING CALL, FRIDAY, MARCH

EX-PRESIDENT TAFT GREETING SOLDIERS AT CAMP CRANE.

EX-PRESIDENT TAFT AND BIG BROTHERS GUESTS IN CAMP CRANE

Big Day Spent With Ambulance Men—Review of Troops, Program of Sports, Soldiers' Mess and Notable Patriotic Address

LEFT TOP: A 1908 campaign ribbon promoting Taft for president. (Courtesy of Kurt Zwikl)

LEFT BOTTOM: A photo in The Allentown Morning Call shows former President Taft on March 14, 1918, greeting soldiers at Camp Crane, which used to be at the Allentown Fairgrounds.

ABOVE: A bugler plays into a huge megaphone at Camp Crane, established at the Allentown Fairgrounds to train the U.S. Army Ambulance Corps. (Courtesy of the Lehigh County Historical Society)

ABOVE: Gen. Harry Trexler leaving the Livingston Club on Seventh Street in Allentown. The club served as an informal headquarters for Trexler as he built his business empire in the Valley. In 1917, future president Warren G. Harding spent the night here. (Morning Call Archives)

RIGHT TOP: President Harding, whose tenure was beset by scandals and is considered one of the low points of the American presidency. He visited the Lehigh Valley once, addressing the Allentown Chamber of Commerce in December 1917.

RIGHT BOTTOM: A Harding campaign button and a Harding-Calvin Coolidge campaign button. (Courtesy of Stephen Cunningham of Nazareth)

HARDING

Warren G. Harding, world in upheaval: 1917

Warren G. Harding was the 29th president and, according to many historians, a failure. But all that was ahead of him when he came to Allentown on Dec. 13, 1917, to speak at the annual Chamber of Commerce banquet at the Odd Fellows Hall on Ninth Street.

The Ohio Republican was a U.S. senator at the time, an affable and well-liked man who must have appeared destined for greater things despite his underwhelming congressional record. Reuben J. Butz, the chamber president and toastmaster, introduced Harding to the Odd Fellows audience of 500 as the man who "may well be the country's next president."

The country had entered World War I eight months earlier and Harding gave what the Allentown Chronicle and News called "a ringing patriotic address."

"All the world is in upheaval," he said. "More than [1.3 billion] people are involved in this gigantic conflict which is transforming everything, and popular government is in the test ... No man is worth anything to the United States if he does not serve. We must win this war of the world."

Harding admitted that he had misgivings about Great Britain and its immense naval power at the start of the war three years earlier. He believed, the Chronicle and News story said, "that she wanted to dominate the commerce of the world."

Now, however, he considered Britain's "bulldog courage" against Germany to be the primary reason that war had not spread to America's very shores.

Harding received warm applause for his remarks, but the evening's greatest ovation was reserved for industrialist Charles M. Schwab, one of the creators of Bethlehem Steel. His company had made millions of dollars supplying the Allies since the onset of the war and stood to make millions more supplying American troops, so he gave a naturally upbeat assessment of its fortunes.

Harding never came to the Lehigh Valley as president. Elected in 1920, his administration was tainted by cronyism and scandal. The so-called Teapot Dome scandal involved the leasing of government oil reserves to private companies without competitive bidding. Harding's secretary of the interior, Albert Fall, was convicted of taking bribes in the case.

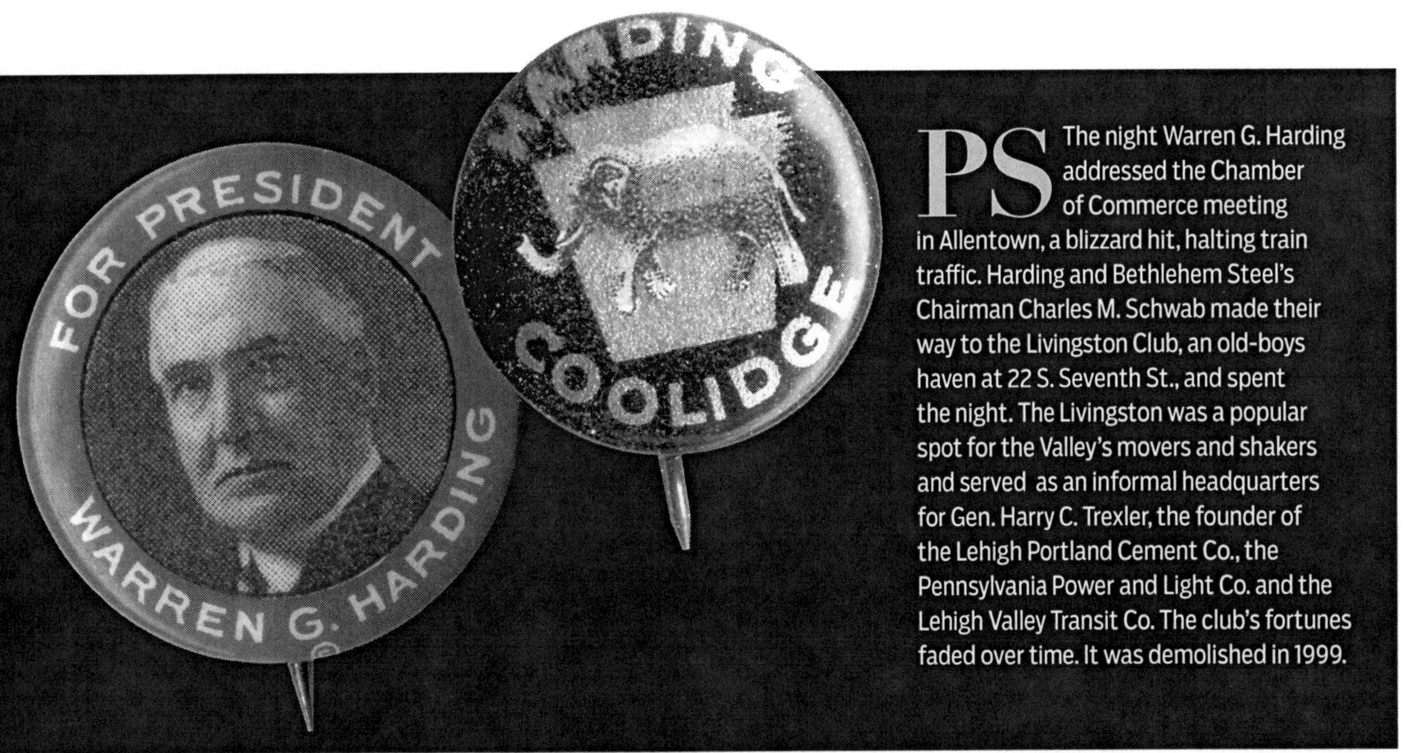

PS The night Warren G. Harding addressed the Chamber of Commerce meeting in Allentown, a blizzard hit, halting train traffic. Harding and Bethlehem Steel's Chairman Charles M. Schwab made their way to the Livingston Club, an old-boys haven at 22 S. Seventh St., and spent the night. The Livingston was a popular spot for the Valley's movers and shakers and served as an informal headquarters for Gen. Harry C. Trexler, the founder of the Lehigh Portland Cement Co., the Pennsylvania Power and Light Co. and the Lehigh Valley Transit Co. The club's fortunes faded over time. It was demolished in 1999.

ALLENTOWN MORNING CALL, SUNDAY, AUGUST 16, 1936

Mauch Chunk Steals Show As President Roosevelt Goes Thru Lehigh Valley Towns

Six Minute Stop in Switzerland of America Where Once Chief Executives Habitually Visited, Gives Carbon County Great Opportunity to Greet the President. Gordon Clay, Lehighton Veteran, Pilots Engine, with Mickey Coyle, 'Democrat in Good Standing' as Fireman

Lichtenwalner In Conference With President

Guest of Mr. Roosevelt During Tour of State's Flood Areas

Part of the Crowd That Awaited Presidential Special at Allentow

Allentonians Defy Storm to Wait For Roosevelt Train Running Late; Many Get Glimpse of Famous Smile And Wave As Special Slows Down

Entire Valley Greets F. D. R.

Not Since T. R. Came Has Valley Seen a President

Phoebe Home Nurse Weds

Charlotte E. Keck Is the Bride of Luther A. Barto

New Hunting Permit Order

License Type Changed and Regulations for Issuance Altered

Band Concert Tuesday Night

Allentown Band to Give First Program at Union Terrace

National Quota Officer Feted

Kathleen Welch, Acting Secretary, Guest of Honor at Tea Here

Knauss - Iobst Family Reunes

Several Hundred Attend 27th

Guard Journey Of President

Lehigh Valley Railroad Takes

As we face serious times, I feel doubly assured that the students who come from the Seminary and College set upon the hill in Bethlehem will, as in ancient times, shine forth giving light, life, and strength to all of those about them.

Very sincerely yours,

Franklin D. Roosevelt

Dr. Edwin J. Heath,
President,
Moravian Seminary and College,
Bethlehem, Pennsylvania.

TOP LEFT: The Allentown Morning Call from Aug. 16, 1936, reporting on the excitement when President Franklin D. Roosevelt's train passed through the region.

TOP RIGHT: A button and ribbon from President Roosevelt's 1941 inauguration. (Courtesy of Kurt Zwikl of Allentown)

BOTTOM: A 1942 letter from President Roosevelt to Edwin Heath, president of the Moravian Seminary and College in Bethlehem, marking its bicentennial. (Courtesy of The Moravian Archives, Bethlehem)

F.D. ROOSEVELT

Hi FDR, bye FDR: 1936

Well, it was better than nothing.

America's longest-serving president, the patrician Franklin Delano Roosevelt, visited Mauch Chunk — present-day Jim Thorpe — on Aug. 15, 1936. But he stayed for only six minutes.

It was enough to thrill a crowd of 5,000 enthusiasts who filled downtown to greet Roosevelt as he made his way on a special Lehigh Valley Railroad train from Wilkes-Barre to Newark, N.J.

The 32nd president, in a duty nowadays carried out from the air, had been touring areas of New York and Pennsylvania that had been stricken by Susquehanna River flooding months earlier. Looking tanned and healthy, he stood on the rear platform of the train for about three minutes, waving and smiling and shaking a few hands.

He offered no remarks, but heard plenty.

"Thanks for the beer," one man shouted, a reference to the end of America's long, disastrous experiment in enforced abstinence from alcohol. Roosevelt, whose 1932 campaign had promised an end to Prohibition as part of a broad strategy to end the Depression, grinned broadly.

A few minutes later, the train departed, heading south into the Lehigh Valley.

In Allentown, nearly 2,000 people turned out to the railroad station on lower Hamilton Street, hoping the president's train might stop.

It didn't. But as it moved slowly through, a smiling Roosevelt waved from inside the observation car, acknowledging the cheers of the crowd.

As the train pulled out of the station, the heavens opened.

"No one seemed to care," the Allentown Morning Call reported. "They had seen the president!"

PS A story in the Aug. 16, 1936, edition of The Allentown Morning Call carried news of the Olympic games in Berlin, including a sidebar tale of a woman who managed to elude Adolf Hitler's blackshirt guards and give the Führer a kiss. "At first embarrassed, the chancellor took the incident good-naturedly," the story said.

TOP: President Roosevelt, America's longest-serving chief executive. He passed through the Lehigh Valley in 1936, waving from his train as it rolled through Allentown, Bethlehem and Easton after a six-minute stop in Mauch Chunk (present-day Jim Thorpe). (Courtesy of the Franklin D. Roosevelt Library and Museum, Hyde Park, N.Y.)

BOTTOM: Roosevelt campaign buttons. (Courtesy of Kurt Zwikl)

ELEANOR ROOSEVELT

First lady 'of the whole world': 1942-56

Jacqueline Kennedy was glamorous. Hillary Clinton was tough. But in the history of first ladies, no one tops Eleanor Roosevelt.

She was a smart, gracious humanitarian and the first presidential spouse to turn that position into one of genuine influence in domestic and international affairs. President Harry Truman would call her the first lady "of the whole world" for her efforts to spread peace and fight poverty.

She would show that on her visits to the Lehigh Valley, and unlike her husband, Franklin, Eleanor did more than roll through on a slow train and wave. She made several visits, most notably to Allentown on May 26, 1942, a spring day in wartime.

The first lady had come to speak at a Muhlenberg College celebration marking 200 years since the arrival of the school's namesake, Henry Melchior Muhlenberg, a German Lutheran missionary to Pennsylvania. About 5,000 were expected to gather that evening in the school stadium to hear her address.

First, however, Roosevelt wanted to visit Allentown's Hanover Acres. Affordable housing was one of her abiding concerns, and Hanover Acres was one of the country's first low-income housing projects, where rents ranged from $18.50 to $23.75 a month.

As her police-escorted car entered the east Allentown project, she turned to her hostess, Reba Tyson, wife of Muhlenberg President Levering Tyson, and said she was glad to see wash on the clotheslines, "where the sunshine and plenty of fresh air can get at it."

No one at Hanover Acres had any idea the first lady was coming for a visit, but word traveled fast. As she met with the housing authority board in the administration building, a crowd gathered outside. The throng followed Roosevelt and her entourage as they made their way to the home of Luther Ebert, a Bethlehem Steel worker.

Ebert was at work, but his wife, Arlene, was at home, ironing. According to The Morning Call, Ebert, "ninety-odd pound mother of six children," nearly dropped the iron when the first lady walked into the kitchen.

"I was so nervous, my hand was trembling when I was shaking hands with her," Ebert said.

Roosevelt questioned the housing authority board about the rent structure and spoke of the need for a nursery school, among other matters. She then departed for Allentown Hospital (now Lehigh Valley Hospital) to visit the ailing Judge Frank M. Trexler, Muhlenberg's oldest graduate. "It was just one of the little niceties Mrs. Tyson switched into the itinerary of a busy day," the Call noted.

That night, before receiving an honorary doctorate, Roosevelt told the Muhlenberg stadium crowd that America had to prepare for a new job after World War II, "the job of being leader in the development of a new world."

"First we must win this war, because if we don't win it, nothing we want can come to pass," she noted, adding that women in particular had a greater role to play in the nation's destiny than ever before. "Since we have equal rights as citizens, we have equal responsibilities and must accept them," she said.

She compared America's educational system to Germany's: "Americans want their children to think for themselves. Hitler wants robots — strong and healthy robots that must act as they are directed."

Roosevelt made several other visits to the Valley. In December 1954, she spoke to 600 people at the Jewish Community Center in Allentown, launching the center's annual lecture series. She touched on a frequent theme: that Americans must look beyond their own culture and borders and gain greater understanding of people elsewhere in the world. Only this way could the nation fully claim moral and spiritual authority, she said.

She also criticized the communist-hunting of U.S. Sen. Joseph McCarthy of Wisconsin. "There is no question in my mind that Sen. McCarthy has hurt our leadership," she said.

In 1956, Roosevelt returned to campaign for Democratic presidential candidate Adlai Stevenson, speaking at the Northampton Memorial Community Center and spending the night at the E. 19th Street home of George Schisler, who owned an oil company in the borough.

LEFT: First lady Eleanor Roosevelt speaks at Muhlenberg College on May 26, 1942. She also visited Hanover Acres in Allentown, one of the country's first low-income housing projects. (Morning Call Archives)

ABOVE: Roosevelt made several trips to the Lehigh Valley, some as first lady. (Courtesy of The Library of Congress)

THE WEATHER
Rain and moderate.

THE MORNING CALL

Lehigh Valley's Greatest Newspaper

VOL. 104, NO. 126 ★ ★ ★ ALLENTOWN, PA., WEDNESDAY MORNING, MAY 27, 1942

Hitler Pressing Laval for Use Of French Navy

German Sailors Being Prepared To Take Ships

Would Threaten Allied Mediterranean Strength

Strength of French Naval Force Secret

Speaking at the Muhlenberg Bicentennial

ANNA ELEANOR ROOSEVELT

Challenge to Americans Given By Mrs. Roosevelt in Address At Muhlenberg Celebration

FDR Jokes with Newsmen About Utopian Shangri La

WASHINGTON, May 26. (AP)—President Roosevelt gave the press a new report today about the fictional Utopia, Shangri La, from which he has insisted the American air raid on Japan was launched.

With evident delight, he told a press conference that he had been informed a southern newspaper editor had been asked by a reader where Shangri La was.

The reader said he had examined every parish in the state of Louisana and had been unable to find Shangri, La.

Then, in a spirit of fun, the President said he was going to look into the question of when an Ambassador from Shangri La would present credentials.

And, to a question whether he had received any cancelled stamps for his collection from the mythical Tibetan retreat, Mr. Roosevelt said the Lama had sent him a special album.

First Lady of Land Comes to Allentown to Take Part in College Bicentennial Observance—Calls Upon People to Prepare for Task That Faces Nation, Job of Winning War and of Becoming Leader in Development of New World

Allentown and Muhlenberg college had an unforgettable day yesterday when America's gracious first lady, Anna Eleanor Roosevelt, came to the college to join in the Nation's tribute to the family whose name it bears.

Beneath the towers of the college that lives as a monument to pioneers who helped found the ideals of freedom and democracy on these shores, the wife of the President of the United States challenged Americans to prepare now for the task that faces this Nation—"the job of being a leader in the development of a new world."

"First we must win this war, because if we don't win it nothing we want can come to pass," Mrs. Roosevelt told an audience of more than 5,000 at last night's bicentennial program in the college stadium.

"At the same time each one of us must think, as we examine ourselves, how we all can be real citizens in a democratic community. In doing that we'll be prepared to meet whatever problems come and face them squarely."

She made a two-fold plea: That Americans direct their thinking in terms of a world economy that will make it possible for people throuhgout the world to work and to live decently; and that they resolve to deal fairly and justly and on an equal basis with people of all races. The future, she said, will be based on both.

Mrs. Roosevelt's visit to Allentown in connection with the Women's Day program of the Bicentennial Week, was a highlight in Allentown's history. Never before has the wife of a President of the United States come to the city while her husband is in office. And probably never before did anyone receive the kind of an ovation in Allentown that was accorded Mrs. Roosevelt from the moment she arrived on the campus at 3:45 o'clock ...

Soviet Forces Press Advance In Kharkov Area

Dig Into Newly-won Positions in Drive Toward City

MOSCOW, Wednesday, May 27. (AP)—Marshal Timoshenko's forces dug into their newly-won positions on the Kharkov front today after a deep advance from previously consolidated points while in the south the Red army is holding off increasingly violent German assaults upon their flank, the Russians announced officially at midnight.

The midnight communique said the Russians were rapidly fortifying their reclaimed positions, which front line dispatches said were gained in a ...

Allied Air Drive Against Germany Is Expected Soon

Top Ranking American Army and Navy Chiefs in London to Map Strategy

Telegraphic News Briefs

Chinese Admit Situation Grave Near Chekiang

Chungking Says Coming Week Will Witness 'Even Fiercer Battles'

Enemy Sub Sunk Off Brazil Coast

U. S. Bomber Pilots Destroy Second Axis Raider in Four Days

US Warship Hit by Torpedo Off Martinique; 10 Missing

Old World War Destroyer Blakeley Damaged While Patrolling Waters Near Island—Makes Way to Harbor At Fort de France—Six of Crew Injured

U. S. Lend-Lease Aid Terms Given Russia By Secretary Hull

Hitler Still Boss

$500 'Boner'

Royal Air Force Attacks Axis Positions in Libya

Duce Has Big Army at French Alpine Border

Invasion of Nice and Corsica Appears Imminent Unless Vichy Grants Demands

Japs Strengthen Island Airfields In South Pacific

Improved Weather Ends A-A Fliers 'Field Day' Enjoyed Since Last Wednesday

TOP FAR LEFT: The Morning Call ran this picture of first lady Roosevelt with the tower of the Lutheran college in Allentown in the background. The occasion was Roosevelt's visit in May 1942.

TOP NEAR LEFT: Teatime at Muhlenberg College in Allentown. Roosevelt visited the college as it celebrated the arrival of its namesake, German Lutheran missionary Henry Melchior Muhlenberg, to America. To her right is Mrs. F. H. Knubel, wife of the president of the United Lutheran Church of America, and on her left is college trustee Howard Shimer. (Courtesy of Muhlenberg College Trexler Library, Special Collections & Archives)

LEFT: First lady Roosevelt arrives at Muhlenberg accompanied by Reba Tyson, wife of college President Levering Tyson. (Courtesy of Muhlenberg College Trexler Library, Special Collections & Archives)

ABOVE: The Morning Call of May 27, 1942, notes first lady Roosevelt's visit to Muhlenberg College, where she received an honorary degree before speaking about women's issues and other topics to a crowd of 5,000.

The LAFAYETTE ALUMNUS . .

President Hutchison, '18, Gen. Eisenhower, '46H, T. Frank Soles, '04, Thomas J. Watson, '34H, in the doorway of Kirby Hall

Area Woman Third In Eisenhower's Calls

Wilbur Shaw, 2 Others Die In Air Crash

'Hello, Mr. President'

ABOVE LEFT: Gen. Dwight D. Eisenhower is flanked by Lafayette College President Ralph Cooper Hutchison on the left and Vice President of the Board Thomas J. Watson on the right a they tour the campus Nov. 1, 1946. (Courtesy of Special Collections & College Archives, Skillman Library, Lafayette College)

ABOVE TOP RIGHT: The Sunday Call-Chronicle of Oct. 31, 1954, leads with Eisenhower making phone calls to 10 voters around the nation. In Pennsylvania, (shown at the bottom of the page) Frances Tyahla of Summit Hill received one of the calls.

ABOVE BOTTOM RIGHT: Campaign buttons for Eisenhower, who was known as "Ike" since boyhood. (Courtesy of Kurt Zwikl of Allentown) An Eisenhower-Nixon button plays on the penchant for rhyming catch phrases. (Courtesy of Stephen Cunningham of Nazareth)

PAGE 45: Gen. Eisenhower speaks at an alumni dinner held in his honor by Lafayette College at the Hotel Easton. "Ike," a war hero, was elected president six years later. (Courtesy of Special Collections & College Archives, Skillman Library, Lafayette College)

EISENHOWER

They liked Ike: 1946

The Lehigh Valley was buzzing on Nov. 1, 1946, and for good reason.

Gen. Dwight D. Eisenhower — six years shy of his election as 34th president, but as famous and admired as any head of state — was coming to visit. The great hero of the war in Europe was to receive an honorary doctorate during Founders' Day ceremonies at Lafayette College in Easton.

The five-star general took a train from Philadelphia to Bethlehem and proceeded by car to Easton, traversing a route mobbed by admirers. By the time he reached Easton's Centre Square, "the progress of his sleek Packard was slowed to a snail's pace," The Morning Call reported.

The general seemed a little surprised by the size of the crowds, but reacted coolly when an 11-year-old boy named Michael Rich — his father, Thomas, had served under Eisenhower in Europe during World War II — jumped onto the Packard's running board.

"The famous Eisenhower handshake was extended, together with a cheerful 'Hi-ya,'" the newspaper reported. "So affected was the youngster that his eyes filled with tears."

At Lafayette, Eisenhower joined trustees for lunch in Kirby Hall, then received his degree in Alumni Memorial Gymnasium.

"The ovation accorded General Eisenhower was a prolonged roll of thunder," the Lafayette Alumnus magazine reported in a story illustrated by photos of the future president among faculty and students.

The laudatory article described the general as a paradoxical figure: "The leader of the strongest, greatest fighting machine ever to take the field in the history of the world is at heart a peace-loving, friendly, human and gentle man."

In his speech, Eisenhower spoke of the American armed forces standing down from war and returning to civilian life, noting how the demobilization after World War I had been accomplished under the guidance of a Lafayette alumnus, Army Chief of Staff Gen. Peyton C. March.

At the time, March had cautioned against isolationism and complacency, Eisenhower noted, but a generation's disregard of that warning had allowed Hitler and Mussolini to rise to power and drive the world into a second conflagration.

Without vigilance, it could happen again, Eisenhower said.

"Gen. March's warning of 27 years ago is far more urgent today," he said. "Our geographic immunity has totally disappeared. Our responsibilities have multiplied. Both selfish interests and the world's future press us to a firm resolve that we shall never again, through our apathy or weakness, permit aggression another chance."

Eisenhower visited the Valley one other time. In 1948, he and wife Mamie, along with her mother, stopped for lunch at a Howard Johnson's restaurant at Airport Road and Union Boulevard in Allentown. They were heading back to Washington, D.C., after visiting their new grandson in New York.

The general was gracious, posing for photos and patiently deflecting the newspapermen who asked about his presidential ambitions.

That question would be answered soon enough. Eisenhower was the Republican candidate in 1952 and defeated Democrat Adlai Stevenson in a landslide. Eisenhower did the same thing, against the same Democrat, four years later.

PS Nobody had better campaign slogans than Dwight D. Eisenhower. "I Like Ike." "Peace and Prosperity." "The Man of the Hour: Eisenhower."

Not that slogans said anything about the quality of the president. James K. Polk gave us one of the catchiest: "54-40 or Fight," a reference to the Oregon Territory dispute with Great Britain. But no one would rank Polk greater than Abraham Lincoln, who offered "Vote Yourself a Farm" during his first campaign, and "Don't Swap Horses in the Middle of the Stream" during his second.

When Republican James Blaine battled Democrat Grover Cleveland in the 1884 campaign, Blaine supporters came up with an unforgettable slogan referring to Cleveland's fathering of an illegitimate child: "Ma, Ma, Where's my pa?" (After Cleveland won, the gibe was appended with "Gone to the White House, Ha ha ha!").
Cleveland's supporters coined a catchy comeback: "Blaine! Blaine! James G. Blaine! The continental liar from the state of Maine."

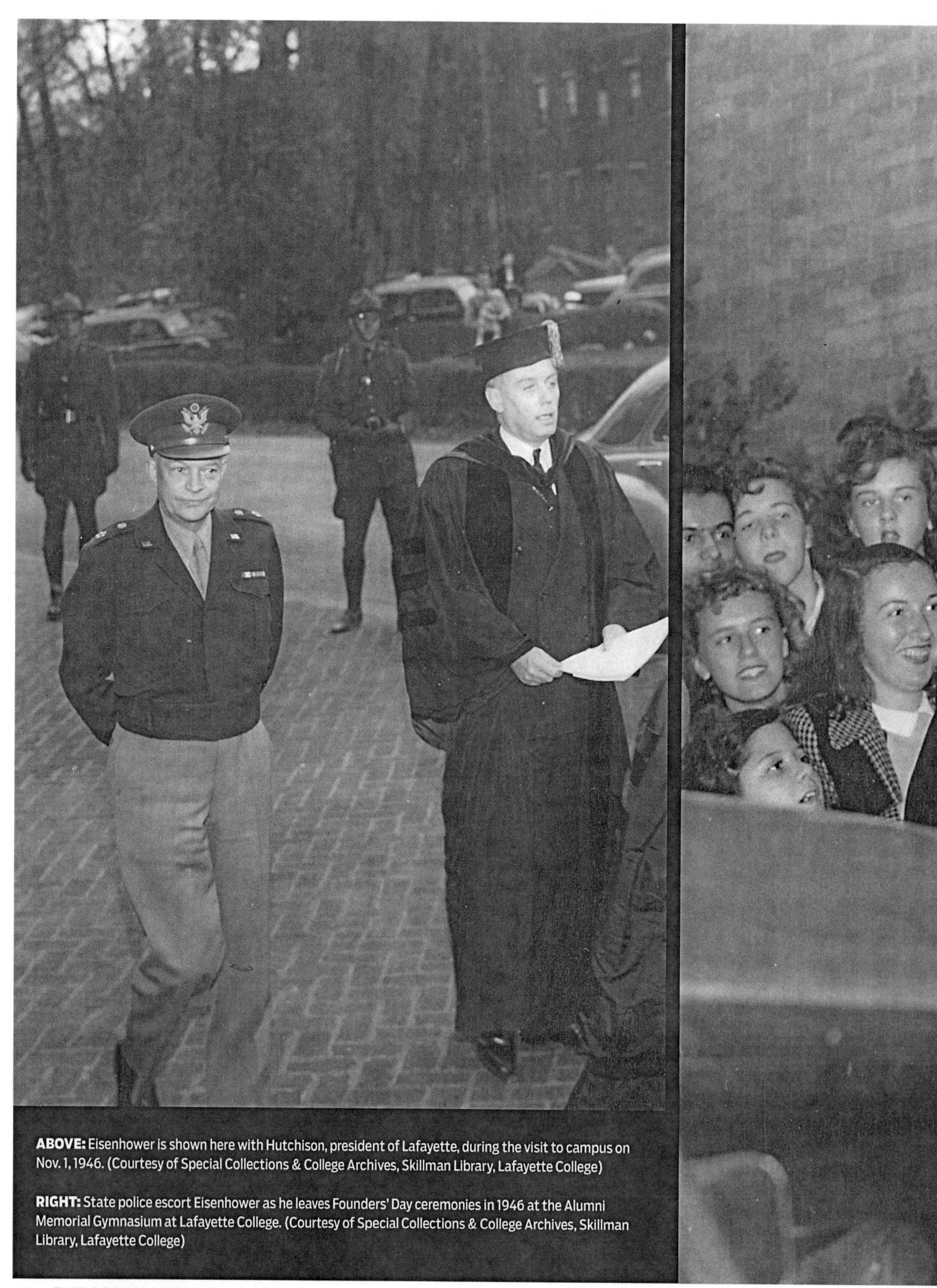

ABOVE: Eisenhower is shown here with Hutchison, president of Lafayette, during the visit to campus on Nov. 1, 1946. (Courtesy of Special Collections & College Archives, Skillman Library, Lafayette College)

RIGHT: State police escort Eisenhower as he leaves Founders' Day ceremonies in 1946 at the Alumni Memorial Gymnasium at Lafayette College. (Courtesy of Special Collections & College Archives, Skillman Library, Lafayette College)

SEAL OF THE PRESIDENT OF THE UNITED STATES

Harry Truman vs. 'do-nothing' Congress: 1948

During the election campaign that was destined to produce the most famous blown call in journalism history, President Harry Truman and his wife, Bess, passed through the Lehigh Valley on a whistle-stop train tour. Truman had assumed the presidency upon the death of Franklin D. Roosevelt in 1945 and was counting on the labor vote to secure his first full term. On Oct. 8, 1948, he found a warm welcome in the heavily industrial Valley, where he addressed crowds estimated at 8,000 to 10,000 in Allentown, Bethlehem and Easton. This was a transitional time, between the cataclysm of World War II and the atomic anxiety of the Cold War. As Americans settled into postwar life and the baby boom continued apace, Congress approved the Marshall Plan to aid European recovery and slow the spread of communism. Israel was born. Mahatma Gandhi was assassinated. In the Valley, Bethlehem Steel and Mack Trucks were among the major employers, so the crowds embraced Truman's labor-friendly rhetoric. He demanded an increase in the 40-cents-an-hour minimum wage, a winning proposition at a time when wages averaged around $2,900 a year. He pushed back against GOP accusations that his proposed federal housing program — with its target of 20 million new dwellings by 1960 — was "socialist." In Bethlehem, with jaw clenched, he condemned the "awful, do-nothing 80th Congress," a Republican-controlled body that rejected universal health care and other elements of Truman's "Fair Deal" agenda. The Morning Call's "Roving Reporter," Charles W. Ettinger, was among a group of Allentonians who rode with the Trumans from the trip's starting point in Reading. The president, Ettinger concluded, was just the kind of man he seemed to be in newspaper and newsreel portrayals: homespun and plain-spoken, with an eagerness to meet and greet people that drove the Secret Service to distraction. "He resents it when we try to keep people away from him," one agent said. "It never occurs to him that anyone might want to hurt him." Sounding a little starstruck, Ettinger wrote about the sense of confidence aboard the Truman train, despite polls showing the president was a distinct underdog in the race against Republican nominee Thomas E. Dewey. The Chicago Tribune was so certain the challenger would win, it went to press on election night with the banner headline, "Dewey Defeats Truman." A famous photograph shows a broadly grinning Truman holding the paper aloft during a train stopover in St. Louis.

LEFT: President Harry Truman and first lady, Bess wave from the rear of the train during the 1948 stop in Allentown. (Morning Call Archives)

RIGHT TOP: President Truman circa 1946. (U.S. Army, courtesy Harry S. Truman Library, Independence, Mo.)

RIGHT BOTTOM: A Truman campaign button. (Courtesy of Kurt Zwikl of Allentown)

PAGES 50-51: Morning Call photographer William Zwikl, at center in front of the pole and holding his Speed Graphic camera, had one of the best seats in town as the Trumans' train stopped at the station in Allentown.

PS

- How Pennsylvania voted in 1948: Thomas E. Dewey, 50.9 percent (1,902,197 votes); Harry Truman, 46.9 percent (1,752,426 votes).
- In Allentown, crowds gathered near the train station on lower Hamilton Street by 9 a.m., four hours before the scheduled arrival of Truman's presidential train.
- In Bethlehem, the Liberty High School Band serenaded Truman with "Hail to the Chief." The president introduced his wife by saying "I want you to meet my boss."

8
9
10

Hailing the chiefs: The Allentown Band

Has any municipal band played for more presidents than the Allentown Band? It's hard to know for sure, but the venerable ensemble has a distinguished record in that regard.

Founded in 1828, it serenaded its first president 11 years later, playing for Martin Van Buren when he visited Allentown.

Abraham Lincoln heard the band in 1861 during flag-raising ceremonies at

Independence Hall in Philadelphia. The band later played at the inaugurations of Ulysses S. Grant (1869), William McKinley (1897), Theodore Roosevelt (1901), Woodrow Wilson (1913) and Warren Harding (1921).

Roosevelt and Wilson also heard the band when they visited Allentown in 1912. So did former President William Howard Taft in 1913.

ABOVE: The Allentown Band is all smiles in this group portait taken in 1891. (Courtesy of The Allentown Band)

PART II

Airplanes

ABOVE: Vice President Richard Nixon is welcomed by fans at Allentown-Bethlehem-Easton Airport in 1960. An enlarged airport and shifting demographics brought a flood of candidates to the Lehigh Valley from this campaign onward. (Morning Call Archives)

PAGE 57: The 1960 presidential tickets, from left, Democratic candidate John F. Kennedy and running mate Lyndon Johnson, and GOP candidate Richard Nixon and running mate Henry Cabot Lodge.

HERE COMES EVERYBODY

Pennsylvania as swing state

For 10 days in October of 1960, the Lehigh Valley hosted an unprecedented run of distinguished guests, including three men who would go on to steer the ship of state through two of America's most tumultuous decades.

The area had welcomed presidents and presidential contenders before, of course, but the visits were occasional and sometimes the product of happenstance, such as Franklin Delano Roosevelt's smile-and-wave roll through Valley train stations in 1936 as he headed from Wilkes-Barre to New York.

The 1960 election was different. Between Oct. 18 and 28, the Valley welcomed all four candidates on the major party presidential tickets: Democrats John F. Kennedy and his running mate, Lyndon B. Johnson; and Republicans Richard M. Nixon and Henry Cabot Lodge, the Massachusetts statesman Nixon had tapped as his running mate in a bid for votes in Kennedy's home state.

Together, the four visitors drew perhaps 200,000 people to the streets, lecture halls and ballrooms of the Valley's cities. In that age before sound bites and truncated attention spans, they offered deep, often lengthy assessments of America's fortunes at home and abroad.

Former Democratic state Rep. Kurt Zwikl of Allentown, an expert on presidential visits to the Valley and on the 1960 campaign in particular, wrote a 1998 study for the Lehigh County Historical Society in which he describes this 10-day period as "the most politically historic occasion in the history of Allentown and the Lehigh Valley.

"Other candidates had come and gone, but never before ... has this area of Pennsylvania been host to the top four candidates for national office within such a short period and at such an important time in our nation's history."

The reason was no mystery, Zwikl concluded. Pennsylvania, long a Republican stronghold, had become a swing state in the 1950s, and by 1960 the number of registered Democrats exceeded the number of Republicans for the first time, albeit by a small margin. According to many polls, the state was a tossup.

That made the Lehigh Valley crucial territory. It was the fourth most-populous region of Pennsylvania at the time, and Allentown's big-circulation newspaper, the Call-Chronicle, reached a large portion of the state's eastern population.

"If Kennedy would carry Philadelphia and Pittsburgh and Nixon would run strong in the suburbs and rural areas of the state, it was reasoned that the Lehigh Valley region might well decide who was going to carry Pennsylvania," Zwikl wrote.

The advent of jet travel had made visiting areas like the Valley a quick and easy matter. Railroad stations had long been the welcoming spot for dignitaries on whistle-stop train tours, but reporters and photographers were now just as likely to be dispatched to Allentown-Bethlehem-Easton Airport, where recent runway expansion made it possible to accommodate candidates' planes.

Pennsylvania, particularly in the last several presidential elections, has retained its swing-state status, and has grown accustomed to repeated visits from high-office hopefuls. In 1960, however, this level of attention was new and enthralling.

The first to arrive was Lyndon Johnson.

28 Evening Chronicle, Allentown, Pa., Wed., Oct. 19, 1960

We Saw You—As Allentown Entertained Senator Lyndon Johnson

ABOVE: A Call-Chronicle page sums up U.S. Sen. Lyndon Johnson's visit to Allentown on Oct. 18, 1960, where he stumped as Democratic presidential candidate U.S. Sen. John F. Kennedy's running mate. Speaking at the old Frolics Ballroom on Union Boulevard, Johnson expressed the hope that voters would look beyond Kennedy's Roman Catholic faith, a source of consternation for many in largely Protestant America.

RIGHT TOP: Johnson in 1960. (Morning Call Archives)

RIGHT BOTTOM: This campaign button refers to Johnson's wife, Claudia "Lady Bird" Johnson. (Courtesy of Stephen Cunningham of Nazareth)

JOHNSON

Lyndon Johnson, a Texan in pajamas: 1960-66

Lyndon Johnson, the big, blunt Texan who would enter the White House in the wake of unspeakable tragedy, got a hearty welcome from Lehigh Valley Democrats on Oct. 18, 1960.

John F. Kennedy's running mate took the podium that Tuesday evening in front of 4,500 partisans at the old Frolics Ballroom on Union Boulevard in Allentown and urged voters to look beyond religion, an issue in the campaign because the nation's Protestant majority viewed Kennedy's Catholicism with suspicion. (Indeed, anti-Catholic literature would be anonymously distributed around the Bethlehem area when Kennedy visited later that month.)

Johnson, at the time a U.S. senator from Texas and majority leader, told the crowd that Kennedy's brother, Joseph, died on a mission during World War II alongside fellow aviator James Wiley, a Texas Baptist.

"They died for you," he said. "They died for America. And there wasn't anybody around the morning they volunteered for that mission who asked, 'What church do you belong to?'"

The next morning, Johnson, clad in pajamas, sat for an interview at the Howard Johnson Motor Lodge near Allentown-Bethlehem-Easton Airport with the Evening Chronicle's Ralph Rosenberger.

The candidate was sucking lozenges to relieve hoarseness — the consequence of making 70 speeches in a week, he said. It was a grueling schedule for a man who had suffered a coronary four years earlier.

"I still watch my food, you know, after that heart attack," the future president said. "I got to like oatmeal when I was just a youngster, and it's still my breakfast mainstay."

Johnson played up his Pennsylvania roots — his Colonial-era ancestors lived near Lancaster — as he discussed the nature of campaigning.

He was an expert on the topic, having watched his father run for the Texas Legislature in 1917 and launching his own career in 1937 by winning a seat in the U.S. House of Representatives.

"It isn't much different," he said. "About the only change is the crowds are a little bigger, the people more interested in what you have to say."

By the time he returned to the region in October 1966, the nation and the world had fundamentally changed. Kennedy's 1963 assassination had elevated Johnson to the White House, and he had won a full term the following year. The war in Vietnam was growing hotter. And the civil rights movement was in full flower.

At the Oct. 16 dedication of Our Lady of Czestochowa, a sprawling Polish Catholic shrine in the countryside near Doylestown, the president urged a crowd estimated at 135,000 to enlist in the struggle for racial equality.

Johnson told the Polish-American crowd that their ancestors were no strangers to discrimination, so they ought to be especially sensitive to the plight of black Americans.

"Their struggle is our own affair," he said. "Let us make it our cause as well."

Johnson had done his part for the cause, signing the landmark1964 Civil Rights Act that outlawed school segregation and other forms of discrimination against minorities. Passing such a law had been one of Kennedy's central concerns before his assassination.

WE
DON'T WANT
LADY BIRD
EITHER

PS The front page of The Morning Call on Oct. 17, 1966, carried the news of President Lyndon Johnson's appearance at the dedication of Our Lady of Czestochowa and a smaller item at the bottom of the page: "Terrorists' Mine Kills GI, wounds 6 others in Saigon." Johnson escalated the American presence in Vietnam from fewer than 20,000 soldiers and advisers in 1963 to more than 500,000 combat troops in 1968. The growing anti-war movement was a key element in his decision not to seek re-election in 1968.

THIRD

THE MORNING CALL

The Weather: Fair and cool today. Fair with frost tomorrow.

DON'T SAY ORANGE! Ask for Orange Crush

Worth Repeating

Lehigh Valley's Greatest Newspaper

NO. 24,820 ★ ALLENTOWN, PA., MONDAY, OCTOBER 17, 1966 10c A Copy 48c Weekly Home Delivered

President Urges Polish-Americans to Aid Negro At Dedication of Bucks County Catholic Shrine

Huge crowd gathers at Polish shrine near Doylestown to hear President.

Procession Colorful

Dedication Mass Viewed by 14,000

By CURT YESKE

Stresses E. Europe Relations

Crowd Put Up to 135,000

By WALTER R. MEARS, Of the Associated Press

Percys Absolved In Slaying

Ceremony Sidelights

Think Packer Line Tough? Secret Service Is Tougher

A Record-Setter

President Starts Asia Trip Today

Turks Seek To Restrict Americans

Move Afoot in U. N. To Pull Out of U. S.

FIRST CALL

Pioneer

PS On Oct. 24, 1964, Lady Bird Johnson drew a crowd of 10,000 people to Center Square in Allentown as she stumped for her husband. President Lyndon Johnson had been elevated to the nation's top office 11 months earlier after the assassination of President John Kennedy and was promoting the Great Society reforms aimed at decreasing poverty and racism. The first lady, addressing a largely female crowd, said it would be women who gave the Great Society "its permanence and continuity." She drew her biggest cheers when she said, "It was a wonderful thrill seeing your beautiful Lehigh County in all its gorgeous autumn colors from the air."

To the President of the United States of America, Lyndon Baines Johnson.

LEFT: As Johnson gets ready to board his plane at A-B-E Airport in October 1960, he says good-bye to two girls dressed as cowgirls. They are Sallie and Catherine Cutshall, daughters of Allan Cutshall, chairman of the Lehigh County Citizens for Kennedy Johnson. (Morning Call Archives)

TOP: The Morning Call front page after President Johnson dedicated the Polish-Catholic National Shrine of Our Lady of Czestochowa outside Doylestown in October 1966. Appealing to the history of discrimination suffered by Poles, Johnson urged the crowd to support equality for African-Americans.

BOTTOM LEFT: The card that accompanied a gift presented to President Johnson at Our Lady of Czestochowa on Oct. 17, 1966. (Courtesy of the LBJ Library)

BOTTOM RIGHT: A cartoon of President Johnson by Morning Call cartoonist Bud Tamblyn. It is signed by the president. (Courtesy of the Lehigh County Historical Society)

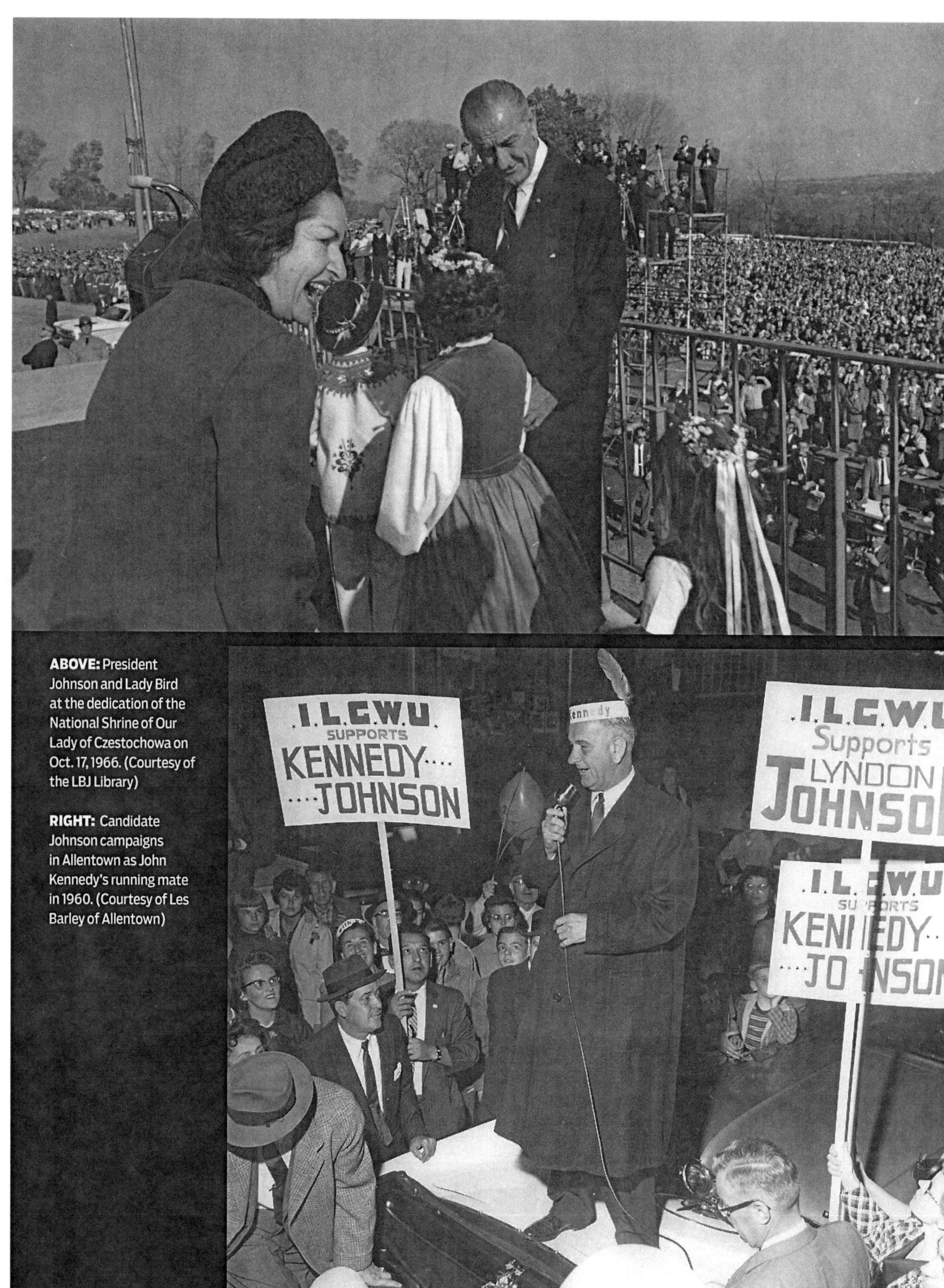

ABOVE: President Johnson and Lady Bird at the dedication of the National Shrine of Our Lady of Czestochowa on Oct. 17, 1966. (Courtesy of the LBJ Library)

RIGHT: Candidate Johnson campaigns in Allentown as John Kennedy's running mate in 1960. (Courtesy of Les Barley of Allentown)

To the Ladies of the Bethlehem Seminary

Washington 7th Novr 1826

The extreme ill health under which I have laboured ever since my return to Washington, has prevented the earlier acknowledgment of the receipt, of the elegant specimen of workmanship so beautifully executed by the Pupils of the Bethlehem Seminary, and presented to me in so very flattering a manner. —

The great interest I must ever take in the exertions of my Sex, to attain excellence and perfection in the cultivation of their minds, and in the acquirement of useful and elegant accomplishments, may perhaps entitle me to express my admiration of the work with which you have honoured me, in which the purest taste and the neatest execution is conspicuous; and return my grateful thanks for the honour thus conferred on me, by the distinction thus bestowed; a sense of which is deeply impressed on my heart. —

With assurances of the highest Respect, permit me to offer to the Ladies of the Bethlehem Seminary, the best wishes for their happiness and prosperity.

Louisa Catherine Adams

Letter from Mrs Adams, Lady of the President of the United States
recd Nov. 12 1826. —

To the Young Ladies of the
Female Seminary at
Bethlehem.
Pennsylvania

ABOVE: The thank-you letter and envelope from first lady Louisa Catherine Adams to Moravian Seminary for Girls (Courtesy of the Moravian Archives)

Gifts from Bethlehem for the first ladies

Students of the Moravian Seminary for Girls in Bethlehem twice presented America's first ladies with gifts of needlework.

The first time was in 1826, when the school sent an elaborate piece of silk embroidery to Louisa Catherine Adams, wife of President John Quincy Adams.

The first lady responded with a thank-you letter, saying how much she appreciated the "elegant specimen of workmanship so beautifully executed by the pupils of Moravian Seminary."

On May 15, 1968 — a time when student protests against the Vietnam War began to reach full boil — Lady Bird Johnson received a similar gift, a petit point quilt presented in person by the young women who made it.

Johnson recorded the event in her diary:

"About 11 I went down to the library to meet some young students from the Moravian Seminary. A class from this same Moravian Seminary had presented to Mrs. John Quincy Adams a needlepoint sampler so popular in that day, and this class wanted to present a similar one to me! They were darling girls — bright-faced, excited at being in the White House. I couldn't imagine one of them walking in a picket line or throwing rocks at their dean. We had iced tea and cookies and they gave me the sampler in a warm little ceremony."

Weather
Cloudy, Warmer

SUNDAY CALL-CHRONICLE

15¢

Lehigh Valley's ONLY Sunday Newspaper

NO. 2046 ★ ★ ★ Telephone HE 3-4241 ALLENTOWN, PA., SUNDAY, OCTOBER 23, 1960 Entered 2nd Class Matter Post Office, Allentown, Pa.

Nixon Welcomed by 100,000, Calls Kennedy Ideas 'Reckless'

FOOTBALL SCORES

(Complete sports coverage on pages 45 to 51)

Coaldale	19
Nesq.	0
Marian	7
S. Hill	0
North.	31
Palm'ton	19
Cass Tp.	32
McAdoo	0
G-burg	14
Muhl.	12
Rutgers	8
Lehigh	0
Leb. Val.	22
Moravian	16
Bucknell	28
Lafayette	0
ESSC	58
Cheyney	0
Illinois	10
Penn St.	8
Navy	27
Penn	0
Iowa	21
Purdue	14
North.	7
N. Dame	6

Vice President Nixon addresses overflow crowd in Muhlenberg Memorial Hall.

Rips Opponent On Cuba Issue

Cites Danger of War In Democrat's Policy

By RALPH ROSENBERGER
Of The Call-Chronicle Staff

Vice President Richard M. Nixon staked out a claim for a four-year lease on the White House last night in Allentown, based on a program founded on the American ideals of "moral and spiritual strength," rather than on the type of Democratic leadership offered by his Democratic opponent Sen. John F. Kennedy on the Cuban issue which Nixon said "could bring civil war in Cuba and easily lead to world war."

It was evident that Nixon had the gloves off and was going to wage a no-holds-barred fight from here on to Nov. 8. He made this plain when he stepped off his plane at the Allentown-Bethlehem-Easton Airport earlier, and told a "We Want Nixon" chanting mob that "it's time for pouring on the coal."

His major speech to a jammed-to-the-rafters Muhlenberg College Memorial Hall, came in the closing moments of a five-hour visit to Allentown that just about outstripped any previous tribute to a national celebrity. It could have been rivaled only by the turnout for Gen. Douglas MacArthur to Allentown on Sept. 21, 1951.

Just before he left last night Nixon remarked, "Wasn't this stupendous! Ithought the entire town turned out."

He could have been right. Police estimates tf the turnout for the vice president were 100,000. These included the crowd at the airport, along the motorcade

See Photos on Pages 4, 5, 29, 39

route into Allentown, at the Americus Hotel and in the field house and the grandstands of the football field at Muhlenberg College.

Nixon's visit here came at the end of a campaign swing through Southeastern Pennsylvania Saturday that brought crowds out ranging in estimates to 240,000.

Throughout his 13-stop trip he kept hammering away at the theme uncovered in the Friday night joint television appearance with Sen. Kennedy, last of the four "great debates," that Kenday's proposals for Cuba were dangerous.

Nixon called Kennedy's ideas of U.S. government support of a revolution in Cuba "the most reckless proposal ever made in our history by a presidential candidate during a campaign."

The vice president said Kennedy's proposals for Cuba show an "immaturity, a rashness, a lack of understanding and an irresponsibility which raises a serious question as to whether he

Highlights and Sidelights

It was just a sliver of a moon that greeted Mr. Nixon at Muhlenberg College and, even that was erased when the colorful pyrotechnic display took place. The vice president blinked at the first salvo.

There was some booing — most of it in the highly Democratic 6th Ward.

The confetti cascade was the work of many young Republicans who worked long hours preparing the shower ingredients for a minute of tribute.

Mr. Nixon's "dinner" at the Americus consisted of a ham and cheese sandwich and a cup of tomato soup. And Mrs. Nixon ordered a club sandwich."

Mr. Nixon's health appeared fine. He was ruddy-cheeked, no lines of care, and only a tinge of gray hair along the temples of his bushy hair. He was clean-shaven. Definitely no signs of a "5 o'clock shadow."

Harry Clark, Americus manager, had a filet mignon ready for the Nixons but never had a chance to serve it. Mr. Nixon's first request upon entering the hotel was for "some hot coffee," the Vice President admitting he was "chilled to the bone."

Mrs. Nixon accepted a bouquet of artificial flowers from the hotel and said "I'll take these back to Washington."

There was much glamour at the airport welcome provided by the 50 Muhlenberg Coeds under di-

Agreement Ends Strike Against GE

NEW YORK (AP) — The International Union of Electrical workers ended its 21-day-old strike against the General Electric Co. Saturday night.

Federal mediators announced the settlement after six hours of talks with both sides.

Some 61,000 workers affected by the strike are expected to return to work Monday.

Union and company negotiators agreed to a three-year contract effective at Midnight Sunday.

It provides for an immediate 3 per cent wage increase.

In addition, the union has 30 days to take one of three options.

The first would provide an additional 3 per cent wage increase in April 1962, an eighth paid holiday, and a fourth week of vacation after 25 years.

The second would provide a 4 per cent increase in April 1962 without additional holiday or vacation benefits.

The third would provide only for a wage reopener clause in April 1962.

General Electric has discharged or suspended an estimated 50 to 100 workers since the strike began Oct. 2. It affected workers in 55 GE plants around the country.

Negotiations had broken down four days ago, but were resumed Friday after mediators met with both sides.

A pact between the union and

An Emotional Tornado

Allentown 'Goes Wild' Over Nixon

By JOHN T. CATHERS
of the Call-Chronicle Staff

Allentown went wild last night over Richard Milhous Nixon.

It wasn't expected to — but, it did!

And there were some 100,000 witnesses.

They just couldn't restrain themselves in their enthusiasm for the Republican presidential candidate.

They jammed themselves together like olives in a jar at the Allentown-Bethlehem- Easton Airport.

They strung themselves out along the five-mile route into the city.

Break Police Barriers

They pushed and cheered. They strained their necks. Jumped onto automobile hoods. Broke through police barriers. They stampeded at some places. Crushed forward at others. Little children were hoisted onto their father's shoulders. Elderly people sat on the curbs in wheelchairs.

They waved flags and banners and released balloons.

They yelled until they were hoarse. And they cried, too. There were copious tears of joy.

They appeared to be caught up in an emotional tornado that increased in fervor at every turn.

At the airport people stood in a chill wind for three hours awaiting the arrival of the Nixon plane, and also the two planes carrying newsmen and photographers attached to the Nixon campaign party.

They didn't mind the iron-gray clouds that sent icicles up and down their spines.

They just waited, and hoped that the wait would be worthwhile.

And it was.

When Nixon's American Airlines flagship "Washington' 'appeared in the northeast and began to circle the field the dying late autumn sun broke through at the same time the crowd spotted the plane.

Across the flat acres of the airport, bordered by golden husks of corn, echoed a common cry of glee:

"Here he comes!"

And the crowd sensed that this was the "moment."

They pressed against the barricades and the police and security officers pushed them back. A little girl was forced under the line and an understanding officer permitted her to stand in front of the others.

Road Clogged

On the airport lawns hundreds of cars were parked. Some arrived shortly after noon, but the great mass clogged Shoenersville road in the hour before the Nixon arrival.

The crowd was orderly at first — cheerfully waving the Nixon colors, and proudly displaying the Nixon-Lodge buttons and the banners that could not be misunderstood: "Experience Counts."

Continued on Page 4, Column 5

Invasion Fear Rises In Havana

Hammers at Foe

Kennedy Asks Nixon For Prestige Report

Eisenhower In Mexico Tomorrow

ABOVE: The Sunday Call-Chronicle of Oct. 23, 1960, sums up the excitement of Vice President Richard Nixon's visit the day before. The candidate spent much of his time hammering his opponent's lack of foreign policy experience and discussing the threat posed by Cuba, where Fidel Castro was creating the Western Hemisphere's first communist regime.

RIGHT TOP: President Nixon.

RIGHT BOTTOM: Vice President Nixon speaks at the Lafayette College commencement in Easton on June 7, 1956. (Courtesy of Special Collections and College Archives, Skillman Library, Lafayette College)

PAGES 66-67: A crowd outside the Americus Hotel at Sixth and Hamilton streets in Allentown welcomes Vice President Nixon and his wife, Pat, on Oct. 22, 1960. (Morning Call Archives)

NIXON

Richard M. Nixon, cheers and tears of joy: 1952-68

By 1960, Richard Nixon had been vice president for eight years, groomed all along to be President Eisenhower's successor. So perhaps it was no surprise that his arrival in the Lehigh Valley on Oct. 22 that year caused such a stir. Some 100,000 people greeted him along the motorcade route between Allentown-Bethlehem-Easton Airport and downtown Allentown.

Nixon had already weathered a minor scandal. In 1952, as Eisenhower's newly minted running mate, he was accused of maintaining a secret political fund and trading favors for donations and gifts. He defused the crisis with a televised speech, emotionally defending himself and famously refusing to return one of the gifts, a dog named Checkers.

That episode was long behind him and the epic Watergate scandal was years in the future when he and his wife, Pat, arrived on the last leg of a campaign swing through southeastern Pennsylvania.

The vice president was scheduled to speak at Muhlenberg College in Allentown after dining at the Americus Hotel at Sixth and Hamilton streets, where banners above the entrance read "Welcome! Pat and Dick" and "Hello! Mr. Nixon."

Nixon had been to the Lehigh Valley before, welcomed warmly in October 1952 — about a month after the Checkers speech — as he campaigned for the vice presidency. In 1956, he visited Easton to speak at Lafayette College's commencement.

The crowds were far bigger and more fervent in October 1960. Because of what Nixon would become — the jowly villain of Watergate and Vietnam — it is hard to imagine his presence driving spectators to cheers and even tears, but it did. Indeed, the Sunday Call-Chronicle reported that some spectators on the motorcade route broke through police barricades for a closer look.

At Muhlenberg, Nixon spoke at length about foreign affairs, particularly tensions with two nations: Red China, which was threatening an invasion of American ally Taiwan, and Cuba, where Fidel Castro and his revolutionaries were establishing the first communist regime in the Western Hemisphere.

Years later in a letter to Kurt Zwikl of Allentown, who was researching the campaign, Nixon said he considered the speech to be aimed at a national audience rather than a local one. "However," he added, "I would not have spoken on such complex issues unless I had felt the Muhlenberg audience was sophisticated enough to want to hear something more than the usual campaign stump speech."

Four days after Nixon's visit, his running mate came to town. Former United Nations Ambassador Henry Cabot Lodge of Massachusetts was tired after arriving at A-B-E at 2 a.m. He spent the night at the Hotel Bethlehem, resting for two scheduled rallies.

The first, in Easton, drew about 3,000 people to Centre Square. Lodge revisited Nixon's Cuba theme, knocking the foreign policy inexperience of the opposition.

"There should be no job training at the White House," he said. He made the same points later to about 5,000 people gathered on Third Street in Bethlehem, then headed back to A-B-E for a flight to Philadelphia.

Nixon returned to Allentown in 1968 during his second run for president as part of a 157-mile motorcade that took him to Reading, Pottsville and Hazleton. At the Allentown Fairgrounds, he told the cheering crowd of 8,000 that it was time to reject the "slap-happy economics" of his Democratic opponent, Hubert H. Humphrey.

Nixon pledged "prosperity without war and progress without inflation." And, in a lighter moment, he said he would be the first piano-playing president in 20 years.

"We'll bring 'The Pennsylvania Polka' right to the White House," he promised.

REYNOLDS
& CO.
WELCOME!
PAT and DICK
AMERICUS
POLICE

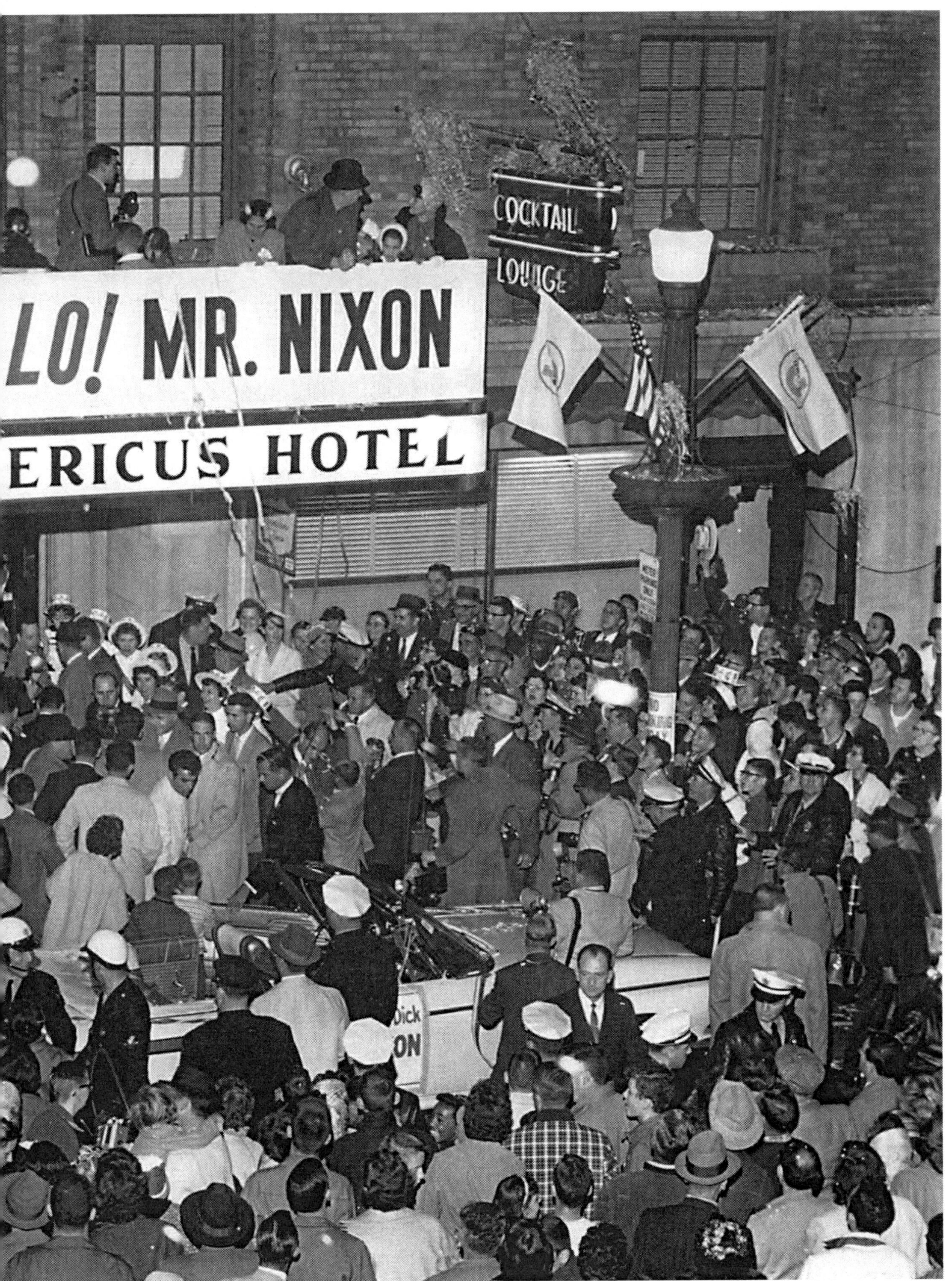
LO! MR. NIXON
ERICUS HOTEL
COCKTAIL
LOUNGE
Dick
ON

MUHLENBERG COLLEGE MEMORIAL HALL
24TH AND LIBERTY STREETS, ALLENTOWN

SATURDAY
OCTOBER
22
1960

Doors Open
6:00 P.M.

VICE PRESIDENT
RICHARD M. NIXON
Meet Pat and Dick!

Republican Committees of Lehigh, Carbon, Monroe
and Northampton Counties

UNION LABEL 3

COMPLIMENTARY

ADMIT ONE

ABOVE: A ticket for Vice President Nixon's talk at Muhlenberg College during the 1960 campaign against U.S. Sen. John F. Kennedy. (Courtesy of Kurt Zwikl of Allentown)

RIGHT: An autographed photo from the collection of Kurt Zwikl shows then U.S. Sen. Nixon campaigning in Allentown in 1952 as Gen. Dwight Eisenhower's running mate. Nixon served as vice president for eight years before making a failed bid for the White House in 1960. Eight years later, Nixon finally reached the promised land. (Photo by William Zwikl)

PAGE 69: A poster advertising Nixon's visit to the Allentown Fairgrounds in the fall of 1968. After years of being groomed for the job, Nixon would finally win the White House that year. (Courtesy of Bill Albert of North Catasauqua)

PAGE 69 BOTTOM: A Nixon campaign button reflecting the voting age in 1960. The war in Vietnam, where soldiers too young to vote could be sent to fight and die, was the impetus behind the movement to lower the age threshold to 18. (Courtesy of Stephen Cunningham of Nazareth)

To Kurt D. Zwikl
With best wishes,
Richard Nixon

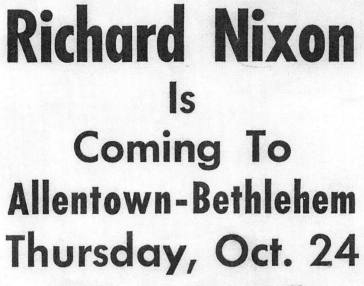

Richard Nixon
Is
Coming To
Allentown-Bethlehem
Thursday, Oct. 24
Come one, come all,
and hear Mr. Nixon at
Agricultural Hall
Allentown Fairgrounds
at 10:15 a. m.
Admission Free

PS Richard Nixon famously taped everything, including an Oval Office meeting with his chief of staff, H.R. Haldeman, on June 23, 1972. Over the course of 90 minutes, the men discuss a broad array of topics and Haldeman at one point refers to "the Democratic break-in thing," a reference to the Watergate burglary that sparked a constitutional crisis and Nixon's downfall.

The president mentions first lady Pat and his oldest daughter, Tricia, who frequently accompanied her father on campaign trips and made many of her own. She had, apparently, run into some unhappy locals on a recent trip to the Lehigh Valley.

"Another point I was going to mention to you, Bob, is the situation with regard to the girls. I was talking to Pat last night. Course Tricia had trouble with (unintelligible) and she mentioned that, she mentioned, Tricia said that apparently when she was in Allentown there were 20 or 30 thugs, labor thugs out booing ..."

IF I
WERE 21
I'D VOTE FOR
NIXON

ABOVE: U.S. Sen. John F. Kennedy addresses a crowd estimated at 85,000 in Allentown's Center Square on Oct. 28, 1960. The soon-to-be president's visit was the culmination of a 10-day period in which all four candidates on the major-party tickets stumped in the Lehigh Valley. (Morning Call Archives)

RIGHT TOP: President Kennedy.

RIGHT BOTTOM: A sticker from the 1960 campaign. (Courtesy of Kurt Zwikl of Allentown)

KENNEDY

John F. Kennedy, 'We want Jack!': 1960

When U.S. Sen. John F. Kennedy came campaigning in 1960, even the seen-it-all reporters of the Lehigh Valley seemed taken aback by the size and enthusiasm of the crowds that turned out: thousands upon thousands of people, young and old, cramming the streets for a look at the handsome presidential hopeful whose youthful Irish face hinted at the promise of the new decade.

Kennedy was already a war hero and a Pulitzer Prize-winning writer for "Profiles in Courage," and now he sought the summit of American achievement.

On Oct. 28, the charismatic Democrat from Massachusetts stood on a platform at the southwest corner of Allentown's Center Square and looked on a sea of cheering, adoring admirers estimated in the tens of thousands. One writer surmised that more people packed the square than at any time since the 1902 dedication of the Soldiers and Sailors Monument.

Confetti poured on the candidate from the top of the old YMCA building. High school bands played a welcoming serenade, but they were hard to hear over the roars of "We want Jack! We want Jack!"

Kennedy had started the day in Bethlehem with a $2-a-plate ham-and-eggs breakfast at the Hotel Bethlehem on Main Street. State Sen. Fred Rooney, dashing around in his eagerness to make sure the event unfolded smoothly, paused to give a reporter his assessment of the importance of the Nov. 8 election: "Our man must win if America is to survive," the Democrat said.

Kennedy told the breakfast's 400 attendees that his Republican opponent, Vice President Richard Nixon, was talking too little about problems at home and far too much about Cuba, where Fidel Castro and his communist revolutionaries were consolidating power. Nixon, the cold warrior, had made that issue central to his address at Muhlenberg College a week earlier.

History would lend that comment an ironic flavor. Kennedy's early presidency was marred by the Bay of Pigs invasion, a failed attempt by American intelligence to inspire the overthrow of Castro. Conversely, one of his shining moments would be his defusing of a nuclear crisis over Soviet missiles on the island nation.

All that was in the future. At the moment, Kennedy was on the verge of winning the White House. He was tired from incessant campaigning but invigorated by the energy of the crowds.

Breakfast in Bethlehem was followed by remarks to a standing-room-only crowd at Moravian College's Johnston Hall. Then it was on to Allentown, where he repeated his critique about Nixon's focus on Cuba and his economic platform for the country. A remark about raising the minimum wage to $1.25 played well in the industrial Valley, where Bethlehem Steel was king despite an industrywide slump that had put many out of work.

"As an American," Kennedy said, "I am not satisfied ... to have only 50 percent of the steel mills of Pennsylvania and the United States operating ... to have 100,000 steel workers out of work ... to build 30 percent less homes this year than last year ... to find that the prestige and influence of the United States, according to studies undertaken by the United States abroad, is lower than it has been in many years.

"I am not satisfied as an American, and I hope you are not, either."

They weren't satisfied, evidently. Kennedy won the White House in a tight race, taking 49.7 percent of the vote to Nixon's 49.5. He did better in Pennsylvania, with 51.1 percent.

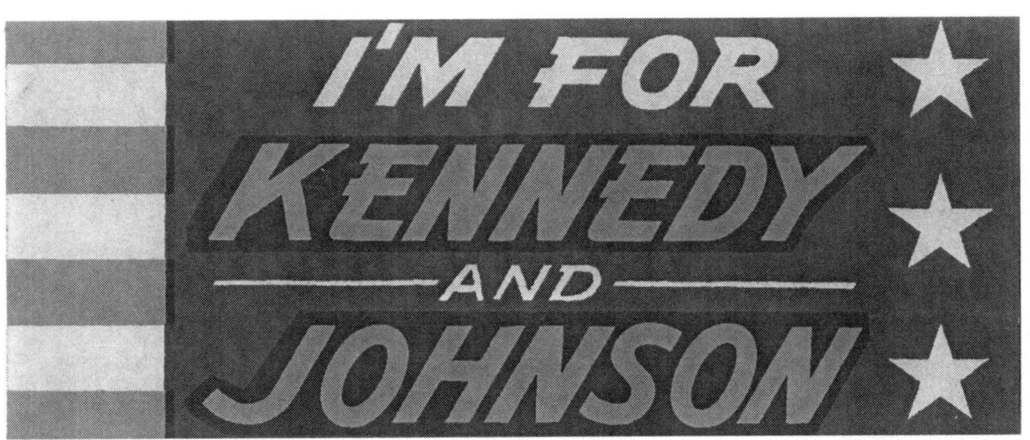

SEE
and
HEAR
(In Person)

SENATOR
JOHN F.

KENNEDY

Democratic Candidate for President

FRIDAY, OCTOBER 28th
10 A. M.

Center Sq., 7th & Hamilton Sts.
Allentown, Pa.

--Public Cordially Invited--

LEFT: A poster advertising candidate Kennedy's visit to Allentown on Oct. 28, 1960. (Courtesy of Kurt Zwikl)

ABOVE: The looks on the faces of the women in the background speak volumes about local reaction to Kennedy during his visit to Allentown. (Courtesy of the Lehigh County Historical Society)

BELOW LEFT: A Kennedy campaign button. (Courtesy of Stephen Cunningham of Nazareth)

BELOW RIGHT: Kennedy in his motorcade on Hamilton Street in Allentown. (Courtesy of the Lehigh County Historical Society)

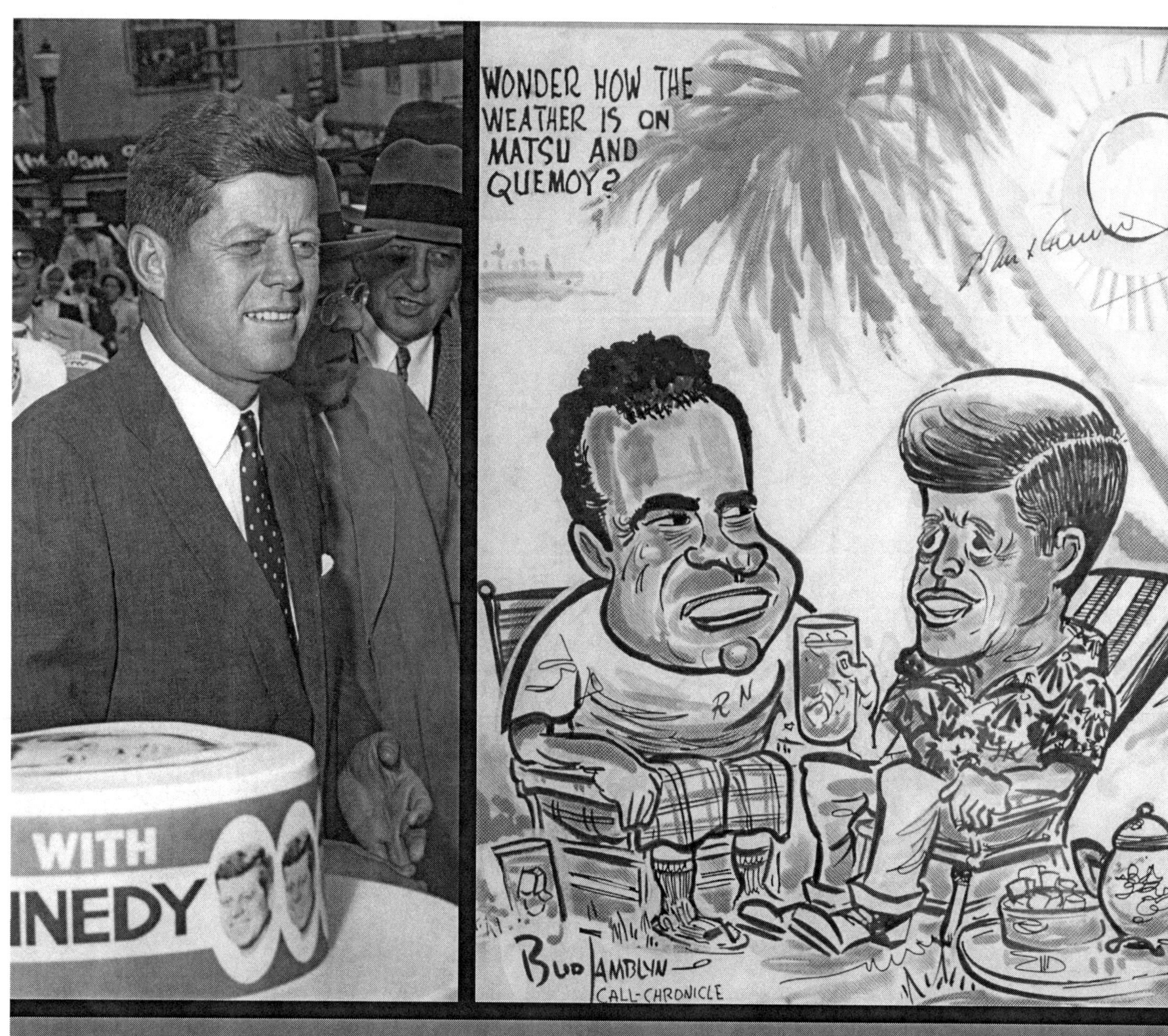

KENNE

FOR PRES

FAR LEFT: Kennedy moves through the crowd in Allentown's Center Square on Oct. 28, 1960. (Morning Call Archives)

LEFT: Call-Chronicle cartoonist Bud Tamblyn imagined the 1960 campaign opponents unwinding on the beach. Matsu and Quemoy were islands off China at the center of a dispute between Red China and Taiwan. They were a hot debate topic.

BELOW: A button from the 1960 campaign that reflected the voting age at the time. It was lowered to 18 in 1971. (Courtesy of Kurt Zwikl)

RIGHT: Confetti falls on Kennedy as he addresses a huge crowd in Allentown's Center Square. (Morning Call Archives)

BOTTOM: A Kennedy bumper sticker from 1960. (Courtesy of Kurt Zwikl)

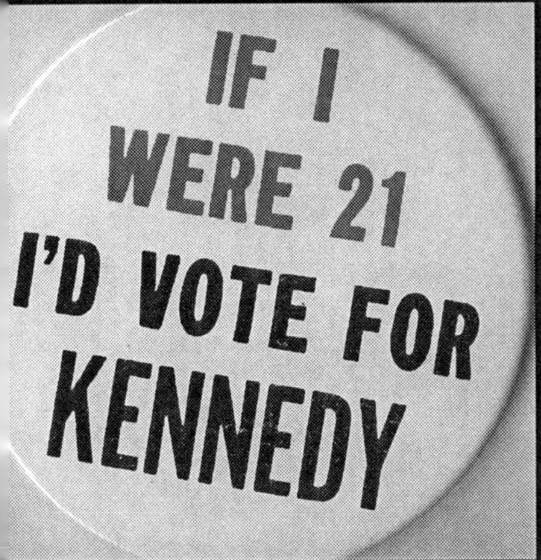

IF I
WERE 21
I'D VOTE FOR
KENNEDY

DY
DENT
CITIZENS FOR KENNEDY AND JOHNSON, 261 CONSTITUTION AVENUE, N.W., WASHINGTON, D.C.

SUNDAY CALL-CHR

'Non-Political' Visit

Goldwater Poses In the Poconos

Arizona's Barry Goldwater has not yet announced his candidacy for the Republican nomination at San Francisco next July. But his supporters are making all kinds of noises to indicate he will certainly do so.

And Sen. Goldwater, although still playing his intentions close to the vest so long as official pronouncements are concerned, acts mighty like one.

For editorial comment on Sen. Goldwater see Page B-10.

Visits Poconos

The senator showed up in the Poconos recently as a guest of John S. Wise Jr., dean of Lehigh Valley fly fisherman, and spent the night at the Wise Tall Timber Camp at Pocono Lake Preserve.

Ostensibly he came for a day or two of rest. But he just happened to have a photographer along from Sports Illustrated magazine. And most of the time he spent was on the Lower Tunkhanna Fishing Association Stream posing for photographs. The photographs taken, he departed early the next morning by private plane from Mt. Pocono.

At his request, the luncheon and dinner conversation and the hour before the Wise fireplace avoided politics for the most part. In a small group, the senator is a quiet man, showing little of his platform fire, though he is an interesting conversationalist with strong opinions on most subjects.

Competent Angler

Mr. Goldwater is a competent fisherman. After watching his host perform he admitted, however, that he still has a long way to go.

"I thought in my life that I had met fishermen," he wrote this week, "but now I know that they were only beginning to learn the art which you understand so thoroughly. I enjoyed every moment of my visit with you, and I hope to have the opportunity of taking advantage of your kind invitation to return sometime this summer.

"I have never fished a more beautiful stream, but more important to me, is the natural way in which you have kept it and I hope you are able to teach thousands of others how to do this so that our streams will not go the way so many have — the beer can, whiskey bottle, dead fish route."

Other Allentonians in the party were Atty. Harold A. Butz and William D. Reimert.

SENATOR - AN
Arizona poses wi
along the Lower
ing trip in the P
maker, of Lanca
subjects.

Allentown, Pa., June 30, 1963 B-5

— Sen. Barry Goldwater of
ost, John S. Wise, Jr., (left)
nna Creek on a recent fish-
. To the right is Sam Slay-
ell-known writer on outdoor

Barry Goldwater's 'Cavalcade of Stars'

Hard to believe after all these years of Barbra Streisand and George Clooney and Brad Pitt, but back in the 1960s, more than a few movie stars fell to the right on the political spectrum. So when Republican U.S. Sen. Barry Goldwater ran for president in 1964 against incumbent Democrat Lyndon Johnson, he enjoyed support from some prominent Hollywood names, from screen star Robert Mitchum to television cowboys Clint Walker and James Drury.

Those three men were slated to be among the luminaries in the "Goldwater-Miller Cavalcade of Stars" that descended on the Lehigh Valley on Oct. 17, 1964, to support the conservative GOP candidate and his running mate, U.S. Rep. William Miller of New York.

Unfortunately, the stars were no-shows, as were starlets Rhonda Fleming and Joanna Dru. The disappointment was palpable when crowds at rally sites in Easton, Bethlehem, Whitehall Township and Allentown learned the big names weren't on hand.

Still, the show went on, with Western musician Perry Botkin, actor Wendell Corey (perhaps best remembered as Jimmy Stewart's detective friend in "Rear Window") and tennis pro Jack Kramer, among others.

The group arrived at Allentown-Bethlehem-Easton Airport, where Corey announced, "Here I am – and I'm for Goldwater."

He went on to accuse the Johnson administration of harboring cheaters and thieves. "If a fish stinks," he said, "it stinks at the head. That's where the blame belongs. At the head."

Ten days after the cavalcade, James Drury made up for his no-show. The star of television's "The Virginian" signed autographs at Hess's Department Store in Allentown, then stood at Ninth and Hamilton streets with two guitar-playing sidekicks and sang a Western tune.

"Over the years it was considered bad taste for Hollywood personalities to actively campaign," he told a reporter from The Evening Chronicle. "But now it's being done for the first time."

He said Goldwater "is the one and only person who can lead us to victory and keep us strong. We are here today because we are frightened Americans – our Constitution and our country are in danger."

Goldwater, who had made a well-publicized but ostensibly nonpolitical fishing trip to the Poconos in 1963, did not campaign in the Valley personally.

He visited five years later, however, as the war in Vietnam raged. Goldwater told a crowd of 2,000 at Lehigh University in Bethlehem that peace in Vietnam without an "honorable settlement" was unacceptable to the United States.

The Weather
Mostly sunny today. Fair and milder tomorrow.

THE MORNING CALL

Lehigh Valley's Greatest Newspaper

NO. 25,448 ★ ★ ★ ALLENTOWN, PA., WEDNESDAY, OCTOBER 30, 1968 10c A Copy 48c

The crowd moves in on Humphrey in hopes of shaking his hand.

5,000 in Bethlehem Hear Humphrey Tell Of Stake in Future

By PHIL STORCH

"Everybody has a stake" in next Tuesday's presidential election and in the future of America, and we must think carefully about who is to provide the leadership for events to come, a crowd of 5,000 was told yesterday by Vice President Hubert H. Humphrey at Moravian College's Johnston Hall, Bethlehem.

The hall was filled to the rafters — and a huge throng milled around outside. Unable, because of space limitations, to crowd into the college athletic building, they waited in the dampness of a wintry day in hope of getting a glimpse of the Democratic presidential candidate.

Humphrey arrived at Allentown - Bethlehem - Easton Airport by jet plane at 2:15 p.m., precisely the time set for arrival. He was whisked away in a motorcade to Bethlehem where a half - hour later he was on the podium. By 4 o'clock, he was back aboard his official plane bound for Philadelphia.

'Basic Goodness'

"I'm convinced there's a basic goodness, a basic greatness in the American people. I seek the presidency of the United States for one reason — to call forth that goodness, that greatness to build strength in our economy, improve our educational program, win world peace and bring about real equality among all peoples of this nation, black and white, rich and poor, North and South."

As he ascended the dais, following introduction by Rep. Fred B. Rooney, of Bethlehem, a mammoth cheer went up from the throats of Humphrey-Muskie supporters, drowning out the beginning of an organized heckling procedure. There were several additional attempts to heckle as time wore on, but Humphrey handled each situation skillfully, driving home his points with such effectiveness that the cheers for the candidate drowned out the detractors.

There were mass demands, "We want Humphrey! We want Humphrey!" as Martin Bechtel, Northampton County Democratic chairman, opened the session. So the candidate at the outset told the crowd, "I want to say if you think you want Humphrey, I want you to know how much I want you." That was greeted with applause.

Speaks for Candidates

He took a moment to speak of the candidacies of Rooney, for re-election to Congress from the 15th District, and Sen. Joseph S. Clark, also seeking re-election. And he commended Dr. Raymond S. Haupert, president of Moravian — who received a standing ovation from students in the assemblage — for building greater what was already a great college. He acknowledged he was aware of Moravian's long and illustrious history.

Then, suddenly, he shouted, "Do you want George Wallace for president?"

"No-o-o-o!" rose a tremendous response.

"Do you want Nixon-Agnew?"

The "no" was even louder because this time no one in the hall was caught napping by the question.

He advised his listeners he was now taking a poll and asked, "Do you want Humphrey and Muskie?"

An overwhelming "Yes" held the scattered "No" votes to a whisper.

In the spirit of the fun resulting from his "poll," Humphrey said, "I accept the results of the election. Thank you very much."

Continued on Page 9, Column 2

Humphrey greets crowd at Johnston H

President, Gen. Abrams Review War

WASHINGTON (AP) — President Johnson met secretly Tuesday with Gen. Creighton Abrams, U.S. military commander in Vietnam, but a White House spokesman said there was "no breakthrough" or change in the Vietnam situation or Paris negotiations.

Abrams had left to return to Vietnam when the White House announced his visit for a "general military review of the situation in Vietnam."

Presidential press secretary George Christian said it was decided over the weekend that Abrams should come to Washington, rather than have the President meet him someplace between here and Vietnam as had been previously considered.

Johnson and the top commander of U.S. forces in the war zone conferred Tuesday at the White House. Abrams met with Pentagon officials, and then joined the regular weekly luncheon at the White House of top military and diplomatic officials.

The group at the luncheon session included Secretary of State Dean Rusk, Secretary of Defense Clark M. Clifford, CIA Director Richard Helms, presidential assistant Walt W. Rostow, Gen. Earle G. Wheeler, chairman of the Joint Chiefs of Staff, Christian and the deputy press secretary, Tom Johnson.

Who's Who Depends on Who's Talking

Saigon Selecting Paris Team; Plan Would Allow NLF Seats

(c) N.Y. Times News Service

SAIGON — The South Vietnamese government was selecting a team of negotiators Tuesday for the peace talks in Paris, apparently on the assumption that North Vietnam might soon accept the latest United States bombing halt proposals.

President Nguyen Van Thieu decided to form the team, according to highly placed sources in Saigon, after quietly agreeing with the United States on a way in which both South Vietnam and the National Liberation Front could be seated at the peace talks.

The seating proposal makes maximum use of semantic distinctions. It would, in effect, give both the South Vietnamese government and the Liberation Front significant representation at the talks, but allow each to ignore the existence of the other.

The Saigon sources emphasized, however, that it was not known definitely here that Hanoi would accept the seating plan.

Thieu has decided to name one general and three colonels to his team, the sources said, and is considering naming Lt. Gen. Vinh Loc, an assistant chief of the Joint General Staff and former commander of Vietnam's 2nd Corps.

In recent days, there has been speculation in both Saigon and Paris that a major obstacle to a conditional bombing halt has been South Vietnam's insistence that the National Liberation Front, or Viet Cong, could not be represented as an organization at the Paris talks.

This would be resolved, from South Vietnam's point of view, under a proposal that is said to have been worked out in conferences between United States Ambassador Ellsworth Bunker and President Thieu.

The complex, semantic plan would allow South Vietnamese and United States negotiating teams to sit side by side at the peace talks, while giving the opposing side the option of regarding them as a single delegation.

The Communist side, for its part, could bring an enlarged delegation to the table and call it two delegations, a joint North Vietnam - N.L.F. delegation, or anything it chose.

However, the United States and South Vietnam would view the opposing negotiators as a single delegation representing "the aggressors from the North." South Vietnam would talk to the North Vietnamese delegates but not to any delegates who referred to themselves as Liberation Front representatives. The United States would talk to any of the delegates but consider them officially as representatives of the North and not of the Liberation Front.

The South Vietnamese representatives would be accepted by the United States as a full autonomous delegation, no matter what the opposing sides choose to call it.

The new seating plan, Saigon sources said, is flexible enough to give all parties freedom to do what they want to do and to allow each opposing side to repudiate the nomenclature used by the other.

Majority Return

Humphrey Tri- Hand at Pollin

By DICK COWEN

Vice President Hubert H. Humphrey took his own poll from the podium at Moravian College.

He asked if the audience wanted George Wallace for president. He got a vigorous "no!"

He asked if the audience wanted Nixon. The Nixon partisans roared "yes!" and waved their banners, with the Humphrey supporters building up their "no" shouts to drown them out.

Then, Humphrey asked if they wanted the Humphrey - Muskie ticket. The vote was "yes" with the Nixon shouting "no" this time.

Humphrey had the c not unanimously, bu whelmingly.

One young man in th ence periodically yelled ing the speech: "What Chicago?"

After a while, a man in an Army uniform lea to the youth and said thing. That stopped tha heckling for the rest speech.

The national press h quently pointed to the h as those opposed to a candidates for president people urging voting An to "drop out" of this pa election.

But the hecklers at M yesterday were Nixon s ers — well - groome dressed, waving their signs and chanting his

Signs and posters w abundance in the hall.

At the back of the hug a large banner read: Valley Welcomes Vice dent Hubert H. Humph

Some of the pro - Hu cardboard posters carri slogans as:

"The apple of our ey . . . Our country need Humphrey . . . Give the HHH . . . Hats off to H

Continued on Page 9, C

Sidewinder Missile Stolen, German Prosecutor Reveals

(c) N.Y. Times News Service

BONN — A 10-foot-long Sidewinder missile was stolen from an allied base in West Germany by three men who trundled it away in a wheelbarrow and drove more than 100 miles with the rocket nose draped in a carpet and protruding from a shattered car window, a federal prosecutor disclosed Tuesday.

The men — including a "Mister X" — stopped en route for gasoline and then packed the dismantled 165-pound weapon off to Moscow by air freight.

Amid mounting concern among West Germans and their allies over the possiblity of an imminent major spy scandal, the prosecutor, Ludwig Martin, also disclosed in Karlsruhe Tuesday two other thefts, of navigational devices, by the same men who smuggled out the Sidewinder.

All three men, he said, are under arrest.

The Sidewinder theft from a North Atlantic Treaty Organization air base called Zell, at Neuberg on the Danube River in Bavaria last year, does not appear to be a major coup for the Russians.

According to a report from Washington Tuesday by the West German news agency, DPA, the rocket is considered a relatively simple device with perhaps two dozen movable parts and no more electronic components than a radio.

First developed in 1953, its main attribute is an infrared guidance system that directs it at heat-giving targets. The system has since been superseded in more advanced weapons.

"We believe the other side had knowledge of these instruments before," the Bonn defense spokesman, Lothar Domrose, said.

The prosecutor's report Tuesday was set against the background of such recent episodes as the escape of six suspected agents to East Germany, three apparent suicides, including that of an admiral, and the arrest of four suspected agents, including the three accused of stealing the Sidewinder. All this has caused an uproar in this espionage-conscious country.

Chancellor Kurt Georg Keisinger phoned Tuesday from Spain, where he is on a state visit, for an urgent report on West German security. It was announced Monday Kiesinger and Vice Chancellor Willy Brandt would take charge

Continued on Page 2, Column 2

Can Settle War, Nixon Tells Rally

SYRACUSE, N.Y. (AP) — Richard M. Nixon, specifically answering the campaign complaints of protesting Syracuse University students, said Tuesday night he can achieve a negotiated settlement in Vietnam —and recommended that the Soviet Union be brought into the peace talks.

For the first time in his campaign, the Republican presidential nominee talked directly to a group of student protestors. The scene was a campaign rally that drew 12,000 persons to the Syracuse War Memorial Auditorium.

Nixon forecast that he will win the Nov. 5 election by a substantial margin. "We will win it quite decisively by between 3 and 5 million votes," he said.

Cites Alternative

He said Democratic nominee Hubert H. Humphrey realizes he cannot win the popular vote, and knows that the only way he can capture the White House is if a deadlock in the Electoral College sends the election to the House of Representatives.

The encounter with the students came about because a group of nearly 1,000 of them had announced in advance plans to march into the hall, sing a song of protest, then listen to the GOP campaigner.

So, Nixon said at the outset that the crowd should listen to the students first. "I'm delighted to hear those differences," he said. "The floor is yours."

The students stood and began to sing. The words of their song, "The Sounds of Silence," could not be made out on the floor of the hall.

The crowd began to boo.

Silences Supporters

Nixon silenced his supporters. "Let them go," he said. "They have indicated that if they are allowed to sing, they will listen."

Their song done, Nixon said he considered it "the very proper right of dissent. In our free society we welcome the right to

Continued on Page 2, Column 2

Youth Group Tells President Ways to Span Generation Gap

WASHINGTON (AP) — A group of young White House fellows gave President Johnson a series of recommendations Tuesday designed to help bridge the generation gap by enabling the voice of youth to be heard in high government councils.

The ideas ranged from appointment of a special assistant to the President for youth affairs to a national television series in which America's youth could bring their questions directly to the chief decision makers.

Johnson launched the program of White House Fellows in 1965 to give promising young men and women one year's experience as assistants to Cabinet officers or in the White House. Sixty-eight of them have formed an association.

Among the recommendations:

That a special assistant to the President for youth affairs to be named to get the concerns of youth to the highest levels of government and develop youth projects, including discussion of the 18-year-old vote.

—That the President establish a National Advisory Commission on Youth to include prominent national figures known for their involvement with youth, including student - body presidents and youth - organization leaders to continue a high-level review of the concerns of youth and to encourage young people to take part in congressional hearings on issues.

—That the President encourage departments and agencies to establish Offices of Youth Affairs.

—That a review be made of the training process for young employes in federal service. This is a step Johnson said he had already taken.

—That a program be established to bring as many as 100 college juniors to Washington annually for a month of in-depth

FIRST CALL

"It's no good, George. You'll have to try a few black keys."

Inside The Call

New 'Personal Distress Call' Button Would Bring Speedy Police Protection

HUMPHREY

Hubert H. Humphrey, the contender: 1966-72

Hubert H. Humphrey was no stranger to the Lehigh Valley. The perennial presidential contender visited several times between 1966 and 1972, drawing big and respectful crowds.

On Oct. 15, 1967, about 6,000 people watched Vice President Humphrey dedicate two new buildings for the Bethlehem Area School District, Freedom High School and East Hills Junior High. The Democrat praised the district's foresight in building the complex, saying it represented a decision to "provide the very best in education."

A little more than a year later, on Oct. 29, 1968, Humphrey returned to the Valley as his party's presidential candidate and addressed 5,000 supporters at Moravian College's Johnston Hall in Bethlehem.

The campaign had been tumultuous. Humphrey had only entered the race in April after President Lyndon Johnson's surprise decision not to seek a second full term.

The primary season had been marked by tragedy. In June, U.S. Sen. Robert Kennedy won the California presidential primary, a potentially game-changing victory. But Kennedy was assassinated moments after giving his victory speech.

Then, in August, massive anti-war riots erupted outside the Democratic convention in Chicago where Humphrey and his running mate, U.S. Sen. Ed Muskie of Maine, won the nomination over Eugene McCarthy of Minnesota and George McGovern of South Dakota, both U.S. senators.

At Moravian, Humphrey looked beyond the tumult of the times and made an ambitious promise: "America will have full employment and economic growth in the Humphrey-Muskie administration — and you can count on it."

He excoriated Republican candidate Richard Nixon for opposing Medicare and other safety-net programs, but the speech was otherwise forward-looking and optimistic.

"I'm convinced there's a basic goodness, a basic greatness in the American people," he said. "I seek the presidency of the United States for one reason — to call forth that goodness, that greatness to build strength in our economy, improve our educational program, win world peace and bring about real equality among all the peoples of this nation, black and white, rich and poor, North and South."

Not everyone on campus was enamored of Humphrey. On the way to Moravian from Allentown-Bethlehem-Easton Airport, the Democrat's motorcade passed a sign reading "Down With Humpty Dumpty."

In the hall, a photo of Republican candidate Richard Nixon hung from the rafters near a "Dump the Hump" placard. Someone held a sign that said "Keep America Hump-free." Someone else called out "We Want Gregory," referring to comedian and third-party candidate Dick Gregory.

Humphrey — who had also sought the presidential nomination in 1952 and 1960 — lost a close race to Nixon.

Humphrey, once again a U.S. senator from Minnesota, visited the Valley again in 1972, speaking at the Northampton Community Center during an unsuccessful primary bid. He considered a candidacy again in 1976, but did not pursue it. In 1978, he died of bladder cancer.

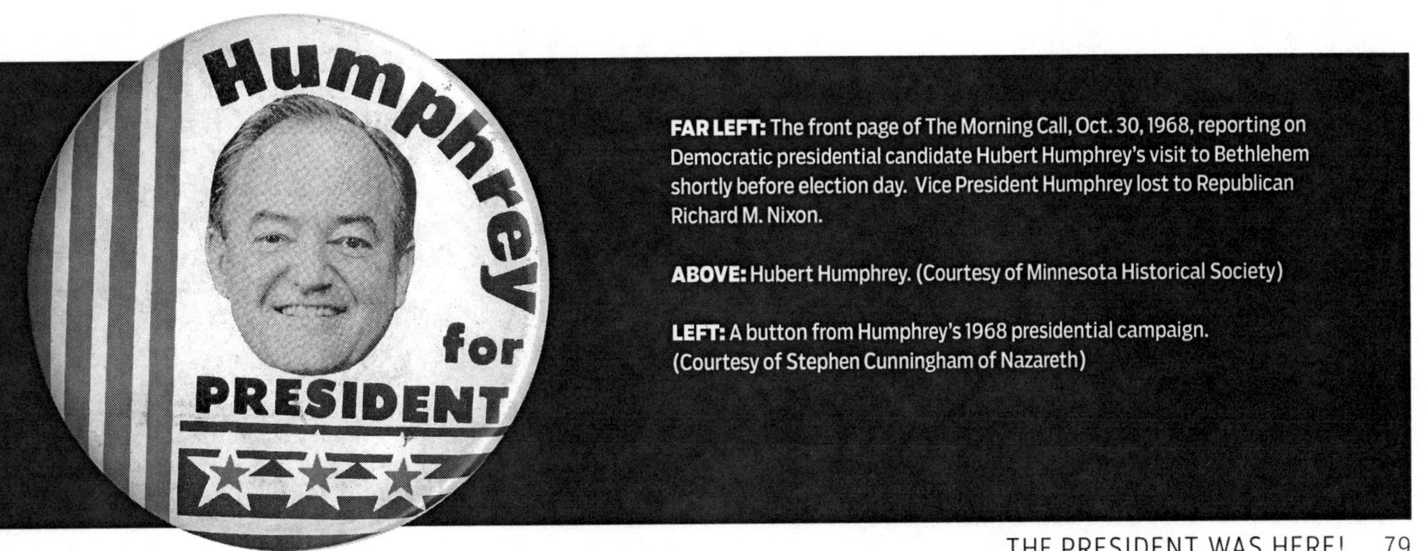

FAR LEFT: The front page of The Morning Call, Oct. 30, 1968, reporting on Democratic presidential candidate Hubert Humphrey's visit to Bethlehem shortly before election day. Vice President Humphrey lost to Republican Richard M. Nixon.

ABOVE: Hubert Humphrey. (Courtesy of Minnesota Historical Society)

LEFT: A button from Humphrey's 1968 presidential campaign. (Courtesy of Stephen Cunningham of Nazareth)

ABOVE: Vice President Humprey addresses a crowd at Muhlenberg College in Allentown in September 1966. (Courtesy of Muhlenberg College Trexler Library, Special Archives & Collections)

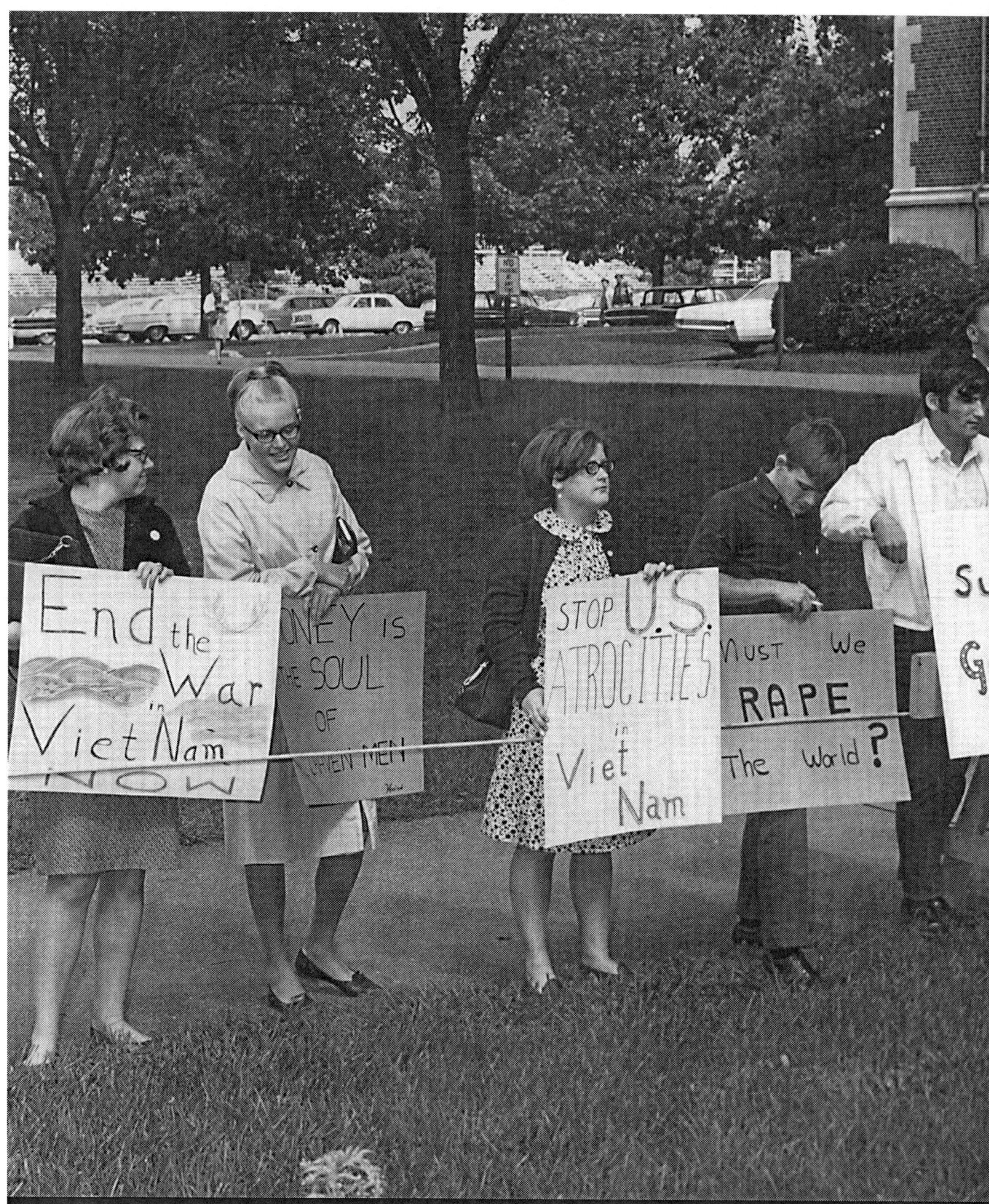

ABOVE: During his September 1966 visit to Muhlenberg College, Humphrey got a taste of a phenomenon that would come to mark political discourse over the next few years: Vietnam War protests. (Courtesy of Muhlenberg College Trexler Library, Special Archives & Collections)

RIGHT: A cartoon by Bud Tamblyn of The Morning Call that is signed by Humphrey. Based on the inscription — "Hello Bud — that's me!" — Humphrey apparently thought Tamblyn captured him well. (Courtesy of the Lehigh County Historical Society)

HUMPHREY
FOR
PRESIDENT
HHH
ell Bud-
thats me!
ny Warm Regards
Hubert H Humphrey
BUD TAMBLYN

FORD

Gerald Ford, the accidental president: 1966-80

When President Gerald Ford died in 2006, Lehigh Valley folk who had been privileged to meet him over the years offered virtually identical assessments of the man: He was humble and gracious, with an innate gift of putting strangers at ease by making them feel like old friends.

Ford came to the Valley five times, tying Teddy Roosevelt for most visits by any president. That included three trips in the 1960s, when the longtime congressman from Michigan was minority leader of the U.S. House of Representatives. In 1966, he spoke to the Lehigh Valley Cooperative Farmers at the Lehigh Valley Dairy. He returned two years later to address students at Lafayette College in Easton.

He came twice in 1969. On May 19, about 350 people at the Jewish Community Center in Allentown turned out to hear him tout President Richard Nixon's proposed $8 billion Safeguard anti-ballistic missile project. It would, he said, protect against an "irrational attack" by Red China, the Soviet Union or any other nation that acquired nuclear missile capabilities.

"It can and will work," Ford declared, "and it will not precipitate another arms race." The Safeguard system was developed but shut down almost immediately after it became operational because Congress had determined it would be ineffectual against a massive Soviet strike.

Ford returned in September to stump for Bethlehem Mayor Gordon Payrow, who was running for re-election. Ford called him "the best of mayors," then took a couple of shots at the Democratic-controlled Congress, which he called "uncooperative" with the Nixon administration. He also predicted that a political settlement could be reached to end the Vietnam War.

Ford made his final visit to the Valley in 1980 to campaign for U.S. Rep. Don Ritter, the Republican who represented Pennsylvania's 15th Congressional District.

The years between visits had been tumultuous, for Ford and the nation.

First, in 1972 he had been named to replace Nixon's disgraced vice president, Spiro Agnew. In August 1974, he replaced Nixon himself, who had resigned after it became clear he would be impeached in the Watergate scandal.

Ford thus became the only man to serve as president and vice president without being elected to either office.

Ford sought a full term as president in 1976, but his decision to pardon Nixon for any crimes he committed was a factor in his loss to Democratic candidate Jimmy Carter.

ABOVE: Former President Gerald Ford campaigns for then state Sen. James Greenwood in Bucks County in October 1992. (Morning Call Archives)

LEFT: Former President Ford greets admirers in the Saucon Valley on Sept. 24, 1980, as he stumps for then U.S. Rep. Don Ritter of Bethlehem, at right. (Morning Call Archives)

RIGHT: A cartoon by Bud Tamblyn of The Morning Call depicts President Ford and his 1976 running mate, U.S. Sen. Bob Dole of Kansas.

PS

• In 1976, the Allen High School Marching Band was selected as one of four Pennsylvania ensembles to play for President Gerald Ford at a campaign event at the Oxford Valley Mall near Langhorne. Allen Principal John McHugh called it a "singular honor" to play for the president. That was a change from 1948, when the Allentown School Board wouldn't allow the Allen band to play for President Harry Truman during his whistle-stop train tour of the Valley.

• When President George W. Bush visited Allentown during the contentious 2004 campaign, Parkland School District Superintendent Louise Donahue declined an invitation for the high school marching band to play at a Lehigh Parkway event. "We don't want to appear to be supporting any particular viewpoint," she said. "We need to remain neutral. We're a public school district." The Saucon Valley and Northampton Area school districts allowed their bands to play.

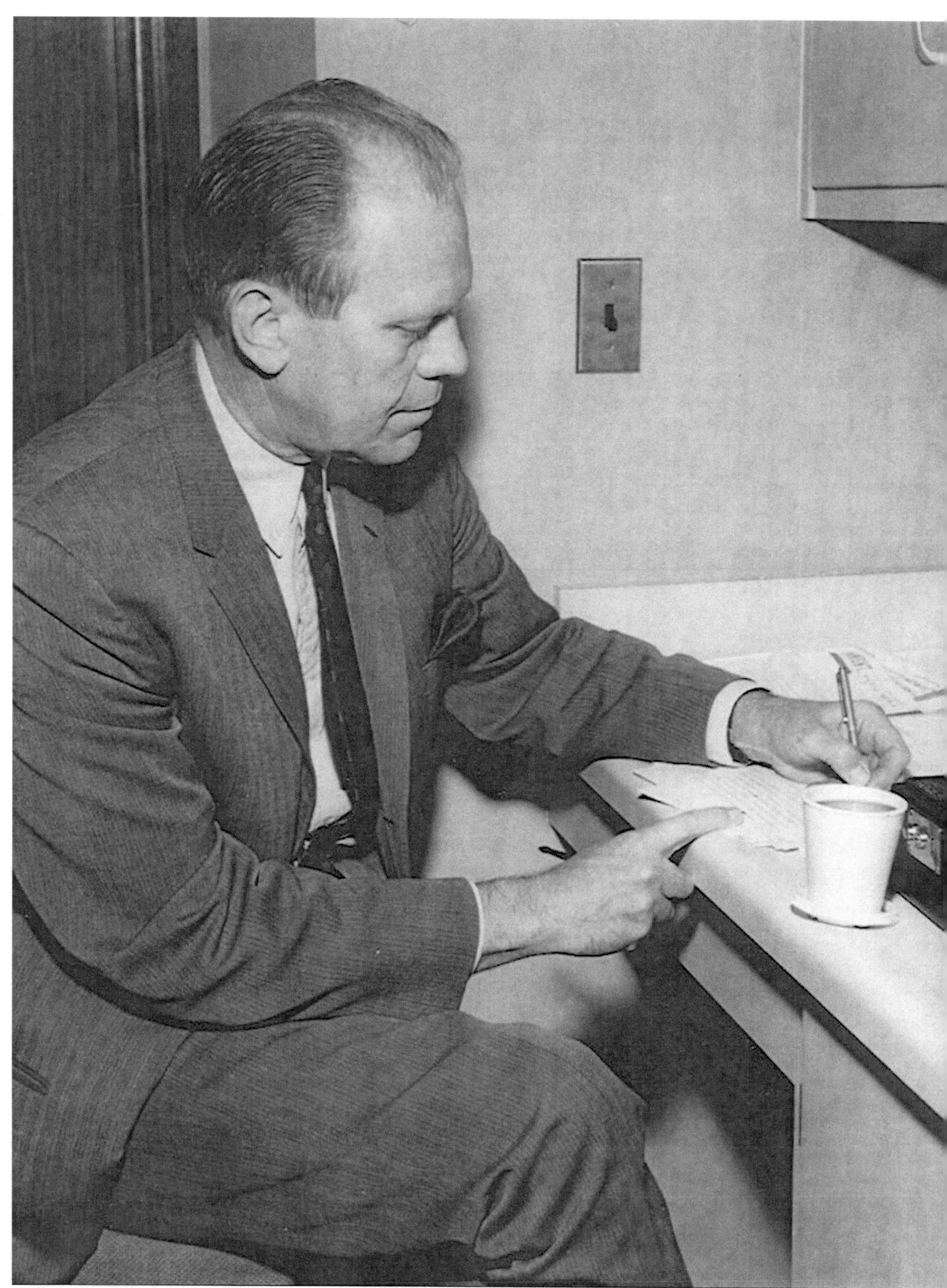

FAR LEFT: U.S. Rep. Ford, the future president, prepares for a speech at Lafayette College in Easton on April 1, 1968. (Courtesy of the Special Collections & College Archives, Skillman Library, Lafayette College)

LEFT: A Ford campaign button. (Courtesy of Kurt Zwikl of Allentown)

ABOVE: President Ford stumps for Congressman Don Ritter, left, during a 1980 visit to a Saucon Valley home. (Courtesy of the Lehigh County Historical Society)

SECOND

Local News

SUNDAY CALL-CHRONICLE

Editorial

ALLENTOWN, PA. SUNDAY, OCTOBER 22, 1972 SECTION B

McGOVERN SUPPORTERS — An estimated 5,000 people, many of them young, jam the Bethlehem City Center yesterday during a visit by Democratic presidential candidate George McGovern. Call-Chronicle photo by Tel Toulomelis.

5,000 Cheer McGovern At Bethlehem

By KATE ZOLL LAEPPLE

A mobbed Sen. George McGovern, on a jet-age whistlestop yesterday in Bethlehem, had a prayer for his 5,000 listeners who jammed the City Center Plaza.

"In 1972, you and I join together to make America the good and decent land we want it to be."

The 50-year-old Democratic presidential hopeful said the Nixon administration has been lax in many ways.

It was a crisp, sunny day, and McGovern's speech matched the mood set by his listeners, many of them young.

"Victory! Victory!" was the chant as McGovern left the platform.

By his side was Sen. Edmund S. Muskie, now an emphatic McGovern supporter.

Muskie had been in Bethlehem earlier this year as a primary election foe of McGovern.

The crowd laughed when he said, "You know McGovern wasn't my first choice. But when that became obvious . . . I'm running for George McGovern!"

Quiet Start

The South Dakota senator, a son of a Wesleyan Methodist minister, came to the Valley in a relatively quiet atmosphere.

His "Dakota II" plane touched down at the Bethlehem Steel Hangar of Allentown-Bethlehem-Easton Airport precisely at noon.

Only Rep. Fred B. Rooney of Bethlehem and Jack Greenblat of Allentown, chairman of the Pennsylvania Tax Equalization Board, greeted the McGovern entourage.

The group had come from the Scranton-Wilkes-Barre area, starting a day that would take them to Kutztown, to Reading, to Johnstown, Cambria County, and then to Pittsburgh for the end of the whirlwind tour.

Tight Security

The dearth of greeters had a purpose. Security was tight — "I never saw security such as this," Rooney observed.

Gov. Shapp, with McGovern throughout the day, led the caravan that threaded its way relatively unobserved along an unannounced route to the City Center.

Waiting outside was a patient, chanting, sign-bobbing crowd. Most of the people had been there two hours.

McGovern's visit was without incident, but there was a moment of doubt. A city detective noticed a "strange-looking" man not far from the dais. He could produce no identification, so he was taken inside for questioning and released.

Beautiful Crowd

Buoyed by the turnout, McGovern said, "This is one of the most beautiful crowds we've ever seen assembled in this campaign. I think we can bring you good news in the Lehigh Valley.

"We are gathering strength all across the country, and what it says to me is that we're going to have a great people's victory on Nov. 7."

On the stage with him were representatives of nearly every major labor union and leading Valley Democratic politicians.

He attacked the Nixon regime on many fronts — the war, jobs, inflation, political espionage — as he's been doing all across the country.

Cued by September's unfavorable inflation report, McGovern

Continued on Page B-2, Col. 1

Veteran's Day Rites On Monday

Allentown Event Is Scheduled At Court Plaza

Veteran's Day — a time for tribute to the men and women who served their country in wartime —will be observed tomorrow in the Lehigh Valley and throughout the nation.

Across the land, most Americans will be expressing their allegiance to the nation, while remembering those who served. (See Story on Page F-1).

In Allentown, Russell T. Olsen Sr., a commander in the Navy Reserve, will be the keynote speaker during Veteran's Day observances tomorrow at the Lehigh County Courthouse Plaza.

The 10:30 a.m. program will be conducted by the United Veterans of Lehigh County. Atty. Richard A. Abbott, program chairman, will be the master of ceremonies.

Taking part in the annual observance will be the Marine Band, directed by Raymond S. Becker; the Rev. C. Harry Kehm, pastor of Grace United Church of Christ; Allentown Mayor Clifford S. Bartholomew; Robert R. Markley, president of

Continued on Page B-3, Col. 3

SEEKING VOTES — Democratic presidential candidate George McGovern and Sen. Edmund Muskie are greeted by supporters yesterday in Bethlehem.

'Biggest Political Crowd'

By TOM SCHROEDER

Sen. George McGovern's Bethlehem visit yesterday brought the presidential campaign spirit to the Lehigh Valley.

"We want McGovern," the crowd chanted at City Center as the Democratic hopeful and his entourage strode from Town Hall to the speaker's platform.

Different Atmosphere

The atmosphere was markedly different from the visit to Bethlehem 11 days ago of McGovern's running-mate, Sargent Shriver.

Shriver's main thrust was directed at two labor meetings, with little public contact.

McGovern's appearance clearly had the thunder of the traditional campaign rally. His listeners had their appetites whetted by a couple hours of waiting, some warmup speeches, band music and slogans.

They were ready for the South Dakotan, and he was ready for them.

McGovern seemed pleased with his reception. So, too, were Gov. Shapp and Rep. Fred B. Rooney of Bethlehem, himself a candidate for re-election.

Cheers rose when McGovern said this was "one of the most beautiful crowds we have seen assembled any place in this campaign."

Shapp declared, "This is the biggest political crowd in the history of this area."

Shapp also remarked, "Thank God we have radicals in this country because it's time for a change."

McGovern aides, attempting to dispel the notion that McGov-

Continued on Page B-2, Col. 6

Stopped by Agents

Angry KSC Fan Leaps at Hopeful

By JOHN H. KOCH

Secret Service agents quickly halted an angry football fan yesterday afternoon when he leaped at Sen. George McGovern as the Democratic presidential candidate made an unscheduled stop at a Kutztown State College football game.

State police at Reading identified the man as William E. Smith, 27, of 526 Spring St., Fleetwood, a Vietnam War veteran.

Smith charged at McGovern with such speed that he nearly collided with the candidate, who was making an appearance during the halftime of the KSC and Cheyney State College football game.

Unexpected Stop

McGovern, en route to Reading after a morning appearance in Bethlehem, unexpectedly stopped at KSC at the request of college President Lawrence M. Stratton, according to McGovern aide Gordon Weil.

The senator arrived just before halftime and waited until play ended for intermission. He was then driven around the track surrounding the field.

Smith reportedly jumped from the northeast section of the stadium on the KSC side, after the senator had gotten out of his automobile and was speaking.

"Get out of here!" Smith shouted, according to one account. A state trooper said Smith shouted, "Get out of here, you dirty Communist!"

Quick Reaction

Reacting quickly, the agents posted themselves in front of McGovern, seized the man and leaned him against a car. Handcuffed, he was led from the field for questioning.

The man was questioned by the Secret Service and state police and released.

In trying to reach McGovern, Smith reportedly knocked over another fan. In their efforts to protect the senator, the agents pushed Smith against the car hard enough to make his mouth bleed.

At the Reading Airport before

Continued on Page B-3, Col. 1

Arson Suspected In Poconos Fire

A "deliberately set" fire early yesterday, the third in about 1½ months, ended the plans of a Stroudsburg R.1 man to open what would have been the Gate Restaurant along Prospect Street in East Stroudsburg.

About 5:50 a.m. a "hit" fire gutted the 40 by 100-foot, one-story frame-and-brick-veneer building for a second time since construction began.

East Stroudsburg Fire Chief William LaBar said, "All three fires in the building were deliberately set."

He has requested the state police fire marshal's office assist him in a probe seeking an arsonist.

The owner of the property, Glenn Detrick, indicated he plans to offer a reward for information leading to an arrest.

LaBar said his department had its first call to the building about 1½ months ago, when a small fire was extinguished in the middle of the floor.

Fire fighters and equipment returned to their quarters only to be recalled about 45 minutes later to find the building interior aflame.

LaBar said when he and his men left after the first call, "The fire was definitely out."

Detrick began refurbishing the structure only to have history repeat itself yesterday.

LaBar said borough police on routine patrol passed the structure about 5:40 a.m. and saw no sign of trouble.

Visitors to Find Game Preserve's Foliage Colorful

"Autumn foliage is gorgeous and will give the photographers many, many opportunities," said Donald B. Hoffman, county commissioner in charge of the Trexler-Lehigh County Game Preserve.

"The preserve will be open at noon today and also at noon on Monday which is a holiday."

Hoffman stressed that the preserve will remain open until November.

Today's Weather

If you thought it was cold yesterday morning, you were correct. Yesterday's low temperature of 23 at 7:30 a.m. was a record for this date, reports the National Weather Service at the Allentown - Bethlehem - Easton Airport. The previous record low of 25 degrees was set in 1952. There will be considerable cloudiness today through Monday with a chance of showers tomorrow. Today's high temperature will be in the middle 50s, dropping to a low tonight in the middle 40s. The high temperature tomorrow will be in the upper 50s. The probability of precipitation is 20 per cent today and tonight.

Temperatures

	High	Low
Allentown	50	23
Atlanta	61	35
Boston	49	33
Chicago	49	42
Denver	58	41
Houston	84	64
Kansas City	54	46
Los Angeles	73	54
Miami Beach	83	78
New Orleans	79	65
Phoenix	71	57
Portland, Ore.	57	49
St. Louis	55	49
Salt Lake	56	41
San Francisco	65	56
Seattle	54	49
Washington	55	32

In the Skies

U.F. Must Raise $260,000 In 3 Days to Reach Goal

Officials of the Lehigh County United Fund faced a major crisis yesterday as they entered the homestretch of the current fund drive $260,000 short.

The 1973 campaign goal is $1,300,000. Officials hope to achieve the goal by Wednesday night when a victory dinner is scheduled at the Allentown Jew-

Some business executives have telephoned the U.F. office asking why their pledges have not been picked up. Houlihan said victory cannot be achieved by Wednesday unless the division chairmen prod their captains and the captains exhort the troops.

The pavement pounder is the

paign Chairman Donald R. Miller of Mack Trucks, Inc., said yesterday the goal is in sight if all prospects are covered by Wednesday. He called for an all-out effort to attain success.

About 85 per cent of the canvass was completed as of last night.

McGOVERN

George McGovern, the peace candidate: 1972

George McGovern's greeting at Allentown-Bethlehem-Easton Airport in April 1972 might have buoyed his hopes that the White House was in his reach.

The U.S. senator from South Dakota was seeking the Democratic nomination to face incumbent Republican Richard Nixon and was campaigning largely on the strength of a potent anti-war message that resonated among young people.

It was a large, boisterous and youthful crowd that met McGovern at the airport and, the Allentown Chronicle said, offered "ecstatic cheers" when he vowed to withdraw all military forces from Vietnam.

McGovern called the war a "tragic mistake" of the government.

"Our first order of business — first on the list of national priorities — will be the ending of the war in Southeast Asia," he said. "Never again will young men of this country die while trying to prop up a corrupt dictatorship."

McGovern won the nomination and returned to the area in October, speaking to supporters outside City Hall in Bethlehem before heading to Reading. On the way, he made an unscheduled stop at a Kutztown State College football game, where a burly 27-year-old Vietnam veteran from Fleetwood named William Smith angrily charged at McGovern, reportedly yelling "Get out of here, you dirty communist!"

Secret Service agents took Smith into custody and released him after 30 minutes of questioning, determining that he posed no real threat. Smith himself, reached by telephone after the incident, told The Morning Call that he was upset McGovern had made a political appearance at a football game.

"I just blew my cool," he said. "I'm not involved in politics. I like to follow it, but I love football, and in my opinion, the two just don't mix."

McGovern went on to suffer one of the worst landslide losses in presidential history, as Nixon swept to a second term with 61 percent of the vote.

ABOVE: George McGovern.

LEFT: The Sunday Call-Chronicle recounts a "jet-age whistlestop" in Bethlehem by U.S. Sen. George McGovern of South Dakota during his unsuccessful 1972 challenge to President Richard Nixon.

RIGHT: Democratic presidential candidate Edmund Muskie, a U.S. senator from Maine, is greeted at Allentown-Bethlehem-Easton Airport during an April 1972 campaign stop. Muskie — who had been Hubert Humphrey's running mate in 1968 — would lose the nomination to McGovern. (Courtesy of the Lehigh County Historical Society)

A presidential portrait gallery

Allentown's Ray Holland was an avid collector, and one of his finest efforts came from his pursuit of presidential portraits. Holland, who built his fortune on the Holiday Hair salon chain, had many different kinds of collections — automobiles, baseball figurines, model trains. In 1999, his interest piqued by a C-SPAN series on the presidents, he set out to obtain an original oil portrait or life-size bust of every chief executive. The collection ranged far beyond that initial ambition and came to include election memorabilia and even a plaster death mask of Teddy Roosevelt. Holland, who once considered opening a public museum to house the collection, sold it in 2009 and has moved to Florida.

RIGHT: A small portion of the Raymond E. Holland Presidential Collection, which began in 1997 and was located in a Victorian home at 111 N. Fourth St. in Allentown. The collection, which has since been sold, consisted of more than 750 paintings and sculptures. The large figure of Andrew Jackson, foreground right, was hand-carved by sculptor Laban S. Beecher in 1834. (Courtesy of John Zolomij of Whitehall)

WITCH PARTY DO YOU BELONG TO?

SCHWETZ NET SO FIEL AND VOTE!

ABOVE TOP: Cartoonist Bud Tamblyn of The Morning Call offered this "spooky" Halloween take on the 1976 showdown between President Gerald Ford and Democratic challenger Jimmy Carter. The Pennsylvania Dutch phrase means "Don't talk so much." (Translation courtesy of the Pennsylvania German Cultural Heritage Center at Kutztown University)

ABOVE: Carter speaks to supporters during a campaign stop at the Hess's store in Allentown in April 1976. (Photo by William Zwikl, courtesy of Kurt Zwikl of Allentown)

RIGHT: President Carter. (Courtesy of Kurt Zwikl)

PAGES 94-95: Former President Carter listens to a rehearsal of the Moravian College Choir during a visit to Bethlehem in October 1990. (Morning Call Archives)

CARTER

Jimmy Carter, a family affair: 1976-80

Jimmy Carter, the Georgia Democrat who seemed to win the White House by the sheer wattage of his smile, visited the Lehigh Valley just once, to shake hands for a couple of hours. But he sent swarms of kin here to spread his message in two presidential campaigns.

Carter's wife, Rosalynn, sons Chip and Jack, mother, Miss Lillian, and daughter-in-law Caron all made stops during his successful 1976 bid and its failed 1980 sequel. (His beer-loving brother, Billy, passed through one day in 1977, holding a jokey press conference on his way to a country music festival in the Poconos. That, undoubtedly to the president's relief, wasn't a political appearance.)

Jimmy Carter was a little-known figure when he emerged on the national stage in the 1976 Democratic presidential primaries. A peanut farmer and one-term governor of Georgia, he wasn't given much of a chance against better-known opponents, including California Gov. Jerry Brown, U.S. Rep. Morris "Mo" Udall of Arizona and U.S. Sen. Henry "Scoop" Jackson of Washington.

Carter, however, used his position as an outsider to his advantage in appealing to a post-Watergate electorate that had grown weary of Washington, D.C.

The president-to-be visited Allentown April 27, 1976, the day of the Pennsylvania primary. He greeted workers outside the Western Electric plant on Union Boulevard (later to become AT&T, Lucent and Agere), visited Hess's Department Store in downtown Allentown and spoke at a press conference at Allentown-Bethlehem-Easton Airport.

There, Carter touched on topics that would come to mark high and low points of his presidency. One was unemployment, which would remain stubbornly high during his administration.

The other was the Middle East. One of Carter's lasting legacies was his negotiation of peace between Israel and Egypt. But the region was also the site of his greatest failure. He was unable to negotiate freedom for 52 Americans held hostage at the U.S. Embassy in Tehran after the Iranian Revolution, and a military rescue attempt ended disastrously with the deaths of eight American servicemen. The hostages were released the day Carter's successor, Ronald Reagan, took office.

Carter won the Pennsylvania primary and the nomination but made no more visits to the Valley. Chip Carter cited the area's lack of a major television station as a factor. "We've got so little money, we've almost got to go where the media is," he said during a visit to Bethlehem.

In the 1980 primary, as President Carter fended off a challenge by U.S. Sen. Ted Kennedy of Massachusetts, he tried a charm offensive.

"The Carter campaign has deployed members of the family like a small army across the state and Lehigh Valley to appeal for support for the president," The Morning Call reported.

First came Miss Lillian, the president's 81-year-old mother, who held an April 3 breakfast meeting with local Democrats at Hess's Patio, the restaurant of the now-gone department store in center city Allentown.

She said she would spend a week shopping at Allentown's premier department store if she had the money. And, sounding quite maternal, she defended the president's 10-cent gas tax. "Ride less, that's all I can say," she said. "Whatever Jimmy does must be right."

Two weeks later, first lady Rosalynn Carter arrived at A-B-E Airport and held a brief press conference. She defended the president's handling of the Iran hostage affair — he had been "very patient," she said — and asked voters to be patient in turn in the face of anti-inflation measures.

Afterward, accompanied by Allentown Mayor Joseph Daddona, state Sen. Henry Messinger and several others, she ate a spinach salad and seafood crepe at Le Crepe Restaurant in the Lehigh Valley Mall. The lunch was a private affair, but the first lady was reported to have been relaxed. "It was like we were having lunch with a friend," said Dorothy Zug, vice chairwoman of the state Democratic Party.

The Carter women's visits were duly reported, but Kennedy created the biggest buzz of the campaign season when he spoke April 4 at Van Bittner Hall in Bethlehem, home of the United Steelworkers of America.

Kennedy was counting on a Pennsylvania primary win to legitimize his run for the White House. He fired up the packed hall by knocking Carter on the domestic economy and foreign policy. He also hit the president for campaigning by proxy in Pennsylvania.

"We saw some Carter supporters out there and we invited them to come in, too," he said. "We invited them to come to our rally because they don't have a rally to go to of their own."

Despite it all — hostage crisis, energy crisis, inflation and a popular challenger — Carter won renomination. But he lost the White House to Reagan in a landslide.

THE MORNING CALL

WEEKENDER

NO. 206 SEPTEMBER 27, 1980 (USPS 047-780) (C) 1980 Call-Chronicle Newspapers, Inc. All rights reserved 20 ce

LEFT TOP: A humorous bumper sticker. Billy Carter was President Jimmy Carter's beer-drinking brother. (Courtesy of Stephen Cunningham of Nazareth)

LEFT BOTTOM: The Morning Call of Sept. 27, 1980, recounts first lady Rosalynn Carter's visit to the Lehigh Valley the day before.

ABOVE: A button from President Carter's unsuccessful 1980 re-election bid. (Courtesy of Stephen Cunningham)

BELOW: Brother Billy held a brief press conference at Allentown-Bethlehem-Easton Airport in 1977 on his way to a country music festival in the Poconos. (Morning Call Archives)

RIGHT TOP: U.S. Sen. Ted Kennedy of Massachusetts mounted an unsuccessful primary challenge against President Carter in 1980. Kennedy's visit to Bethlehem caused quite a stir. (Morning Call Archives)

RIGHT BOTTOM: A poster from President Carter's doomed 1980 campaign. His running mate, Walter Mondale, would unsuccessfully challenge President Ronald Reagan in 1984. (Courtesy of Kurt Zwikl)

Kennedy captivates Bethlehem throng

DAVID DAWSON
Chronicle staff writer

Whether it was his politics, celebrity status or charisma, Ted Kennedy created more excitement during his visit to Bethlehem yesterday than have all the political events to date this year combined.

An hour before he arrived at United Steelworkers Hall on Lehigh Street, people began to gather around the main entrance and in the hall where he was to speak.

Candidates in local Democratic races and their workers took advantage of the political gathering to hand out leaflets and shake a few hands.

People without passes to enter the hall scouted around the building, hoping to find an unguarded door where they could slip in to see the senator from Massachusetts, the man whose brother became president 20 years ago, the man who is banking on the Pennsylvania primary to make his run for the White House a legitimate one.

See Page 17, Column 1

Photography by TOULOMELIS

EDWARD KENNEDY...blasts Carter

רייגן
Reagan

KEEP AMERICA GREAT
RE-ELECT REAGAN-BUSH in '84

INAUGURATION DAY
Jan. 20th, 1981
Ronald Reagan
Our 40th President

Reagan visits Bucks

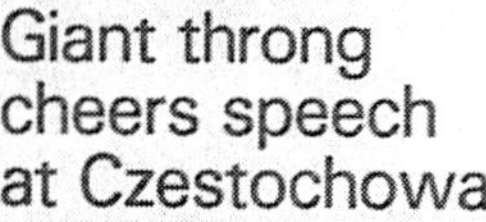

Giant throng cheers speech at Czestochowa

▶More photos on shrine **B1**

By BILL GERNERD
Of The Morning Call

President Reagan defended his administration's buildup of the military and his foreign and economic policies before a crowd repeatedly estimated at "100,000-plus" yesterday at the National Shrine of Our Lady of Czestochowa near Doylestown.

Reagan arrived by helicopter from Camp David. Then a motorcade carried him to a stage set up at the base of a hillside below the shrine, where he was greeted by Gov. Dick Thornburgh, who made introductory remarks along with Cardinal John Krol of Philadelphia.

As Reagan took the stage, tens of thousands in the audience waved American flags and the first of repeated chants of "four more years" went up from the crowd.

He took over at the sun-baked podium with the observation, "I'm out of uniform," and he proceeded to shed his suit coat.

Noting that the Polish people still "suffer under the oppressor's boot in Poland," Reagan admonished, "I believe you'll agree that we should never be afraid to stand up in the international debate and vigorously defend the cause of freedom and our national interests.

Please See **REAGAN** Page **A2** ▶

Morning Call photos—Dick Mantz and Burt Swayze

A crowd (above) at the National Shrine of Our Lady of Czestochowa listens to President Reagan.

Mondale to announce deficit plan

The Washington Post

WASHINGTON — Walter F. Mondale will be in Philadelphia today to unveil his federal budget deficit-reduction plan that calls for budget cuts and tax increases of roughly $175 billion in fiscal 1989, and will include a "pay-as-you-go" pledge that any new programs proposed by a Mondale administration would be financed by spending cuts or tax increases, sources familiar with the plan said yesterday.

The sources also said that tax increases account for slightly less that half of the deficit package and would be earmarked for deficit reduction, rather than for additional government spending.

That commitment, Democratic strategists say, is designed to inoculate Mondale against the expected Republican charge that the tax increase proposals represent a rerun of past Democratic "tax and spend" policies.

In his weekly paid radio address yesterday, Mondale repeated his contention that no matter who wins the presidency, taxes will have to be raised next year to close the "nearly three-quarters of a trillion dollars" deficit that the Reagan administration has built up.

"Everyone knows that taxes will go up. But who will pay?" Mondale asked. "If you have a president who favors millionaires and big corporations, he'll sock it to the families of average income and leave his friends alone. That's Mr. Reagan — not me."

Campaign chairman James Johnson said in an interview that tax increases will fall most heavily on those in the upper-income brackets.

Please See **MONDALE** Page **A2** ▶

Reagan (above) removes jacket under sunny skies as he prepares to speak.

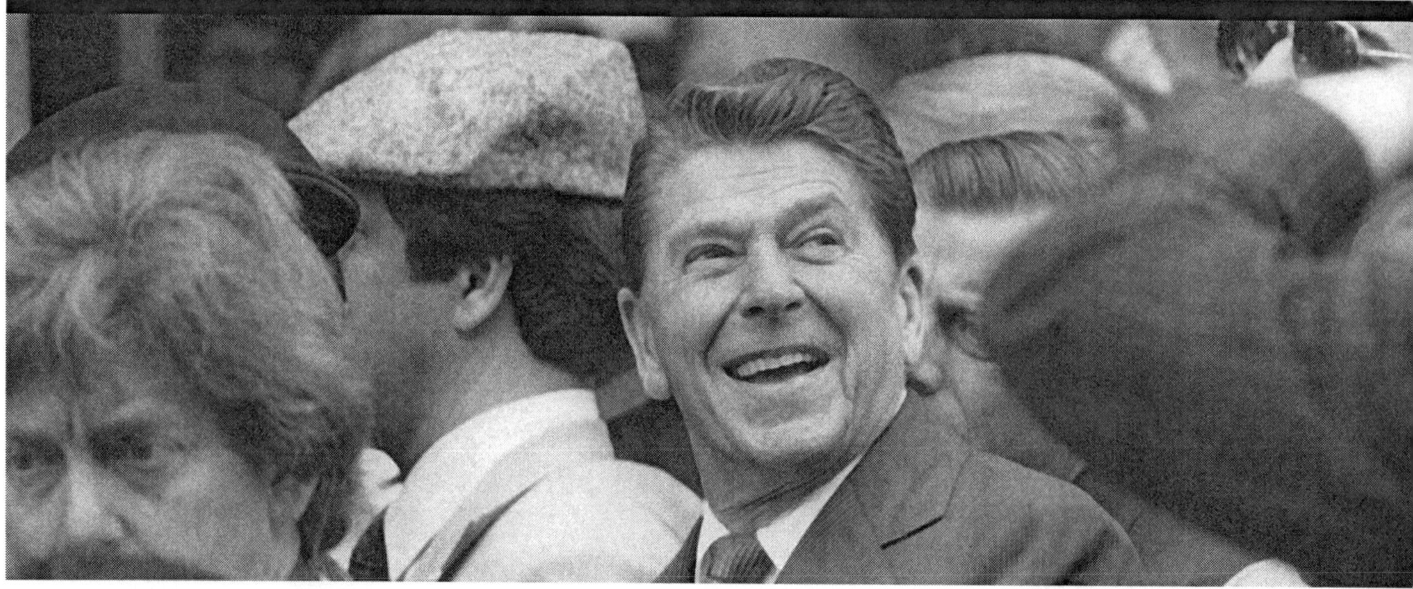

REAGAN

Ronald Reagan, making them swoon: 1957

Ronald Reagan's only visit to the Lehigh Valley came long before the presidency that would transform him into the ultimate conservative icon.

In the 1950s, Reagan was in the midst of a Hollywood career that had high points ("Knute Rockne: All American") and low ("Bedtime for Bonzo") but was merely a prelude to politics.

He was famous enough, though, to make female workers swoon when he stopped at General Electric's small appliance factory on S. 12th Street in Allentown on March 12, 1957.

"Slightly Agog," read the caption on an Evening Chronicle photo showing Reagan greeting one employee, a punch press operator named Dolores Long. Her open-mouthed reaction was "typical of the reception the handsome actor received throughout his day-long appearance in the city."

The visit was part of a national tour Reagan had undertaken as host and program director of television's "General Electric Theater." After the factory tour, he addressed about 200 business leaders at a Chamber of Commerce luncheon at the Lehigh Valley Dairy on MacArthur Road in Whitehall Township.

There, he gave a hint of the themes that would mark his run for the White House more than two decades later, excoriating "government harassment and government interference" of industry.

Leaders of the motion picture industry "have never asked the government to sit down on our side of the table, because we always suspected when you invite government to help, you end up with a partner," Reagan said.

Reagan's wife, Nancy, campaigned in the Valley on his behalf on April 8, 1980. "He has a basic integrity [people] find whether they agree with him or not," she said, explaining her husband's broad appeal.

Reagan came close to the Valley a couple of times during his presidency. On Sept. 9, 1984, during his re-election campaign against Democratic challenger Walter Mondale, a throng estimated at more than 100,000 cheered him at the National Shrine of Our Lady of Czestochowa outside Doylestown.

The president, who famously defined the Soviet Union as an "evil empire," defended his administration's military buildup, reminding the largely Polish-American crowd that Soviet-dominated Poland was still "under the oppressor's boot."

Near the end of his White House tenure, in October 1988, Reagan visited Upper Darby High School in Delaware County. He had launched his presidential bid there eight years earlier, and reminisced about the accomplishments of his two terms.

He told students who were of age to get out and vote, and to urge their friends and family to do the same.

By voting, he said, Americans "determine the course of history and protect those liberties that have made this good and gentle land the envy of the world."

FAR LEFT, FROM TOP: A Reagan-Bush campaign button from 1980, which features the word Reagan spelled in Hebrew script. (Courtesy of Kurt Zwikl of Allentown) The Reagan-Bush team would win in a landslide over challenger Walter Mondale and his running mate, Geraldine Ferraro. (Courtesy of Stephen Cunningham of Nazareth) A commemorative button from Ronald Reagan's first inauguration. (Courtesy of Stephen Cunningham) A cartoon by Bud Tamblyn of The Morning Call shows President Reagan receiving a bag of his favorite candy, jelly beans. (Courtesy of the Lehigh County Historical Society)

NEAR LEFT TOP: The Morning Call from Sept. 10, 1984, recounts President Reagan's visit to the National Shrine of Our Lady of Czestochowa outside Doylestown.

LEFT BOTTOM: President Reagan during his September 1984 trip to the National Shrine of Our Lady of Czestochowa outside Doylestown.

ABOVE: President Reagan.

RIGHT: Nancy Reagan made a daylong visit to the Lehigh Valley on April 8, 1980, to campaign for her husband. (Morning Call Archives)

Answering questions, Mrs. Reagan is joined by State Sen. Richard S. Schweiker and State Rep. George J. Kanuck Jr.

Photography by BURT SWAYZ

Need 'maturity in the White House,' Nancy Reagan claims at whistlestop

By TED MELLIN
News Editor

Nancy Davis Reagan, wife of Republican presidential hopeful Ronald Reagan, said yesterday she feels the age of her husband is not an issue in the campaign.

Whitehall Township during a daylong visit in the Lehigh Valley.

Later, during a meeting with Rea-

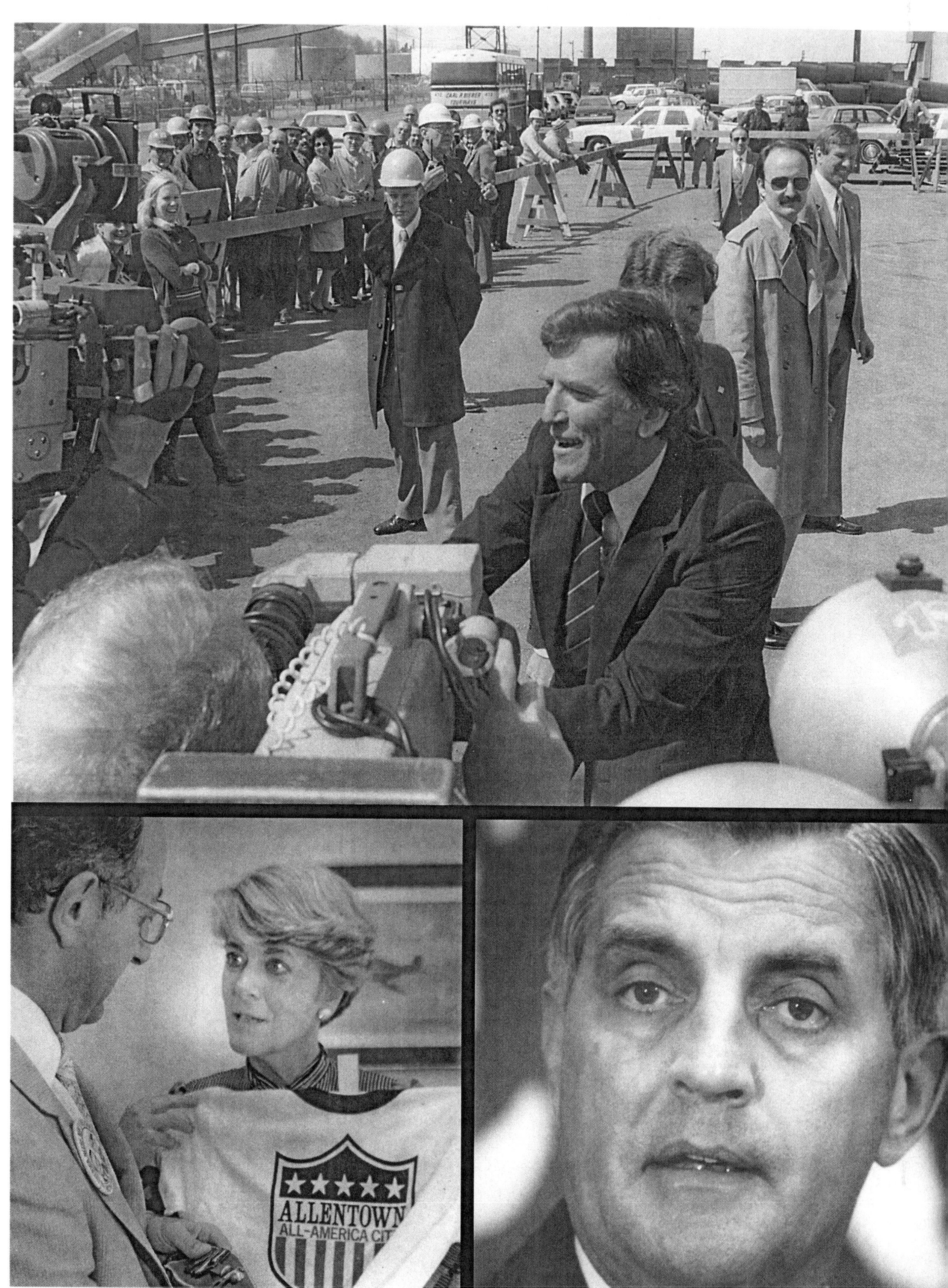
ALLENTOWN
ALL-AMERICA CIT

JACKSON, HART, MONDALE & FERRARO

Steel a hot topic of Democratic contenders: 1984

In 1984, the presidential candidates who visited the Lehigh Valley talked steel, steel, steel.

The Rev. Jesse Jackson came first. The sometimes controversial civil rights figure was the first black man to seek the Democratic presidential nomination and would make a surprisingly strong run, placing third in the primaries behind U.S. Sen. Gary Hart of Colorado and eventual nominee Walter Mondale, the former vice president under Jimmy Carter.

On Feb. 25, three months into the groundbreaking campaign, Jackson fired up a crowd of about 2,500 at Lafayette College, condemning nuclear proliferation and excessive military spending and calling on the government to protect the steel and food industries through subsidies.

"Our steel and our food are part of our national security," Jackson said. That remark reads poignantly today, given that Bethlehem Steel would be all but dead within 15 years of Jackson's appearance.

At the time, though, steel was still the Valley's central industry. Hart showed up at Bethlehem Steel's main plant on April 9, the day before the Pennsylvania primary, to plead for votes among steelworkers whose union bosses were backing Mondale.

Hart said he wanted to "make this country a leader again" in steel production and it had to happen "not in the 1990s but in the 1980s ..."

Once again, a sigh-worthy sentiment. Hart narrowly lost the nomination to Mondale. Hart made another presidential bid in 1988, but it ended disastrously with the exposure of his marital infidelities.

Jackson wasn't the only political groundbreaker in 1984. U.S. Rep. Geraldine Ferraro of New York became the first woman on a major party presidential ticket when Mondale tapped her as his running mate.

When she visited Bethlehem's Moravian College on Oct. 15, Ferraro thrilled the crowd of 4,000 with a blunt and fiery condemnation of the Reagan administration. She called the president's environmental record "the worst since Gen. Sherman marched through Georgia." And she said his attitude toward the struggling steel industry was "let it rust."

Mondale himself made only one appearance in the Lehigh Valley that year, a brief campaign stop at Allentown-Bethlehem-Easton Airport. He greeted local Democratic leaders and, like other candidates, spoke of the importance of steel. A story in The Morning Call said Mondale appeared "optimistic but not glowingly confident."

Rightly so. Reagan won in a historic landslide, with Mondale taking only his home state of Minnesota and the District of Columbia.

LEFT TOP: U.S. Sen. Gary Hart of Colorado greets the crowd during a primary campaign visit to Bethlehem in April 1984. (Morning Call Archives)

FAR LEFT BOTTOM: Vice presidential candidate Geraldine Ferraro, Walter Mondale's 1984 running mate, accepts a T-shirt from Allentown Mayor Joe Daddona during a campaign stop in October 1984. Ferraro was the first woman on a major party presidential ticket. (Morning Call Archives)

NEAR LEFT BOTTOM: Presidential candidate Walter Mondale.

ABOVE: The Rev. Jesse Jackson, a civil rights leader and 1984 Democratic presidential candidate, speaking at Lehigh University in November 1986. (Morning Call Archives)

BOTTOM: A Jackson campaign button. (Courtesy of Stephen Cunningham of Nazareth)

TOP: President George H.W. Bush's visit to Allentown in April 1992 drew cheers — and protests. A woman holds a sign reading "Read my Lips ... No More Bush," a play on the president's famous broken promise of "Read my lips — no new taxes." (Harry Fisher, The Morning Call)

ABOVE LEFT: The future first lady, Barbara Bush, looks out the window of the former Sheraton Inn at Fourth and Hamilton streets in Allentown during a visit on April 17, 1980. She was campaigning for her husband, who mounted an unsuccessful bid for the Republican presidential nomination that year. (John Simitz, The Morning Call)

ABOVE RIGHT: Workers get ready for President Bush's 1992 visit to Allentown, where he touted his education programs. (Chuck Zovko, The Morning Call)

RIGHT TOP: President George H.W. Bush. (Morning Call Archives)

G.H.W. BUSH

George H.W. Bush, 'Nice to see yah': 1980-2000

The Lehigh Valley got its first close-up look at George H.W. Bush when he visited in 1980 as a Republican presidential contender.

On a three-hour swing through Bethlehem and Allentown on April 9, he took a few jabs at GOP front-runner Ronald Reagan but mainly focused his criticisms on President Jimmy Carter and his "disastrous economic policies."

Bush joined a Lehigh Valley Homebuilders Association demonstration on Allentown's Hamilton Mall — the group was protesting high interest and mortgage rates — and later spoke to reporters at City Hall.

"After three years of Jimmy Carter, the housing industry faces collapse and families can't afford to buy houses," he said. "Inflation threatens the very heart of America."

Afterward, Bush greeted campaign volunteers and had lunch at the old Sheraton Inn on Hamilton Street, then headed to Bethlehem Steel where he stood in a light drizzle. "Hello, I'm George Bush, nice to see yah," the candidate said time and again as he shook hands with departing workers.

Bush lost the nomination to Reagan but had the consolation of being picked as vice presidential candidate. In that role, he returned to Bethlehem Steel in October to watch a steel-pouring operation and to once again excoriate Carter, who had proposed a steel bailout plan that Bush said was a carbon copy of earlier Reagan proposals.

Bush served with Reagan for two terms and succeeded him in 1988. As president, he made one visit to the Valley, speaking at Allentown's Dieruff High School on April 16, 1992, to celebrate the first anniversary of his education initiative, America 2000.

It was the first Valley visit by a sitting president since Harry Truman's whistle-stop train tour in 1948, and it generated plenty of excitement.

"Love him or loathe him, Bush was the hot ticket on the East Side," The Morning Call reported. "Neighbors stood three and four deep along sidewalks ... Ritter Elementary students waved U.S. flags and chattered while waiting in the off-and-on rain under a dismal gray sky. Protesters carrying placards blasted Bush for claiming the 'education president' mantle. And people clutching cameras recorded Bush's arrival for posterity."

An overwhelmed short-order cook at an east Allentown diner went through 34 gallons of pancake batter and 400 eggs feeding Secret Service agents, reporters, police officers and teachers in the hours leading up to the speech.

In a packed Dieruff gymnasium, Bush promoted a plan to give $25,000 in college student aid to every American and praised Lehigh Valley 2000: Business Education Partnership, a local reform effort he called one of the most advanced in the nation.

He praised the Dieruff band as "first class" and asked the students to take a long view of history.

"Look now at the world you'll soon call your own, at the pace of change that we've come to expect," he said. "Each day we see history played out in the headlines, literally. Old empires expire; new worlds are born. In the past six months alone we've seen the birth of 18 new nations. Who knows how many there will be by the time you take your big geography final a few weeks from now."

Bush was commencement speaker at Easton's Lafayette College on May 23, 1998. And he returned to the Valley on Oct. 26, 2000, to stump for his son, George W. Bush, who was locked in a tight race with Vice President Al Gore. At a short but boisterous rally at Cedar Crest College in Allentown, the former president predicted — correctly, it turned out — that he would be "the happiest father in America" come Election Day.

PS George H.W. Bush's challenger in 1988, Massachusetts Gov. Michael Dukakis, was often criticized as stiff and excessively businesslike during campaign appearances. But when he visited Bethlehem Steel's Grace Auditorium on April 23 during primary season, he charmed the crowd. Sharing the stage with Lehigh University President Peter Likins, the 5-foot-8-inch candidate said he and the equally diminutive Likins "make up for in quality what we lack in height."

Later, during a rally at Allentown-Bethlehem-Easton Airport, Dukakis mocked the notion that he was too businesslike.

"How could a Greek be unemotional?" he said. "Charisma is a Greek word, isn't it?"

Crowds jam Center Square as lead elements of protest parade heads east

Heavy equipment parades through center city in builder-Realtor protes

GOP candidate Bush joins homebuilders' protest march

DAVID DAWSON
Chronicle staff writer

Although the event was "non-political" in the words of James Molinaro, president of the Lehigh Valley Home Builders Association, there was no shortage of politicians taking part in the association's protest march today.

Getting most, if not all of the attention was George Bush, Republican presidential candidate whose campaign depends upon success in the Pennsylvania primary.

Addressing a crowd of media representatives and building tradesmen in Allentown City Council chambers, Bush said, "Those of you in the housing industry are forced to carry a disproportionate share of economic hardship because Jimmy Carter doesn't know what to do."

Although the event featured political conservatives as speakers Mayor Frank Fischl and U.S. Rep. Don Ritter also took to the podium the atmosphere was charged.

"After three years of Jimmy Carter's disasterous econon policies the housing industry faces a collapse in this country," Bush s — words repeated by Molinaro later in the program.

"I believe in the family and the ability to buy a home threatens t family," the candidate said.

Bush blamed the housing industry's woes on the current hi inflation rate and the "credit crunch that strikes at only some causes inflation and threatens the very heart of the housing industry."

Bush noted that the highest interest rates in 150 years are now effect; building costs have gone up 20 percent — "thanks to Jimn Carter"; the price of a new home has increased 50 percent in thr years, and mortgage rates have doubled in some areas in the san period.

The candidate proposed "supply side tax credits" as a way to g the housing industry back on its feet. Such a policy would stimula investment, he said, and have an immediate effect on the housi industry.

Bush also called for policies to prevent steel dumping in th country by foreign nations.

He then spoke against overregulation, singling out OSHA ar environmental regulations as particularly harmful to economic develo ment.

"I supported OSHA (the Occupational Safety and Health Act) in i inception, but it's gone too far," he said.

Bush concluded by commenting, "It's great to take part in th grass-roots expression of the need to get this industry back on track."

As soon as he finished his speech, he left council chambers by a sic door to meet with campaign staffers across the street at the Sherat Inn. He was scheduled to shake hands with steelworkers at the 3 p.n Bethlehem Steel shift change this afternoon.

Molinaro read a letter and resolution to be sent to the president, ar handed them to Rep. Ritter, who promised to read them on the Hou floor.

"I'd like to make one thing very clear — the home builders and th construction industry did not cause inflation," Ritter said.

Citing some of the current administration economic policies, Ritt called them "tantamount to economic vandalism."

Molinaro then read a telegram of support from Sen. Edwar Kennedy, who said he supported the association's action and would hav been present if his schedule permitted.

Chronicle photos/DON UHRICH

U.S. Rep. Don Ritter, far left, and GOP presidential candidate George Bush, flanked by Mayor Frank Fischl and city Treasurer Robert Smith, arrive at City Hall for press conference after builders-Realtors protest parade in Allentown.

ABOVE: The Evening Chronicle reports on Republican presidential candidate Bush's campaign visit to Allentown on April 9, 1980. Bush would lose the nomination to Ronald Reagan that year, then accept an invitation to run as vice president.

RIGHT: Future first lady Barbara Bush during a visit to the Private Industry Council in Allentown in April 1988. (Naomi Halperin, The Morning Call)

PAGE 105 TOP: Candidate Bush on Hamilton Street in Allentown during a 1980 primary campaign visit. (Morning Call Archives)

PAGE 105 BOTTOM: Massachusetts Gov. Michael Dukakis, who lost the 1988 presidential election to Bush, addressed a crowd at Bethlehem Steel in April of that year. (Harry Fisher, The Morning Call)

STEEL

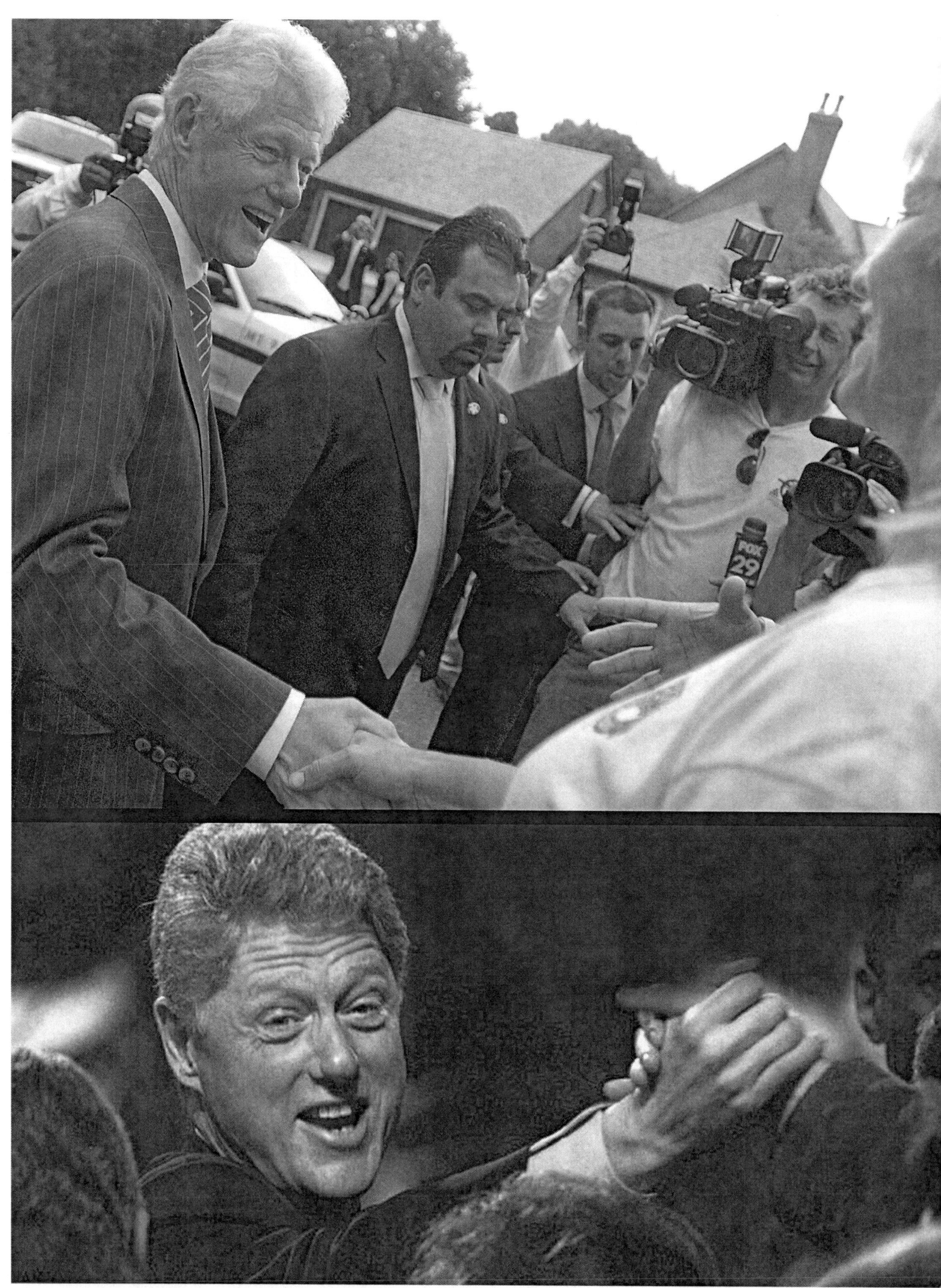
FOX
29

CLINTON

Bill Clinton grabs a cup of coffee: 1995–2010

One day in 1995, lightning struck a Wescosville diner called the Charcoal Drive-In. Not actual lightning, but the kind of dumb luck that plucks a nondescript business out of obscurity and puts it on the front page.

The president stopped by.

It was Jan. 25, a Wednesday. Bill Clinton had delivered a speech at Kutztown University and now his motorcade was heading east on Route 222 toward Lehigh Valley International Airport. The cars pulled into the diner parking lot, and the chief executive popped in for a cup of coffee.

Like most political events, it wasn't nearly as spontaneous as it seemed. Art Metzgar, who owned the now-defunct diner and who has since died, told The Morning Call that Secret Service agents had checked the place out a few days earlier. They were "oddball types, just walking around," he said.

Metzgar, however, said it was mere chance that his diner had been chosen for the stop out of all the eateries between Kutztown and the airport.

The president ordered a decaffeinated coffee – he told Metzgar he'd grown allergic to caffeine – and made small talk with 15 or so customers. The excited waitresses forgot to top off his coffee, so Clinton slipped behind the counter and did it himself.

Clinton returned to the Valley in 2008 to campaign for his wife, U.S. Sen. Hillary Clinton of New York, who was competing in the Democratic primary against fellow senator Barack Obama of Illinois.

On March 19, the former president stumped at the Hotel Bethlehem and Muhlenberg College in Allentown, telling crowds that his wife would return America to the peace and prosperity it had known during his own White House tenure.

He accused President George W. Bush of profligate spending, criticized the president's No Child Left Behind education policy and promised his wife would bring troops home from Iraq "responsibly."

Clinton returned on April 15, telling a crowd at Easton Area High School that Hillary was "the greatest changemaker" he had ever known.

"I'm telling you, if you vote for her you will always be proud you did, and you will be able to say you did something which guaranteed that you are leaving the future of our children in better, stronger hands," he said to raucous cheers.

LEFT TOP: Former President Bill Clinton shakes hands during a visit to Salisbury Township on Aug. 10, 2010. Clinton was stumping for Democratic congressional candidate John Callahan. (Abby Drey, The Morning Call)

LEFT BOTTOM: President Clinton greeting the crowd during his visit to Kutztown University on Jan. 25, 1995. (Donna Fisher, The Morning Call)

ABOVE: Former President Clinton during a visit to Northampton Community College on Oct. 28, 2010, where he stumped for Callahan, the mayor of Bethlehem. (Morning Call Archives)

BOTTOM: A 1996 Clinton-Gore button. (Courtesy of Stephen Cunningham of Nazareth)

PS President Bill Clinton's 1995 visit to the Charcoal Drive-In was lighthearted, but it followed close on the heels of a more serious episode. As the motorcade passed through Trexlertown on Route 222, two police officers spotted a man with a gun in his waistband and wrestled him to the ground.

The man was involuntarily committed to a mental hospital for five days. He was never charged with a crime – he had a permit to carry the gun – and successfully had the commitment expunged from his record. In 2000, he died at a Whitehall store when his gun accidentally fell to the floor and discharged.

ABOVE: Crowds gather around the motorcade during President Clinton's 1995 visit to Kutztown. (Morning Call Archives)

PAGE 109 TOP: A special guest ticket to President Clinton's speach at Kutztown University Fieldhouse. (Courtesy of Kurt Zwikl of Allentown)

PAGE 109 BOTTOM: William Albert of North Catasauqua holds a President Clinton doll, part of his vast collection of presidential memorabilia. (Harry Fisher, The Morning Call)

- Special Guest -

KUTZTOWN UNIVERSITY

presents

President Bill Clinton

Kutztown University Fieldhouse

Wednesday, January 25, 1995

Doors Open 10:00 a.m. - Program Begins 11:30 a.m.

First Come, First Served

ADMIT ONE - FREE ADMISSION

Carpooling Recommended!

Kutztown University
State System of Higher Education

Len
GRUP
State Repres
AMERICAN
US
LEGION

Bob Dole in the Hall of Fame

Bob Dole, the longtime U.S. senator from Kansas and 1996 Republican presidential candidate, has a quiet connection to the Lehigh Valley. He is a member of Good Shepherd's Hall of Fame.

The Allentown rehabilitation hospital has long honored people who have achieved great things despite disabilities. Dole, an Army veteran, lost the use of his right arm during World War II when he was hit by machine gun fire during battle in Italy in April 1945.

Dole, who spent 39 months in a hospital recovering from his injuries, was inducted into the Good Shepherd Hall of Fame in 1983. An issue of the hospital's "Sweet Charity" magazine from that year recounted his life after the war:

"Sen. Dole never let the handicaps that remained following his injury deter him. In 1951, while still in college, he was elected to the Kansas Legislature and was elected to the U.S. House of Representatives in 1961. He became a member of the United States Senate in 1968."

Dole was President Gerald Ford's running mate in the 1976 loss to Jimmy Carter. Dole was the GOP nominee in 1996, losing to President Bill Clinton.

A plaque honoring Dole hangs in the Health and Technology Center of the hospital's south Allentown campus.

LEFT: Bob Dole speaks at American Legion Post No. 9 in Palmer Township, stumping for George W. Bush in 2000. (Ed Koskey, The Morning Call)

KUTZTOWN
UNIVERSITY
AMERICA
SAFER, STRONGER, BETTER
WWW.GEORGEWBUSH.COM

G.W. BUSH

George W. Bush battles for a swing state: 1988-2004

When he came to the Lehigh Valley as the Republican presidential nominee on Sept. 5, 2000, Texas Gov. George W. Bush was in the thick of a tight race against Vice President Al Gore. Tighter, it turned out, than anyone could have imagined.

Bush and running mate Dick Cheney visited Gross Towers, a senior citizens high-rise in Allentown, to tout a massive Medicare reform proposal. Afterward, Bush campaigned at a $5,000-per-person reception and a $500-per-person lunch at the Holiday Inn of Bethlehem in Hanover Township, Northampton County.

Gore followed on Oct. 27, drawing a crowd of several thousand to Stanley Avenue Park in Fountain Hill. The Democrat got off on the wrong foot — "I'm happy to be in Allentown," he said, drawing boos from borough partisans — but won the crowd over with promises of middle-class tax cuts, Social Security protection and education reform.

The election, of course, turned out to be one for the ages: a deadlock decided in Bush's favor by the U.S. Supreme Court.

When Bush returned to Allentown in 2004, he was completing a first term marked by the Sept. 11 terrorist attacks and the invasions of Afghanistan and Iraq. This time around, the president was vying against Democrat John Kerry, the U.S. senator from Massachusetts.

Kerry had drawn 12,000 people to the Allentown Fairgrounds on Sept. 10, bashing Bush's policies on job growth and health care and calling the decision to depose Iraqi dictator Saddam Hussein "the worst of all the choices" the president had made.

On Oct. 1, about the same number of people jammed Lehigh Parkway in Allentown to see Bush, whose motorcade from Lehigh Valley International Airport had received a mixed greeting. In Hanover Township, a group of reservists lined Postal Road to salute the commander in chief. But in front of a store on Lehigh Street in Allentown, a white panel truck bore the message "Where's Osama?" — a reference to 9/11 mastermind Osama bin Laden, who had eluded capture even as the administration pursued war in Iraq.

Inside the Lehigh Parkway, the crowd milled excitedly under a bright blue sky. "Bush, Bush, Bush," cheered Bailey Shiban, a 7-year-old from Lower Saucon Elementary School who had "W" painted on her right cheek and "04" on her left. "Bush is in the house!"

The president, fresh from debating Kerry on television the night before, seemed relaxed and confident. Accompanied by a one-time primary rival and future presidential candidate — U.S. Sen. John McCain of Arizona — Bush knocked Kerry on foreign policy, which had been the major theme of the debate.

"I've never seen a meeting that would depose a tyrant or bring a terrorist to justice," the president said, mocking Kerry's suggestion to hold an international summit on rebuilding Iraq.

To that point in his presidency, Bush had visited Pennsylvania 38 times, underscoring its importance as a swing state. Against Kerry, he would lose the state but win the election.

LEFT TOP: President George W. Bush holds a town hall-style meeting at Kutztown University on July 9, 2004. (Donna Fisher, The Morning Call)

LEFT BOTTOM: President Bush speaks during a campaign rally at Lehigh Parkway in Allentown on Oct. 1, 2004. The night before, Bush had debated Democratic challenger John Kerry. (Morning Call Archives)

ABOVE: Before the White House: Bush at the Sheraton Jetport in Hanover Township, Lehigh County, during a 1988 campaign visit on behalf of his father. (Morning Call Archives)

RIGHT: A Bush-Cheney inaugural button. (Courtesy of Harry Fisher)

Kutztown, Pennsylvania Welcomes

PRESIDENT GEORGE W. BUSH

FRIDAY, JULY 9, 2004

DOORS OPEN AT 8:30 AM
PLEASE ARRIVE NO LATER THAN 10:15 AM

KUTZTOWN UNIVERSITY
KEYSTONE HALL
SOUTH CAMPUS DRIVE
KUTZTOWN, PA 19530-0151

164870

ADMIT ONE

Non-Transferable

TOP: An invitation to President Bush's 2004 visit to Kutztown University. (Courtesy of Kurt Zwikl of Allentown)

BOTTOM: President Bush chats with Dale and Sharon Stump of Bethel, Berks County, during a brief visit to the Hometown Diner near Trexlertown on July 9, 2004. (Douglas Benedict, The Morning Call)

Sunny

70° / 45°

Forecast, B12

mcall.com

The Morning Call's online source

http://www.mcall.com

WEDNESDAY

SEPTEMBER 6, 2000

NO. 39,420

THE MORNING CALL

50¢

BUCKS
MONTGOMERY
BERKS

EDITION

Index on A2

Bush pushes Medicare plan

CESAR L. LAURE / The Morning Call

Republican presidential candidate George W. Bush greets the crowd outside the Gross Towers senior citizens center in Allentown during a campaign stop Tuesday.

■ He unveils proposal detailing medical makeover to Allentown senior citizens.

▶ Latino leaders undecided A3

By JOE McDERMOTT
Of The Morning Call

George W. Bush, surrounded by two dozen residents of an Allentown senior citizens high-rise, proposed a $158 billion Medicare makeover that local elder advocates worry is too complicated for many and too undependable for most.

Bush called for $110 billion to modernize the program created in 1965 and $48 billion for a prescription drug plan that would cover the first four years of a transition to a better Medicare program.

"Medicare is a vital program, too vital to be neglected," the Texas governor said in a long-awaited campaign policy speech Tuesday morning at Gross Towers on Allen Street.

The Republican presidential nominee later touted his plan while campaigning at a $5,000-per-person reception and a $500-per-person lunch at the Holiday Inn of Bethlehem in Hanover Township, Northampton County.

ELECTION 2000

Hammered in recent weeks by opponent Vice President Al Gore for a lack of specifics on his Medicare and prescription drug plans, Bush accused the Clinton administration of squandering chances to revive an ailing program over the past eight years.

"At first, the Clinton-Gore administration proposed an ill-advised government takeover of American medicine that was wisely rejected by Republicans, Democrats and the American people," Bush said. "Since then, the administration has been too partisan — playing politics at the expense of reform."

Bush's visit to Gross Towers was brief. He was accompanied by his wife, Laura, and running mate Dick Cheney. Bush entered, shook a few hands, made his 30-minute speech and left without answering questions.

Yet his address was well-received by the small group of tenants invited to the crowded community room, where they were almost outnumbered by Republican leaders who included Gov. Tom Ridge; U.S. Rep. Pat Toomey, R-15th District; Allentown Mayor William L. Heydt; and state Sen. Charles Dent, R-Lehigh.

The seniors — and the Republican VIPs — were downright

See BUSH Page A3 ▶

At fund-raiser in Valley, Republicans greet Bush with open arms, wallets

By RON DEVLIN
Of The Morning Call

Adam Ballek's not even old enough to vote, but there he was — hobnobbing with the two biggest Republicans in the land at a $500-a-plate lunch in the Holiday Inn of Bethlehem.

His parents bought the Lower Saucon Township teen a ticket for his 17th birthday, and the self-described "die-hard conservative" made memories that will last a lifetime.

In a dark pin-striped suit, executive written all over him, Ballek brushed elbows with Texas Gov. George W. Bush and former Secretary of Defense Dick Cheney — perhaps the next president and vice president of the United States. "I can't vote yet," said Ballek, a junior at Allentown Central Catholic High School, "but I'd do anything to support a campaign like this one."

A lot of Lehigh Valley Republicans — and a few Democrats in attendance — apparently agree.

More than 300 donated at least $500 apiece for a meal of herbed chicken with hostess potatoes and a chance to meet the GOP presidential and vice presidential candidates.

An additional 25 paid $5,000 a couple, an organizer said, to attend a private Lehigh Room reception with Bush and Cheney before lunch at the inn in Hanover Township, Northampton County.

Conservatively, that would add about $200,000 to Victory 2000, the state Republican Committee election initiative — not the Bush campaign.

"It's soft money," said John Brinson, owner of the Allentown and Bethlehem Racquetball and Fitness Clubs.

See MONEY Page A4 ▶

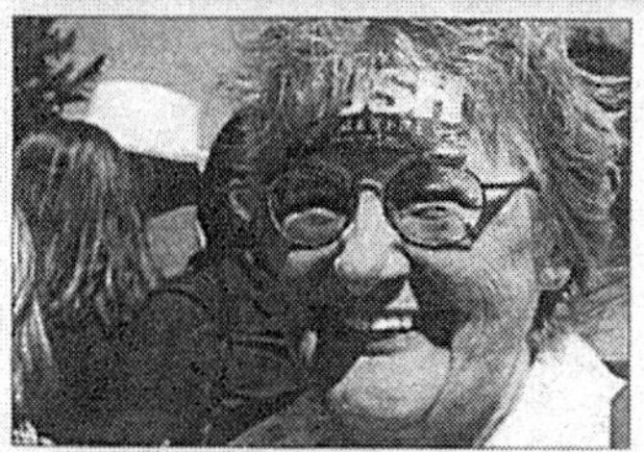

Above, George W. Bush is heckled during a speech Tuesday at the Holiday Inn of Bethlehem. Story, A3. At left, Agnes Gackanbach of Emmaus shows her support for Bush outside the hotel.

BETTY E. CAULER / The Morning Call

ABOVE: On Sept. 5, 2000, Republican presidential candidate Bush unveiled a massive Medicare reform proposal at Gross Towers, a senior citizens high-rise in Allentown. (Morning Call Archives)

FIRST SECOND

MIDEAST: *Four die, more than 100 hurt in latest attack, A*

DRUCE: *Disgraced ex-lawmaker gets 2-4 years, B1*

TINGLY

58°/ 33°
Page **B2**

PULLOUT SECTION
Local, Classified
Section B follows Page A38
Complete index Page A2

6 73249 00050 8

THE MORNING CALL

SATURDAY
October 28, 2000
No. 39,472

50¢

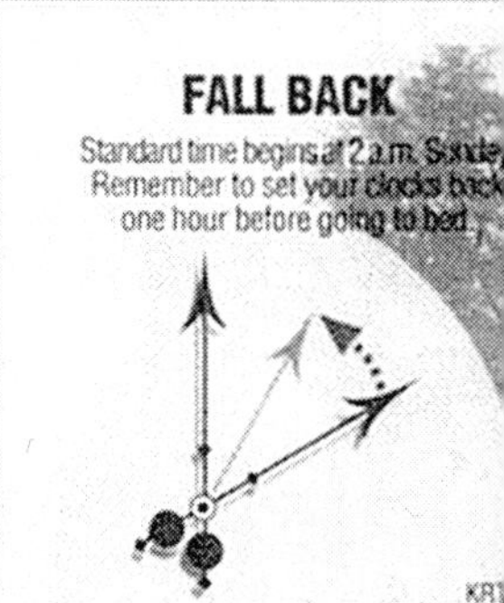

FALL BACK
Standard time begins at 2 a.m. Sunday. Remember to set your clocks back one hour before going to bed.

KRT

Gore on tour

Vice president visits Valley trying to sway undecideds in a key state
Page **A3**

A patriotic Bryan Redding, 7, adjusts his hat while waiting with brother Andrew, 10, to get into Stanley Avenue Park in Fountain Hill, where Al Gore was to speak Friday. The brothers, both from Fountain Hill, waited for more than three hours.
DOUGLAS BENEDICT
The Morning Call

PAGE 116: The Morning Call front page after Vice President Al Gore, Democratic candidate for president, visited the Lehigh Valley in October 2000. The Bush-Gore election would be a historic one, a deadlock ultimately decided by the U.S. Supreme Court in Bush's favor.

ABOVE LEFT: Former Vice President Al Gore speaking at Northampton Community College on Oct. 17, 2002. Gore was stumping for congressional candidate Ed O'Brien. (Morning Call Archives)

ABOVE RIGHT: President Bush speaks during a campaign rally at Lehigh Parkway in Allentown on Oct. 1, 2004, a day after debating Democratic challenger John Kerry. (Douglas Benedict, The Morning Call)

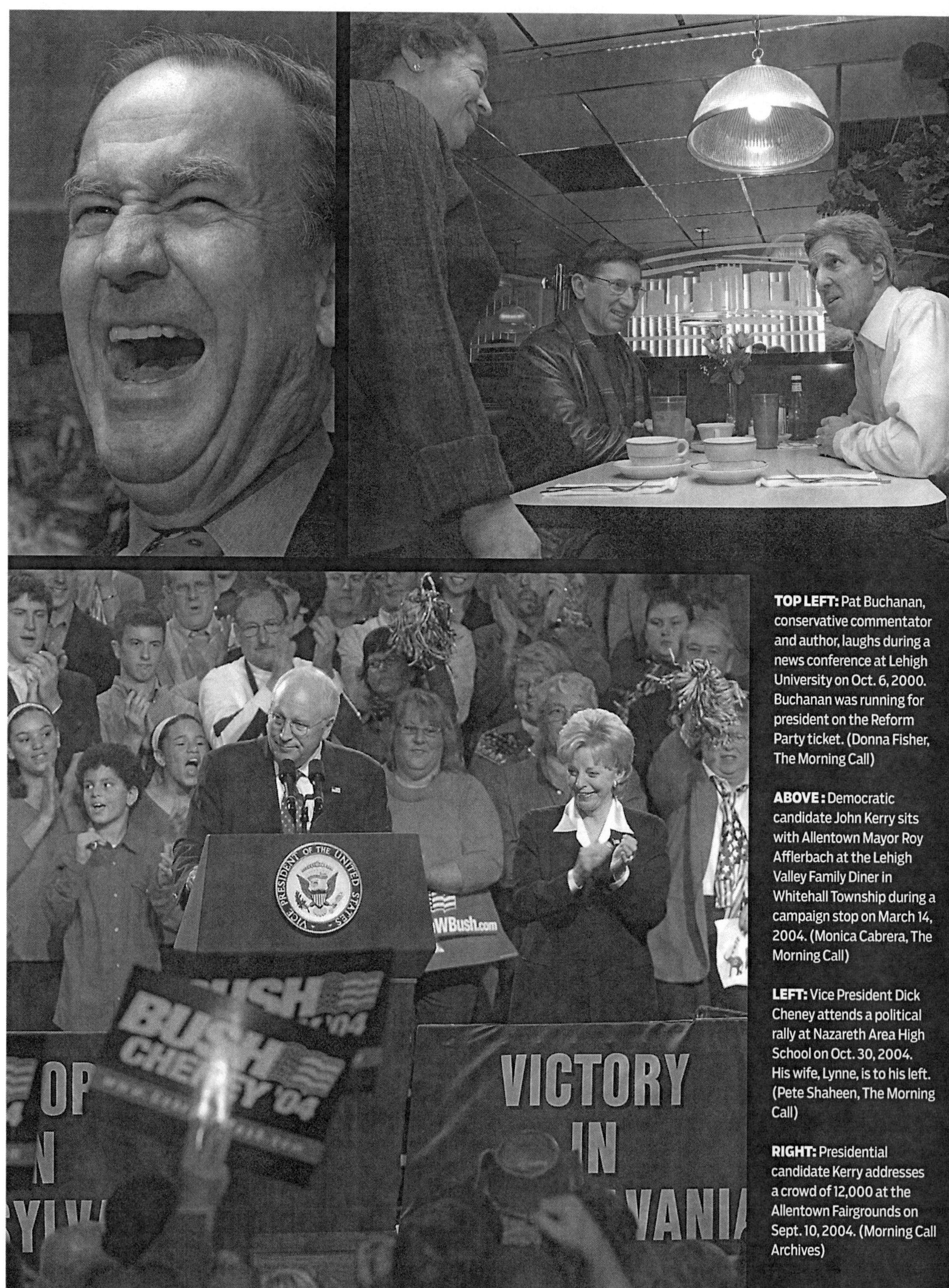

TOP LEFT: Pat Buchanan, conservative commentator and author, laughs during a news conference at Lehigh University on Oct. 6, 2000. Buchanan was running for president on the Reform Party ticket. (Donna Fisher, The Morning Call)

ABOVE: Democratic candidate John Kerry sits with Allentown Mayor Roy Afflerbach at the Lehigh Valley Family Diner in Whitehall Township during a campaign stop on March 14, 2004. (Monica Cabrera, The Morning Call)

LEFT: Vice President Dick Cheney attends a political rally at Nazareth Area High School on Oct. 30, 2004. His wife, Lynne, is to his left. (Pete Shaheen, The Morning Call)

RIGHT: Presidential candidate Kerry addresses a crowd of 12,000 at the Allentown Fairgrounds on Sept. 10, 2004. (Morning Call Archives)

A STRONGER AMERICA
JOHNKERRY.COM
REFRESHMENTS
Kerry
Edwards
TRONGER AMERICA
JohnKerry.com

Soldiers' and S
Centr
H BROS - CLOTHIERS
KOCH BROS

' Monument and Allen Hotel,
iare, Allentown, Pa.

Presidential eateries

Two centuries from now, will people wander into the Bethlehem Brew Works on Main Street and ask to see the spot where Barack Obama sat and sipped a beer?

Could happen. After all, people today visit the Sun Inn, just across the street from the Brew Works, to see the rooms where George Washington and John Adams dined in the 1770s and 1780s.

The Sun Inn was the original hot spot for Valley visitors. But in the years since the Founding Fathers visited, plenty of other eateries have hosted presidential patrons.

Martin Van Buren ate at George Haberacker's inn, which once stood at the northeast corner of Seventh and Hamilton streets in Allentown. The Hotel Allen would occupy the same spot decades later and host Teddy Roosevelt, Woodrow Wilson and others.

In 1948, before he was president, Dwight D. Eisenhower ate at a long-gone Howard Johnson's at Union Boulevard and Airport Road in Allentown.

In 1980, President Jimmy Carter's mother, Miss Lillian, ate breakfast at Hess's Patio, the restaurant in the late, lamented department store in downtown Allentown.

Bill Clinton put the now-defunct Charcoal Drive-In of Wescosville on the map when he stopped for a cup of coffee there in 1995.

Obama visited the Bethlehem Brew Works as a candidate in 2008 and Allentown's Hamilton Family Restaurant as president in 2009.

Brew Works owner Michael Fegley said he still has Obama's beer glass, chair and other memorabilia from that day, "all tucked away for my great-grandkids. Actually, someday we might donate it to a museum."

LEFT: A postcard of the Hotel Allen on the northeast corner of Center Square in Allentown. Woodrow Wilson, Teddy Roosevelt and other presidents slept and ate here, making it one of the Lehigh Valley's original dining hot spots for chief executives. The hotel was built in 1888 and was torn down in the late 1940s.

ABOVE: Presidential candidate Barack Obama makes a stop on Main Street in Bethlehem on April 20, 2008. Obama's surprise visit coincided with a speech at Liberty High School by his chief opponent in the Democratic primary, U.S. Sen. Hillary Clinton. (Cesar Laure, The Morning Call)

TOP RIGHT: President Obama smiles as a crowd at Lehigh County Community College welcomes him on Dec. 9, 2009. It was one of five stops on a busy day as Obama crisscrossed the Lehigh Valley, seeking to boost confidence in the shattered economy. (Morning Call Archives)

RIGHT: Clinton speaks at a 2008 campaign rally at Liberty High School, Bethlehem. (Michael Kubel, The Morning Call)

OBAMA

Barack Obama, here, there and everywhere: 2008-09

On Dec. 4, 2009, Barack Obama made what had to be the most wide-ranging presidential visit in Lehigh Valley history.

In five hours he visited a steel manufacturer, a community college, a diner, a job center and a pet food factory. He shook hands with blue-collar workers, cooed at babies and commiserated with the unemployed at a job center.

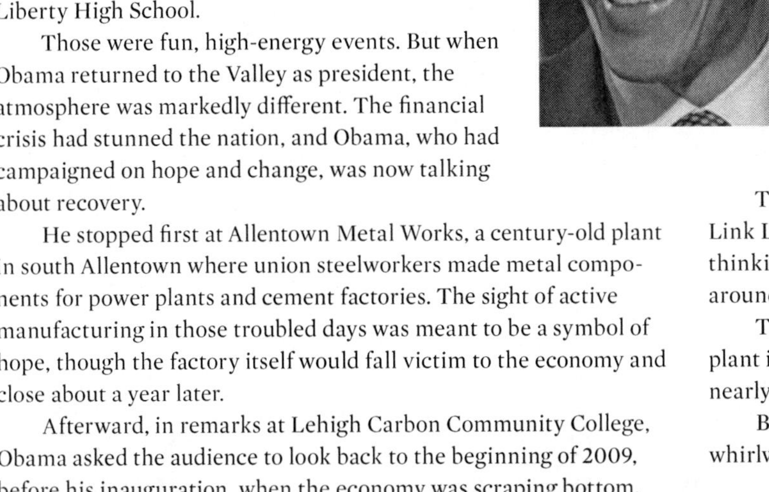

Obama had visited the Valley twice as a candidate. On March 31, 2008, the U.S. senator from Illinois addressed 3,500 fired-up supporters at Muhlenberg College in Allentown. And on April 20, he made a surprise visit to Bethlehem, sipping beer at the Bethlehem Brew Works just hours after his Democratic primary opponent, U.S. Sen. Hillary Clinton of New York, greeted screaming supporters at the city's Liberty High School.

Those were fun, high-energy events. But when Obama returned to the Valley as president, the atmosphere was markedly different. The financial crisis had stunned the nation, and Obama, who had campaigned on hope and change, was now talking about recovery.

He stopped first at Allentown Metal Works, a century-old plant in south Allentown where union steelworkers made metal components for power plants and cement factories. The sight of active manufacturing in those troubled days was meant to be a symbol of hope, though the factory itself would fall victim to the economy and close about a year later.

Afterward, in remarks at Lehigh Carbon Community College, Obama asked the audience to look back to the beginning of 2009, before his inauguration, when the economy was scraping bottom.

"We were losing more than 700,000 jobs a month," he said. "That's roughly half the [population] of Philadelphia each month. Our financial system was on the verge of collapse. Economists were warning of a second Great Depression. You remember."

The latest jobs report, released that day, showed jobs were still disappearing, albeit at a much slower pace. Indeed, it was the best such report in two years, and Obama called it a sign that his efforts to revive the economy were working.

His greeting at the college mirrored the issues facing him in his first year. Supporters beseeched him for help in finding a job or getting health care coverage, other supporters criticized him for increasing the number of American troops in Afghanistan. At other Valley stops, protesters slammed him for both his handling of the economy and the growing national debt.

At lunchtime, Obama huddled at the iconic Hamilton Family Restaurant in Allentown, dining on a cheeseburger and fries with the city's mayor, Ed Pawlowski, and several politicians and business owners.

Then he headed to the Workforce Investment Board's CareerLink Lehigh Valley office on Union Boulevard in Allentown. "I'm thinking about you every day," he told the job seekers clustered around the center's computer terminals.

The president made one last stop: the Nestle Purina PetCare plant in South Whitehall Township, where he shook hands with nearly 200 workers at the 3 p.m. shift change.

By 4 p.m., the president was back aboard Air Force One. The whirlwind was over.

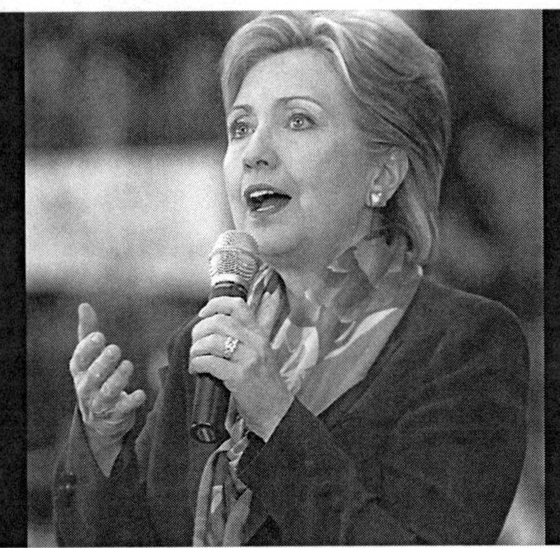

PS When Hillary Clinton took the stage at Liberty High School during the 2008 primary campaign, she attacked Barack Obama for his position on universal health care.

The Morning Call summarized the issue: "Both Clinton and Obama favor extending health coverage to the uninsured by opening up the benefits plan offered to members of Congress and federal employees. The difference: Clinton's plan would require those without coverage to purchase it."

Obama, of course, would make that requirement central to his own health care reform law. The whole matter ended up in front of the U.S. Supreme Court, which ruled the law constitutional.

Clinton won the Pennsylvania primary decisively, by 10 percentage points. "The road to the White House runs through Pennsylvania," she said at her victory party April 22. But in the end, it was Obama, not Clinton, who followed that road to its finish.

ABOVE: A crowd gathers around Democratic presidential candidate Obama during a surprise visit in April 2008 to Bethlehem's Main Street, where he sipped beer at the Bethlehem Brew Works. (Emily Robson, The Morning Call)

OBAMA

THE LEHIGH VALLEY'S GREATEST NEWSPAPER

THE MORNING CALL

SATURDAY

DECEMBER 5, 2009

1 75¢

themorningcall.com

Rain/Snow 39° | 25°
FORECAST Sports 8

WHITE HOUSE TO MAIN STREET TOUR

From LCCC to the Ham Fam, he hears what's on people's minds

OBAMA STOPS BY

"You can't keep just printing money. I love this country, but I want to see it stronger, not weaker."

— Pat Moe, Wilson, waiting outside an Obama event

"The two things that derail presidents are bad economies and unpopular wars. He's got both on his plate."

— Chris Borick, Muhlenberg College

"I've never felt so nervous. This is a story I can't wait to share with my grandson."

— Tracey Hicks, Hamilton Family Restaurant waitress

NICHOLAS KAMM / GETTY IMAGES

President Barack Obama greets a baby before delivering remarks on the economy at Lehigh Carbon Community College in Schnecksville.

President gathering ideas for jobs initiative

The president visits Allentown Metal Works on S. 10th Street on his fast-moving visit to the Lehigh Valley.

MONICA CABRERA / THE MORNING CALL

By Spencer Soper, John L. Micek, Daniel Patrick Sheehan and Brian Callaway
OF THE MORNING CALL

Barack Obama returned to the Lehigh Valley as president Friday to say his administration has rescued the economy from a disastrous tailspin and now needs to get Americans back to work.

Friday's dip in unemployment is progress, Obama said, but he made clear he understands many out-of-work people still face a serious lack of opportunities.

he said. "Every one of us knows [them]."

Candidate Obama visited the Valley twice last year. President Obama's motorcade crisscrossed the region Friday, with stops that included a pet food plant in South Whitehall Township, a metal fabrication plant in Allentown and the Hamilton Family Restaurant in the city. His appearance before about 1,000 at the community college was the main event.

Obama's 50-minute give-and-take came at a critical time for the administration. He wants to convince the public he is focused on

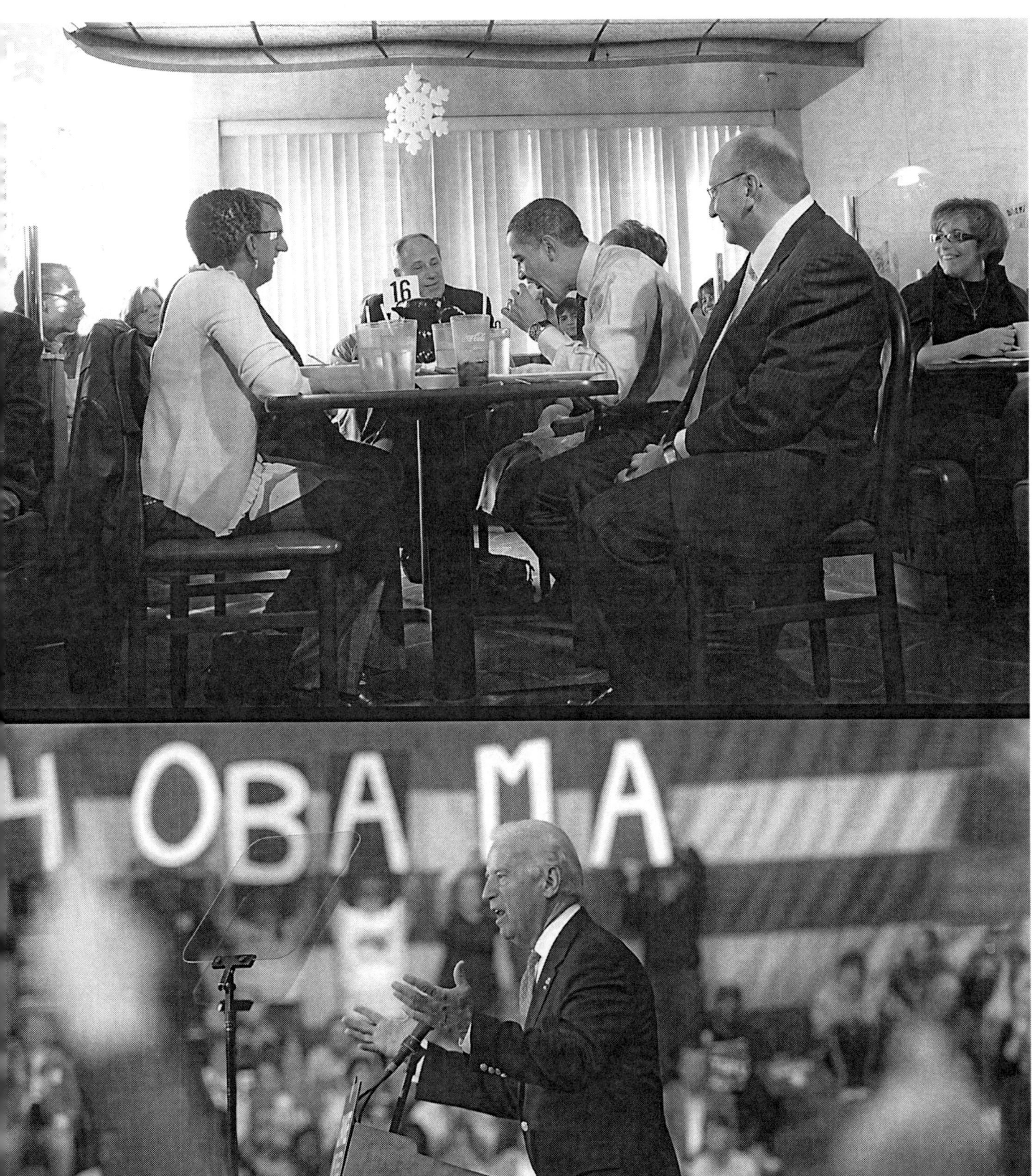

LEFT: The front page of The Morning Call recounts President Obama's wide-ranging visit to the Lehigh Valley on Dec. 4, 2009.

TOP: President Obama enjoys a hamburger at the Hamilton Family Restaurant in Allentown during a 2009 visit. Mayor Ed Pawlowski is seated to his left. (Monica Cabrera, The Morning Call)

BOTTOM : The Democratic vice presidential candidate, U.S. Sen. Joe Biden of Delaware, speaks at Muhlenberg College on Oct. 30, 2008. (Michael Kubel, The Morning Call)

First lady makes her pitch

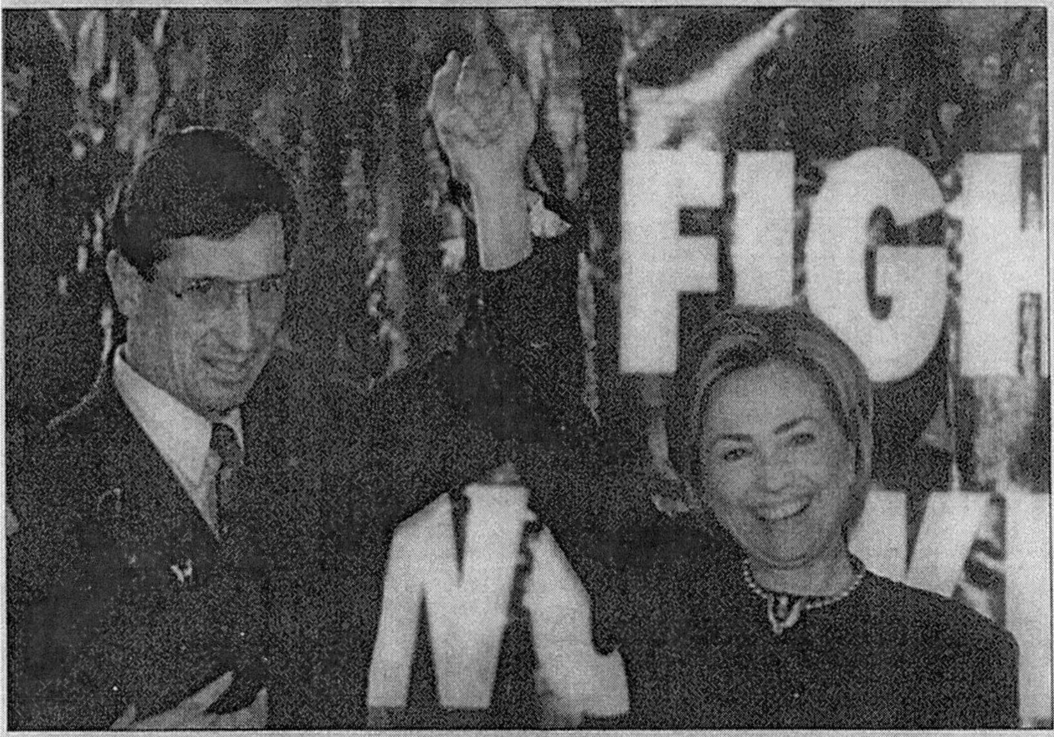

■ At UAW hall, she sings the praises of congressional candidate Roy Afflerbach.

By MARTIN PFLIEGER
Of The Morning Call

After watching one Republican heavyweight after another campaigning in recent weeks on behalf of his opponent, Democrat Roy Afflerbach took his turn Sunday basking in the spotlight of a political star.

In a visit designed to boost Afflerbach's campaign for Congress just 48 hours before Tuesday's election, first lady Hillary Rodham Clinton came to Allentown on Sunday for a rally and fund-raiser and to push the Democratic Party agenda.

Standing at a podium before about 500 cheering party faithful in the United Auto Workers union hall on Mack Boulevard, the first lady called Afflerbach, a state senator, the clear choice over Republican Pat Toomey.

"You have someone with a proven record, experience, with accomplishments and with a vision about what is best for improving the lives of people here in this district," she said. "Now that says a lot to me, because he isn't a rookie.

"It's an election not just between two candidates," said Clinton, who was interrupted often by applause and whistles. "It's a fundamental choice between progress and partisanship, between putting people's interests first and politics as usu

Please See FIRST LADY Page A8 ►

Above, first lady Hillary Rodham Clinton gives a hand of support to Democratic candidate Roy Afflerbach at the UAW hall on Mack Boulevard, Allentown, Sunday. At right, Hispanic Political Caucus member Sainz De La Pena holds a sign for Clinton.

HARRY FISHER
The Morning Call

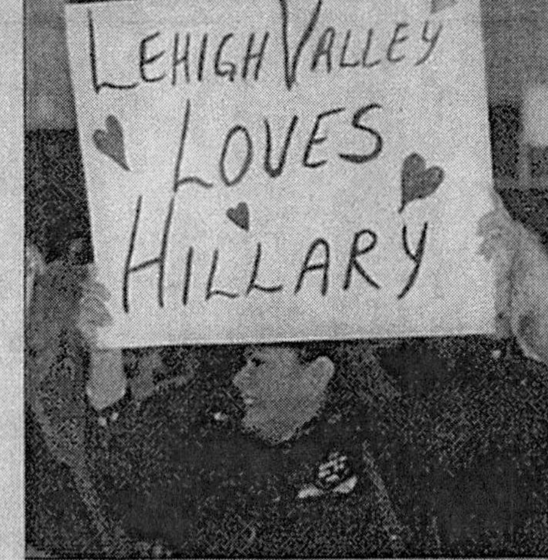

Visit attracts supporters, sightseers, protesters

■ Some outside Democratic rally sought glimpse of first lady; others hope to see the last of her husband.

By ANN WLAZELEK
Of The Morning Call

While hundreds of Democratic ticket-holders filed inside the United Auto Workers' union hall Sunday morning for a rally featuring Hillary Rodham Clinton, a smaller group of protesters, supporters and sightseers collected across the street.

Some came to make a statement against abortion and for impeaching the president. Some stumped for congressional candidate Roy Afflerbach, other Democrats and the need to vote. Others just hoped for a glimpse of the first lady.

Michael Brack walked his 8-year-old daugter Alecia a few blocks from home for a chanc to see Clinton. Waiting on the sidewalk in fro of Mack Trucks World Headquarters, the closest they got was seeing her ride by in a black sedan behind an Allentown police car.

"I never saw her before, only pictures," Alecia said, after removing a lollipop from he mouth.

Brack, a machinist for a company in Trumbauersville, said, "I think it's neat that the president's wife comes to Allentown, a small town."

Without a ticket, the two were not permited inside the hall.

Please See RALLY Page A8

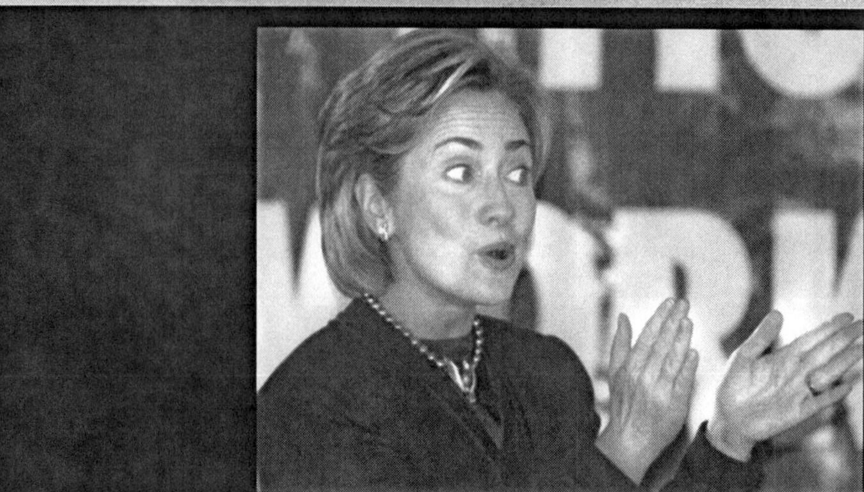

ABOVE: A page from The Morning Call highlights first lady Clinton's visit to Allentown on Nov. 1, 1998. Clinton stumped for Democratic congressional candidate Roy Afflerbach.

LEFT: Clinton claps during the 1998 visit to Allentown.

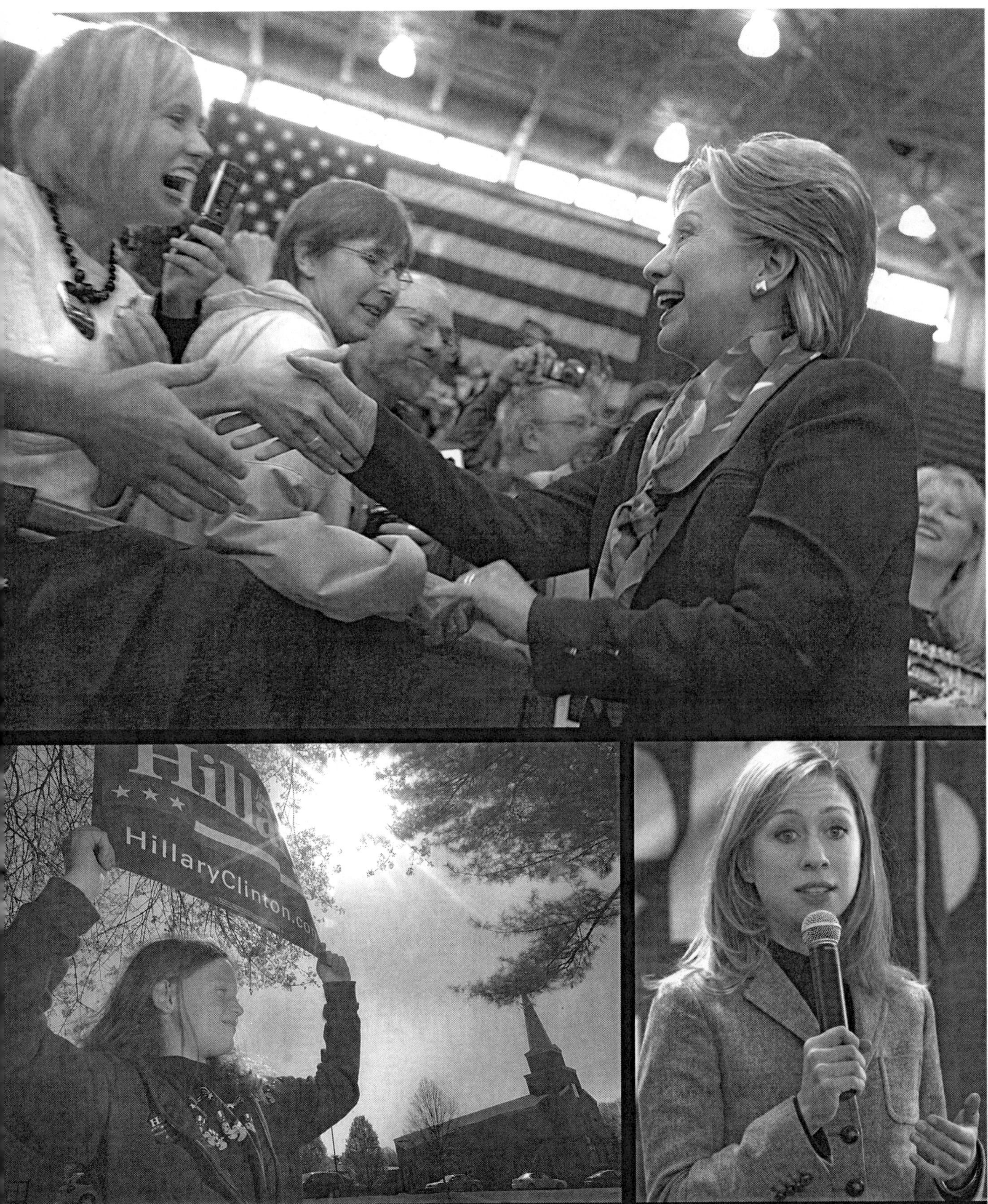

TOP: Sen. Clinton greets gleeful supporters on April 20, 2008, during her presidential primary campaign appearance at Liberty High School in Bethlehem.

ABOVE LEFT: Clinton campaign volunteer Christine Olsen, 11, stands outside Wesley United Methodist Church in Bethlehem during the Democrat's April 2008 visit.

ABOVE RIGHT: Chelsea Clinton campaigns for her mother at Northampton Community College in Bethlehem Township on March 28, 2008.

COUNTR

LEFT: U.S. Sen. John McCain of Arizona and his running mate, Alaska Gov. Sarah Palin, hold a rally at Stabler Arena in Bethlehem on Oct. 8, 2008. McCain had plucked Palin out of obscurity to share the ticket and created a media phenomenon. (Monica Cabrera, The Morning Call)

RIGHT: Gov. Palin waves as she arrives at Lehigh Valley International Airport on Oct. 8, 2008. McCain, the GOP presidential candidate, and Palin drew a crowd of 6,000 to Stabler Arena later that day. (Monica Cabrera, The Morning Call)

McCain & Palin

The Republican presidential ticket of John McCain and Sarah Palin rallied a crowd of 6,000 at Lehigh University's Stabler Arena on Oct. 8, 2008.

It was the third campaign visit to the Valley for McCain, the U.S. senator from Arizona, and the first for Palin, the governor of Alaska.

With the financial crisis in full swing, the team outlined a plan to help homeowners refinance their mortgages. One of the major elements of the crisis was the decline in housing values, which left many homeowners owing more than their homes were worth.

"The dream of owning a home should not be crushed under the weight of a bad mortgage," said McCain, who had debated Democratic candidate Barack Obama of Illinois the night before. "The moment requires that government act, and as president I intend to act, quickly and decisively."

In her 15-minute introduction of McCain, Palin called the election a choice between "a politician who puts his faith in government and a leader who puts his faith in you."

Such knocks on Obama, at the time one of McCain's colleagues in the Senate, brought the crowd to its feet.

"We have all heard what he has said, but it is less clear what he has done or what he will do," McCain said. "What Sen. Obama says today and what he has done in the past are often two different things."

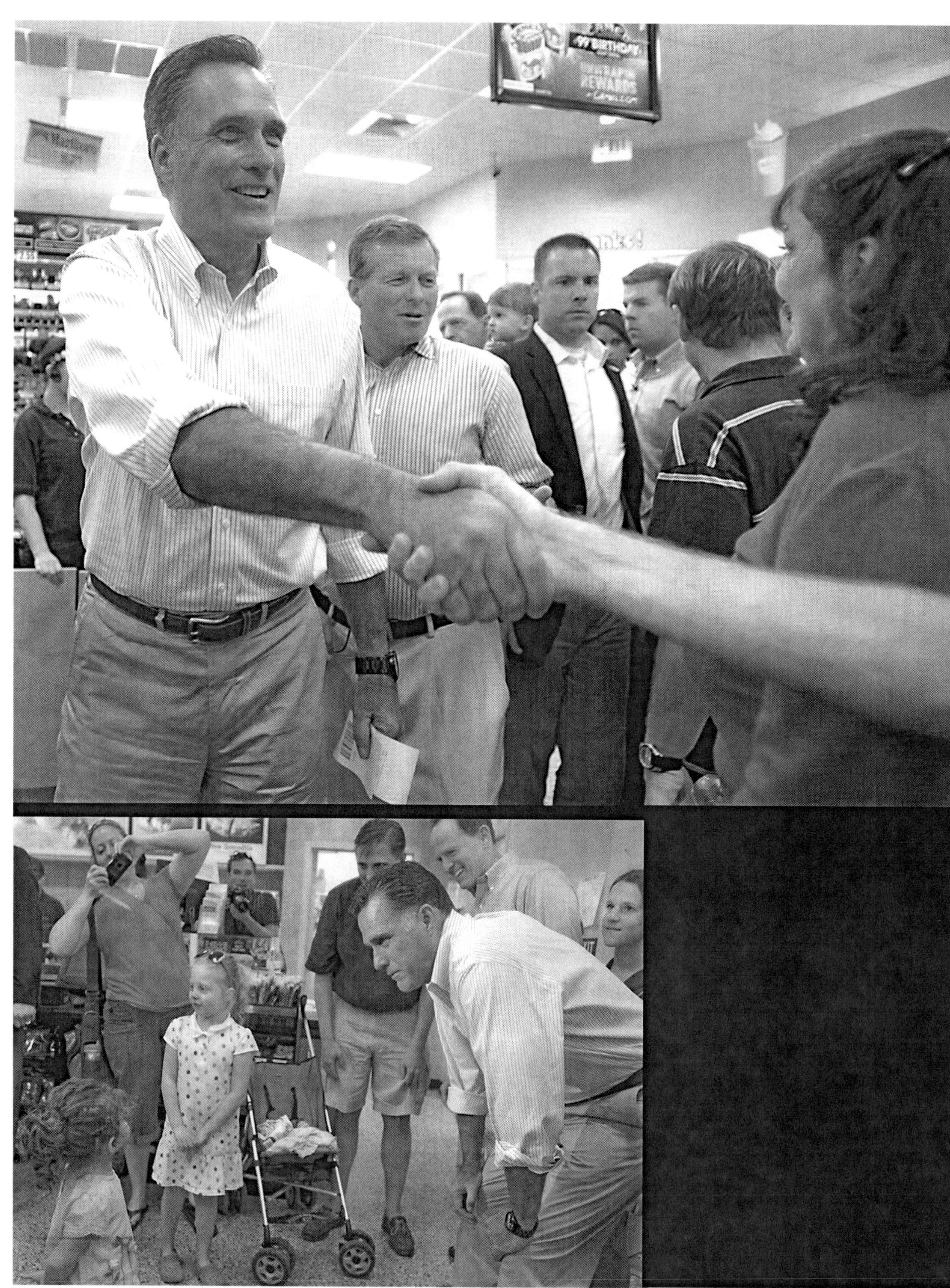
99¢ BIRTHDAY
REWARDS
Marlboro

BIDEN & ROMNEY

Joe Biden, Mitt Romney and a look ahead: 2012

In the Lehigh Valley, the first real event of the 2012 presidential campaign was Vice President Joe Biden's May 2 appearance at Lafayette College in Easton. More than 3,100 people crowded the Kirby Sports Center to hear the Scranton native imagine a future in which cars go 1,000 miles on a single electric charge and medicine has all but conquered cancer.

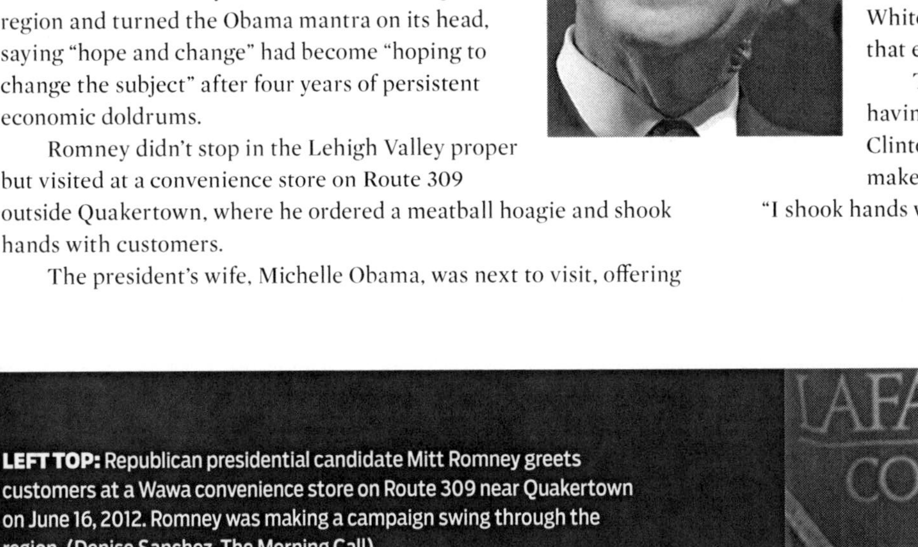

"You have to have imagination," Biden said. "You have to ask yourself the question – not only 'What if we do' [but] 'What if we don't?' Tell me what happens if we don't."

It was a hopeful speech, recalling the rhetoric of Barack Obama's "hope and change" campaign in 2008.

On June 16, 2012, presumptive Republican nominee Mitt Romney took a bus tour through the region and turned the Obama mantra on its head, saying "hope and change" had become "hoping to change the subject" after four years of persistent economic doldrums.

Romney didn't stop in the Lehigh Valley proper but visited at a convenience store on Route 309 outside Quakertown, where he ordered a meatball hoagie and shook hands with customers.

The president's wife, Michelle Obama, was next to visit, offering a fiery message on Aug. 9 to a packed gym at Moravian College in Bethlehem.

"We can't afford to turn back now, not now, not when we have come so far, but we have so much work to do," the first lady exhorted 2,400 screaming enthusiasts in Archibald Johnston Hall.

From the early going, the 2012 campaign promised to be a tough one. But presidential politics has always been tough, ever since Thomas Jefferson's campaign characterized John Adams as a "hideous hermaphroditical character" with neither the "force and firmness of a man, nor the gentleness and sensibility of a woman." President Obama's attacks on Romney's role in outsourcing American jobs seem quite tame in comparison.

Campaign hardball can taint what ought to be a dignified process, but in the end, whoever wins the White House is afforded a special kind of respect, one that extends beyond the person to the office itself.

The most ardent partisan of whatever stripe, having shaken the hand of a Ronald Reagan or a Bill Clinton, a George W. Bush or a Barack Obama, will make the same proud boast to family and friends: "I shook hands with the president."

LEFT TOP: Republican presidential candidate Mitt Romney greets customers at a Wawa convenience store on Route 309 near Quakertown on June 16, 2012. Romney was making a campaign swing through the region. (Denise Sanchez, The Morning Call)

LEFT BOTTOM: Candidate Romney chats with 2-year-old Abby Petrille of Bedminster at the Wawa near Quakertown. Romney was on a campaign swing through the region. (Denise Sanchez, The Morning Call)

RIGHT TOP AND BOTTOM: Vice President Joe Biden gives a lecture at a packed Kirby Sports Center at Lafayette College in Easton on May 2, 2012. Biden told the audience that American imagination and inventiveness can mean a brighter future for the world. (Emily Robson, The Morning Call)

PART III

More than 100 years of history in front pages

Few things return one directly to the biggest days in history as do those newspaper front pages that first reported the wars, the disasters, the losses and gains that have marked the turning points of our society. Whether such events carry the import of the end of war, the wrenching loss of life to natural disaster, or the death of a leader, these landmark events hold fast to the public mind as though they just took place.

Following are 40 front pages that serve as milestones to more than 100 years of history — from the sinking of the battleship Maine in 1898 to the firing of Penn State football coach Joe Paterno in 2011. They are all from The Morning Call archives. Along with Morning Call front pages, you'll find images of the Evening Chronicle, The Sunday Call-Chronicle and The Allentown Morning Call — all predecessors or sister papers to The Morning Call.

Page through and consider what a tumultuous backdrop history presented to the presidential campaigns that brought so many leaders to the Lehigh Valley. Consider what unknown challenges these men and women who would lead the nation throw themselves into should they win the presidency.

IS TRADE DULL?
Try an advertisement in the Morning Call.

MORNING CALL.

If it's worthy it's here.
If it's here it's worthy.

NEW SERIES—VOL. XV., NO. 38. ALLENTOWN, PA., THURSDAY MORNING, FEBRUARY 17, 1898. PRICE 2 CENTS.

THE MAINE DISASTER.

Frightful Loss of Life by the Explosion Which Sunk Our Cruiser at Havana.

MORE THAN 200 MEN ARE MISSING.

Various Theories in Explanation of the Awful Casualty—It Couldn't Have Been Spontaneous Combustion, as the Maine Used Only Hard Coal.

Special to the "Morning Call."

WASHINGTON, D. C., Feb. 17, 2.20 a. m.—Reports have been received from Consul General Lee at Havana in which he states that 200 of the "Maine's" crew are drowned or dead, 29 are badly injured and in the hospital at San Ambrosio and 30 slightly injured in the hospital at Alphonso XIII. All but five officers and those of the crew that are injured and slightly injured have been taken to Key West.

LOOKS LIKE SPANISH TREACHERY.

The consul general is not yet prepared to report on the cause of the disaster. The impression seems to be popular in this city that the explosion was not due to accident, but to Spanish treachery. Navy department officials are extremely reticent to-night in giving out information regarding the cause of the disaster and many eral explosions occurred. Magazines were burst open, and explosives were thrown overboard. In half an hour it was apparent nothing could save the ship. The first explosion wounded and disabled many, but how many it is impossible to say. Many were struggling in the water. I was crowded overboard and remember no more until reaching the wharf."

An engineer confirms the previous story regarding the explosion and said when he started for the deck water was already in the engine room. He helped fight the fire for a short time, when another explosion occurred, and when he recovered he found himself in the water.

As these officers were talking boats from various ships in the harbor were bringing wounded and half drowned men ashore. Several were dead, while others were dying. It is impossible at

THE BATTLESHIP MAINE.

THE RESULT IN THE COUNTY.

The following is the result in the township and borough.

A NUMBER OF ACCIDENTS

Which Occurred in This City and Other Places.

HE FLEW THROUGH THE AIR

Brakeman, Richard McGee, of This City, Had a Thrilling Experience Yesterday in New Jersey—A Fireman Badly Burned.

Richard McGee residing on Turner street between Ridge avenue and Second street and who is a brakeman on the Jersey City fast freight on the Central Railroad of New Jersey that left this city at 5 o'clock yesterday morning had an exciting experience yesterday.

He was standing on the top of a box car at High Bridge (N. J.) when the fierce wind lifted the roof of the car off its bearings and in a moment roof and the brakeman were sailing through the air. The car top landed nearly a hundred feet away with McGee still on top. In striking the ground, however, he was badly bruised and was sent home on the next passenger train that arrived in Allentown at noon. He is confined to the house in consequence of his injuries.

A FIREMAN BADLY BURNED.

T. W. Burkholder, fireman on the Perkiomen Railroad, while fixing his fires at Palm Station on Tuesday night, was painfully burned by flames and steam that shot out of the fire box. He was brought to this city and removed to his home, No. 430 Maple street.

A SAWMILLER'S CLOSE CALL.

John Schneck, the sawmiller of Schnecksville, while sawing timber on the Balliet estate, near Ballietsville, fell from the car-

STRUCK BY A COAL TRAIN

An Unknown Tramp Injured at Laury's.

ON THE VALLEY RAILROAD

He Was Acting Suspiciously in the Village and After Being Ordered Out of a Shop Attempted to Jump on a Cowcatcher.

Last evening at 6.05 a man was struck by a Lehigh Valley coal train at Laury's, but is not supposed to be fatally injured. He acted somewhat mysteriously before he was struck. He arrived there with a freight train in the afternoon and went into the cooperage shop of the mill where he tried to hit another man with a coal scuttle. When warned he left and when the coal train arrived he attempted to jump on the cowcatcher, but was unsuccessful and fell to a side. His forehead was badly cut.

Dr. Horn, of Coplay, was called and temporarily dressed the wound. The man was sent to St. Luke's Hospital on a later train. His name is not known. He is a stout, well-built man and swore in the worst manner after he had been struck.

A CHILD POISONED.

A Fatal Mistake in the Family of J. H. Fisher, of Graterford.

A sad mistake occurred in the family of Josiah H. Fisher, of Graterford, Montgomery county, in which they lost, by death, their only child, a daughter, less than a year of age. Mrs. Fisher being sick and unable to attend to her household duties, her mother, Mrs. Kratz, was looking after her household affairs.

WINTER SOCIAL FUNCTIONS

The members of the Mercury Wheelmen gave their third annual dance to their lady friends last evening. The rooms were elaborately decorated for the occasion. Twenty-five couples participated. Euchre was also indulged in. Professor E. Lehman Rube's Orchestra furnished music. The affair was in charge of the following committee: W. P. Sterner, chairman; E. Lehman Rube, Frank Heffner, Fred Balliet and Jacob Goundie.

A GOLDEN WEDDING CELEBRATED.

Rev. and Mrs. Edmund Butz, the former one of the oldest United Evangelical ministers in active service in this section, celebrated their golden wedding at their home, No. 21 North Eleventh street, with a reunion of their nearest friends on Thursday evening. Rev. D. A. Medlar and family were also present. A splendid dinner was served and the couple received a number of gold presents. Rev. and Mrs. Butz are 73 years old and both are in good health. Mrs. Butz's maiden name was Leah Mertz. The couple were married along the Cedar creek by Rev. Kramer.

NEW PAPER PATTERN DEPARTMENT.

W. R. LAWFER & CO. MAKE

ROYAL BAKING POWDER

Get What You Want. A Call Classified Ad Will Help You. The Cost Is Small.

THE ALLENTOWN MORNING CALL

SWORN DAILY CIRCULATION FOR 3 Months of 1912 13,374

VOL. XLIV, NO. 89. 16 PAGES—4 A. M. EDITION ALLENTOWN, PA., TUESDAY MORNING, APRIL 16, 1912. 16 PAGES—4 A. M. EDITION TWO CENTS.

1,200 REPORTED LOST ON TITANIC

Only 866 Passengers, Some of World-Wide Prominence, Are Known to Be Saved.

GREATEST DISASTER IN MARINE HISTORY

White Star Officials Admit "Horrible Loss of Life."

VESSEL WAS ON MAIDEN VOYAGE

Was Bound From Liverpool to New York and Crashed Into Iceberg, Sinking Four Hours Later Off New Foundland Banks—Largest Ship Afloat

Boston, April 15.—A wireless message picked up late to-night, relayed from the Olympic, says that the Carpathia is on her way to New York with 866 passengers from the steamer Titanic aboard. They are mostly women and children, the message said, and it concluded:

"Grave fears are felt for the safety of the balance of the passengers and crew."

While the fate of the majority of the 2100 persons on board the mammoth White Star Liner Titanic which sank early yesterday on the New Foundland banks after a collision with an iceberg, ...

CAPTAIN OF THE TITANIC.

CAPT E. J. SMITH

Captain E. J. Smith of the ill-fated steamship Titanic, which struck an iceberg off Cape Race, had in his care some of the most noted people in the country and his bond was for the complete safety of all on board the vessel ...

THE WHITE STAR LINE STEAMSHIP TITANIC.

MESSAGE FROM OLYMPIC REPORTS 1,800 LOST

Hoped to be Erroneous Unless Titanic Had More Than 2,170 People on Board

PARISIAN AND VIRGINIAN MAY HAVE SURVIVORS

PARTIAL LIST OF PASSENGERS SAVED

AMATEURS INTERFERE WITH THE WIRELESS

STEAMER VIRGINIA SENDS GOOD NEWS

FIRST NEWS OF DISASTER COMES FROM CAPE RACE

CAPTAIN HADDOCK REPORTS ALL ON BOARD WERE SAVED

SURVIVORS SUFFER GREAT HARDSHIPS

EVERY EFFORT MADE TO GET IN TOUCH WITH OLYMPIC

DEATH-BED OF TITANIC TWO MILES BELOW THE SURFACE

BIG FLUCTUATIONS IN PRICE OF WHEAT

WILLIAM A. LATHROP BURIED AT FORTY FORT

TEDDY CHARGED WITH TRYING TO WRECK G. O. P.

In Statement Issued From Taft Bureau After Officials' Visit to White House

"NO WORD OR DEED TOO MENDACIOUS

Or Mean to Accomplish End in View on Part of Under-Strappers," the Statement Continues—Says Wm. L. Ward Is Engineering Campaign.

WM. A. DORR SOUGHT FOR MARSH MURDER

Abandoned Auto Located in Boston Garage.

TO INQUIRE INTO MENTAL CONDITION OF HARRY THAW

DALZELL DEFEATED FOR CONGRESSMAN

THE WEATHER.

MEMBER OF THE ASSOCIATED PRESS—The Associated Press is exclusively entitled to the use of republication of all news dispatches credited to it or not otherwise credited in this paper and also the local news published herein.

THE ALLENTOWN MORNING CALL

THE DAILY CIRCULATION of the Allentown Morning Call for the Month of October, 1918, was.......... 23,512

VOL. LVII, NO. 113 | SECOND EDITION | ALLENTOWN, PA., MONDAY MORNING, NOVEMBER 11, 1918 | TWO CENTS A COPY—TEN CENTS A WEEK

ARMISTICE IS SIGNED

(By Associated Press.)

Washington, Nov. 11—The world war will end this morning at six o'clock Washington time, 11 o'clock Paris time. The armistice was signed by German representatives at midnight. This announcement was made by the state department at 2:50 o'clock this morning.

The terms of the armistice, it was announced, will not be made public until later. Military men here, however, regard it as certain that they will include:

Immediate retirement of the German military forces from France, Belgium and Alsace-Lorraine.

WILHELM II ABDICATES

(By Associated Press.)

London, Nov. 10, 2:04 p. m.—Emperor William signed a letter of abdication on Saturday morning at the German grand headquarters in the presence of Crown Prince Frederick William and Field Marshal Hindenburg, according to a despatch from Amsterdam to the Exchange Telegraph Company.

The German crown prince signed his renunciation to the throne shortly afterwards.

It is believed that King Ludwig, of Bavaria, and King Frederick August, of Saxony, also have abdicated.

The ex-kaiser and the former crown prince were expected to take leave of their troops on Saturday but nothing has been settled regarding their future movements.

Before placing his signature to the document an urgent message from Philipp Scheidemann, who was a Socialist member without portfolio in the imperial cabinet, was handed to the emperor. He read it with a shiver. Then he signed the paper saying, "It might be for the good of Germany."

The emperor was deeply moved. He consented to sign the document only when he got the news of the latest events in the empire.

Serious food difficulties are expected in Germany owing to the stoppage of trains. The council of the regency will take the most drastic steps to re-establish order.

Basel, Switzerland, Nov. 10, (Havas) —Wilhelm II, the reigning king of the monarchy of Wurtemberg, abdicated on Friday night.

Copenhagen, Nov. 10, 8:30 p. m.—News of Emperor William's abdication was received on Saturday afternoon at Berlin with general rejoicing, which was tempered by the fear that it had come too late.

Washington, Nov. 10.—William Hohenzollern arrived this afternoon in Holland and is proceeding to Middachten Castle in the town of DeSteeg, according to a despatch received by the American army staff from the Hague based on press reports in the Netherlands capital. The despatch dated today says:

Press reports state that the Kaiser arrived this morning at Maastricht, Holland, and is proceeding to Middachten Castle in the town of DeSteeg, near Utrecht.

DeSteeg is on the Guelders Yessel, an arm of the Rhine river about forty miles east of Uetrecht and 12 miles east of the German border. The chateau Middachten, to which the former emperor is reported to be proceeding, belongs to Count William Frederick Charles von Bentinck. He is a member of the Prussian guards and before the war was attache of the German embassy in London and a member of the English Turf and Automobiles. He is thirty-eight years old. He belongs to the famous Anglo-Dutch-German house of Bentinck, the continental branch of the family of the Duke of Portland.

Middachten Castle dates back to the year 1697.

London, Nov. 11, 12:31 a. m.—The former German emperor's party which is believed to include Field Marshal Von Hindenburg, arrived at Eysden, on the Dutch frontier, at 7:30 o'clock Sunday morning according to Daily advices.

Virtually the whole German general staff accompanied the former emperor and ten automobiles carried the party. The automobiles were bristling with rifles and all the fugitives were armed.

The ex-kaiser was in uniform. He alighted at the Eysden station and paced the platform, smoking a cigarette.

Eysden lies about midway between Liege and Maastricht on the Dutch border.

London, Nov. 10 (midnight). Both the former German emperor and his eldest son, Frederick William, crossed the Dutch frontier Sunday morning according to advices from the Hague.

MATHIAS ERZBERGER, Secretary of State and leader of the Centrist or Moderate Party, who heads the German truce delegation.

FORTRESS OF MAUBEUGE CAPTURED BY BRITISH

London, Nov. 9. The British forces have captured the fortress of Maubeuge, Field Marshal Haig announced today.

South of Maubeuge the British are pushing forward and are well beyond the Avesnes-Maubeuge road.

Maubeuge was the most important French fortress in the hands of the Germans. Before the war it was considered a fortress of the first class, and it guarded the Namur-Charleroi route into France by way of the Sambre river.

The town is situated on both banks of the Sambre and was founded in the seventh century. Several famous battles of French history prior to 1800 are in the provinces to Maubeuge.

Maubeuge was taken by the Germans after heavy fighting with the British and French late in August, 1914.

CAPITAL OF LUEBECK FALLS TO SOLDIERS' COUNCIL

(By Associated Press.)

Amsterdam, Nov. 10—The Rhenish Westfalian Zeitung, of Essen, announces that Lubeck, the capital of the principality of Lubeck is in the hands of the Soldiers' council. Many persons, both civilians and military, have been shot.

Marriage Banns Announced.

Banns of marriage between Miss Theresa, the accomplished young daughter of Mr. and Mrs. B. J. O'Neill, of No. 442 Chew street, and one of this city's talented soloists, and Theodore Englehardt, of No. 123 North Fifth street, a rising young businessman, associated with the Seventh street Bedding Company, were announced yesterday morning in the Church of the Sacred Heart of Jesus. Wedding arrangements are being made for the Thanksgiving season.

Slight Sunday Fire.

A rubbish fire on the second floor of the rear porch of the house at 230 North Fifth street, owned by George W. Fetzer and occupied by Traffic Officer Charles Lawall, caused a fire alarm yesterday at 12:40 p. m. The fire was put out with a few buckets of water. The loss was trifling.

EVENTS IN GERMANY RAPIDLY DRAWING TO A PEACE CLIMAX

(By Associated Press.)

William Hohenzollern, the former German emperor and king of Prussia, and his eldest son, Frederick Wilhelm, who hoped some day to rule the German people, are reported to have fled to Holland.

The revolution which is in progress throughout Germany, although it seemingly is a peaceful one, probably threw fear into the hearts of the former kaiser and the crown prince and caused them to take asylum in a neutral state.

Wilhelm II, reigning king of the monarchy of Wurttemburg, is declared to have abdicated Friday night, and reports have it that the grand duke of Hesse, ruler of the grand duchy of Hesse, has decreed the formation of a council of state to take over the government there. Every dynasty in Germany is to be suppressed and all the princes exiled, according to Swiss advices.

People's governments have been established in the greater part of Berlin and in other cities of the kingdom and empire. Leipsic, Stuttgart, Cologne, Essen and Frankfort have joined the revolution. In Berlin there has been some fighting between the revolutionists and reactionaries in which several persons were killed or wounded. The palace of the crown prince has been taken over by the revolutionists. "Long live the republic" and the singing of "the Marseillaise" have been heard in streets.

Frederick Ebert, the Socialist leader, has been appointed imperial chancellor and has issued a proclamation saying it is his purpose to form a people's government which will endeavor to bring about a speedy peace.

Meanwhile the terms of the Allies by which Germany may have an armistice, have reached German headquarters by courier but thus far there is no indication that a reply has been received by Marshal Foch. Whether the terms have been sent on to Berlin for action by the new chancellor is problematical. The time limit for a reply expired Monday morning.

On the battlefront the Germans everywhere continue to suffer defeat at the hands of the British, French and American forces.

In the north Field Marshal Haig's forces have driven the enemy beyond the Franco-Belgian frontier south of the Sambre canal and now are almost within gun range of Brussels. Large quantities of supplies, including much rolling stock, have fallen into the hands of the British.

Likewise the French still are in pursuit of the enemy who is abandoning guns and supplies of all descriptions. In many instances, entire railroad trains have been left behind. All the enemy's lines of communication now have been captured except the road leading northward from the Mezieries.

General Pershing's troops continue to make progress on both sides of the Meuse river and the American second army has launched an attack west of the Moselle river and gained its objectives. On the Meuse the town of Stenay has been captured by the Americans after violent opposition. In the Moselle sector several woods and heights have been cleared of the enemy by the Americans including the Bois de Waville, from the northern fringes of which the great German fortress of Metz is only ten miles distant.

THE REVOLUTION IN GERMANY COMPLETELY UPSETS OLD ORDER

(By Associated Press.)

The German people for a generation the obedient and submissive servants of their war lord, for more than four years his pliant instruments in ravaging the world, have spoken a new word and the Old Germany is gone. From the confused, sometimes conflicting and often delayed advices from Germany in the last two days it now has become apparent that William, emperor and king, has been stripped of his power. He now is plain William Hohenzollern, a fugitive in Holland. With his fall topples into ruin William's mad design to rule the world.

Little is known of the situation today in Germany for that country is in the first days of its new adventure. It is not clear whether the old regime has been permanently dislodged, or whether the new authorities, with the unscrupulous which has long marked German politics, merely are sacrificing the chief figureheads of Kaiserism in the hope of obtaining an easier peace. It appears probable that no one in Germany knows, and that it still is to be determined which of the contending elements will gain the upper hand.

Revolution is spreading rapidly and from the fact that a Socialist now is chancellor it may be gathered that the object of the revolution is not merely the quick ending of the war but the complete severance of the political ties which still bind the nation with its past.

For the Allies the problem has changed. The countries which fought Germany and her vassals for more than four years have emerged from the war completely triumphant but in the borders of countries which menaced the peace of the whole world dispatches reveal famine and anarchy. The entente's next task may be to restore order in the desolate central empires. It may be the lot of the forces who have successfully contested Germany's forces to save her from the fate she imposed on Russia. Likewise, help will have to be given to Austro-Hungary, Bulgaria and Turkey, whose ruin Germany wrought.

The German empire was the last of the great autocracies whose fall marks the real significance of the war. In Russia, Austria Hungary and finally in Germany, irresponsible power gave way before the irresistible forces of democracy. Germany holding on to the last, kept up the hopeless struggle until Field Marshal von Hindenburg's prophetic words, early in the war, came true. The side with the strongest nerves, said he, would win. It was the crumbling of the home front which made it impossible for Germany, notwithstanding her great armies in the field, to carry on any longer.

The virtual ending of this greatest of conflicts has come with dramatic swiftness. Four months ago today the German military power apparently was at its heights. The unchecked forces of the enemy had battered their way through the French and British lines until Paris was in peril and the British were fighting with their backs to the wall to prevent themselves from being forced to the sea. Late in July the world was thrilled with the news of an Allied counter-attack between the Aisne and the Marne. The Germans were hurled back along the whole sector, and since that day the victorious progress of the Allies has been maintained.

Various causes have contributed to this reversal. The entrance of America into the struggle, with her vast resources of men and materials is conceded by the Allies to have turned the scale. One of the most important effects of this country's act was the heartening to an enormous extent of the wearied Allied nations and a corresponding deterioration of German morale. Exhaustion of German raw material and years of semi-starvation assisted in the process of beating down the enemy to a submissive frame of mind. It also is significant that the establishment of unquestioned allied supremacy in the field almost synchronized with the unification of military control and the appointment of General now Marshal Foch to the post of supreme command. Military commentators without exception lay stress upon the importance of single leadership and the genius of Foch in stemming and finally turning the tide.

Germany, at the beginning of 1918 announced her purpose to end the war by an offensive in France. It was her last mighty effort and for weeks the world wondered when the enemy hordes would be stopped. The turn in the fighting came on July 18 when Marshal Foch launched the Americans and French in an attack. Since that fateful day for Germany the Allied armies on all fronts have met with continued success.

Germany's ultimate defeat became more certain as the summer advanced. The first break in the ranks of the Central powers came with the defection of Bulgaria late in September. Turkey signed armistice terms the last of October and Austria-Hungary tendered the white flag to Italy on November 4, when hostilities ceased on all the Austrian fronts. Germany attempted to bring about a negotiated peace but how great was her failure is shown by the fact that her emissaries now are at Marshal Foch's headquarters for the last scene of the great world tragedy.

WIDE FRONT OF AMERICAN ARMIES IN FRANCE

(By Associated Press.)

With the American Army in France, Nov. 10—The First and Second American armies, in their attacks today, extending along the Moselle and the Meuse, advanced on a front of approximately 115 kilometres (seventy-one and a half miles).

GERMAN PEOPLE'S GOVERNMENT IS IN SADDLE IN BERLIN AFTER SEVERE FIGHTING IN STREETS

MILITARY DELEGATE OF THE GERMAN ARMISTICE ENVOYS—Gen. K. A. von Winterfeld is the chief army representative of the enemy commission sent to receive the terms. He was formerly military attache at Paris.

Many Killed and Wounded in Revolutionary Riots—"The Marseillaise" Sung in Streets of Capital—General Strike Called

(By Associated Press.)

Copenhagen, Nov. 10, 8:15 p. m.—Berlin was occupied by forces of the Soldiers' and Workmen's Councils on Saturday afternoon, according to a Wolff bureau report received here.

Berlin, Saturday, Nov. 9, 12:56 p. m.—(German wireless to London, Nov. 10)—The German people's government has been instituted in the greater part of Berlin. The garrison has gone over to the government.

The Workmen's and Soldiers' Council has declared a general strike. Troops and machine guns have been placed at the disposal of the council. Guards which had been stationed at the public offices and other buildings have been withdrawn.

Friedrich Ebert (vice president of the Social Democratic party) is carrying on the chancellorship.

The text of the statement issued by the people's government reads:

"In the course of the forenoon of Saturday the formation of a new German people's government was initiated. The greater part of the Berlin garrison and other troops stationed there temporarily went over to the new government.

"The leaders of the deputations of the Social Democratic party declared that they would not shoot against the people. They said they would, in accord with the people's government, intercede in favor of the maintenance of order. Thereupon in the offices and public buildings the guards which had been stationed there were withdrawn.

The business of the imperial chancellor is being carried on by the Social Democratic deputy, Herr Ebert.

It is presumed that apart from the representatives of the recent majority group three independent Social Democrats will enter the future government.

London, Nov. 10, 8:57 a. m.—Severe fighting took place in Berlin between six and eight o'clock last night and violent cannonade was heard from the heart of the city.

The revolution is in full swing in Berlin and the Red forces occupy the greater part of the German capital according to a Copenhagen despatch to the Exchange Telegraph Company quoting Berlin advices sent from there at three o'clock this morning.

The crown prince's palace was seized by the revolutionists. The people shouted "Long live the Republic" and sang the "Marseillaise."

When revolutionary soldiers attempted to enter a building in which they supposed a number of officers were concealed shots were fired from the windows. The Red then began shelling the building.

Many persons were killed and wounded before the officers surrendered. The Red forces are in control and have restored order. Strong guards marched thru the streets. When the cannonade began, the people thought the Reichsbank was being bombarded and thousands rushed to the square in front of the Crown Prince's palace. It was later determined that other buildings were under fire.

CHANCELLOR EBERT SEEKS TO BRING ON A SPEEDY PEACE

Copenhagen, Nov. 10.—Frederick Ebert, the Socialist leader, has been appointed chancellor. He has issued a proclamation saying that he plans to form a people's government which will endeavor to bring about speedy peace. Chancellor Ebert said he would endeavor to fortify the freedom which the people had won. He begged support in the hard work ahead and appealed for co-operation in the country and cities in the problem of provisioning.

Herr Ebert declared that Prince Maximilian of Baden had transferred the chancellorship to him, all the secretaries of state having given their consent. The new government, he added, would be in agreement with the various parties.

BIG KRUPP STEEL WORKS SEIZED BY REVOLUTIONARIES

(By Associated Press.)

London, Nov. [illegible] p. m.—Essen, where the great Krupp steel works are situated, is reported to be in the hands of the revolutionaries, says a despatch from Amsterdam to the Exchange Telegraph Company.

Lieutenant Krupp von Bohlen and Halbach, the head of the Krupp works, and his wife have been arrested.

This news was brought from Essen to [illegible] arriving by special train at [illegible] on Saturday.

POLAND TAKES OVER GALICIA

(By Associated Press.)

Amsterdam, Nov. 10. Prof. Lammasch, the Austrian premier has received official notification, says a despatch from Vienna, that Poland has assumed sovereignty over Galicia.

Galicia is a crown land of Austria Hungary north of the Carpathians. It has an area of 30,307 square miles and in normal times had a population of some 7,000,000.

WORLD'S CHAMPION TROTTING STALLION DEAD

New York, Nov. 8.—Lee Axworthy, 1:58¼, world's champion trotting stallion and winner of six heats in 2 minutes or faster, died of hemorrhage early Wednesday morning at David M. Look's Castleton Farm, near Lexington, Ky.

Kiel Crews Join Revolution.

(By Associated Press.)

Copenhagen, Nov. 10. The crews of the German dreadnoughts Posen, Ostfriest, Nassau and Oldenburg in Kiel harbor have joined the revolution. Marines occupied the lock gates at Ostmor and fought down a coast artillery division which offered resistance.

Came for Trucks

A detachment of eight colored soldiers from Camp Dix arrived in this city last evening and enjoyed a fine supper at the Rescue Mission. The men were on their way to Camp Crane where they slept over night, returning today to Wrightstown with eight army trucks, to be used at the Jersey camp.

TRAMP STEAMSHIP SUNK ON HITTING MINE

Ocean City, Md., Nov. 9—Twenty minutes after striking what is believed to have been a mine the American 500-ton tramp steamship, Saetia sank twenty-five miles off shore here at 9:05 o'clock a. m. today. Thirty-seven of the crew are missing. Forty-seven men were landed at this city this afternoon. The chief engineer, Charles Tormey, of Hartford, Conn., was injured. The sinking of the ship was preceded by an explosion a few minutes after 9 o'clock. A few minutes later two more violent explosions followed. Although the ship was light, having just left an American convoy off the Delaware Capes, she went down within twenty minutes, according to her master, Captain W. S. Lynch, of Pleasantville, N. J., who landed at this place.

Washington, Nov. 10—Eighty-one persons aboard the Saetia, have been safely landed. In making this announcement tonight the navy department said this accounted for "approximately all" of those aboard.

POLISH REPUBLIC UNDER PRESIDENT DASYNSKI

Amsterdam, Saturday, Nov. 10—A message from Cracow announces the formation of a Polish republic under the presidency of Deputy Daszynski.

AMERICAN ARMY ATTACKS IN LORRAINE

With the American Forces on the Lorraine Front, Nov. 10, 8:40 p. m.—The Second American army this morning launched its initial attack in Lorraine. Its objectives were limited. The villages of St. Hilaire and Marcheville were captured as also were a number of woods.

SOLDIERS' COUNCILS OCCUPY R. R. STATIONS

Copenhagen, Nov. 10—The railway stations in the entire industrial districts of Germany from Dortmund to Duisburg have been occupied by Soldiers' Councils, according to a despatch from Essen. There were no disorders.

British in Close Chase.

London, Nov. 10—Field Marshal Haig's forces are closely following up the retreating Germans along the entire front in Flanders. The official statement issued today by the war office announces the British troops have occupied the Fauburg de Bertaimont, on the Southern outskirts of Mons, Belgium.

PRINCE HENRY ESCAPES ATTEMPT ON HIS LIFE

(By Associated Press.)

Copenhagen, Nov. 10—Another attempt on the life of Prince Henry, of Prussia, has been made at Flensburg where he was in seclusion in a villa. The result of the attempt is not known but it is believed that he escaped.

Prince Henry, brother of the former emperor, was attacked by marines while fleeing from Kiel in an automobile flying a red flag on Wednesday last. A dozen shots were fired at him and his chauffeur was wounded.

COUNCIL OF STATE IN GRAND DUCHY OF HESSE

(By Associated Press.)

Amsterdam, Saturday, Nov. 9.—An official despatch from Darmstadt, capital of the grand duchy of Hesse, announces that the grand duke of Hesse has decreed the formation of a council of state to take over the business of the government "until a final settlement of the questions arising from the present situation."

GERMANS BALK ON BEING KILLED ON LAST DAY

(By Associated Press.)

With the American Army on the Sedan Front, Nov. 9—"What is the use of staying out there to be killed the last day?" was the comment of scores of prisoners brought in yesterday by the Americans. The captured Germans were more discouraged than usual. Most of them declared that since their government is quitting—and they appear to be convinced that it is—it was absurd for them to neglect the opportunity to surrender.

Austrian Soldiers Hurry Home.

(By Associated Press.)

Innsbruck, Austria, Saturday, Nov. 9, via Basel, Switzerland, Nov. 10—Bavarian troops have occupied the railroad station here.

Austrian troops are returning from the former front in swarms, clinging to the cars wherever they can get hold. Many have been crushed or decapitated by the trains passing through tunnels. Bodies to the number of 273 were picked up on a single day on the railroad tracks near Innsbruck.

Princess Heinrich Wounded.

(By Associated Press.)

Copenhagen, Nov. 10, 8:50 a. m.—According to a frontier message Princess Heinrich, wife of the grandson of Ludwig III, of Bavaria, was wounded in the arm when fired upon as she was fleeing from Munich. She and her husband now are hiding in southern Bavaria with Princess Adelheid, wife of Prince Adalbert, Emperor William's third son.

THE WEATHER

(By Associated Press.)

Washington, Nov. 10.—Fair Monday and Tuesday, not much change in temperature.

SCHLESWIG-HOLSTEIN TO PROCLAIM REPUBLIC

(By Associated Press.)

London, Nov. [illegible] a. m.—Schleswig-Holstein, the Prussian province which formerly belonged to Denmark, is to be proclaimed an independent republic, says an Exchange Telegraph despatch from Copenhagen.

GEN. GOURAUD ENTERED SEDAN YESTERDAY AFTERNOON

(By Associated Press.)

With the French Army in France, Nov. 10. The French General Gouraud made his official entrance into Sedan at two o'clock this afternoon.

BRITISH FORCES ALMOST WITHIN GUN FIRE OF BRUSSELS

(By Associated Press.)

London, Nov. 10. The British have crossed the Franco-Belgian frontier south of the Sambre river, Field Marshal Haig reports from headquarters tonight. They have advanced four miles east of Renaix, bringing them almost within gunfire of Brussels.

Americans Take Stenay.

(By Associated Press.)

With the American Forces on the Meuse Front, Nov. 10, 6 p. m.—General Pershing's troops this afternoon captured Stenay on the east bank of the Meuse, notwithstanding terrific opposition.

Pottsville Trolley Strike Off.

(By Associated Press.)

Pottsville, Nov. 9—The strike on the local trolley lines ended at 3 o'clock this afternoon, when the cars started to run after being motionless for three days. The trolleymen agreed to a fifteen-day trial of a new cash-register, the cause of the walkout.

AUSTRIA PROTESTS GERMAN INVASION OF TYROL

Amsterdam, Nov. 9. With respect to the Austrian protest to the German government against the invasion of northern Tyrol by Bavarian troops it is explained in Berlin that the crossing of the frontier was designed to keep disorganized and undisciplined Austrian troops from German territory and that it will not obstruct the demobilization of the Austrian forces.

The German Field Marshal von Mackensen's troops, it is reported, will force their way through Hungary to Germany with their arms despite the intention by the Hungarian government that arms must be discarded when German troops cross Hungarian soil.

Albert Ballin Dead.

Copenhagen, Nov. 10. Albert Ballin, general director of the Hamburg American Steamship company, died suddenly on Saturday according to an announcement made in Berlin.

Germans Falling Back.

(By Associated Press.)

With the Allied Forces in Belgium, Saturday, Nov. 9. There are many indications that the Germans do not intend to make a protracted stand this side of Brussels and Charleroi.

28 Killed at Kiel.

Copenhagen, Nov. 10—Up to Friday night the number of persons killed at Kiel was twenty-eight, according to information received here. The majority of these were officers.

THE WEATHER
Increasing of cloudiness and rising temperature today is to be followed by rain or snow tomorrow.

ALLENTOWN MORNING CALL

PHONE BELL 4241
A Call Want Ad will doubtless solve the one problem that may be before you right now.

VOL. LXXII, NO. 24 — ALLENTOWN, PA., SUNDAY MORNING, JANUARY 24, 1926 — PRICE FIVE CENTS

ELEVEN KNOWN DEAD IN LAFAYETTE HOTEL HOLOCAUST

ANTHRACITE OPERATORS AGREE TO NEW WAGE PARLEY ASKED BY LEWIS

Owners and Miners Will Again Meet in Joint Conference in a Few Days for Another Battle to End Long-Drawn-Out Strike

OBSERVERS, HOWEVER, NOT VERY OPTIMISTIC

Employers Accept Call Requested by Mine Workers' Leader to Consider Scranton Publisher's Plan but Deny Accepting Proposal 'in Principle'—Union Suggests Open Session to Avoid Misunderstanding.

Philadelphia, Jan. 23 (AP)—Anthracite miners and operators will again meet in joint conference in a few days for another battle to end the long coal strike. The meeting will be held at the request of John L. Lewis, president of the United Mine Workers; but the operators have already served notice that the plan on which the call for further conference is based is fundamentally unsound and does not afford a satisfactory basis for a contract.

The call for the meeting is expected to be issued from Hazleton late tonight or early Sunday morning by Alvan Markle, chairman of the joint conference of operators and miners. Many interests, it was said, had to be consulted before the time and place could be fixed. It probably will be held in New York next week.

President Lewis suggested any coal region city or New York City as the operators preferred.

The request for the meeting was made by Mr. Lewis in a letter to Mr. Markle early in the day in which he stated that both W. W. Inglis, chairman of the operators' negotiating committee, and the miners had accepted "in principle" the plan offered by E. J. Lynett, publisher of the Scranton Times.

Mr. Lewis notified Mr. Markle that the miners would move that the conference be open to the public press because of "many misleading statements as to what actually transpired in the recent conference in New York and which have caused confusion and misunderstanding in the public mind."

Members of the operators' negoti-

(Continued on Page Three)

Day's News Features

Cardinal Mercier, primate of Belgium and heroic figure of the World War, dies at Brussels, after lingering illness, aged 74; United States sends condolences.

Head of Miss Anna May Dietrich, whose dismembered body was found near Media, Pa., discovered under railroad trestle near Elwood, a Philadelphia suburb, with no indications as to how she met death.

John L. Lewis, international president of United Mine Workers of America, requests that joint conference of anthracite operators and miners reconvene to discuss strike settlement, newspapermen to be admitted to sessions.

Laboratory at Princeton, N. J., announces discovery of factor missing from German formula for recovery of nitrogen from the air, long sought by scientists.

Roald Amundsen, Norwegian explorer, discoverer of south pole, after interview with Dr. Frederick Cook, in Leavenworth prison, says claims of latter to discovery of north pole are as sound as those of late Admiral Peary.

SOVIET GOVERNMENT SENDS TRITE MESSAGE TO CHINESE DICTATOR

Gives Pekin Government 72 Hours to Release Russian Head of Railroad

ISSUE ARISES OVER FREE TROOP TRANSPORTATION

'White' Manager Named by Marshal Chang to Operate International Railway

Moscow, Jan. 23 (AP)—Events having to do with the Chinese Eastern Railroad difficulty between Russia and China, assumed a grave character with the dispatch of a note by M. Tchitcherin, Soviet foreign minister, ...

(Continued on Page Two)

SPANISH AVIATORS AT CANARY ISLANDS

Will Continue Trans-Atlantic Adventure Today if Weather is Propitious

ROSS AGAIN PULLED FROM CHAIR'S SHADOW

Announcement of Reprieve Halts Execution For Third Night in Succession

MARYLAND MAYOR HELD AS DRY LAW TRANSGRESSOR

Wife Said to Have Furnished Home-Brew Recipe to Federal Agents

FRENCH ATTACK REBELLIOUS TRIBESMEN IN SYRIA

Natives Caught Between Two Fires and Driven Back Into Hills

SIR WM. HAGGARD DIES

Brother of Late English Novelist Succumbs at Age of 80

THE LAFAYETTE HOTEL, 117 YEARS OLD— AS IT APPEARED AFTER YESTERDAY'S FIRE

An exterior view of the gutted hostelry taken from across the street. To the reader's left are the two fire escape exits which were cut off by the flames almost immediately after the fire started. The death toll was confined to these two floors.

CARDINAL MERCIER, WORLD WAR HERO, SUCCUMBS IN BELGIUM

Famous Prelate Loses Long Fight For Life in 75th Year

Desire Mercier

POLICE FIND HEAD OF SLAIN WOMAN HID UNDER BRIDGE NEAR MEDIA

Discovered Wrapped in Paper and Jammed Beneath Wooden Support at Railroad Trestle. No Marks Indicating How She Was Killed

Woman Beaten With Switches by 17 Masked Amazons Near Ocala, Fla.

TARDIEU SAYS BRIAND LACKING IN COURAGE IN FINANCIAL CRISIS

Premier's Vacillation Leading to Chaotic Condition, Says French Publicist

By ANDRE TARDIEU

REFORMERS BLAMED FOR CRIME INCREASE

Committee On Citizenship of N. Y. Bar Association Says in Report

SECTION HANDS' CAR HITS REAR OF FREIGHT TRAIN

GRIST MILL AT DuBOIS DESTROYED BY FLAMES

BRITISH ARTISTS IN SAD PLIGHT AT HOME LONDON EDITOR SAYS

Countrymen Do Not Buy Their Paintings But Prefer to Patronize Foreigners Instead

By A. G. GARDINER

John D. G. Rutter Dies

BROADCASTING OF HEAT ONLY MATTER OF TIME ENGINEER PREDICTS

Problem 'Only in Thought Stage Now,' However, Technical Expert Admits

ROYALTY FAR FROM DEAD IN GERMANY HARDEN DECLARES

Two Dethroned Czars and One Duke Living in Coburg, Noted Publicist Finds

By MAXIMILIAN HARDEN

SEA PLANE FORCED DOWN

TWO BODIES UNIDENTIFIED; SIX LODGERS STILL UNACCOUNTED FOR

Search for Missing Bodies Ended Until Dangerous Ruins Can Be Dynamited Today—Heart-Rending Scenes at Morgues as Relatives Identify Bodies or Fail to Find Missing Ones. Some Bodies Burned Beyond Hope of Recognition

Eleven known dead and about twenty injured are the gruesome figures that tell the tale of the most horrible tragedy visited upon Allentown in the burning of the Lafayette Hotel, 133-37 North Seventh street, early Saturday morning.

Nine of the dead have been identified in various city morgues; two charred bodies are yet to be named, while the work of check up is being carried on at a rapid pace in an effort to learn the exact extent of the injured and missing. Up to late last night six persons were unaccounted for. As many as a half dozen are believed to be dead amidst the ruins.

Loss on the building, which was built in 1809 and remodeled in 1890 from a three to a five story structure, is estimated at more than $200,000, with comparatively little insurance. The hostelry was probably the oldest in the city, known more than a century ago as the Black Horse Inn.

All day Saturday the work of reclaiming the dead was carried on at a furious pace by the city fire and police departments, while immense crowds of curious and horror stricken residents stood silently by as one by one the long wicker baskets, carried hurriedly from building to hearse, told of another life snuffed out by the angry flames.

Five of the known dead are from Allentown, three from other points in Pennsylvania, and another's address is unknown. The fact that many of the guests were from out of town makes the work of identification doubly difficult.

What remains of the structure will be dynamited this morning in order to make the work of rescue more safe. C. V. Weaver, a representative of the DuPont Powder company, and an expert in his line, arrived in this city last night and will have the work in charge.

By five o'clock in the morning three bodies had been discovered and were removed. This work continued as the smouldering walls and floors cooled with other bodies coming to light until at one o'clock three bodies were discovered by Hibernia firemen on a section of the flooring on the fifth story.

Shortly afterward work was begun on the tearing down of the west wall of the building, which had been dangerously weakened. With the aid of the Hibernia hook and ladder apparatus, men were raised to the fifth floor where they fastened ropes ...

... der when the grip of his rescuer weakened. He too dropped and was taken to the hospital. Just which of the injured he was is not known.

The identity of the rescuer is unknown as well. He came from the ladder, however, weeping and crying, "I should have held him, I should have held him," and was taken away and comforted.

Many of the guests reached the balcony in safety coming down ladders, held by firemen and policemen, who had to hold them up in their hands because of the great distance to the fourth floor.

First Alarm at 2.20 a. m.

Horrible Sights and Sounds

Elevator Shaft Ablaze

Ice and Cold a Handicap

Survivors Scantily Clad

Man Killed in Fall

A Second Man Drops

(Continued on Page Two)

COLD WEEK FORECAST

Snows or Rains Likely at Beginning Middle and End

THE WEATHER

MAY 7, 1937

THE WEATHER
Fair today and tomorrow, slightly warmer tomorrow.
(Weather Details on Page 5)

ALLENTOWN MORNING CALL

Lehigh Valley's Greatest Newspaper

VOL. XCIV, NO. 127 ★ ALLENTOWN, PA., FRIDAY MORNING, MAY 7, 1937 SINGLE COPY Three Cents | DAILY & SUNDAY 15 Cents Week | DAILY 12 Cents Week

Zeppelin Hindenburg Explodes; 33 Die

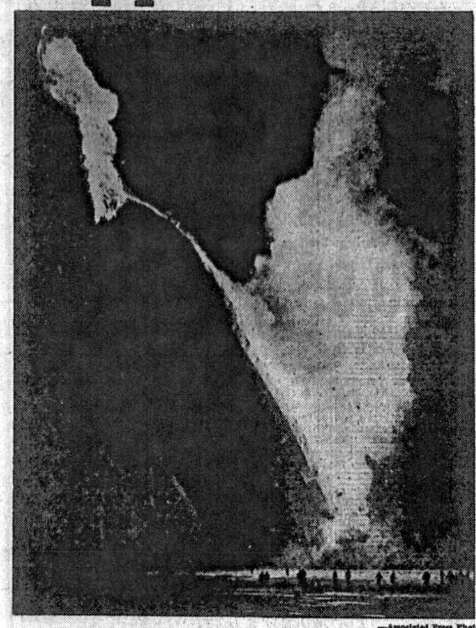

—Associated Press Photo.

LAKEHURST, N. J., May 6.—Her tail in the ground, her nose in the air, the flaming giant Hindenburg crashed to earth, a mass of ruins after an explosion rent her in mid-air. The number of fatalities was placed by Zeppelin Co. officials at 33.

—Associated Press Photo

LAKEHURST, N. J., May 6.—Bursting into flames as it nosed toward the mooring mast at the Naval air station here, the giant German Zeppelin, Hindenburg, was caught by an Associated Press photographer on the scene for the docking.

Italian Troops Massed in Rebel Drive on Bilbao

Rome Reveals Volunteer Battalion, 'Black Arrow,' Ready for Big Push

ROME, May 6. (AP)—Italian correspondents today saw the forthcoming Spanish insurgent attack on Bilbao as the possible climax of the civil war and revealed Italian volunteers in the insurgent ranks were massing for the drive.

Torrential rains held up the push on the Basque capital, the correspondents reported, but added Italian brigades, headed by a crack battalion called the "Black Arrow," was ready for the fight.

The "Black Arrow" legion was cited today for its part in the capture and defense of Bermeo.

Describing the capture of trenches in Mount Sollube and the occupation of several crossroad settlements, Renzo Segala, writing in Corriere Della Sera of Milan, says:

"Both these operations were the work of a mixed brigade which was composed predominantly of Italian

(Continued on Page Twenty-nine)

Telegraphic News Briefs

ROME, May 6. (AP)—Two Italian air-force pilots and a mechanic were killed when their bomber lunged into the sea a few miles south of Naples today.

QUITO, ECUADOR, May 6. (AP)—Priests, ministers, women and communists were barred from voting today in a decree by Dictator Frederick Paez which set July 11 for election of deputies to the assembly—the voters limited to those listed by the military who can read and write.

CASTEL GANDOLFO, May 6. (AP)—Archbishop Giuseppe Pizzardo, vatican undersecretary, headed the papal mission to King George's coronation which departed for London today.

TOKYO, May 6. (AP)—Police disclosed today arrest in Kanagawa prefecture of 156 village assemblymen, farmers, firemen and insurance brokers charged with starting 28 fires since 1934 and defrauding insurance companies.

TOKYO, May 6. (AP)—One sailor was drowned today when a Japanese naval plane collided with a launch from the cruiser Isuzu.

MOSCOW, May 6. (AP) — Norman Thomas and his wife departed for Leningrad and Helsingfors today after a week's sightseeing on their first visit to the Soviet union, where they saw no government officials, but had "an excellent time," Thomas said.

KIEL, GERMANY, May 6. (AP)—Reichsfuehrer Adolf Hitler journeyed through the Kaiser Wilhelm canal aboard the cutter "Grille" to this important naval base today, his first visit to Kiel since he repudiated control over Germany's inland waterways under the Versailles treaty.

Many Passengers Leap To Safety from Airship

Happy Shouts of Arriving Passengers Turn to Shrieks of Dying Men and Women as Series of Explosions Demolish Queen of Skies

LAKEHURST, N. J., May 6 (AP)—The queen of the skies—German dirigible Hindenburg—sailed serenely into Lakehurst tonight, its silver bag gleaming despite the sullen atmosphere.

Passengers stood at the windows, waving gaily.

There were few spectators on the broad sandy field to wave a return greeting, for the comings and goings of the queen of the skies, which 10 times before had dropped to earth here, were considered now of little more significance than the docking of an ocean liner.

The ship's motors droned loudly. Two nose lines were dropped. In a few more minutes, the ship would be fast, the passengers departing.

It was 6:23 p. m. (EST).

An explosion rent the air—so loud one person said he heard it at Point Pleasant, 15 miles away.

The stern broke into flames.

Bystanders, unable to comprehend it, unable to believe it, gasped.

The happy shouts of arriving passengers turned to shrieks of dying men and women. Smiling faces of spectators became tear-splotched.

More explosions followed—intermittently they continued for hours.

There was confusion, but the ground crew made the best of the situation.

After a first should "run for your lives," they ran to the ship as fast as they had retreated—doing rescue work now instead of mooring.

"The Navy boys dove into the flames like dogs after rabbits," was the way Gill Robb Wilson, state aviation commissioner described it.

Passengers and crew—those who were elsewhere than in the blazing stern—jumped.

"I landed on my stomach, and crawled 30 or 40 yards to escape the flames," Philip Mangone of New York told his two daughters at Paul Kimball hospital, Lakewood.

Two stewards and a little cabin boy jumped from a window—saved.

Murray Becker, an Associated Press photographer, said that in the twinkling of an eye, "there was nothing left but the skeleton.

"There wasn't much smoke," he said. "I saw a man walking toward me, assisted by two men. He had no clothes on. I saw a woman lying on a stretcher. There were screams from men and women on the field."

Another photographer, Larry Kennedy, said the ship burst as though it "were made of paper."

"Pieces of fabric fell on us," he said. "I saw one fellow jump or fall out."

"A noise that sounded like bullets coming out of the gondolas," was the way Robert Seelig, another cameraman, described it.

One witness said the ship buckled as the flames spread.

"I saw the ship just sink down and the flames go through it." He said. "The fabric burned away in a few seconds. I turned back with others to go as close to the ship as possible to pick up the survivors."

Herbert O'Laughlin of Chicago, one of the survivors, said there was "a blinding flash, but the people on the ground would know more about it than we would on the ship."

Roosevelt Expresses Sympathy to Hitler

GALVESTON, TEX., May 6. (AP)—President Roosevelt, learning of the disaster to the dirigible Hindenburg at Lakehurst, N. J., tonight sent a message to Chancellor Hitler in Berlin expressing his "deepest sympathy" to the German government and people.

In a brief statement made public through temporary White House headquarters here, the President also extended his sympathy to the families of those who lost their lives in the explosion.

The message to Hitler follows:

"I have learned of the disaster to the airship Hindenburg and offer you and the German people my deepest sympathy for the tragic loss of life which resulted from this unexpected and unhappy event."

The public statement said:

"I am distressed to hear of the tragedy of the Hindenburg and extend by deep sympathy to the families of the passengers, officers and crew who lost their lives."

Other pictures of the Hindenburg explosion on Pages 16 and 23

Hindenburg Survivor Takes Plane for Chicago

LAKEHURST, N. J., May 6. (AP)—Herbert O'Laughlin, Chicago, one of the survivors of the Hindenburg disaster, boarded a plane at Newark for Chicago tonight a few hours after the tragedy.

O'Laughlin said "there was a blinding flash but the people on the ground would know more about it than we would on the ship."

Asked how he escaped, he said he jumped when the ship was about ten feet from the ground.

Backfire of Engine May Have Caused Blast

WASHINGTON, May 6. (AP)—First reports received in German circles here indicated that the Hindenburg disaster may have been caused by the backfire of a single engine.

The dirigible, according to the word received here, was approaching the mooring mast and had shut off all of its engines.

As it floated lower, it was said, a single motor was started to afford steerage way, when, suddenly, the entire ship burst into flames.

Attaches of the embassy, lacking complete reports, attributed the disaster to a leak in a hydrogen cell, freeing gas which was ignited by the backfire of the motor as it was turned on.

Zeppelin Made 10 Trips Across Ocean Last Year

'Flying Hotel' Built Especially for Trans-Atlantic Service

NEW YORK, May 6. (AP)—The Zeppelin Hindenburg, Germany's "flying hotel" which burst into flames at Lakehurst today after a long fight against the North Atlantic's headwinds, was built at Friedrichshafen in 1936 especially for the trans-Atlantic service.

She made ten trips across last year, carrying from 21 to 57 passengers each time and had been hailed by German and other experts as an example of perfection in air travel.

A stickler for promptness, the vessel's voyages ordinarily were run off like clockwork.

Her fastest crossing was from Lakehurst to Frankfort in July, last year. Leaving Jersey July 6 with 50 passengers, 291 pounds of mail and 230 pounds of express, she nosed over her German base 45 hours and 43 minutes later, breaking her own May 14 record and that set by the Graf Zeppelin the year before.

Previously, on her initial voyage, she left Friedrichshafen May 9 and made the westward crossing in 61 hours, 38 minutes, shattering a record which had been held by the American Los Angeles since 1924.

Then, leaving Frankfort June 22, she broke her own record, settling at Lakehurst 60 hours later.

The five round-trips were made between May 9 and July 17, 1936, the service giving way then to the fear of ice borne on the North Atlantic's fall and winter gales.

On two of her voyages she carried 57 passengers—Lakehurst to Frankfort June 26 and Lakehurst to Frankfort July 17, her last successful crossing. The smallest booking she ever had was 21 from Frankfort to Lakehurst July 2.

For the five westbound voyages she completed she averaged 41.4 passengers, 647.2 pounds of mail and 628.4 pounds of express, while her eastward sailings averaged 52.8 passengers, 638.4 pounds of mail and 645.6 pounds of express.

On one trip to Germany, May 23, 1936, she carried an airplane among other express.

Another airplane, belonging to Gilbert Miller, theatrical producer, news reels, a gown which was to have been worn Monday by an American woman in connection with the British coronation, radio parts, silk hosiery, tobacco and grain samples were among the items consigned at Lakehurst today for the homeward trip which never will be made.

Lakehurst Station Closed For an Indefinite Period

NEW YORK, May 6. (AP) — The naval air station at Lakehurst, N. J., tonight was closed to the public for an indefinite period.

As thousands of curiosity-seekers swarmed toward the field upon hearing of the Hindenburg explosion, commander Rosenthal announced that the station would be "entirely closed to the public until further notice."

To assist in controlling crowds and guarding the station, 50 patrolmen left Manhattan police headquarters shortly before 8 o'clock for Newark, N. J., where they took airplanes for Lakehurst. An inspector, a captain, a lieutenant and a sergeant commanded the detail.

Says 'Something Strange' About Hindenburg Blast

LAKEHURST, N. J., May 6. (AP)—Gill Robb Wilson, New Jersey aviation director, describing the wrecking of the German dirigible Hindenburg, said there was "a hydrogen explosion in No. 2 cell from the rear."

"There was something very strange about the explosion," he said. "The Hindenburg had stopped completely and was preparing to hitch when flames broke out from the rear.

"The only persons possibly saved were those who were in the engine gondolas.

"Those in the belly of the ship absolutely had no chance.

"In all my 21 years of flying experience I have seen crackups, explosions, flaming airplanes, but nothing measures up to the explosion of the Hindenburg.

"I cannot be too loud in my praise of those navy boys who dove into the flames like dogs after rabbits in their rescue work.

"There will be investigations by the federal bureau of air commerce and the State of New Jersey.

"I repeat there was something strange that caused the tragedy."

Luxury Airship 803 Feet Long In Service Year

Considered Greatest Product of Science in Aircraft Construction

NEW YORK, May 6. (AP)—The Hindenburg, considered the greatest product of the science of airship construction, was the largest zeppelin ever built—803 feet long.

Powered with four huge 1,000-horsepower Diesel enines, it had a maximum speed of 84 miles an hour and carried a crew of 42 besides 50 passengers.

Its payload capacity of 15 tons constituted the largest combination of passengers, freight and mail ever lifted off the ground by aircraft.

As a "flying hotel," it was the most luxurious of the 150-odd airships built in the 36 years since Count Ferdinand von Zeppelin made his first historical dirigible flight.

Elaborate interior decorations, featured by murals depicting the history of aviation, embellished the spacious passenger quarters.

(Continued on Page Twenty-eight)

The Call's Index

Blast Wrecks Airship Landing at Lakehurst

70 Planned Return Trip On Hindenburg

Waited at Lakehurst to Board Airship for Eastward Crossing

NEW YORK, May 6 (AP)—They thought it was a joke.

Seventy men and women, watching their bags "weighed in" for the outgoing trip at midnight, wouldn't believe the Hindenburg had exploded.

Waiting in the lobby of the Biltmore

(Continued on Page Twenty-eight)

List of Major Dirigible Disasters in 23 Years

WASHINGTON, May 6. (AP)—There have been 18 major dirigible disasters in the last 23 years—three of the major ones involving the United States dirigibles Akron, Macon and Shenandoah.

The disaster list:

Feb. 12, 1935—The navy dirigible Macon destroyed off the Pacific coast. Two killed, 81 saved.

April 4, 1933—United States navy dirigible Akron crashed in electrical storm off New Jersey coast; 73 dead, 3 survivors.

Oct. 4, 1930—British dirigible R-101 exploded over France while en route from England to India; 48 dead.

May 25, 1928—Italian dirigible Italia crashed in Arctic in flight to North Pole; 8 dead.

Sept. 3, 1925—United States dirigible Shenandoah, formerly ZR-1, wrecked in storm in Ohio; 14 killed.

Dec. 21, 1923—French dirigible Dixmude, presumably struck by lightning over Mediterranean; 52 killed.

Feb. 21, 1922—United States dirigible Rome, bought by United States from Italy, crashed in flames near Hampton Roads army base; 34 killed.

Aug. 24, 1921—Dirigible ZR-2, bought in England for United States, frame buckled over Humber river; 42 killed.

Jan. 29, 1921—British dirigible R-34, wrecked in gale in Howden, England; no lives lost.

July 21, 1919—Dirigible burned over Chicago; 10 killed.

July 15, 1919—British airship NS-11 struck by lightning over North sea; 12 killed.

June 20, 1914—Airship and airplane collided at Vienna; 9 killed.

Sept. 9, 1913—Zeppelin L-1 destroyed off Heligoland; 15 killed.

Oct. 17, 1913—Zeppelin L-2 exploded over Johannisthal airdrome; 28 killed.

July 2, 1912—Balloon Akron exploded at Atlantic City; 5 killed.

Besides the Zeppelins L-1 and L-2, Count Zeppelin lost four other great peace-time dirigibles in accidents, the Zeppelins 3 and 6 and the Deutschlands 1 and 2.

Spark Believed to Have Set Off Hydrogen Gas

Ropes Already Thrown to Ground Crew When Explosion Near Tail of Ship Rocks 'Flying Hotel' — Several Other Blasts Follow

LAKEHURST, N. J., May 6 (AP)—Germany's great silver Hindenburg, the world's largest dirigible, was ripped apart by an explosion tonight that sent her crumpling to the Naval landing field a flaming wreck with horrible death to about a third of those aboard her.

Exactly how many died was still in dispute as the flames licked clean the twisted, telescoped skeleton of the airship that put out from Germany 76 hours before on its opening trip of the 1937 passenger season.

The American Zeppelin Co., through its press representative Harry Bruno, placed the death toll at 33 of the 97 aboard.

The company listed 20 of the 36 passengers and 44 of the 61-man crew as the disaster's survivors.

These figures were at slight variance with unofficial estimates of the number of dead.

In the crowded hospitals in the communities neighboring this hamlet in the pine covered New Jersey coastal plain, many of the survivors were in critical condition, a number suffering from excruciating burns.

Some were so gravely injured, among them Capt. Ernest Lehmann, that the last rites of the Roman Catholic church were administered to them.

Lehmann, skipper of the ship's 1936 flights, made the ill fated flight as an observer.

Captain Max Pruss, the commander, was listed among the injured survivors.

Storms and buffeting headwinds had delayed the slim, graceful ship far behind her schedule for the maiden trip, and she nosed down in the early evening to keep the unexpected rendezvous with disaster.

She had been due to tie up at the snub mooring mast at 5 a. m. (EST) but radioed last night that the bad weather had retarded her speed so much that she would land around sunset.

Cruises Over New York

After cruising down over New York's crowded streets in the afternoon, she hove into sight at the air station here at 3:12 p. m. but landing conditions were not favorable and she circled around idly in full view of the small crowd of spectators who had assembled for what was to be a routine hurry-up arrival and departure.

A rain storm came up and whipped across the field and Capt. Pruss decided to ride it out to make sure of most favorable landing conditions.

Rain was still falling lightly when she headed into the mooring circle shortly after 6 o'clock, nosing down gracefully and with the nice precision that had marked so many of her arrivals last year.

The ground crew of sailors, soldiers and marines moved out onto the field to handle her landing ropes.

Lower she nosed, her Deisel motors throttled down.

Passengers, gaily waving at the crowd, lined the long lounge windows which show like transparent slits in the great silver belly of the ship.

Craft Bursts Into Flames

The spider-like web of landing ropes snaked down the little trap doors in the nose. Men of the ground

(Continued on Page Twenty-eight)

DECEMBER 8, 1941

THE WEATHER
Cloudy and warmer today; Tuesday, cloudy and colder with snow flurries in mountains.

THE MORNING CALL

Lehigh Valley's Greatest Newspaper

THIRD

VOL. 103, NO. 137 ★ ALLENTOWN, PA., MONDAY MORNING, DECEMBER 8, 1941 Entered as Second-class Matter Post Office, Allentown, Pa. | SINGLE COPY Three Cents | DAILY | DAILY & SUNDAY

Japan Attacks Hawaii, Guam, Philippines, Causing Heavy Damage and 350 Deaths; Roosevelt May Ask Declaration of War

Enemy Planes Bomb Islands In Philippines

White House Announcement Says 'No Essential Damage Reported'

WASHINGTON, Dec. 7. (AP)—The White House announced tonight that during President Roosevelt's conference with legislative leaders and members of the cabinet he received word from General Douglas MacArthur that "enemy planes were over central Luzon in the Philippines about 3 p.m., Eastern standard time; that a bombing attack has been made on Davao at the southern end of the southern island of Mindanao, and that another attack has been made on Camp John Hayes at Baguio in the northern mountains of Luzon.

"So far," the White House announcement said, "no essential damage had been reported."

Japanese Forces Invade Malaya Near Singapore

British Aircraft Bomb Ten Jap Ships Attempting Thailand Invasion

SINGAPORE, Monday, Dec. 8. (UP)—Japanese expeditionary forces landed on beaches in northeast Malaya and were strongly attacked by British land and air forces, a communique said today shortly after an enemy air raid on the big naval base of Singapore.

Ten Japanese ships also were attacked by British aircraft off Bangkok, where they apparently were attempting an invasion of Thailand.

(The British radio reported without confirmation that Bangkok had been attacked from the air, CBS said.)

Some of the landings in Malaya were repulsed but fighting was still in progress near Kota Bharu, the communique said.

Enemy airplanes raided Singapore shortly before dawn, causing slight damage and some civilian casualties.

(Singapore is the Great British naval base in the Far East and strong British fleet units, including the 35,000-ton battleship Prince of Wales, arrived there last week.)

The communique said that enemy troops landed on a beach near Padang Sabek and were reported trying to work toward Kota Bharu. (The town of Kota Bharu is a railroad junction almost in the northeast corner of Malaya, close to the Thailand border.)

Landings made by enemy troops shortly after 1 a. m. were repulsed, the communique said. The defenders used small arms against the attacking forces, which also were bombarded by airplanes.

The 10 ships reported further north in the Gulf of Siam, off Bangkok, also were attacked by British airplanes.

(Japanese ships previously had been reported steaming toward the Gulf of Siam. They were said to include both warships and transports.)

In connection with the enemy landing at Sabek, the communique said that "contact was made by both our aircraft and our land forces and fighting is occurring on the beach."

A Hudson (American-made) bomber was reported to have scored a direct hit on a barge filled with enemy troops on a river in Kelantan. (Kelantan is the northernmost of the Federated Malay States. Kota Bharu is one of its principal towns.)

No Information Received On Casualties in Hawaii

WASHINGTON, Dec. 7. (AP)—The War and Navy Departments issued the following announcement tonight:

"The War and Navy Departments tonight announced they are receiving many inquiries regarding personnel stationed in the Hawaiian island area.

"No information has been received about casualties.

"Families will be notified promptly as soon as definite word regarding casualties becomes available.

"Both departments request individual inquiries be not sent at this time."

The Call's Index

Berlin Fails to Clarify Intentions; Declares FDR 'War Incendiary'

BERLIN, Monday, Dec. 8. (AP)—Obligated under the three-power pact to go to Japan's assistance if Japan is "attacked," Germany referred early today to hostilities in the Pacific as "clashes".

A special communique failed to clarify Germany's intentions, but termed President Roosevelt a "war incendiary."

Article three of the tripartite pact, signed by Italy, Germany and Japan on Sept. 27, 1940, provided that those three countries "undertake to assist one another with all political, economic and military means" if one of the three contracting parties was attacked by a power not then involved in the European or Asiatic wars.

"The war monger Roosevelt has reached his aim," said the Berlin statement.

Bulletins

NEW YORK, Monday, Dec. 8. (AP)—NBC reported from Manila early today that it had received a report that the U. S. Transport General Hugh L. Scott, formerly an American President liner, had been sunk about 1,500 miles from Manila.

NBC relayed another report from Manila that the former President Harrison, now a transport which has been sent to China to evacuate Americans, "had been either seized or sunk in the Yangtse river, just south of Shanghai."

NEW YORK, Dec. 7. (AP)—All three major networks—National Broadcasting Co., Columbia Broadcasting System and Mutual Broadcasting System—will carry President Roosevelt's message to Congress at 12:30 p.m. (EST) tomorrow.

BATAVIA, NETHERLANDS EAST INDIES, Monday, Dec. 8. (AP)—The Netherlands East Indies declared war on Japan today and immediately proclaimed a state of "danger of air attack."

The declaration called upon people of these islands for an all-out war against the Japanese empire. The Aneta agency said all Japanese living in the Netherlands East Indies had been interned.

OTTAWA, Dec. 7. (UP)—Canada came quickly to the support of the United States tonight with an announcement that a state of war exists between the Dominion and Japan.

The action, taken at an emergency session of the cabinet, was the first such move by a member of the British commonwealth of nations.

NEW YORK, Dec. 7. (AP)—An Axis-controlled radio station at Shanghai broadcast a Japanese report tonight saying "a large number of Thai military forces have commenced moving towards the border of Burma."

The broadcast, sent out by Shanghai station XGRS and heard here by CBS, quoted Domei, the Japanese news agency, as adding: "This is most significant, as Reuters news agency (British) reports that British forces have completed preparations on the Malayan border for an invasion of Thailand."

WASHINGTON, Dec. 7. (AP)—Authoritative information was received here tonight that from three to five Japanese ships had attacked the town of Kota Bharu on the Malay peninsula north of Singapore and that an attempt was made to land troops.

The outcome of the expedition was not learned here immediately. Kota Bharu is a port on the Gulf of Siam in British Malaya.

LOS ANGELES, Dec. 7. (AP)—A broadcast from Tokyo said tonight that 63 American soldiers had been disarmed at the International Settlement in Tientsin, China.

The broadcast, picked up by the

Continued on Page 15, Column 7

Sen. Wheeler Advocates Immediate Declaration Of War Against Japan

BILLINGS, MONT., Dec. 7. (AP)—Senator Wheeler (D-Mont) tonight advocated an immediate declaration of was against Japan and united support of the administration in Washington.

"In view of the vicious and uncalled for attack upon the United States by the Japanese government, Congress must declare war upon that government," said the isolationist bloc leader in an interview.

"The Japanese have chosen war. We must now exert our every energy not only to win but to give the Japanese such a whipping that they will not want war again. I had sincerely hoped that we could avoid war both in the Atlantic and the Pacific. War seldom, if ever, settles anything and it is inconceivable to me that the Japanese government would be foolish enough to want war with this country.

"Everyone, regardless of party affiliations, must back up the administration to the end that we win. This applies to labor, capital and all other classes."

Wheeler, cutting short a Montana visit, will return at once to Washington by train.

Battleship Oklahoma Which Japs Claim to Have Sunk

—U. S. Navy Photo

Pictured above is the U. S. Battleship Oklahoma which the Japanese claim to have sunk yesterday in Pearl Harbor along with the battleship West Virginia and several destroyers.

Arbitration Board Awards 'Union Shop' to Workers In Nation's Captive Mines

Draft Deferment for Men Over 28 Ceases If U.S. Declares War

WASHINGTON, Dec. 7. (AP)—Immediate and vast expansion of the Nation's armed forces, was regarded in military circles tonight as certain.

It was believed that one of the first steps would be to call all enlisted reserves to active duty. This would mean a return to Army posts for those selective service trainees who recently were discharged from active duty because of being past the age of 28 or for other reasons.

Army officials at Fort Lewis, Wash., were reported already to have issued calls to such men.

Officials at the War Department here said, however, that no general order calling in enlisted reserves had been issued. They understood such a call would have to come from the War Department.

With a declaration of war by the United States, men in the age bracket between 28 and 35 and registered under the draft act would be liable for immediate call to training.

These men were given a deferred classification by congressional act a few months ago. The legislation, however, specified that this deferment would cease automatically if the Nation went to war.

Before the Japanese attack, plans were to release more than a third of the Army's 1,600,000 officers and men for the Christmas holidays. They were to be given leave periods ranging from ten days to a month.

Many of these men may be given their scheduled Christmas holiday leaves, the War Department indicated tonight, regardless of the sudden emergency.

Other officials said that in the meantime local commanders who had granted holiday leaves were authorized to rescind them without reference to the War Department. Dispatches indicated such action was taken promptly at various posts.

Chairman May (D-Ky) said it would take the House Military committee "only an hour or two" tomorrow to approve legislation to remove the present prohibition against use of the Army's National Guard and selectees outside the western hemisphere.

Nation, Stunned by Jap Attack, Springs to Alert

By The Associated Press

Like a momentarily stunned giant, the Nation awakened last night to the grim fact of war in the Pacific and Americans of all classes and ranks responded immediately to the necessity of repelling attacks on the far-flung ocean ramparts of their homeland.

On the whole the reaction was calm. Amid the hurried recall of all the Nation's military elements, citizens gathered in small and usually silent groups to watch news bulletins, buy newspaper extras or listen to their radios.

The western coast of the country, where the warfare was closest, sprang immediately to the alert. Air raid listening devices went into action and huge aircraft factories took precautionary steps to guard against the possibility of sabotage.

From the Atlantic seaboard, the director of national civilian defense, Mayor F. H. LaGuardia of New York, warned against any feeling of security on the eastern coast and notified his regional directors to take all necessary measures for civil precautions.

In the Nation's capital, from which much intelligence of the Pacific developments emanated, President Roosevelt as commander-in-chief of the armed forces conferred long hours with his military and naval chiefs and with the heads of other governmental branches including the cabinet.

From hamlets and villages, cities and state capitals; from governors, senators and representatives and persons prominent in public life came messages to the President assuring him of a united country.

Senator Burton K. Wheeler, leader of the opposition to the government's foreign policy, from his home in Billings, Mont., declared "the only thing now is to do our best to lick hell out of them." In New York Wendell Willkie said "there is not the slightest doubt as to what a United America should and will do."

Former President Herbert Hoover called for an all-out fight against the Japanese, saying "American soil has been treacherously attacked by Japan. Our decision is clear."

With lightning speed, all military and naval personnel were ordered to the colors. Naval districts and army posts, army and navy air bases recalled men on weekend leaves and all furloughs were cancelled. A steady stream of sailors returned to their ships and stations during the day.

The vast industrial might of the Nation, straining at capacity for months, was thrown under increased surveillance and the Federal Bureau of Investigation called in its agents in many sections to direct counter-sabotage strategy.

Armed guards patroled industrial plants from Maine to California and details of watchmen were increased. In many states, state police and special police units aided in the industrial patrol.

New York City's great aggregation of auxiliary firemen, 25,000 strong, were ordered to report nightly to their respective firehouses and the fire commissioner announced that all plans were ready for a "blackout" of the Nation's largest city should it become necessary.

The Fight for Freedom Committee in New York, ardent anti-isolationist group, issued a statement saying: "It's America first now," and added: "Japan's war on the United States is a last desperate effort of Hitler to turn American attention from the center of war against our world. That center is Berlin."

There was no immediate comment from the America First Committee, isolationist organization, nor from Charles A. Lindbergh, one of its leading spokesmen.

Steel-helmeted guards of the provost marshal's office began to patrol the War and Navy Departments in Washington and the entire capital went on a war-time basis. Officers of all services were ordered into uniforms. They had hitherto worked in mufti.

Mrs. Franklin D. Roosevelt, the Nation's first lady, departed from her regular Sunday night broadcast to speak to mothers with sons in the armed forces: "You can not escape anxiety," she said. "You can not escape the clutch of fear at your heart, and yet I hope that certainty of what we have to meet will make you rise above those fears."

Steelman Votes With Lewis On Issue

8 Steel Firms Compelled To Abide by the Decision

NEW YORK, Dec. 7. (AP)—The United Mine Workers of America (CIO) tonight won a 2-to-1 arbitration board decision awarding a union shop in captive mines owned by the country's major steel producers.

The decision was announced by Dr. John R. Steelman, chairman of the board who was granted a leave of absence as director of the U. S. conciliation service to head the arbitrators.

John L. Lewis, president of the union, agreed with Steelman in the majority opinion. Benjamin F. Fairless, president of the United States Steel Corp., dissented and returned a minority opinion.

The eight steel companies, having previously agreed to abide by the decision of the board appointed by President Roosevelt after the recent captive mine strike, will be compelled as a result of the board's award to sign the Appalachian wage agreement which is in effect between the union and all but a negligible portion of the country's coal producers.

The steel companies already had separate stipulations with the union which had placed into effect wage scales and conditions of the Appalachian agreement in the captive mines owned by the companies. Coal produced in the captive mines is used exclusively by the steel companies owning them.

Only the issue of the union shop was involved in this dispute. The union's definition of the union shop describes it as the type in which a workman immediately upon going to work for a company automatically becomes a member of the union.

Fifty-three thousand miners will be covered by the steel companies' forthcoming signing of the Appalachian agreement. The decision was the climax of the union's 40-year-old battle for a union shop in the captive mines.

Companies involved were: United States Steel Corp., Bethlehem Steel Corp., Republic Steel Corp., Woodward Iron Co., National Steel Corp., Youngstown Sheet and Tube Co., Crucible Steel Co. and the Wheeling Steel Corp.

The Semet-Solvay Co. of New York, a commercial coal concern selling its product to steel producers, was also covered by the decision. The Carter Coal Co., originally a party to the dispute, did not agree to abide by the decision of the board. This company sells a part of its product to the steel companies for captive use.

The companies in signing the Appalachian agreement will give the union the union shop until April 1, 1943, expiration date of the agreement. This agreement covers more than a half million miners throughout the country.

In dissenting, Fairless, referring to the shop as a "closed shop," said his dissent did not affect the position of the United States Steel and that his company would sign.

Fairless said the decision "further imposes an unregulated labor monopoly upon the entire bituminous coal industry" and that it violated a fundamental right of the American worker "to a job regardless of membership or non-membership in any organization."

Lewis made only this one brief statement: "I feel that the award justifies the position assumed by the United Mine Workers of America in regard to this conference."

F. D. R. Will Address Joint Session of Congress Today; U. S. Warship Reported Afire

War Measures

WASHINGTON, Dec. 7. (AP)—Hostilities with Japan were followed by the following measures in this country:

Censorship was imposed on all outgoing communications.

Amateur radio operations were halted except for those specifically authorized in connection with the emergency.

All Army and Navy officers were ordered to wear their uniforms instead of civilian clothes.

Suspicious aliens were rounded up on the Pacific coast and in Alaska, Hawaii and the Panama Canal Zone.

Industrial plants were directed to guard against sabotage.

Departure of Japanese from the United States and financial transactions by Japanese were banned.

Armed guards were thrown around key buildings in the capital.

The Securities Commission was reported to be studying whether to close security exchanges tomorrow.

Mayor Angelo J. Rossi of San Francisco declared the city in a state of emergency.

The police chief of Norfolk, Va., ordered all Japanese arrested.

New York firemen were ordered to stand by for a "blackout if one became necessary."

Attack Centers On Hickam Field, Big Army Airport

A. P. Reporter Hints at Naval Engagement in Last Dispatch

HONOLULU, Dec. 7. (AP)—War struck suddenly and without warning from the sky and sea today at the Hawaiian islands. Japanese bombs took a heavy toll in American lives.

Cannonading offshore indicated a naval engagement in progress.

Wave after wave of planes streaked over Oahu in an attack which the Army said started at 8:10 a. m., Honolulu time, and which ended at around 9:25, an hour and 15 minutes later.

Witnesses said they counted at least 50 planes in the initial attack.

The attack seemed to center on Hickam field, huge Army airport three miles northwest of Honolulu, and Honolulu, where the islands' heaviest fortifications are located.

The planes streamed through the sky from the southwest, their bombs shattering the morning calm. Most

Continued on Page 15, Column 1

Panama Canal Zone Is Placed On War Footing

Army and Navy on Alert as Police Round Up All Japanese in Area

BALBOA, CANAL ZONE, Dec. 7 (AP)—The Panama canal zone, all-important link for United States naval operations in the Atlantic and the Pacific, was placed on a wartime footing tonight for all-out protection.

The Army and Navy were placed on full alert, the zone was blacked out and Japanese were rounded up by police in neighboring Panama.

U. S. naval and military authorities said they were "ready for anything."

Aircraft steadily patrolled the skies over the canal. All sailors and officers were understood to have returned to their ships, and soldiers who were weekending in Panama rushed back to their posts.

The Panama cabinet met in emergency session, and Panama police, in addition to beginning a round-up of Japanese, guarded the Japanese, German and Italian legations.

The cabinet was considering internment of all Axis elements.

The streets of Panama, usually gay over the weekend, were dark and semi-deserted. Army posts cancelled Sunday night movies.

Heavy patrols of military police were on duty.

Caribbean defense headquarters had an increased guard, and all civilians were barred.

Panama police announced they already had detained about 100 Japanese residents of the republic.

It was understood the Japanese would be turned over to the United States quarantine station. U. S. Army trucks and personnel stood by at the police station, but the roundup was being handled by Panama police.

Anti-aircraft posts, off-shore patrols and other defenses of the Army and Navy are held ready to combat any attempt against the canal or the canal area.

Number of Attacking Planes Shot Down in Dog-fights Over Honolulu; American Gunboat Is Captured at Shanghai. Four Governments Declare War on Nippon After Attack on United States Pacific Possessions

By The Associated Press

Japanese warplanes made a deadly assault on Honolulu and Pearl Harbor Sunday in the foremost of a series of surprise attacks against American possessions throughout the Pacific.

Three hours later the Japanese government declared war on the United States and Great Britain.

Soon a second wave of Japanese bombers roared over shocked Honolulu.

The Japanese aggression, which the United States officially and unequivocally described as treacherous and utterly unprovoked, bore these first fruits for the empire, as summed up from official and unofficial sources:

Up to 350 U. S. soldiers killed and more than 300 wounded at Hickam field, Hawaiian Islands;

The U. S. battleship Oklahoma set afire and two other U. S. ships at Pearl Harbor attacked;

Heavy damage to Honolulu residence districts, where there were unnumbered casualties;

Torpedoing of a lumber-laden U. S. Army transport between Hawaii and San Francisco;

Bombing of the Philippine Islands;

Capture of the U. S. Pacific islet of Wake and bombing of Guam;

Seizure of the international settlement at Shanghai;

Capture of the U. S. gunboat Wake at Shanghai and destruction of the British gunboat Petrel nearby.

Troops Carry Out Secret Orders

There was little news of U. S. defensive actions, except the report that a number of the attacking planes at Honolulu had been shot down in dog-fights over the city; an unconfirmed report that a Japanese aircraft carrier had been sunk off Hawaii; and announcement that U. S. Army and Navy forces had started carrying out secret instructions long since issued to them in event of just such an emergency.

A formal U. S. declaration of war could not come until today (Monday) at the earliest, and Britain summoned her Parliament to meet today for similar action. President Roosevelt, the cabinet and congressional leaders met Sunday night.

WASHINGTON, Dec. 7. (UP)—President Roosevelt tomorrow is expected to ask a joint session of Congress for a declaration of war on Japan as result of a "treacherous" Japanese attack on United States Army and Navy bases in Hawaii and Guam.

The decision was believed reached at a momentous White House conference tonight among the President and his congressional and cabinet advisers, called a few hours after the announcement of the Japanese attacks.

Legislative leaders said the President's request would be approved quickly and by an overwhelming vote.

The Dutch government in London, the Dutch East Indies, Canada and the little Central American nation of Costa Rica, near the blacked-out Canal Zone, quickly declared war on Japan.

At the exact moment Japan was irrevocably embarking on her course of "conquer or die," her emissaries in Washington were seeking still another appointment to continue the peace talks with which they have consumed the time since last August, with every protestation of good faith.

Hull Flays Japanese Attitude

Finally, when they saw Secretary of State Hull and gave him the latest statement of Japan's position, he told them he never had seen a document "so crowded with falsehoods and distortions."

With embarrassed smiles, the Japanese left.

First announcement that the Japanese had attacked Manila in the Philippines appeared premature, but subsequently a pro-Axis radio station in Shanghai declared there had been an attack which caused great damage.

In both Manila and Honolulu, said the Shanghai broadcast, the Japanese used dive-bombers to cause terrific destruction and many deaths.

Germany, officially and gleefully, declared:

"As a result of constantly increasing warmongering of the American President Roosevelt in recent weeks, the first clashes between Japanese and United States armed forces occurred today."

Details of Japan's explosive rupture of the peace of the Pacific came from many sources.

A Reuters (British news agency) dispatch from Shanghai quoted unconfirmed reports saying the Japanese had occupied U. S.-owned Wake Island, between Guam and Hawaii.

Japanese troops in Shanghai seized the waterfront of the international settlement and sank the British gunboat Petrel nearby.

The U. S. gunboat Wake, lying not far from the Petrel, was undamaged. A pro-Axis radio broadcast from Shanghai, however, said Japanese troops had captured the American gunboat.

Panama Canal Blacked Out

A blackout of the Panama Canal Zone, vital link between the Atlantic and Pacific, was ordered, starting at 6:30 p. m. tonight.

Gov. Poindexter of Hawaii reported to President Roosevelt late today that heavy damage had been inflicted on life and property in Honolulu.

He said a second wave of Japanese planes was just coming over.

In the Panama Canal Zone, Panama police swiftly acted to protect the vital canal by rounding up all Japanese and taking them to Colon under heavy guard.

Continued on Page 7, Column 1

THE WEATHER
Partly cloudy and humid today with slightly cooler temperature. Yesterday's temperatures: Maximum, 83; minimum, 54.

THE MORNING CALL

FIRST SECOND

Lehigh Valley's Greatest Newspaper

VOL. 108, NO. 135 ★★★ ALLENTOWN, PA., WEDNESDAY MORNING, JUNE 7, 1944

Fresh Reinforcements Reported Streaming Into France As Allies Battle Their Way Inland Along Normandy Coast; 11,000 Planes, 4,000 Ships Revealed in Invasion Drive

Allied Planes Win Air Mastery Over Large French Area

10,000 Tons of Bombs Crash Down To Clear Way for Invasion Forces

LONDON, Wednesday, June 7. (AP)—Supreme headquarters announced today that more than 1,000 troop-carrying aircraft delivered the largest air-borne force in history into France yesterday as other Allied planes—in the war's greatest air operation—ruled not only the invasion beaches but also far inland.

The aerial phase of the invasion saw 10,000 tons of bombs crash down clearing the way for the ground troops. The attacking planes which swept through French skies found that only 50 German planes had come up to meet them.

Day and Night Watch

"Continuous fighter cover was maintained over the beaches and for some distance inland, and over naval operations in the channel," the supreme headquarters communique said. Night raiders protected the troop-carrier force, which included gliders, and reconnaissance aircraft maintained a day and night watch over shipping and ground forces.

Naval Casualties Off France Held Very Light; Two Destroyers Down

Nazis Welcome The Final Test, So They Say

De Gaulleites Resent Timing of Invasion

Flying Officer Denies Nine Serious Charges

Start of History's Greatest Military Enterprise

Embarking on the greatest military enterprise in history, American troops at an English port clamber aboard the shallow landing craft that took them across the English Channel to invade several points on the French coast between Le Havre and Cherbourg. Supported by 11,000 planes and strong naval forces, the landing, according to Prime Minister Churchill, have been "successfully effected." An announcement by the Nazi radio states that Allied paratroops in great numbers also have made landings in great depth." U. S. Signal Corps Radiophoto. (International Soundphoto)

FDR Sees War Heads, Says Operations Up to Schedule

WASHINGTON, June 6. (UP) — President Roosevelt, in his first report on the invasion of western Europe, said today that operations are running "up to schedule" — which, he ...

... Ernest J. King, commander-in-chief of the U. S. Fleet, and General H. H. Arnold, chief of the Army Air Forces.

King had said on leaving the White House that the invasion "is doing all ...

Eisenhower Uses Motor Trailer As Quarters

By STANLEY BURCH

Invasion Brings Call To Union Seamen To Man Any Ship

Badoglio to Form Italian Government With New Leaders

Liner Gripsholm Back With 131 Exchanged Prisoners of Axis

Allied Armies Use Many Secret Weapons

Liberation of Rome Praised by Stalin

Allied Invasion Leader

GENERAL DWIGHT D. EISENHOWER

Pope Pius Receives Many U. S. Soldiers

Fighting Proceeds On 100-Mile Front; Casualties Light

Germans Claim Strong Allied Naval Forces Off Dunkerque-Calais Area

SUPREME HEADQUARTERS, ALLIED EXPEDITIONARY FORCE, Wednesday, June 7. (AP)—United States, British and Canadian troops battled inland against Nazi defenses of Normandy across the white-capped English channel today to expand an invasion operation which Prime Minister Churchill said was proceeding "in a thoroughly satisfactory manner" and with unexpectedly light casualties.

Channel Weather Deteriorates

Channel weather was adverse, a strong northeaster kicking up the waves. But this was not permitted to halt the stream of reinforcements and supplies for the forces hacking out positions along a 100-mile front between Cherbourg and Le Havre.

The German radio expressed fear of further landings. Fresh and strong naval forces were reported sighted this morning off the Dunkerque-Calais area opposite Dover and some 200 miles airline northeast of Cherbourg.

The Nazi-controlled Paris radio said "an important American-British naval squadron was cruising off Cherbourg two hours after midnight."

Eisenhower Confident

General Dwight D. Eisenhower, supreme commander, was serene and confident of success in the great land, sea and air blow, launched before dawn Tuesday under a screen of bombs and shells from 4,000 warships and 11,000 warplanes.

The Allied high command disclosed that more than 1,000 troop-carrying aircraft, including gliders, bore fighting specialists on invasion missions and said this phase was executed with "unexpected success." Allied bulldozers slashed out coastal landing strips.

Germans Predict Further Allied Landings

"The Germans expressed fear of additional operations and said "fresh and strong naval units approached the Calais-Dunkerque area (northeast of the Normandy bridgehead) this morning."

"Under cover of heavy naval guns, the Allies are bringing up fresh troops," said a DNB dispatch broadcast from Berlin.

Continued on Page 9, Column 3

Rommel Commands Nazi Ground Forces In Northern France

The Call's Index

Phone 4141 for Want Ads.

THE WEATHER
EASTERN PENNA.: — Increasing cloudiness and not so cool tonight; Tuesday showers, followed by cooler.

Evening Chronicle

FIRST

VOL. 126—NO. 107 ★★ ALLENTOWN, PA., MONDAY, MAY 7, 1945

GERMANY QUITS

Doenitz Orders Armies to Accept Unconditional Terms of Big Three

Foreign Minister von Krosick Declares 'We Have Succumbed;' High Command Gives Up to Eisenhower at Reims; London Goes Wild; Conflict Lasted 5 Years, 8 Months, 6 Days; U-boats Called Off

London. (AP)—The war against Germany, the greatest in history, ended today with the unconditional surrender of the once mighty Wehrmacht.

The surrender to the Western Allies and Russia was made at General Eisenhower's headquarters at Reims, France, by the German high command.

The British government announced that tomorrow will be celebrated as V-E Day. Prime Minister Churchill will broadcast at 9 A.M. Eastern War Time and King George VI at 3 P.M., EWT.

In Washington microphones were made ready for a broadcast by President Truman. Prime Minister Churchill, after a busy day at 10 Downing St., went to see King George VI.

News of the surrender came in an Associated Press dispatch from Reims, at 9:35 A.M., Eastern War Time, and immediately set the church bells tolling in Rome and elsewhere.

In the hour before the news from Reims, German broadcasts told the German people that Grand Admiral Karl Doenitz had ordered capitulation of all fighting forces, and called off U-boat warfare.

Joy at the news was tempered only by the realization that the war against Japan remains to be resolved, with many casualties still ahead.

The end of the European warfare, greatest, bloodiest and costliest war in human history—it has claimed at least 40,000,000 casualties on both sides in killed, wounded, and captured—came after five years, eight months, and six days of strife that overspread the globe.

Hitler's arrogant armies invaded Poland on Sept. 1, 1939, beginning the agony that convulsed the world for 2,076 days.

The historic news began breaking with a Danish broadcast that Norway had been surrendered unconditionally by its conquerors.

Then the new German Foreign Minister, Ludwig Schwerin von Krosick, announced to the German people, shortly after 2 P.M. (8 A.M. Eastern War Time), that "after almost six years struggle we have succumbed."

Von Krosigk announced Grand Admiral Karl Doenitz had "ordered the unconditional surrender of all fighting German troops."

The world waited tensely. Then at 9:35 A.M., E.W.T., came the Associated Press flash from Reims, France, telling of the signing at General Eisenhower's headquarters of the unconditional surrender at 2:41 A.M. French time (8:41 A.M., E.W.T.) Germany had given up to the Western Allies and to Russia.

London Goes Wild

London went wild at the news: Crowds jammed Piccadilly Circus. Smiling throngs poured out of subways and lined the streets.

(Cheers went up in New York, too, and papers showered down from skyscrapers.)

ANNIVERSARY

New York, (AP) — Germany's unconditional surrender today came on the 30th anniversary of the U-boat sinking of the Lusitania—Britain's express of the seas—which caused the death of 1,198 persons, including 124 Americans.

The big luxury liner was torpedoed May 7, 1915, 10 miles off Kinsale Head, Ireland. It sank in 20 minutes. Perhaps no other one act of the first World War did more to alienate from Germany the sympathy of neutral nations.

Theodore Roosevelt called it the "greatest act of piracy in history." In Germany there was exaltation.

Allies Ready To Land In Norway, Swedes Say

London. (UP)—The Swedish home radio service said today that an Allied naval force of 48 ships has been sighted at the entrance to Oslo fjord and that a landing on Norwegian soil is expected at any moment.

London. (UP)—The Oslo radio broadcast this proclamation today by Major Vidkun Quisling, pro-Nazi Premier of Norway:

"In this grave hour I appeal to all Norwegians to maintain calm and order and to avoid everything which might endanger public security.

"On my part, I will make all arrangements which will guarantee the peaceful development of the interests of the country."

Spain Breaks With Reich

Little Red School House Scene for Capitulation

By EDWARD KENNEDY

REPORT FINDING GOEBBEL'S BODY

CITY TAKES SURRENDER REPORT IN FULL STRIDE

Awaits Official V-E Day Announcement; Mack Plant Shuts Down

Victory in Europe was in the air in Allentown today.

Everybody talked in terms of V-E Day—but it's still not official, even though nobody in Washington, London or Moscow would issue an official denial to the Associated Press report that the Germans had surrendered unconditionally.

Tension Increases

Victory tension, building up for several weeks, increased tremendously this morning as an anxious world awaited the official V-E proclamation. The announcement didn't come, but the people who gathered in little groups on street corners were sure tomorrow would be the day.

Tuesday Will Be V-E Day, London Says

LONDON, (AP) — The British Ministry of Information announced that tomorrow will be treated as V-E Day.

The Ministry said officially that, "in accordance with arrangements between the three great powers, the Prime Minister will make an official announcement at 3 p. m., British double summer time, (9 a. m., eastern war time), tomorrow, the 8th of May."

The announcement said that the Prime Minister "will broadcast at 3 p. m. and His Majesty, the King, will broadcast to the peoples of the British Empire and the Commonwealth tomorrow at 9 p. m., British double summer time (3 p. m., E.W.T.)"

The text of the Ministry of Information announcement:

"It is understood that in accordance with arrangements between the three great powers, an official announcement will be broadcast by the Prime Minister at 3 o'clock tomorrow afternoon the eighth of May, (9 a. m., E.W.T.).

"In view of this fact tomorrow, Tuesday, will be treated as Victory-in-Europe Day and will be regarded as a public holiday.

"The day following, Wednesday the ninth of May, will also be a holiday.

"H.M. the King will broadcast to the peoples of the British Empire and Commonwealth tomorrow Tuesday at 9 p. m. DBST (3 p. m. E.W.T.).

"Parliament will meet at the usual time tomorrow."

LONDON. (AP)—E. P. Stackpole, Press Association correspondent in the Parliament lobbies, wrote today that "although the war is over, I understand there will be no official announcement of this until tomorrow afternoon."

The Lord Mayor of London, Sir Frank Alexander, told a cheering crowd:

"We have had the announcement of the cessation of hostilities in Europe through the papers and we feel that this is, indeed, a joyous moment."

The crowds dispersed quickly after he finished. Workmen covered the decorations on the balcony with tarpaulins.

Surrender Story Not Denied, But Termed 'Unauthorized;' Report Stalin Delays V-E Day

Chinese Destroy Jap Force Pushing Toward U. S. Base

How They Stood— Pre-Surrender Dispatch Shows Status Of European Fronts When the End Came

Today's Chronicle

White House Marking Time, Arrangements Completed To Proclaim End of Hostilities

WASHINGTON, May 7 (AP)—President Truman said today he had agreed with the London and Moscow Governments that he would make no announcement on the surrender of enemy forces "until a simultaneous announcement can be made by the three governments."

Washington, (AP)—The White House marked time today on a momentarily expected victory in Europe proclamation—but arrangements were complete for President Truman to go on the air when it is issued.

Broadcasting equipment was readied for use in the White House diplomatic room, usual site of presidential radio addresses.

Shortly before noon, boxes of sandwiches were carried into the office of Jonathan Daniels, presidential press secretary, indicating no one planned to go out for lunch. The usual parade of official visitors trooped in and out of President Truman's office.

SAN FRANCISCO. (AP)—The office of Secretary of State Edward Stettinius said today he has "no comment" to make on the end of the European war because he has not yet been officially notified.

To Ask Moscow For Evidence in Polish Arrests

San Francisco. (AP)—The United States and Britain were reported by ...

MORE CIVILIAN GOODS DUE—WPB

Aussies Preparing Tarakan Air Field For Fighter Bases

THE WEATHER
Clear and a little cooler followed by sunny, pleasant skies with moderate temperatures and low humidity.

THE MORNING CALL

Lehigh Valley's Greatest Newspaper
SECOND

VOL. 111, NO. 33 ★ ★ ALLENTOWN, PA., THURSDAY MORNING, AUGUST 9, 1945 Entered as Second-class Matter Post Office, Allentown, Pa. | SINGLE COPY Four Cents | DAILY 18 Cents a Week | DAILY & SUNDAY 25 Cents a Week

Russians Attacking Japanese

Atomic Bomb Kills All Life In Hiroshima

Too Many Dead To Be Counted Tokyo Says

SAN FRANCISCO, Aug. 8. (AP)—Destruction of "practically all living things" in atom shattered Hiroshima, city of 343,000, was reported by Japan today in broadcasts picturing such confusion that a definite check on causalties was impossible.

Persons outdoors were "burned to death while those indoors were killed by the indescribable pressure and heat" generated by the Atomic bomb dropped on the city in Monday's historic raid, one broadcast said.

While "authorized quarters" charged America with violation of international law in using the bomb, a special meeting of government officials considered a report on the "disastrous ruin" that befell Hiroshima.

Tokyo's reports, monitored by the FCC, said of the stricken city:

'Dead Too Numerous'

"Practically all living things, human and animal, were literally seared to death" by the "new type bomb." Use of the term "atomic bomb" was carefully avoided in domestic broadcasts.

Houses and buildings were crushed and "all the dead and injured were burned beyond recognition."

"The dead are too numerous to be counted" and "authorities are having their hands full in giving every available relief possible under the circumstances."

"The destructive power of these bombs is indescribable."

Monitored Japanese domestic transmissions appeared more moderate and restrained, after yesterday's propaganda pattern of vivid accounts of destruction and charges of American atrocities.

Voice broadcasts and wireless transmissions aimed at North America and Europe meanwhile seemed to be trying to establish the propaganda point

Continued on Page 7, Column 5

Truman Reports To Nation Tonight

WASHINGTON, Aug. 8. (UP)—President Truman, preparing to report to the nation at 10 p. m. EWT tomorrow on recent momentous developments, today received latest information on the atomic bombing of Japan and then conferred lengthily with Secretary of State James F. Byrnes.

Secretary of War Henry L. Stimson's bombing report to Mr. Truman was interrupted by Undersecretary of State Joseph C. Grew, who hastened into the President's office with a small sheaf of papers, remained only long enough to deliver them and departed without comment.

Presidential Secretary Charles G. Ross had no explanation of the hurried visit.

Byrnes added to the mystery when he refused to tell reporters whether he and Mr. Truman had discussed the atomic bombing.

"Ask the President," he replied. "He's doing the talking now."

Meanwhile, Senator Harly M. Kilgore, D., W.Va., predicted after a conference with the Chief Executive that Congress may be called into session before Oct. 8, the scheduled date, if the new bomb speeds victory over Japan.

(A Stamford, Conn., dispatch said Rep. Clare Boothe Luce, R., Conn., had cancelled her next week's appearances in a play there because she expects to be called back to Congress.)

White House officials indicated there was nothing specific about recalling the legislators, but it was pointed out that Congress naturally would be reconvened if the Japanese surrender.

Petain Secretly Aided Britain, Witness Says

PARIS, Aug. 8. (UP)—Marshal Henri Philippe Petain's top military advisers in the Vichy regime testified today that the old marshal never believed in a German victory, approved plans for a secret mobilization of the French army and supplied military information to Britain while pretending to cooperate with the Germans.

General Jacques Campet, for three years chief of Petain's military household in Vichy, and Airforce General Jean Bergeret, were the latest to testify in the long procession of defense witnesses.

There was some doubt that their testimony that he played a double game in Vichy for four years would win an acquittal for Petain. Those who have watched the trial for 15 days note an obvious hostility among the jurors toward defense witnesses. Defense Counsel Fernand Payen has complained repeatedly that Judge Pierre Mongibeaux showed prejudice in favor of prosecution witnesses.

Public opinion polls show the French man-in-the-street is even fore convinced of Petain's guilt than he was last September. A survey by the French Institute of Public Opinion showed 76 per cent in favor of conviction, 15 per cent for acquittal. Thirty-seven per cent favor a death sentence. Last September only 32 per cent thought the marshal guilty.

Five defense witnesses testified today, starting with Bergeret who said that with Petain's full knowledge and approval, the French air force kept a close check on Luftwaffe activities during the occupation and sent the information to London. Petain, he said supplied funds for these operations up to the time Bergeret left the air ministry in April, 1942.

No Radioactivity From Atomic Bomb

WASHINGTON, Aug. 8. (AP)—Fears that deadly after-effects of the new atomic bomb might linger for years were calmed today by the man in the best position to know.

The War department quoted Dr. J. R. Oppenheimer, head of this phase of atomic research, in denying published reports that blasted-out areas might continue to emit killing radioactive rays for years.

Dr. Harold Jacobson of Columbia university, one of those who participated in the atomic research, had expressed the opinion that rays from the atomic bomb dropped on Hiroshima might persist for 70 years. His views were expressed in a story distributed yesterday by the International News Service.

The War department said in a statement today:

In the opinion of the most competent experts who have been studying all phases of the effects of the bomb for a number of years there is no basis for Dr. Jacobson's speculation with respect to radioactivity. There has been no expectation by these same experts of any such radioactive phenomena as he describes.

Dr. J. R. Oppenheimer, the head of this phase of work, when asked for his views said: "Based on all of our experimental work and study, and on the results of the tests in New Mexico, there is every reason to believe that there was no appreciable radioactivity on the ground at Hiroshima and what little there was decayed very rapidly."

In New York, Dr. Jacobson said in a statement today that his connection with the atomic project was in a minor official capacity and that the material in his story "represents my opinions rather than confidential information."

"I find that as a result of later information eminent and qualified scientists do not agree with some of my opinions," he said.

"I am surprised and pleased to learn that the results of the July experiment indicate that only minor amounts of radioactivity are present after the explosion and that these quickly disappear."

Japanese Lose 11,200 In Lower Burma Trap

CALCUTTA, Aug. 8. (AP)—The Japanese have lost more than 11,200 men, including 744 captured and the rest killed, in attempts to escape a trap in lower Burma between the Mandalay-Rangoon road and the Sittang river, Southeast Asia Command headquarters said today.

A communique said isolated groups of the enemy and stragglers still were being mopped up in this area.

Liberators of the Air Command yesterday bombed Benkoelen airfield on the southwest coast of Sumatra. Mosquito bombers on the preceding day struck Japanese troops and ammunition dumps east and southwest of Moulmein in Burma.

Assault Follows Red Declaration Of War on Nips

Tokyo Reports Fighting Along Manchurian Border

NEW YORK, Aug. 8. (AP)—The Tokyo radio said tonight that the Soviet Army suddenly launched an attack against Japanese forces on the Eastern Soviet Manchukuo border early Thursday morning, Japanese time.

According to a communique released by Kwantung army headquarters at 3:30 a. m. Thursday, Japanese time, the broadcast said, the Soviet army suddenly opened the attack against Japanese forces with its ground forces.

Simultaneously, the broadcast said the communique added, a small number of Soviet aircraft started bombing attacks on Manchukuo territory.

There was no indication of the exact location of the attack.

The broadcast was recorded by the Associated Press.

The text of the Domei English-language dispatch, recorded also by the FCC:

"Flash! Hsinking, Aug. 6 (Japanese time)—The Soviet army suddenly launched an attack against Japanese forces on the Eastern Soviet-Manchukuo border shortly after midnight last night.

"According to a communique released by the Kwantung army headquarters here at 3:30 this morning, Aug. 9, the Soviet army suddenly opened an attack against the Japanese forces on the eastern border at one this morning with its ground forces.

"The communique added that simultaneously a small number of Soviet aircraft started bombing attacks on strategic points in Manchukuo territory."

The eastern border of the Jap puppet territory lies within about 30 airline miles, at the nearest point, of the great Soviet Pacific base at Vladivostok. The Eastern Manchukuo border area also includes the Changkufeng area, near the northern tip of Korea, where the Jap Kwantung army was defeated in a "vest pocket" undeclared war with Soviet Far Eastern forces before the war in Europe began.

Where Nips Report Border Attack by Soviet Forces

U.S.S.R.
SIBERIA
MANCHURIA (JAP.)
KOREA (JAP.)
CHINA
JAPAN
KAMCHATKA (U.S.S.R.)
SAKHALIN (U.S.S.R.)
KARAFUTO (JAP.)
KURILE ISLANDS (JAP.)
Sea of Okhotsk
Sea of Japan
Pacific Ocean
Yellow Sea
VLADIVOSTOK
HAKODATE
NAGOYA
OSAKA
YOKOHAMA
HAMAMATSU
AP Newsfeatures
MILES 0 400

Atomic Bomb Hits Nagasaki

Says Atomic Bomb 'Blew Joe Off Fence'

WASHINGTON, Aug. 8. (AP)—Commenting on Russia's entrance into the war with Japan, Senator Wiley (R-Wis) said today:

"The atomic bomb which hit Hiroshima also blew Joe off the fence."

B-29s and Fleet Planes Attack Honshu

GUAM, Thursday, Aug. 9. (AP)—Admiral Halsey's Third Fleet returned to its terrific carrier plane devastation of the Japanese homeland today, adding its weight to 400-plane B-29 raids, the wrecking of Hiroshima with the world's first atomic bomb and entry of Russia into the war against Japan.

Admiral Nimitz' communique reported that American and British carrier pilots launched "strong attacks" on shipping, air installations and other military targets on the northern part of Honshu island at dawn.

Attacks Continuing

The attacks are continuing, Nimitz added, and announced that a battleship and lesser fleet units shelled Wake island yesterday, destroying ammunition dumps and anti-aircraft emplacements and inflicting other damage.

Halsey's force was swinging into action for the first time in 10 days, during which it rode out a typhoon in the Western Pacific and undoubtedly refueled and resupplied itself for renewed efforts to attempt to knock Japan out of the war in coordinated assaults with the B-29s and other forces.

More than 400 Superforts, intensifying the fury of attacks while the high command prepares for its next atomic bombing, cascaded fire and demolition bombs yesterday on four cities. It was the third straight day B-29s had attacked the enemy homeland.

The carrier plane strike followed by only about 20 hours a Navy department warning from Washington that Halsey's Third Fleet was off the Japanese homeland and would strike again soon.

Although Nimitz did not identify Halsey's targets, it was believed that wave after wave of his planes were aiming bombs against approximately 30 air fields.

The attack on Wake was strictly a surface bombardment. There was no report of Japanese interference although they replied briefly with anti-aircraft guns.

By WILLIAM F. TYREE

GUAM, Thursday, Aug. 9. (UP)—The second mighty new atomic bomb to rock Japan fell on the teeming war city of Nagasaki at noon today and first reports indicated that the attack was as successful as the explosion that devastated Hiroshima.

The seventh largest city of Japan, Nagasaki was struck by the same type of weapon which crushed buildings like match boxes at Hiroshima and killed almost every living thing within its range.

For the second time in four days, Japan felt the stunning effect of the terrible weapon.

General Carl A. Spaatz, commander of the Strategic Air forces, announced the second use of the atomic bomb in a brief special communique which said:

"The second use of the atomic bomb occurred at noon of Aug. 9 at Nagasaki. Crew members reported good results. No further details will be available until the mission returns."

How destructive the atomic bomb had been grimly demonstrated at Hiroshima. In Nagasaki's jammed shipyards and war plants, the most terrible explosive force ever loosed by man would find greater targets than those used for the first war test of the bomb.

Nagasaki has a population of more than 250,000. It is located on Kyushu, Japan's southernmost home island.

Tokyo said disastrous and utter ruin struck Hiroshima Monday when a lone Superfortress unleased the first new bomb on the important Imperial Army base. It appeared probable that Nagasaki also has been turned into a desolate area of destruction.

Japan, already battling Soviet Russia's ground and air forces in Manchuria, had been told she had but little time to choose between surrender or destruction. The empire had been warned that Marianas-based Superfortresses were poised to carry the atomic bomb against Japan in the most fearful obliteration campaign ever envisioned in war.

Today, at noon, Nagasaki saw these grim promises come true.

Sixty per cent of Hiroshima's built-up area was leveled Monday and as many of 200,000 of that city's 300,000 residents preished or were injured under the impact of history's greatest explosion.

There was little doubt that the second atomic bomb blast would prove every bit as effective as the first.

The second bomb fell on Nagasaki, site of great shipbuilding yards, while Japan still sought to survey the seared and blistered corpses—"too numerous to count"—scattered amidst the wreckage of what once was Hiroshima.

Pearl Harbor Flag Flies Over White House

WASHINGTON, Aug. 8. (AP)—A flag that flew over Pearl Harbor Dec. 7, 1941, over the United Nations Charter meeting at San Francisco and over the Big Three conference at Potsdam was unfurled over the White House today.

It was hoisted at sunrise, 6:15 a. m. EWT.

U. S. Air Forces Believed Based In Russia

LONDON, Aug. 8. (UP)—American air forces may already be based in Far Eastern Russia poised for action against Japan as part of the deadliest and most concentrated attack in the history of warfare, military quarters believed tonight.

U. S. Prepared for Months

It is now possible to reveal that for months there have been detailed reports in Allied capitals of preparation for American aerial activity from Russian bases after a Russian declaration of war on Japan.

Nothing naturally was published regarding the reports so long as Russia maintained her neutral relations with Japan—relations which, it was known, were not friendly.

The continuance of America lend-lease aid to Russia through far eastern ports after VE-day was taken as evidence if not tacit confirmation that the Soviet Union was preparing to enter the Pacific war.

But at the same time there were reports also that preparations on an extensive basis, involving many thousands of men, were under way in the vast Russian Far East to care for a big air force.

Scores of Soviet Airfields

There are scores of airfields concentrated in Russian Siberia and their development for use by American air fleets would serve a double purpose.

They would give our planes a starting point only 650 airline miles from Tokyo and would bring Japan's newly-developed Manchurian war industries under close bombardment to support strategically the expected Russian land campaign in the Far East.

The situation also appears to be naturally suited for the shuttle bombing of Japan such as was worked out by the U. S. 8th and 15th Air forces in Europe.

There has been some speculation that the establishment of shuttle bases in Europe was partly experimental for projected use against the Japanese in the east.

Targets Within 300 Miles

The distance from Vladivostok to Okinawa is only 1,600 miles. The 8th Air force in Europe shuttle-bombed Germany with full fighter escort from Britain to Russia, covering a distance approximately the same. Also many rich Japanese targets lie as close as 300 miles to Russian bases on or near the Manchurian border.

There also is the possibility that American and British planes have been shuttled directly across Russia to the Far East bases from the European theatre of operations.

Although such a movement naturally would be a top secret, it appears certain that Russia would make sure she had ample and close aerial support at hand in the Far East for the moment when she was ready to strike.

Russia never has developed long range bombing fleets comparable to those of the Allies, and yet Allied experts have stated that Russian air power could shorten the war by months. This undoubtedly calls for the use of Russian bases by huge American bombing fleets.

Red Declaration Followed Plea By Truman

WASHINGTON, Aug. 8. (UP)—Russia declared war on Japan today at the request of President Truman.

The President's part in bringing Russia's vast might into the Pacific War was revealed by Secretary of State James F. Byrnes three hours after Mr. Truman summoned newsmen into his office at 3 p. m. (EWT) and made this brief announcement: "Russia has declared war on Japan—that's all."

Mr. Truman gave no details.

But Byrnes disclosed that the President had proposed a Russian declaration of war at the recent Big Three conference at Potsdam.

Hailing the Russian action, Byrnes said it "would materially shorten the war and save the loss of many lives."

He warned the Japanese that there is "still time—but little time—to save themselves."

Washington jubilantly hailed Mr. Truman's announcement as meaning that the war, already shortened by the atomic bomb, was nearing its end.

Typical congressional reaction was summed up in these words:

"It won't be long now."

Some Congressmen believed the end might be a matter of days.

Soviet Tightens Allied Blockade Of Japan

WASHINGTON, Aug. 8. (AP)—Russia's entry into thhe Pacific war tightens a strangling blockade which already is denying the Japanese home islands the food and raw materials they need to wage war.

In effect, Japan is now completely encircled. On the east and south American forces control the waters and the air right up to the Japanese islands themselves from the Aleutian islands in the north to Okinawa and the Philippines.

On the west, Japan now is confronted by a Soviet enemy on the Asiatic mainland stretching in a great arc across the Sea of Japan from her.

There appears scant possibility that the Japanese can hope to get more than a trickle of supplies from the continent by way of Korea and the China mainland.

The United States has bene endeavoring to cut off Japan-Asia traffic by air patrols and mines in Japanese waters. A recent Navy estimate was that this had succeeded to the point where Japan was unable to bring in as much as she used, thus necessitating depletion of stock piles.

Soviet Subs Ready

To back up the American efforts, the Soviets have a submarine fleet, authoritatively estimated at more than 100, based in Far Eastern waters and presumably already deployed in the Japan sea. They are reported also to have a large number of fast patrol boats.

In addition, Russian planes based in Siberia and on the Kamchatka peninsula also may be expected to aid in the blockade.

Rear Admiral John H. Cassady, assistant deputy chief of naval operations for air, commented tonight that Russian's entry removes the risk of taking U. S. ships into the narrow sea of Japan. He said in a radio broadcast:

"Japan now has on her northwestern flank not only one of the great armies of the world but also a huge area capable of mounting tremendous additional air attacks against her home industries and military installations.

"We can now settle down to the task of preparing Japan for invasion with increased confidence."

Russian Embassy Calm As War Is Declared

WASHINGTON, Aug. 8. (AP)—The ornate Russian embassy was as stolid as usual on the day Moscow declared war on Japan.

Guards at the door declared acting Charge d'Affaires Nikolai V. Novikov was "too busy" to be photographed or interviewed.

An attendant with a thick accent showed the only evidence of interest in the event. He wanted to know whether the papers were out yet with "thees news." He moved quickly—but with dignity—through the door to hunt a copy.

Allies Sign Master Plan for Mass Trial Of Nazi War Chiefs Before World Court

LONDON, Aug. 8. (AP)—A master plan for the mass trial of Germany's arch criminals before an international military tribunal was signed today by the legal representatives of the United States, Great Britain, Russia and France.

The historic document, setting legal and military precedents, gives the high tribunal sweeping powers to punish by death, deprive the convicted of stolen property, disregard "technical rules of evidence" in the interests of speed and take strict measures to prevent delays.

First Trial in Nuernberg

Under the agreement the permanent seat of the tribunal is to be established in Berlin, but the first trial will be held at Nuernberg, long the seat and meeting place of the Nazi party.

The tribunal itself is to consist of four members, each with an alternate representing the four big powers. Before this body will be arraigned such Nazi bigwigs as Reichsmarshal Hermann Goering, former Foreign Minister Von Ribbentrop, Rudolf Hess, Franz von Papen, former ambassador to Turkey, Labor Front Leader Robert Ley, Julius Streicher, the Jew-baiter, and Hans Frank, Nazi governor of Poland.

Arch Nazis in Jail

Some of these are now housed—or will be soon—in the Nuernberg jail to await trial. There they will lose status as prisoners of war and be treated as civil criminals.

The agreement—reached after three weeks of conferences which once approached a stalemate broken only by the intervention of the Big Three during the Potsdam conference—contains 30 articles, ranging from the constitution of the court to a plan for handling the expenses of the trial.

The plan—made public in Washington, London, Paris and Moscow—was accompanied by a statement by Supreme Court Justice Robert H. Jackson, chief U. S. war crimes prosecutor, in which he declared: "the definitions under which we will try the Germans are general definitions. They impose liability upon war-making statesmen of all countries alike. The action of the masses of men are the result of their thinking.

"If we can cultivate in the world the idea that aggressive war-making is the way to the prisoner's dock rather than the way to honors

Continued on Page 7, Column 5

Singing Soviet Troops March In Moscow

MOSCOW, Aug. 8 (AP)—Long columns of singing Red army men tramped through the heart of Moscow tonight, 45 minutes after the Soviet radio announced to the people of Russia that the nation would be at war with Japan at one second after midnight.

People piled out of buildings and apartments to cheer the marching soldiers of the Red army, whose force was being turned against the Japanese, the Soviet government said, at the request of the Allies to speed "universal peace."

Japs Sought Red Aid

Foreign Commissar Vyacheslav Molotov disclosed Japan had asked the Soviet Union to mediate in the war in the Pacific but said Tokyo's rejection of the Potsdam ultimatum to surrender made her proposals "lose all significance."

Molotov revealed that the Japanese request for mediation came from Emperor Hirohito "about mid-June." Molotov said President Truman, Winston Churchill then prime minister, and Clement Attlee, who succeeded Churchill, had been informed, and also their respective foreign secretaries.

7 Hours Warning

Russia gave the Japanese seven hours warning she meant to strike. Molotov handed Russia's declaration of war to Japanese ambassador to Russia Naotake Sato at 5 p. m., Russian time. Three hours later, the Moscow radio broadcast the news to the world, and at 8:30 p. m. Molotov called in correspondents.

In a jovial mood he leaned across a birch table, lighted up a long Russian cigarette and made his announcement. He was perfectly informal as he asked permission to read the text of the declaration.

Loyal Allied Duty

Russia went to war as her "loyal Allied duty" after she was asked to do so by the United States, Britain and China and had rejected Tokyo's suggestions she mediate the war, Molotov said.

Immediately Russia made her decision the ambassadors of the three great Allied countries warring with the Japanese were informed. They expressed "satisfaction."

Molotov had summoned Japanese Envoy Sato to the Kremlin and read him the declaration of war, which Sato was to relay to Tokyo. The declaration said Russia would consider herself at war Aug. 9, tomorrow.

Molotov reminded Japan that after the defeat and capitulation of Germany, Japan was the only great power "which still insisted on the continuation of war."

He reminded the Japanese that they had rejected the American-British-Chinese surrender ultimatum issued at Potsdam July 26.

"Thus a proposal which the Japanese government made to the Soviet Union concerning mediation in the war in the Far East loses all basis," Molotov said.

By DOUGLAS B. CORNELL

WASHINGTON, Aug. 8. (AP)—Russia joined the war against Japan tonight and a few hours later the Tokyo radio said the Soviet army was attacking on the Eastern Manchurian border.

The enemy broadcast declared a ground assault was launched while a small number of Russian planes began bombing strategic points in the big Asiatic mainland province.

Report Unconfirmed

The radio report, unconfirmed in Allied quarters, gave it as a Kwantung army communique. Supposedly started shortly after midnight Thursday, Japanese time, the exact location of the attack was not stated. Eastern Manchuria (Manchukuo) faces the big Soviet base of Vladivostok.

Mighty Russia's entry into the conflict brought applause from America and the Allied world. Early doom of the enemy was expected.

Russia declared war at the request of the United States, Britain, and China, as of 5 p. m. (EWT). That was midnight in Russia.

President Truman announced the decision in mid-afternoon.

Secretary of State Byrnes followed through with a declaration that there is "still time—but little time—for the Japanese to save themselves from the destruction which threatens them."

'Duty as Ally'—Molotov

Foreign Commissar Molotov proclaimed in Moscow that Russia had been "true to her duty as an ally."

Swift and sure was Washington's reaction that the Soviet decision to fight once more, along with the unwrapping of the terrible new weapon of atomic bombing, signifies that Japan cannot long survive.

For not only are Russian legions set to strike on the Asiatic mainland, but Russia's Siberian air bases are available for loosing her bombs on the nearby Nipponese islands.

Japan thus was all but cut off from the continent, from its rich supplies and the fastness from which she might have hoped to prolong her resistance.

Byrnes voiced a hope in a formal statement that "the people of Japan now realize that further resistance to the forces of the nation now united in the enforcement of law and justice will be futile."

Put Squarely Up to Reds

Byrnes didn't call it an ultimatum but government agencies set to work to get the word to the Japanese people.

He disclosed that President Truman had put it squarely up to Russia at the Big Three conference at Potsdam to team up again with the Allies with whom she operated so successfully against Germany.

Mr. Truman cited a section of the United Nations charter which gives to Russia, Britain, China, France and the United States the duty of enforcing world peace until a new world organization is ready to take over the task.

He cited, too, the Moscow declaration of Oct. 30, 1943, in which Russia,

Continued on Page 7, Column 1

Baby Rescued from House Blaze on First Birthday

PITTSBURGH, Aug. 8. (AP)—Christine Orlowski's first birthday anniversary today was observed by her rescue from a fire which swept the home of her uncle, Adam Wojno, 52.

The child and her mother both trapped by smoke on a second-floor landing, were aided out of the house by a cousin, Betty Wojno. Adam Wojno was burned about the arms and shoulders in trying to extinguish the flames.

The Call's Index

Phone 4241 for Want Ads

The Weather
Increasing cloudiness with showers likely by afternoon. Tomorrow, cloudy, showers and colder.

THE MORNING CALL

Lehigh Valley's Greatest Newspaper

Jobs Open?
There'll be some new faces in the higher echelons of both political parties in near future, is Robert Allen's prediction on today's editorial page.

NO. 21,763 ★ ★ Telephone HE 3-4241 ALLENTOWN, PA., WEDNESDAY, NOVEMBER 7, 1956 Entered 2nd Class Matter Post Office, Allentown, Pa. 5c a Copy 30c Weekly

Eisenhower Again in Landslide

Cease-Fire in Suez

North Half Of Canal Captured

British, French Control Canal, Silence Guns

By NATHAN POLOWETZKY

LONDON, Wednesday, Nov. 7 (AP)—French and British forces seized effective control of the Suez Canal today and declared a cease-fire.

Just before the deadline they announced the capture of Ismailia, midway control point on the 103-mile canal. (The time was 2 a.m. in Egypt, midnight in London, 7 p.m. Tuesday EST).

Egypt announced it would accept the U. N. request for a cease-fire if all foreign troops withdraw from Egyptian soil and if other conditions are met.

The capture of Ismailia gave British and French forces the northern half of the waterway after two days of battle.

Port Said, the northern terminal, was overrun yesterday.

Objective Achieved

The French said the cease-fire was possible because the British and French have achieved their main objective of restoring the canal to international control.

The next step is to turn control of the waterway over to a U. N. police force now being organized swiftly.

Cairo radio interrupted a program to read the U. N. announcement that Britain and France agreed to a cease-fire.

Then the radio announcement laid down these conditions of acceptance previously insisted upon by Egypt:

1. The cease-fire must be immediate.

2. All foreign troops must be withdrawn from Egypt.

3. Combatant forces must withdraw behind the 1948-49 armistice lines.

4. There must be no outside help to combatants.

5. Free safety of passage through the Suez Canal must be assured.

Britain and France announced they would be willing to pull out once U. N. police forces can take control in the canal zone.

Hint of Fighting On

Israel has announced it agrees to a cease-fire. It has said nothing about giving up any of the Sinai Peninsula wrested from Egypt last week.

Egypt gave indications of fighting on, apparently in the belief that all its conditions will not be met.

Cairo dispatches said total mobilization was proceeding.

The Egyptian capital was taking on the appearance of an armed camp. Workmen dug trenches and gun emplacements.

A French Defense Ministry communique said the cease-fire was possible because the British and French had attained this objective.

"To re-establish the rule of international law in this part of the world and to put an end to the arbitrary acts of a man who no longer knew how to respect the rights of others."

This meant President Nasser.

Continued on Page 12, Column 1

President Dwight D. Eisenhower

U.S. Senate Fight Runs Nip-and-Tuck

WASHINGTON, Nov. 6 (AP) — A nip-and-tuck battle developed tonight for control of the Senate in the 85th Congress.

The lineup now is 49 to 47 Democratic, so a net Republican gain of one would give the GOP control if Vice President Nixon remained to cast his tie-breaking vote.

In early returns, Republicans were leading in fights to take these seats now held by Democrats: two in Kentucky, and one each in Nevada, West Virginia and Oregon.

On the other hand, Democrats held margins in these states now represented by Republicans: Pennsylvania, South Dakota, Ohio, Idaho and Illinois.

Nothing Conclusive

None of these races appeared conclusive, however. Returns from Nevada, Oregon and South Dakota were fragmentary. In Pennsylvania and Illinois, the Democratic candidates piled up early margins in the traditionally Democratic big cities, but these could be wiped out by votes from outstate.

In New York state, Mayor Robert F. Wagner was leading in the fight to retain the seat being vacated by Democratic Sen. Herbert Lehman, but the bulk of the votes from the traditionally Republican upstate area remained to be counted.

Eight Democrats and four Republicans won Senate seats in the early returns. All of the Democrats were from southern or border states and five had no opposition.

Ride GOP Bandwagon

The Republicans reelected were in Vermont, Connecticut, Maryland and Indiana. Democrats had hoped to knock off Sen. Prescott Bush in Connecticut and Sen. John M. Butler in Maryland, but both rode the Eisenhower bandwagon to easy victories.

In addition to the races already decided, Republican incumbents appeared to be safe in Wisconsin, New Hampshire and North Dakota.

Democratic senators were running well ahead in Arizona, Missouri and North Carolina.

In the House, which had four vacancies, the Republicans are outnumbered by the Democrats 230-201, but GOP strategists predicted they would gain at least 25 seats. Democrats maintained they would increase their present majority.

While all 435 House members are elected every two years, party control usually is determined by the outcome in about 60 districts where the winner normally receives less than 55 per cent of the votes.

Senators are elected for six

Continued on Page 6, Column 2

Javits Wins Senate Bid In New York

Compiled From Wire Reports

NEW YORK, Nov. 7 (Wednesday)—Mayor Robert F. Wagner early today conceded his defeat for a U. S. Senate seat at the hands of Republican State Atty. Gen. Jacob K. Javits.

With 8,275 out of New York state's 11,132 districts reported, Javits had 2,373,655 votes to 2,367,878 for Robert F. Wagner.

NEW YORK, Nov. 6 (AP)—President Eisenhower took a strong lead over Adlai Stevenson tonight in their bid for New York's 45 electoral votes — largest bloc of any state.

Republican Atty. Gen. Jacob K. Javits was behind Democratic Mayor Robert F. Wagner of New York by a narrow margin for the U.S. Senate in early returns.

For president, 3971 districts of 11,132 gave: Eisenhower 1,373,544; Stevenson 1,083,890.

For the Senate, 3,148 districts of 11,132 gave: Wagner 977,803; Javits 930,483.

Victory Predicted

Javits and Wagner vied for the seat held by retiring Democratic Sen. Herbert H. Lehman.

All four New York morning newspapers—the Times, Herald-Tribune, Daily News and Daily Mirror—predicted an Eisenhower victory. All supported Eisenhower.

Some seven million votes were cast in the state in summerlike weather.

Poll Cited

Polling hours in New York were from 6 a.m. to 9 p.m.

The New York Daily News said yesterday its poll of 30,000 voters throughout the state favored the Republican President over his Democratic opponent by 58.6 per cent to 40.4 per cent.

Eisenhower and Stevenson have campaigned actively in New York. Both have addressed Madison Square Garden rallies.

From the start, Stevenson was faced with the task of trying to overcome the huge plurality Eisenhower amassed upstate four years ago.

At no time during the campaign

Continued on Page 6, Column 1

Boy Swallows GOP Line Whole

NEW ULM, Minn., Nov. 6 (AP)—Mike Lloyd of New Ulm swallowed the Republican line whole. Today he's carrying around in his stomach a boast on a small button it will be "Ike in '56."

The only disappointment for the GOP cause is that Mike isn't old enough to vote. The 5-year-old boy found the button in his older brother's bedroom.

Mike accidentally swallowed it. His father took Mike to the doctor. The physician saw the button in a fluoroscope and said "everything will come out all right."

U. N. Speeds Suez Police Force Plans

UNITED NATIONS, Nov. 6 (AP) — The United Nations moved tonight for quick organization of a Middle - East peace police force as Britain and France declared a cease-fire in Egypt.

The U. N. secretariat published a plan suggesting the force should watch over a general cease-fire and withdrawal of British, French and Israeli troops from Egypt. It would not have the right of "enforcing a withdrawal of forces."

Later seven countries circulated a resolution calling on the General Assembly, now in emergency session on the Middle - East crisis, to approve this plan. The Assembly has approved the idea of a police force.

Advisory Committee

The resolution proposed setting up an advisory committee empowered to convene the Assembly again whenever questions of "urgency and importance arose on the functioning of the police organization."

Sponsors of the resolution were Argentina, Burma, Ceylon, Denmark, Ecuador, Ethiopia and Sweden. Countries on the committee would be Brazil, Canada, Colombia, India, Iran, Norway and Pakistan.

The assembly was called to meet at 9:30 p.m. on request of the Asian-African group of delegations. Later the meeting was postponed to 10:30 a.m. tomorrow. The U. N. apparently will have little trouble recruiting a police force.

Eight Nations Ready

Eight countries were quick in announcing their readiness to contribute. They were Canada, New Zealand, Colombia, Denmark, Norway, Pakistan, Sweden and Finland.

India, a leading power in the Asian-African group, agreed to contribute forces on one condition, Indian sources said. The condition is that the force would not remain in permanent possession of the Suez Canal.

Others are expected to be added as the peace momentum of the force grows. U. N. officials expressed the hope the police patrol can be on the spot within a short time, maybe in two or three days. At least they would like for the United Nations Command under Maj. Gen. E.L.M. Burns of Canada, to set up headquarters in the area at the earliest possible moment.

As these developments occurred, diplomats expressed deep worry about the Russian threat to intervene in the Middle East in force. The cease - fire agreement appeared to ease the situation somewhat but this did not allay the apprehension that the Russians might try some other way to exert a stronger influence in the troubled zone.

Secretary General Dag Hammarskjold, speaking calmly but with deep emotion, read to a hurriedly summoned news conference a letter from Britain's Sir Pierson Dixon announcing the joint decision of the British and French. His hand shook slightly as he read the document. He made a brief statement and correspondents ran for the door.

Continued on Page 12, Column 4

Electoral Vote By States

(Needed to Elect — 266)

On the basis of incomplete returns at 2 o'clock this (Wednesday) morning, President Eisenhower had won or was leading in 42 states with a total electoral vote of 470. Adlai Stevenson led only in six states with 61 electoral votes. In 1952 Stevenson carried nine states with 89 votes. Three of these, Kentucky, Louisiana and West Virginia appeared to be in the Eisenhower column.

Eisenhower	
Arizona	4
California	32
Colorado	6
Connecticut	8
Delaware	3
Florida	10
Idaho	4
Illinois	27
Indiana	13
Iowa	10
Kansas	8
Maine	5
Maryland	9
Massachusetts	16
Michigan	20
Minnesota	11
Missouri	13
Montana	4
Nebraska	6
Nevada	3
New Hampshire	4
New Jersey	16
New Mexico	4
New York	45
North Dakota	4
Ohio	25
Oklahoma	8
Oregon	6
Pennsylvania	32
Rhode Island	4
South Dakota	4
Tennessee	11
Texas	24
Utah	4
Vermont	3
Virginia	12
Washington	9
Wisconsin	12
Wyoming	3
Total	442
Stevenson	
Alabama	11
Arkansas	8
Georgia	12
Mississippi	8
North Carolina	14
South Carolina	8
Total	61
Undecided	
Kentucky	10
Louisiana	10
West Virginia	8
Total	28

Election At Glance

By THE ASSOCIATED PRESS

Associated Press returns on the 35 Senate contests at 11:15 p.m., EST Tuesday, showed:

Republicans elected 2; holdovers 30; total 32.

Democrats elected 8; holdovers 31; total 39.

Needed for majority 49.

Republicans leading in 13 states, Democrats in 11.

Returns on the 435 House seats at 11:15 p.m. Tuesday showed:

Republicans elected 30, Present Congress 201, vacancies 2.

Democrats elected 109. Present Congress 230 vacancies 2.

Needed for majority 218.

Republican gains 2, losses 1.

Democratic gains 1, losses 2.

Republicans leading 62, including 6 in districts now Democratic.

Democrats leading 36 including 8 in districts now Republican.

President Leads in 42 States; Congressional Control Still in Doubt

By THE ASSOCIATED PRESS

Dwight D. Eisenhower won reelection to the presidency early today by the massive, overwhelming vote of a nation that heard and heeded his pledge of peace and prosperity.

Deep beneath an avalanche of Eisenhower's victory votes were buried the presidential ambitions of Democrat Adlai E. Stevenson — now and probably for all time.

Stevenson conceded at 1:20 a.m. EST a defeat that had been obvious and inevitable almost from the moment the ballot counting from yesterday's election got under way.

Control of Congress, now in Democratic hands, still dangled in tantalizing doubt.

But for Eisenhower there was a clear-cut, resounding vote of confidence from the great American electorate — and one of the most crushing landslide victories in the nation's political history.

The soldier-statesman became the first Republican to win a second term since another general, Ulysses S. Grant, was reelected in 1872.

470 Electoral Votes

At the instant of Eisenhower's victory, this was the box score, with returns in from 74,331 of the nation's 154,744 polling places: Eisenhower 18,621,742 votes leading in 42 states with 470 electoral votes.

Stevenson 13,976,811 votes; leading in 6 states with 61 electoral votes.

Needed to win 266 electoral votes. In 1952, Eisenhower won by 442-89.

It was a runaway race, a romp from the start. Stevenson gave up at a time when Eisenhower had:

Cracked the solid South once more. That broke the backbone of Democratic strength.

Seized Pennsylvania and built up heavy leads in such other big states as New York, Ohio, California, Massachusetts and Stevenson's own home base of Illinois. Democratic leaders figured they were done if they lost Pennsylvania, California or Massachusetts.

Marched out in front in the Corn Belt, where the Democrats had counted on a "farm revolt" to give them a hand. They got one, in spots, but not enough of one.

Peace, Prosperity

It appeared to be adding up to a victory even more mammoth, in electoral votes, than the one Eisenhower marked up four years ago. He won then by taking 39 states with 442 electoral votes to 9 states with 89 votes for Stevenson.

It added up, too, to an impressive demonstration that the bulk of the American people prefer the Eisenhower version of peace and prosperity to the vision of a "New America" Stevenson futilely unfurled before the voters.

Over this election hung the pall of gun smoke from Egypt in the Middle East and from Hungary, fighting for freedom against impossible odds. Unquestionably this meant votes for the man who has served his country in uniform and in the White House.

From Eisenhower had come assurances to the voters that peace was the paramount aim of his administration.

In vain Stevenson tried to convince the country that the Eisenhower administration had swept perilously close to war with a foreign policy Stevenson said had "fluffed and blundered the United States into a shattering diplomatic disaster."

In state after state, people turned out in record or near-record numbers. And in state after state, Eisenhower crashed into a lead and kept it.

The tide began with fragmentary returns from New Hampshire and other New England spots. It fanned out to the Midwest and South and finally spanned the nation.

Dab of Dixie for Adlai

As it poured over the Deep South, Eisenhower swept up Virginia, then Florida, Texas and

Continued on Page 6, Column 1

Clark Defeating Duff by 59,000 In Senate Race

PHILADELPHIA, Nov. 6 (AP)—President Eisenhower tonight carried Pennsylvania with its important 32 electoral votes, apparently by an even larger margin than four years ago.

With three quarters of the state vote counted and the remainder mainly from normally Republican quarters, the President rolled up a lead of better than 292,000 over his Democratic opponent, Adlai Stevenson. In 1952, Eisenhower won Pennsylvania by 260,000 votes.

The count in 6,078 of the state's 8,808 precincts was:

Eisenhower 1,698,560
Stevenson 1,406,337

Still at issue was the race for the U.S. Senate seat now held by Republican James H. Duff, who was running 59,630 votes behind former Philadelphia Mayor oJseph S. Clark.

These figures were based on returns from 7,009 precincts of 8,808.

JOSEPH S. CLARK JR.

Stevenson carried Philadelphia as expected but the margin there appeared below the Democrats' prediction of 160,000 or more.

Democratic pre-election prediction were for a Philadelphia victory ranging up to 160,000 votes. With two thirds of the city vote tabulated Stevenson was 86,000 ahead of President Eisenhower.

Continued on Page 6, Column 5

Eisenhower Wins Praise Of Stevenson

CHICAGO, Nov. 6 (AP)—Adlai E. Stevenson conceded tonight his second defeat for the presidency.

Here is the text of a telegram sent by Stevenson to President Eisenhower:

"You have won not only the election, but also an expression of great confidence of the American people. I send you my warm congratulations.

Americans All

"Tonight we are not Republicans and Democrats, but Americans.

"We appreciate the grave difficulties your administration faces, and, as Americans, join in wishing you all success in the years that lie ahead."

Talking to a group of volunteers at the Conrad Hilton Hotel, Stevenson said:

"I want to express my respect and thanks to a gallant partner in this great adventure—Estes Kefauver."

Stevenson went on to say:

"I wish there was some way I could properly thank you, one by one. I wish there was some way I could make you feel my gratitude for the support, the encouragement, the confidence that has sustained me through these weeks and months and years that I have been privileged to be your leader."

Earlier, Stevenson watched returns over a television set in the

Continued on Page 6, Column 8

Four Demos Lose Seats in Assembly

HARRISBURG, Nov. 6 (AP) — Four incumbents — all Democrats — were defeated today in reelection bids to the 1957 Legislature.

The early returns showed:

Senate —
Republicans elected 1; holdovers 11; total 12.
Democrats elected 4; holdovers 12; total 16.
House —
Republicans elected 20.
Democrats elected 12.

Win Reelection

Preliminary figures showed 23 House incumbents — 11 Republicans and 12 Democrats — and four state senators winning reelection.

Rep. George J. Sarraf (D-Allegheny), chairman of the House Ways and Means Committee in the last session, was chosen in a special election in the 38th Senatorial District to fill the seat vacated by Elmer Holland. Holland is now a congressman.

Twenty-six votes are necessary to control the Senate and 106 to organize the House.

Lehigh County

Two of the defeated House incumbents, Samuel Frank and Mary E. Leiby, lost in the Republican sweep of Lehigh County. Taking their seats were Reginald Stimmel and Paul DeLong, the candidates they defeated two years ago.

The other House members losing their seats were Michael J. Needham, Lackawanna County, and John F. Bonner, Carbon County.

Among these reelected to the Senate were Joseph M. Barr, state Democratic chairman, who had an 11,000 lead over his Republican opponent, James F. Coyne, in incomplete returns from the 43rd Senatorial District.

Other Senate Winners

Other Senate members winning new four-year terms were: Peter J. Camiel, and Israel Stiefel, Philadelphia Democrates; and G. Robert Watkins, Delaware County Republican.

Sarraf's term in the special election is the 38th district is for two years.

Republicans picked up two seats in Lehigh County making that county's delegation 4 Republicans and no Democrats.

Three of the elected Democrats ran without opposition.

The three, who won write-in Republican nomination at the May primary, were all incumbents.

Rep. Julian Polaski won his ninth consecutive two-year term from Erie County's Second District. He was chairman of the State Government Committee during the last session.

Rep. Harold B. Rudisill, a first-term member in 1955, was elect-

Continued on Page 6, Column 2

Global Traffic

WASHINGTON, Nov. 6 (AP)—The Civil Aeronautics Administration reports that civil aircraft flights across the North Atlantic during July and August averaged 88 a day, or one every 16 or 17 minutes.

Of the 5,337 flights in the two-month total, 2,373 were by U. S. scheduled airlines, 2,412 by foreign airlines, and the remainder by nonscheduled airlines. The CAA total did not include military flight, or flights by private individuals or business firms.

Today's Index

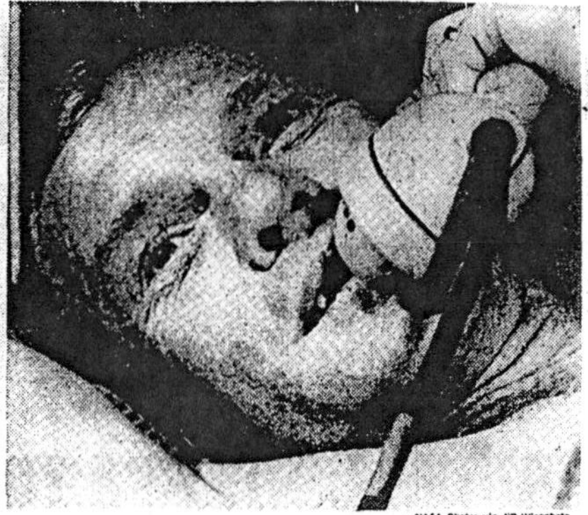

After his space capsule is pulled out of water, John Glenn stands on deck of Destroyer Noa and later talks to President. —NASA Photos via AP Wirephoto

The Weather
Increasing cloudiness, snow beginning tonight, probably changing to rain tomorrow.

PARKWAY REST HOME
395-4011

THE MORNING CALL

Lehigh Valley's Greatest Newspaper

Worth Repeating
Slander is a vice that strikes a double blow, wounding both him that commits, and him against whom it is committed. —Jacques Saurin

NO. 23,388 ★ Telephone 433-4241 ALLENTOWN, PA., WEDNESDAY, FEBRUARY 21, 1962 Entered 2nd Class Matter Post Office, Allentown, Pa. 5c a Copy 30c Weekly

U.S. Hails Glenn Orbit Flight, Bullseye Landing; Globe Circled 3 Times in Less Than 5 Hours

On Urban Agency

President Loses Senate Skirmish

By JAMES D. CARY

WASHINGTON (AP)—President Kennedy lost the first big political skirmish of the year Tuesday—an effort to force a quick Senate floor test of his plan to create a Cabinet department of urban affairs and housing.

The move was defeated 58 to 42 by Republicans and Southern and Western Democrats. It was the first time since 1936 all senators—including one in a wheelchair—have voted on an issue.

The defeat did not kill the reorganization plan creating the department that will go into effect automatically March 31 if not voted down before then by either House or Senate.

But it did sidetrack administration efforts to record all senators for or against the department before the House votes and probably kills the plan, perhaps Wednesday. House Speaker John W. McCormack of Massachusetts has acknowledged he doesn't have sufficient votes for approval.

Hot Political Issue

The urban affairs department mushroomed into a hot political issue because it could affect the 1962 congressional elections. Kennedy had announced he planned to appoint Robert C. Weaver, a Negro, to head the 11th Cabinet agency if created.

The vote was on a motion to discharge the Senate Government Operations Committee from further consideration of a resolution opposing the department. Senators consider discharge an unusual procedure and many objected strongly.

Sen. John McClellan, D-Ark., the committee chairman, shouted that the discharge motion was an attempt to crucify his committee and "an unwarranted and wanton attack" upon the committee system of Congress. He said the committee had diligently processed the disapproval resolution, "but instead of praising us you want to condemn and punish us."

Senate Majority Leader Mike Mansfield of Montana argued that discharge provided the only opportunity to go on record for or against the department.

"You can talk all you want about technicalities, but you can't have it both ways," he said. "You are either for a department of urban affairs or you are against it."

He said if the Senate didn't vote to sustain the President "they will kill the measure over there," meaning the House.

Sen. Spessard L. Holland, D-Fla., said the Senate should vote on pending legislation to create the department regardless of what the House does. The legislation is another way to create

Continued on Page 38, Column 2

Debt Ceiling Hike Voted By House

WASHINGTON (UPI) — The House passed and sent to the Senate a bill raising the national debt ceiling to a record $300 billion. The roll call vote on the administration bill was 251 to 144.

The debt — now at its peak—is pressing close to the present $298 billion legal limit. The House-passed bill would raise the ceiling to the $300 billion mark until June 30.

The Treasury has urged Congress to complete action on the legislation by the first week of March and the Senate probably will comply.

Some House Republicans who reluctantly supported the $2 billion boost served notice they may vote "no" when President Kennedy seeks approval this spring of his proposal that the legal ceiling be boosted to $308 billion for the fiscal year starting July 1.

Congressional action on a second bill will be necessary, since the debt limit otherwise will drop on July 1 to its permanent level of $285 billion.

Destroyer Noa crewmen secure Mercury capsule, with Glenn inside, to ship. (AP)

Perth Glows For Glenn

PERTH, Australia (AP) — The people of Perth turned on their lights for John Glenn and received the astronaut's thanks as he passed overhead.

Glenn said in his first orbit "I can see the lights of Perth on the coast. Thank everyone for turning on the lights."

Tense Nation Explodes Into Cheers and Tears

By FRANCIS STILLEY

NEW YORK (AP)—Breathlessly, Americans waited.

With mounting tension they clung to their television and radio sets.

Then they prayed.

And then they cheered.

"Go! go! go!" arose their cries.

"Make it John! God bless you!"

Across the nation, citizens united to form a vast rooting section. America had put its man into space orbit at last.

Business workers, government officials and just plain people dropped everything where possible to follow the proceedings second by second.

Stores were empty in spots. Telephone activity came to a virtual halt in some places. Housewives deserted the dishpan. School classwork was curtailed. In Reno, Nev., gamblers quit the gaming tables.

President Kennedy arose to watch the preparations on a TV set in his bedroom from 7:15 a.m. to 8:50. He phoned Cape Canaveral to make a personal check on the situation. Otherwise, official Washington come to a virtual standstill.

Some 5,000 commuters halted their morning dash to work upon arrival in New York's Grand Central Terminal to watch the rocket firing on a huge television screen. At the climactic moment, women wept, men's eyes moistened and scores prayed together. Then a mighty roar erupted from the crowd.

Passengers Pray

People on New York streets and in cars were seen with tiny radios glued to their ears. Passengers in the subways were kept informed by loudspeakers — and asked to pray. Many did.

In Nebraska, an executive of

Continued on Page 38, Column 2

U.S. Prestige Overseas Receives Mighty Boost

By United Press International

American astronaut John H. Glenn Jr. drew cheers around the world Tuesday for his history-making voyage through space. The triumphant flight in the full glare of world-wide publicity was hailed as a tremendous boost for United States prestige.

Millions of Western Europeans followed Glenn's progress minute-by-minute by means of live radio broadcasts from Cape Canaveral. From the moment of blastoff Europeans reacted with American type enthusiasm.

A French observatory spokesman summed up general Western European feeling when he called Glenn's trip into space "a great step forward for the whole world." West German Chancellor Konrad Adenauer said it was "a great deed."

Russians Beam News

In Moscow, the Soviets broke into regular television and radio programs to bring the news of Glenn's flight to the Russians from launching to landing. The

Continued on Page 38, Column 6

Ready, Set —Blackout

PHILADELPHIA (AP) — A Philadelphia Electric Co. work crew cut power to make routine repairs Tuesday, silencing radio and television sets in 30 North Philadelphia homes.

At the time power was cut, the countdown before astronaut John Glenn's space flight was at 25 seconds.

By the time power was restored 15 minutes later, Glenn was soaring over Africa.

'Couldn't Feel Better,' Says Space Pilot

By CHARLES W. CORDDRY

CAPE CANAVERAL (UPI)—Astronaut John H. Glenn Jr. whirled three times around the earth Tuesday in his tiny Mercury capsule, landed smack in an Atlantic Ocean bullseye, and reported to a joyous nation that "I couldn't feel better."

Blazing a space trail for the United States and the free world, the 40-year-old Marine lieutenant colonel completed his spectacular orbital mission in excellent shape.

After spending four hours and 56 minutes whizzing above oceans and continents, he came down in the prime recovery zone 800 miles southeast of here and was picked up with an old fashioned block and tackle by the delighted crew of the Navy destroyer Noa.

Within three hours he was on board the big carrier Randolph, eating a dinner of filet mignon, and then was flown back to land at Grand Turk Island in the Bahamas.

He stepped down on Grand Turk slightly less than 12 hours from the moment a gleaming, white Atlas missile boosted him and the capsule into the blue Florida skies for his great ride into space and the history books.

The nation, from President Kennedy to the people in New York who showered their streets with ticker tape, shared in the delight of Glenn's success.

In addition it was a singular triumph for the Project Mercury team of scientists, engineers and astronauts, who started from scratch only three years ago and wound up with a near-perfect achievement Tuesday.

"I feel fine. I feel just wonderful. I couldn't feel better," said Glenn as he landed at an Air Force range tracking station at the tiny, British-owned Bahaman island of Grand Turk.

He will spend the next two days describing to space agency personnel his experiences of spending nearly five weightless hours in the capsule, of the searing return to the earth's atmosphere, and of the sights he saw on his voyage.

Even as he began to relax after the trip, the National Aeronautics and Space Administration was getting ready for more orbital flights in the near future. Next on the list is Donald K. Slayton, who may go into orbit

Related News, Photos and Comments on Pages 5, 6, 8, 9, 13, 14, 32, 38, 46 and 54.

within the next two months, and who flew to Grand Turk to hear firsthand from Glenn what to expect.

Grand Turk is only some 160 miles from the watery landing

Continued on Page 38, Column 1

'We Express Our Thanks'

WASHINGTON (AP) — Following is the text of a statement by President Kennedy on the orbital flight of astronaut John H. Glenn Jr:

"I know that I express the great happiness and thanksgiving of all of us that Col. Glenn has completed his trip and I know that this is particularly felt by Mrs. Glenn and his two children.

"A few days ago Col. Glenn came to the White House and visited me and he is—as are the other astronauts — the kind of American of whom we are most proud.

"I also want to say a word for all those who participated with Col. Glenn in Canaveral. They have faced many disappointments and delays — the burdens upon them were great—but they kept their heads and made a judgment, and I think their judgment has been vindicated.

"We have a long way to go in this space race. We started late. But this is the new ocean, and I believe the United States must sail on it and be in a position second to none.

"Some months ago I said that I hoped every American would serve his country. Today Col. Glenn served his, and we all express our thanks to him."

Inside Labor

Secret Steel Deal Reported

This is another in a series of articles about the steel contract negotiations. The column, Inside Labor, is a regular feature of The Morning Call's editorial page.

By VICTOR RIESEL

NEW YORK — The deal on steel has been made. It is all over but the pouting. From the executive suite in that house on the Potomac and in steel company and union headquarters on the Monongahela and in that financial capital stretching here from the East River to the Hudson, the word has come. The final settlement will average somewhere between 10 and 11 cents an hour per man.

That will mean the package will grow to some 33 cents-an-hour jump over three years — same size package which Walter Reuther's auto union got from the car industry.

In addition, the industry will agree not to raise prices — except on special types of steel. Not for a while anyway.

That is the package which President Kennedy and Labor Secretary Arthur Goldberg thought was not too heavy for the nation's economy to carry.

The "deal," it is reported, was made in the White House in January. The 10 to 11 cents an hour covers everything.

If it sets a pattern for the rest of the country, it means the average increase for millions of industrial workers over the next few years will total from four to four and a half dollars a week each year.

But not in cash.

Bargaining Procedure

At this point it is important to know how the bargaining goes on behind those "closed doors" in Pittsburgh, New York or Washington. The Big Eleven steel corporations decide in their finance committees just how much money they believe they can spend on additional labor costs and still make a profit. The union decides on the basis of its braintrust—statisti-

Continued on Page 13, Column 4

$947 Million in Appropriations

State Senate Votes Funds

HARRISBURG (AP) — The Senate, between occasional breaks to check the progress of America's first orbital space flight, passed $947 million worth of appropriations bills Thursday.

The historic feat of astronaut John Glenn attracted as much, if not more, attention in the Senate than Gov. Lawrence's $910 million general spending bill for 1962-63.

The general appropriations bill, which goes back to the House for agreement on a $50,000 increase, passed on a vote of 49-1 minutes before Glenn was scheduled to land in the Atlantic Ocean.

A recess lasting an hour was declared before the Senators took up and passed a $20.2 million appropriation for Pennsylvania State University and a $9.1 million additional school subsidy bill.

Groups of senators held private "caucuses" on the floor during debate on some measures, following progress of the flight on transistor radios. During the hour's break they watched on television.

At the start of the session in the morning the Senate observed a minute of silent prayer for the safety of Glenn. After he landed the chamber unanimously adopted a resolution praising him and members of the team which thrust him into three orbits of the globe.

In other action, a month-long Republican roadblock to the reappointment of A. D. Cohn of York as chairman of the State Liquor Control Board was dissolved on a vote of 48-2.

Action on the appropriation bills cleared the way for possible adjournment of the 1962 session next week. Democratic leaders of both houses have tentatively set Wednesday Feb. 28 to end the constitutionally restricted ses-

Continued on Page 39, Column 3

Allentown Stores Plan Washington's Birthday Sale Tomorrow

OCTOBER 23, 1962

The Weather
Windy and cool, chance of showers today. Windy, cooler tomorrow.

Lehigh Valley Vitamin D Milk in the new Plastic Container

THE MORNING CALL

Lehigh Valley's Greatest Newspaper

Worth Repeating
To be doing good is man's most glorious task. —Sophocles

NO. 23,594 ★ ★ Telephone 433-4241 ALLENTOWN, PA., TUESDAY, OCTOBER 23, 1962 Entered 2nd Class Matter Post Office, Allentown, Pa. 5c a Copy 30c Weekly

President Orders Blockade of Cuba to Halt Shipment of Offensive Weapons by Russians

U.S. Ready To Sink Ships Defying Search

WASHINGTON (AP) — The United States is ready to sink every Communist bloc ship headed for Cuba which refuses to stop and be searched under the blockade, a defense spokesman said Monday night.

He said this country's blockade fleet, now being deployed, will order any ship of any nation obviously bound for Cuban ports to stop and undergo search by a boarding party if necessary.

A spokesman, under a barrage of questions, made it clear that force would be used if necessary in any case.

Procedure Outlined

In discussing the big force of blockade ships now steaming toward intercept position, the spokesman outlined the procedure this way:

Air and sea patrols will be watching vessels move toward Cuba. Their positions will be reported by observation planes and ships. Warships will move in to intercept. They will hail the Cuban-bound ship.

If it stops, a boarding party will be sent aboard to look over the manifest.

If offensive weapons or long-range missiles or strategic-type aircraft, for instance, are found, the captain of the ship will be told he can head for any port other than Cuba.

If he refuses to change his course, "We will use force to compel him." Force also will be used if a ship refuses to stop for search.

A reporter asked the spokesman "Are you prepared to sink Soviet ships?" The spokesman replied with one crisp word:

"Yes."

A Defense Department spokesman said Soviet missilemen are manning 1,200-mile-range rockets in Cuba on mobile launch pads aimed at key American cities including Washington.

The spokesman showed reporters reconnaissance photographs of mobile medium-range missiles in place near their launchers.

He said this country has no firm information on whether nuclear warheads are there, too, but that it was "inconceivable" that the missiles would be emplaced without accompanying warheads.

The spokesman said U.S. aerial reconnaissance, sharply increased on President Kennedy's orders last week, also had spotted the early stages of construction of longer range missiles which it is estimated could reach more than 2,200 miles and threaten all but the northwest corner of the United States.

The reconnaissance photographs, enlarged 30 times, showed two launchers with several missiles on trucks nearby.

It was indicated that the presence of these offensive-type missiles was definitely established to the government's satisfaction only Sunday, after nearly a week of round-the-clock study by literally hundreds of photo interpretation experts.

The spokesman declined to say how the photographs were taken other than to describe the planes which did the work as military reconnaissance crafts.

'Rather Recently'

The spokesman said the mobile medium-range missiles were installed "rather recently."

He said that in a matter of perhaps 24 hours U.S. surveillance spotted an increase of perhaps 50 per cent in missile equipment.

Continued on Page 6, Column 1

The President speaking to nation.

Acts to Prevent Buildup Of Missile Launch Base Against Hemisphere

By LEWIS GULICK

WASHINGTON (AP) — President Kennedy ordered a U. S. "quarantine" blockade of Cuba Monday night, saying the Soviets are sending Prime Minister Fidel Castro offensive weapons able to rain nuclear destruction on all the Americas.

Kennedy spoke in a grim emergency nationwide radio-television address in which he disclosed that, despite past Soviet assurances to the contrary, offensive atomic missiles sites are being built in Cuba and Soviet jet bombers capable of carrying nuclear weapons have arrived there.

Kennedy outlined a 7-point program for fast military and diplomatic action to stop Cuba from being built up as a Communist launching base against the hemisphere and sent a letter to Soviet Premier Khrushchev calling for a halt.

Kennedy Text, Related News Photos on Pages 6, 7, 8

Speedy developments amid an atmosphere of deep crisis followed the President's somber announcement:

—A Defense Department spokesman said the United States is ready to sink every Communist bloc ship headed for Cuba which refuses to stop for a search. The blockade, which could apply against planes later, applies against offensive weapons but not nonmilitary necessities like food or medicine.

—The Navy said at San Juan, Puerto Rico, that the more than 40 ships and 20,000 men assembled for announced annual Caribbean exercises now are "sustaining the blockade" of Cuba.

—The United States summoned the Organization of American States (OAS) to an emergency session here at 9 a.m. Tuesday in expectation that the inter-American group will approve the U.S. program, thereby giving it international legal standing.

—Canada said it has stopped Soviet planes bound for Cuba and the Caribbean from landing at Canadian air bases, such as Gander, Nfld.

State Department officials prepared a formal proclamation to be issued Tuesday after the OAS action.

Kennedy used the word "quarantine" to describe the naval ring around Cuba, since "blockade" implies an act of war. State Department authorities said, however, that the U. S. act included the essential elements of a blockade — inspection, visit and search.

At the United Nations, U.S. Ambassador Adlai E. Stevenson called for an emergency meeting of the U. N. Security Council, which is expected to take place Tuesday afternoon. He sought a Security Council order for "immediate dismantling and withdrawal" of all offensive weapons in Cuba.

Full Retaliation

Kennedy warned in his speech that any atomic attack against any nation in the Western Hemisphere would bring full retaliation against the Soviet Union.

He coupled with this an invitation to Khrushchev to join in "a search for peaceful and permanent solutions."

About the time of Kennedy's 7 p.m. broadcast duplicates of a Kennedy letter to Khrushchev and copies of his speech were reported delivered to the Soviets — by the U. S. Embassy in Moscow and by Secretary of State Dean Rusk to Soviet Ambassador Anatoly F. Dobrynin here.

Kennedy's letter was described as similar to the speech. U. S. authorities said it included the possibility of a Kennedy-Khrushchev meeting if such would be fruitful, though a two-man summit conference was not directly proposed.

Foreign reaction to Kennedy's

Continued on Page 6, Column 4

Britain Set To Give India Military Aid

LONDON (AP) —Britain accused Communist China Monday of aggression against India and

Related News on Page 12

stood ready to hurry weapons and other military aid to her threatened Commonwealth partner.

Intensified fighting along the wild, disputed frontiers of the two Asian giants brought these developments:

1. The Foreign Office went out of its way to remind newsmen that Britain regards India as the victim of Red Chinese aggression.

2. The Defense Ministry announced that Admiral of the Fleet Earl Mountbatten, chief of the defense staff, will visit New Delhi among other Asian capitals early next month.

3. Qualified officials reported after informal exchanges that the British government soon is likely to announce its readiness to meet some of India's most urgent military needs, including aircraft supplies.

4. The British hustled into consultations with the United States and other allied and Commonwealth nations on all the implications of the dangerous situation developing in the Himalayas.

5. Prime Minister Harold Macmillan conferred urgently with Home and Commonwealth Relations Secretary Duncan Sandys and afterward officials said a government statement may soon be issued. This is expected to affirm British readiness to discuss ways of helping the Indians because of the circumstances of the crisis.

Kennedy Cancels Political Trips

WASHINGTON (AP)—President Kennedy canceled Monday night all remaining engagements on his political barnstorming schedule this fall.

The White House announced Kennedy called off all political appearances shortly after the President told the nation the United States would place a naval ring around Cuba to halt the Soviet military buildup there.

Press secretary Pierre Salinger said Vice President Lyndon B. Johnson also has canceled his political schedule.

In Face of Cuban Missile Buildup

7 Steps to Meet Threat to Peace

By the Associated Press

President Kennedy told the nation Monday night unmistakable evidence has established that offensive missile sites—both medium range and intermediate range — are being built in Cuba and jet bombers are being uncrated there capable of carrying nuclear weapons.

This, he said, constitutes an explicit threat to the peace and security of all the Americas.

The President said these initial steps are being taken:

1. A strict quarantine on all offensive military equipment under shipment to Cuba is being initiated. All ships of any kind bound for Cuba, from whatever nation or port, will, if found to contain cargoes of offensive weapons be turned back.

2. Kennedy has directed continued and increased close surveillance of Cuba and its military buildup.

3. "It shall be the policy of this nation to regard any nuclear missile launched from Cuba against any nation in the Western Hemisphere as an attack by the Soviet Union on the United States requiring a full retaliatory response upon the Soviet Union."

4. The U.S. naval base at Guantanamo, Cuba, has been reinforced, dependents of military personnel there have been evacuated and additional military units have been ordered on an alert basis.

5. The United States is calling for an immediate meeting of the Organization of American States, "to consider this threat to hemispheric security. . ."

6. The United States is asking that an emergency meeting of the Security Council "be convoked without delay to take action against this latest Soviet threat to world peace." Ambassador Adlai Stevenson took such action immediately after Kennedy spoke.

7. Kennedy has called on Soviet Premier Khrushchev "to halt and eliminate this clandestine, reckless and provocative threat to world peace and to stable relations between our two nations."

Both Parties Laud Action

Kennedy Decision Wins Full Support of Congress

By ALVIN SPIVAK

WASHINGTON (UPI) — Congressional leaders of both parties Monday night overwhelmingly endorsed President Kennedy's decision to impose a blockade on arms shipments to Cuba.

The seven top Republican leaders who conferred with Kennedy at the White House said "Americans will support the President on the decision or decisions he makes for the security of our country."

The statement was signed by Senate GOP Leader Everett M. Dirksen, Ill., Sen. Bourke Hickenlooper, Iowa, Sen. Leverett Saltonstall, Mass., Sen. Alexander Wiley, Wis., House GOP Leader Charles A. Halleck, Ind., Rep. Leslie C. Arends, Ill., and Rep. Robert B. Chiperfield, Ill.

Sen. George A. Smathers, D-Fla., secretary of the Senate Democratic Conference, said that both GOP and Democratic leaders had assured the President they would stand solidly behind him.

White House Press Secretary Pierre Salinger said the President had asked the congressional leaders to remain in Washington for an indefinite time and they had agreed.

Salinger stopped short of indicating that Kennedy meant for the leaders to remain here without further participation in the campaign. Dirksen and Wiley are engaged in hot campaigns for reelection.

The strong endorsement Kennedy received from the legislators was similar to the overwhelming votes by which Congress approved its fight-if-we-must resolution on Cuba.

Rep. William E. Miller, N. Y.,

Continued on Page 6, Column 2

U.S. Bombers Put on Alert Around Globe

WASHINGTON (UPI) — The United States has ordered the Strategic Air Command and other military forces on a more vigilant alert around the world, a Pentagon spokesman said Monday night.

He indicated the alert of SAC's nuclear bombers and missiles and of U.S. forces, including those in Berlin and West Germany, was a precautionary measure in case the Russians should make any countermove.

Britain Reaction Cautious

West Germany Welcomes 'American Determination'

By United Press International

West Germany's government Monday night welcomed "the determination of the American government to meet the dangers arising from this situation" in Cuba.

Britain, reacting more cautiously, declared in a Foreign Office statement that President Kennedy's "revelation of the Soviet buildup in Cuba will come as a shock to the whole world."

These were the first reactions of the Allies to the U.S. declaration of a quarantine around Cuba.

A French government spokesman refused all comment but there were informed indications Paris had been informed in advance.

In Bonn, a government press spokesman said simply:

"The federal government welcomes the determination of the American government to meet the dangers arising from this situation."

Macmillan Briefed

In London the Foreign Office revealed that Prime Minister Harold Macmillan had been personally briefed at mid-day by U.S. Ambassador David K. E. Bruce.

"British ministers will consider the matter further in the morning," the Foreign Office statement said, and there would be no additional comment.

It was just on midnight in Europe when President Kennedy began speaking.

Foreign ministers of the six European Common Market nations broke up a night session in Brussels. Belgium, early to listen to a direct broadcast from Washington. They generally declined comment on the Kennedy declaration pending talks Tuesday morning.

Continued on Page 6, Column 7

Plane Ditches in North Pacific —All 103 Aboard Quickly Saved

SITKA, Alaska (UPI)—A Northwest Orient Airlines DC7 military charter plane ditched Monday in the chilly waters of the North Pacific about 17 miles from here. All 103 persons aboard were quickly rescued.

Ninety-six passengers, including one infant, and a crew of seven were put aboard a 50-foot supply boat that was only 400 yards from the plane when it hit the water.

The plane was en route from McChord Air Force Base, Wash., to Elmendorf AFB, near Anchorage.

Two twin-engine amphibian planes and a small seaplane belonging to Alaska Coastal Ellis Airlines were standing by as passengers and crewmen took to their life rafts.

All passengers and crewmen were transferred to rescue vessels by the time the airliner sank, 23 minutes after ditching. The supply boat, Fedair One, operated by the Federal Aviation Agency, was on a supply run to tiny Biorka Island, west of here.

The infant and a male passenger were flown here for medical attention. It was not known whether the two were injured or whether they required treatment from exposure to cold water. There were no other reports of passengers or crewmen requiring medical attention.

The Coast Guard cutter Sorrell arrived at the scene soon after the rescue and took aboard all passengers.

Airline officials said the plane was forced to ditch because of a runaway propeller. Reports indicated that one engine caught fire while the pilot was trying to reach the Sitka Airport for a forced landing.

Door Left Open

WASHINGTON (UPI) — President Kennedy sent a letter to Soviet Premier Nikita Khrushchev informing him of the U. S. action against Cuba, officials said Monday night.

The letter's implication left the door open for Kennedy-Khrushchev talks, officials said.

Your Money's Worth—2

Tax Break Given Self-Employed

Some important changes in the tax statutes have just been enacted by Congress. A leading financial writer, whose column is a regular feature of The Morning Call's editorial page, discusses them further in this second article of an eight-part series.

By SYLVIA PORTER

If you are one of America's millions of self-employed professional and businessmen, you may, if you wish, set up a tax-sheltered retirement program beginning with 1963.

Porter

For years, many self-employed have envied the special retirement plan tax breaks which have been limited to employes and corporation executives. But their requests for a law to give them somewhat similar benefits have been turned down again and again by Congress. Now, though, Congress has passed and the President has signed the Retirement Act of 1962 to give you a retirement plan tax benefit of your own — although it is not as sweet as the one available to the corporation executive.

Here, in brief, is how the new tax break will work.

You will, as a self-employed person, whether a professional or an unincorporated businessman, be able to set aside and deduct a certain portion of your earned income each year for retirement purposes.

While your retirement fund is accumulating and the money is being invested, the income earned by the fund will be tax-free.

When you retire and start drawing on your retirement fund, you will pay tax on the amount which you originally deducted and on the fund income you accumulated tax-free.

Generally, every self-em-

Continued on Page 12, Column 3

Violent Reaction Indicated

Moscow Asleep for News

By PRESTON GROVER

MOSCOW (AP)—President Kennedy's speech declaring a blockade to Cuba came through to Moscow Tuesday on news services two hours after midnight and found the city asleep.

But violent Soviet reaction to the stop-and-search blockade of aggressive arms headed for Cuba seemed inevitable.

The Soviet radio and official press agency Tass Monday carried reports of the American operations in the Caribbean.

"Washington is once again raising its armed fist over Cuba and once again threatening the peace and tranquility of the people." said a Moscow radio commentator some hours before the Kennedy speech.

The Kennedy speech was given too late for any Soviet paper to give much of the text, even if it chose to hold open for an extra hour or two.

Moreover, it appeared likely nothing would be said until Premier Khrushchev had an opportunity to bring his advisers together for consultation.

He likely was advised of the general nature of the Kennedy program in advance since the Soviet ambassador was called to the State Department in Washington Monday afternoon. That was late evening in Moscow.

The Weather
Windy and mild with occasional showers today. Clearing and colder tonight and tomorrow.

THE MORNING CALL

THIRD

Lehigh Valley's Greatest Newspaper

Worth Repeating
Our minds are like our stomachs; they are whetted by the change of their food, and variety supplies both with fresh appetite. —Quintilian

NO. 23,929 ★ Telephone 433-4241 ALLENTOWN, PA., SATURDAY, NOVEMBER 23, 1963 Entered 2nd Class Matter Post Office, Allentown, Pa. 5¢ Copy 30¢ Weekly

Suspect Charged in President's Slaying; Johnson Takes Oath as Chief Executive

SWORN ABOARD JET — Lyndon B. Johnson is sworn in as the 36th President of the United States as Mrs. Jacqueline Kennedy stands by his side. Performing the ceremony is Judge Sarah T. Hughes. (AP)

Grim Texan Pledges Best For Nation

First Conference Brings McNamara To White House

By ROBERT BARKDOLL

WASHINGTON (UPI) — Lyndon B. Johnson took over the burdens of the presidency Friday night, pledging to do his best in the nation's highest office with the help of God and the American people.

Still stunned by the assassination of John F. Kennedy, the new President began his White House tenure by meeting with Defense Secretary Robert S. McNamara and presidential aide McGeorge Bundy shortly after his arrival in the capital from Texas.

The former vice president, known as an exacting taskmaster, also summoned Democratic and Republican congressional leaders to the White House for a mid-evening conference on the difficult legislative problems he faces.

Johnson Takes Oath

Johnson, only a few cars back when an assassin's bullet felled his predecessor in a Dallas, Tex., motorcade, already had been sworn into presidential office by a woman judge before he left on the capital-bound plane that bore the body of President Kennedy.

John F. Kennedy died at 2 p.m. Lyndon Johnson was sworn in at 2:39 p.m. EST., and left Dallas immediately for Washington.

He arrived in the capital at 5:58 p.m. and was at work almost at once. He flew to the White House from Andrews Air Force Base in a helicopter and touched down on the grounds of the mansion at 6:27 p.m. for the first time as President of the United States.

Under floodlights at Andrews Air Force Base just outside Washington, the grim Texan

Continued on Page 11, Column 1

JOHN FITZGERALD KENNEDY

Shots Fired In Ambush Kill Kennedy

By FRANK CORMIER

DALLAS (AP) — A gunman assassinated President Kennedy from ambush Friday with a high-powered rifle. Nearly 12 hours later, a 24-year-old man who professed love for Russia was charged with murder.

The charge was filed against Lee Harvey Oswald, 24. Officers said he was the man who hid on the fifth floor of a textbook warehouse and snapped off three quick shots that killed the President and wounded Gov. John B. Connally of Texas.

As the shots reverberated, blood sprang from the President's face. He fell face downward in the back seat of his car. His wife grasped his head and tried to lift it, crying, "Oh, no!"

Half an hour later, John F. Kennedy was dead and the United States had a new president, Lyndon B. Johnson.

Within the hour, police had arrested Oswald following the killing of a Dallas policeman. He was charged with the murder of the officer and several hours later with murder in the assassination of the President.

Police dragged Oswald from a tiny movie theater after a fight.

"I did not kill the President. I did not kill anyone," Oswald told newsmen.

Dist. Atty. Henry Wade said the case against Oswald in the slaying of the President probably would go to a grand jury next week.

Wade refused to say whether fingerprints found on the murder weapon matched those of Oswald.

"I don't want to go into that," he said.

Police figured the man who slew the President had to be calculating.

Four years ago Oswald said he had sworn allegiance to Russia and wanted Russian citizenship. He has a Russian wife.

The assassination occurred just as the President's motorcade was leaving downtown Dallas at the end of a triumphal tour through the city's streets.

His special car — with the protective bubble down — was moving down in an incline into an underpass that leads to a freeway route to the Dallas Trade Mart, where he was to speak.

Witnesses heard three shots. Two hit the President, one in the head and one in the neck.

The third shot wounded Gov. John B. Connally of Texas in the chest but his condition was reported not critical.

The motorcade slowed and then sped forward at breakneck speed to Parkland Hospital near the Trade Mart.

Onlookers, terrified at the sight and sound of the assassination, dived faced forward for protection onto a grassy park at the entrance of the underpass, fearing more shots. Police swarmed into the scene.

It seemed evident that there was some planning behind the assassination. In the Texas School Book Depository building, overlooking the underpass, officers found an old .30 calibre Enfield rifle with telescopic sights, spent cartridges and

Continued on Page 2, Column 1

Connally's Condition Satisfactory

DALLAS, Tex. (AP) — Gov. John B. Connally of Texas, wounded by the sniper who assassinated President Kennedy, was in stable and satisfactory condition Friday night. He apparently had not learned of the President's death, doctors said.

Dr. Robert W. Shaw said Connally, who underwent surgery for more than an hour, was "in better spirits." He said he did not anticipate Connally getting any worse, and no further surgery was planned.

Shaw, the attending physician said the governor apparently was struck by just one bullet that traveled through his chest, hit his wrist and lodged in his thigh.

"The bullet emerged from his chest and struck his wrist and thigh. The thigh wound is trivial.

"In making a wound in the chest, the fragments from the rib caused considerable tissue damage. It was found there was a tear in a part of the lung and a small hole in the lower lobe."

Shaw said, "From what we know about his condition at the present time, he will completely recover without a disability of any sort."

Connally rode in the same car with Kennedy.

"How's Nellie?" Connally asked after coming out of surgery, speaking of his wife. "How are the kids?"

Connally, former secretary of the Navy under Kennedy, has been governor of Texas since January 1962. He resigned as Navy secretary to make the race.

A temporary governor's office was set up across the hall, but all major functions of the governor's office were canceled.

Johnson's Statement

WASHINGTON (AP) — President Johnson's first statement to the American people:

"This is a sad time for all people. We have suffered a loss that cannot be weighed.

"For me it is a deep personal tragedy. I know the world shares the sorrow that Mrs. Kennedy and her family bear.

"I will do my best. That is all I can do.

"I ask for your help — and God's."

Capital Shocked To Near Standstill

WASHINGTON (AP) — The news of President Kennedy's assassination struck Washington like a bombshell Friday.

Virtually every agency of the federal government came to a temporary standstill as officials and employes high and low reacted in shocked disbelief.

Quickly then the thread was taken up and the things that had to be done were done.

Word flashed out to an airplane over the Pacific recalling six members of the President's cabinet who were en route from Honolulu to a trade conference in Tokyo.

Acting Secretary of State George W. Ball, whose chief was among those aboard the plane, summoned an emergency meeting of top State Department officials to determine what steps needed to be taken before secretary Dean Rusk arrived back in Washington.

For one thing, the State Department sent out official notification of the President's death to the heads of all diplomatic missions in Washington and all U.S. ambassadors abroad.

The Secret Service set up a guard in the office of Speaker of the House John W. McCormack, who is next in the line of presidential succession after the new President, Lyndon B. Johnson.

The 71-year-old McCormack, who like Kennedy is a Massachusetts Democrat and a Roman Catholic, was at lunch in the House restaurant when news-

Continued on Page 14, Column 2

Funeral Monday In Washington

WASHINGTON (AP) — President Kennedy's funeral will be held Monday at St. Matthew's Roman Catholic Cathedral, the White House announced Friday night.

The body of the slain President will lie in repose at the White House on Saturday and will lie in state in the rotunda of the Capitol on Sunday and Monday.

The President's body will be taken a couple of miles to the cathedral at 11 a.m. Monday. There, Richard Cardinal Cushing, archbishop of Boston and close friend of the Kennedy family, will celebrate a Pontifical Requiem Mass at noon.

Burial Site Uncertain

Acting White House press secretary Andrew T. Hatcher said he did not know where Kennedy will be buried. There has been one report, still unconfirmed, that burial would be in the family plot in Brookline, Mass.

The President's body will be moved from the White House in an official cortege to the Capitol rotunda at 1:00 p.m. Sunday. This ceremony will be attended by members of the Kennedy family, government leaders, Supreme Court justices, members of Congress and foreign diplomats.

The public will be permitted to file past the bier shortly after its arrival until 9 p.m. Sunday and from 9 until 10 a.m. Monday, the White House said.

Kennedy's body will lie in repose in the East Room of the

Continued on Page 11, Column 8

Russian Girl, Diplomats Weep

All World in Tears, Silence and Prayer

By the Associated Press

Word of President Kennedy's assassination struck the world's capitals with shattering impact, leaving heads of state and the men in the street stunned and grief-stricken.

While messages of condolence poured into the White House from presidents, premiers and crowned heads, the little people of many lands reacted with numbed disbelief.

Pubs in London and cafes in Paris fell silent, as the news came over radio and television.

In Moscow, a Russian girl walked weeping along the street. At U.N. headquarters in New York, delegates of 111 nations bowed their heads in a moment of silence.

In Buenos Aires, newspapers sounded sirens reserved for news of the utmost gravity.

Britain's Prime Minister Douglas-Home sent condolences and Sir Winston Churchill branded the slaying a monstrous act.

"The loss to the United States

Continued on Page 14, Column 1

News Kept From Children

Jacqueline Kennedy Goes Into Seclusion

Compiled From Wire Reports

WASHINGTON — Mrs. John F. Kennedy went into seclusion Friday night and she is not expected to return to the White House for some time.

Her two young children, John Jr. and Caroline, who are observing their 3rd and 6th birthdays respectively next week, still were not aware of their father's death Friday night, Kennedy's assistant press secretary Andrew Hatcher said.

The children were taken from the White House about a half hour before the presidential jet plane arrived at Andrews Air Force Base carrying their father's body home to Washington.

"I'm not at liberty to say where they are," Hatcher told reporters.

Mrs. Kennedy, holding tightly to the hand of the president's brother, Atty. Gen. Robert F. Kennedy, had accompanied her husband's body from the Maryland airport to Bethesda Naval Hospital.

She was still wearing the

Continued on Page 11, Column 1

Anger Follows Initial Shock as News Of Assassination Flashes Across U.S.

By the Associated Press

The nation reeled in stunned disbelief Friday at the news that President Kennedy had been shot and killed by an assassin. Business came to a near standstill from coast to coast.

"Is it true?" a New York judge asked.

"How did it happen?" was another question.

But the big question in those first numbing moments of the momentous news from Dallas, Tex., was:

"Is he alive?"

More than an hour passed before the feared answer came: The President is dead.

Anger followed the initial shock.

In Downtown Manhattan's criminal courts building, a man slammed a newspaper violently onto a desk and ran from a room in near hysteria.

The stock market closed early. Three governors attended the Midwest Governors Conference in Omaha, Neb., stood quietly around a television set.

In Hyannis Port, Mass., where the President planned to spend Thanksgiving, a workman told the President's mother and father about the shooting. It was reported that neither commented.

Kennedy's father, a semi-invalid as the result of a stroke, was napping when the news came.

From all across the country came reports of stunned disbe-

Continued on Page 11, Column 5

Related News

Other news and photos on the assassination of President Kennedy and a biography of his life, and reactions from Lehigh Valley and Pennsylvania residents can be found on Pages 2, 5, 7, 8, 9, 10, 11, 15, 17 and 21.

White House flag.

AFTER FATAL SHOT—In this photo, taken an instant after the President was shot, Kennedy's head is obscured by the car's rear view mirror. The arrow points to the arm of a Secret Service man who grasped the lapel of the slumping Kennedy. The V-shaped white spot directly below the arrow is the gloved hand of Jacqueline Kennedy, also reaching to grasp her husband. The head seen at the left of the mirror is that of Texas Gov. John Connally, who was also shot. Two Secret Service men are shown looking to see where the shots came from. (UPI)

Suspect Dropped From Service As Undesirable

WASHINGTON (UPI) — Marine Corp records show that Lee Harvey Oswald, held in the investigation of President Kennedy's assassination, was given an undesirable discharge from the Marine reserves in 1960.

A corps spokesman said this discharge was a result of Oswald's renunciation of U.S. citizenship when he turned in his passport in Moscow in 1959 and said he would stay in Russia.

Oswald twice received summary courts-martial while serving on active duty with the Marine Corps in Japan, the spokesman said.

He qualified as a "marksman" with the M1 rifle while in the Marines, rating neither low nor high as a rifleman, the spokesman told newsmen.

Oswald's record, as described by the spokesman, included these items:

Oswald was born in New Orleans on Oct. 18, 1939, his mother is Mrs. Marguerite Oswald, whose address at the time of his enlistment was given as 4936 Collingwood St., Fort Worth, Texas. He enlisted Oct. 24, 1956 at Dallas.

ASSASSIN? — Lee Harvey Oswald, 24, has been charged with the assassination of President Kennedy.

FIRST

THE MORNING CALL

Lehigh Valley's Greatest Newspaper

The Weather
Clearing today, windy and cooler. Fair and seasonable tomorrow.

Worth Repeating
A farmer may be sincere in planting thistles, but he will not raise corn.
—Bishop Fulton Sheen

NO. 25,273 ★ ★ ★ ALLENTOWN, PA., FRIDAY, APRIL 5, 1968 10c A Copy 48c Weekly Home Delivered

Dr. Martin Luther King Slain in Memphis; National Guard Called in to Enforce Curfew

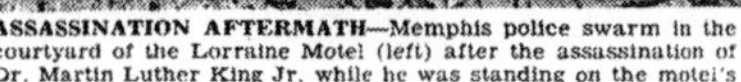

ASSASSINATION AFTERMATH—Memphis police swarm in the courtyard of the Lorraine Motel (left) after the assassination of Dr. Martin Luther King Jr. while he was standing on the motel's second-floor balcony. At right, a Memphis detective examines the gun used in the crime. (AP)

Mourning Associates Urge Calm

Police Seek White Suspect

By EARL CALDWELL
(C) N.Y. Times News Service

MEMPHIS — The Rev. Dr. Martin Luther King Jr., who preached nonviolence and racial brotherhood, was fatally shot here Thursday by a distant gunman who then raced away and escaped.

Four thousand National Guard troops were ordered into Memphis by Gov. Buford Ellington after the 39-year-old Nobel Prize-winning civil rights leader died.

A curfew was imposed on this shocked city of 550,000 inhabitants, 40 per cent of whom are Negro.

Police Director Frank Holloman said the assassin might have been a white man who was "50 to 100 yards away in a flophouse." Holloman said two persons had been taken into custody, but he also said the police had no definite lead.

King was shot while he learned over a second-floor railing outside his room at the Lorraine Motel, chatting with two friends just before starting for dinner.

King's mourning associates sought to calm the people they met by recalling his messages of peace, but there was widespread concern by law enforcement officers here and elsewhere over potential reactions.

In a television broadcast after the curfew was ordered here, Holloman said "Rioting has broken out in parts of the city." He asserted, "looting is rampent."

The police issued an alarm seeking a young white man reported to have rushed out of a building across the street after the shooting, who might have dropped a Browning Automatic Rifle with a telescopic sight before leaping into a car.

Arkansas State Police, across the Mississippi River from Memphis, received an alert to watch out for a white car driven by a white man, dark-haired and dressed in a dark suit.

Dr. King had been bleeding profusely from what appeared to be a huge wound in the right jaw or neck area as he lay face up on the concrete walkway before he was taken away in a fire department ambulance.

His eyes appeared first half-closed and then open but staring. One of his closest aides, James Bevel, grief - stricken, said after Dr. King was removed, "I think he's gone."

Dr. King had come back to Memphis Thursday morning to organize support once again for 1,300 sanitation workers who have been on strike since Lincoln's Birthday. Just a week ago he led a march on behalf of the strikers that ended in violence with a 16 - year - old Negro killed, 62 persons injured and 200 arrested.

Police poured into the area around the Lorraine Motel on Milberry Street where Dr. King was shot. They carried shotguns and rifles and sealed off the block, refusing to allow entry to newsmen and others.

Dr. King had been in his sec-

Continued on Page 6, Column 1

DR. MARTIN LUTHER KING

Voice of Negro
The Crusader For Equality

By MURRAY SCHUMACH
(C) N.Y. Times News Service

To many millions of American Negroes, the Rev. Dr. Martin Luther King Jr. was the prophet of their crusade for racial equality. He was their voice of anguish, their eloquence in humiliation, their battle cry for human dignity. He forged for them the weapons of nonviolence that withstood and blunted the ferocity of segregation.

And to many millions of American whites, he was one of a group of educated Negroes who preserved the bridge of communication between races when racial warfare threatened the United States in the 1960's, as Negroes sought the full emancipation pledged to them a century before by Abraham Lincoln.

To the world Dr. King had the stature that accrued to a winner of the Nobel Peace Prize; a man with access to the White House and the Vatican; a veritable hero in the African states that were just emerging from colonialism.

Caught in Crossfire

In his determined dedication to nonviolence, Dr. King was caught in the crossfire between white and Negro extremists as the racial tensions erupted into arson, gunfire and looting in many of the nation's cities during the summer of 1967.

Militant Negroes, with the cry of, "burn, baby burn," argued that only by violence and segregation, could the Negro attain self - respect, dignity and real equality in the U.S. and white extremists, not bothering to make distinctions between degrees of Negro militancy, looked upon Dr. King as one of their chief enemies.

At times, in recent months, efforts by Dr. King to utilize nonviolent methods exploded into violence. On March 28, when he led a massive protest march through downtown Memphis, in support of the city's striking sanitation workers — mostly Negro—a group of Negro youths suddenly began breaking store windows and looting and one Negro was shot to death.

Miscalculation

Two days later, however, the minister said he would stage another demonstration and blamed the violence on his own "miscalculation."

At the time he was assassinated in Memphis, Dr. King was involved on a plan to dramatize the plight of the poor and stir Congress to help Negroes. He called this venture the "poor people's campaign." It was to be a huge "camp-in" either in Washington or in Chicago dur-

Continued on Page 17, Column 1

King Aware Of Threats, Unworried

MEMPHIS, Tenn. (AP) — "It really doesn't matter what happens now. I've been to the mountaintop."

The speaker was Martin Luther King Jr. It was Wednesday night.

Less than 24 hours later, the nation's foremost apostle of nonviolence was dead — the victim of an assassin's bullet—as he stood on the threshhold of the biggest test of the theories he espoused.

King said Wednesday night that he was aware the threats had been made on his life. But he said he had seen the fulfillment of his goals of nonviolence, and did not worry about the future.

"And there have been some threats around here," he added. "We've got some difficult days ahead, but it really doesn't matter now," King said. "Because I've been to the mountaintop."

Will Leave Today
President Postpones Trip

WASHINGTON (AP) — President Johnson Thursday night postponed his departuer for Hawaii for a Vietnam strategy conference because of the slaying of Dr. Martin Luther King Jr. in Memphis, Tenn.

Johnson had been scheduled to leave at midnight. He now intends to leave some time Friday.

There was growing caution here about the prospects of preliminary peace talks.

The White House announced that, on his way, Johnson will stop at March Air Force Base, Calif., Friday to talk with former President Dwight D. Eisenhower. It was disclosed also that South Korea's president, Chung Hee Park, will join the weekend Hawaii meeting Sunday.

Shortly before Johnson's scheduled late-night departure, Hanoi charged that American planes bombed a North Vietnamese town northwest of the country's Capital—deep inside the territory the President had declared off limits to U.S. air raiders.

The Pentagon quickly disavowed any "present knowledge of any such U.S. attack since the President's speech Sunday night" in which he proclaimed the curtailment of U.S. bombing of North Vietnam.

"Nonetheless an immediate investigation has been ordered," Asst. Secretary Phil G. Goulding said in issuing the Defense Department statement.

Johnson met for an hour Thursday with U Thant, secretary-general of the United Nations, to discuss peace prospects in Vietnam.

The session was held at the U.N. headquarters in New York after the President had attended ceremonies at St. Patrick's Cathedral marking the installation of the Most Rev. Terence J. Cooke as Roman Catholic archbishop of New York.

The meeting was suggested by U.N. Ambassador Arthur J. Goldberg while he was with Johnson at the cathedral.

A U.N.-White House announcement said the two men discussed peace, that Goldberg and Undersecretary-General Ralph Bunche participated, and that the meeting lasted from 3:53 p.m. to 4:55 p.m.

Pressed for details, a U.N. spokesman said "The conversations were strictly private."

En route back to Washington, Johnson told reporters:

"He gave me his assessment of the situation that developed since Sunday night and the attitudes among the U.N. missions, as well as his own. He was encouraged by it."

Johnson said it was a good meeting, very helpful and very constructive. He added he is going to ask U Thant to visit him in Washington later.

The Honolulu meeting of the President with his top Washington and Saigon advisers follows Johnson's pattern for such get-togethers every half year or so for an across-the-board review of the Southeast Asian conflict. Such sessions have been held before in Hawaii, Guam and Washington.

But this week's spectacular developments toward direct negotiations with Hanoi have greatly heightened the potential of this weekend's parley.

This time the U.S. strategists must weigh what shifts may be necessary in the conduct of the war to accompany possible developments on the diplomatic front.

White House sources indicated, too, that the choice of a successor to the U.S. commander in Vietnam, Gen. William C. Westmoreland, would be on the agenda.

After four years at Saigon, Westmoreland is returning to Washington to become Army chief of staff in July. The U.S. commander in the Pacific, Adm. U. S. Grant Sharp, also is due for replacement by July.

Westmoreland and Ambassador Ellsowrth Bunker will be in the U.S. contingent from Saigon. Flying out from Washington are Secretary of Defense Clark M. Clifford, Gen. Earle G. Wheeler, chairman of the Joint Chiefs of Staff, and William P. Bundy, assistant secretary of state for East Asian affairs.

Arriving at Honolulu Saturday night from a foreign ministers' meeting in New Zealand is Secretary of State Dean Rusk.

Administration authorities took some pains to divorce Park's trip to Honolulu from the all-U.S. meetings which will precede his arrival. This was to avoid pressure from other allied

Continued on Page 6, Column 7

Johnson Says Nation 'Saddened'

WASHINGTON (AP) — President Johnson spoke Thursday night of an "America shocked and saddened" by the assassination of Dr. Martin Luther King as he condemned violence, lawlessness and divisiveness.

In a brief, solemn message to the nation, Johnson disclosed that because of the slaying at Memphis he had canceled plans for a political appearance Thursday night and postponed until Friday his scheduled midnight departure for Hawaii and a Vietnam strategy conference.

The President appeared in the doorway of the White House offices, stern-faced and spoke on all television and radio networks.

"I ask every American citizen," he said, "to reject the blind violence that has struck down Dr. King, who lived by nonviolence."

The President urged prayers

Continued on Page 6, Column 6

Saigon Aide Asks Peace With Honor

WASHINGTON (AP) — South Vietnam's deputy ambassador said Thursday any call for a coalition or a neutralist government in the South "is merely wishful thinking from a minority of naive liberals who persist in forgetting the painful lessons of the past."

In a statement apparently aimed at presidential aspirants Robert F. Kennedy and Eugene J. McCarthy, Dr. Ngo Ton Dat said the Vietnamese people "honestly desire peace with honor but not a peace which eventually means enslavement.

He did not mention any political candidate by name.

The embassy statement said the people of South Vietnam are the innocent victims of a Communist strategy of conquest not limited to their nation alone.

Dat said any negotiations should include discussions on a halt to infiltration by North Vietnamese troops, their withdrawal from South Vietnam, and the cessation of aggression and all other acts of guerrilla warfare and subversion.

Relief Force Within Sight Of Besieged Khe Sanh Base

By EDWIN Q. WHITE

SAIGON (AP) — A U.S. task force pressed close to the Marine combat base at Khe Sanh on Friday, the fifth day of a drive to lift the long siege of the battered fortress in South Vietnam's northwest corner.

At last report, lead elements of the relief force were within half a mile Thursday night of the Khe Sanh perimeter and were poised for a final push.

The relief force has met only light opposition from artillery and mortar fire since jumping off from Ca Lu, 12 miles away, on Monday. Soviet reports in London said Thursday that the North Vietnamese were beginning to withdraw as a good-will gesture, but there was no confirmation from Hanoi.

Another reason advanced for the lack of sizeable opposition was the incessant American bombing by planes and from artillery in Khe Sanh itself, of North Vietnamese positions during the past three months.

In other developments early Friday:

Allied military spokesman said the Viet Cong shelled 11 U.S. and South Vietnamese military positions Thursday night and early Friday. The targets, ranging the length of the country, included the big Tan Son Nhut air base on Saigon's outskirts. The heaviest shelling was at a U.S. Army base camp 11 miles northeast of Saigon, but even there casualties and damage were reported light.

Navy Bombs North

In the newly curtailed U.S. air campaign against North Vietnam, Navy fliers ranged 225 miles north of the demilitarized zone Thursday for a third successive day. They bombed a railroad siding 12 miles northeast of Thanh Hoa and just a mile below the 20th parallel which President Johnson set as the northern limit under his order to de-escalate the air war.

In a late report, the U.S. Command said Marine units ranged out of Khe Sanh on Thursday and, meeting no resistance, occupied a hill 1½ miles to the south as the relief troops pushed closer.

The 6,000 Marines inside Khe Sanh watched through field glasses as the relief columns moved into view—Marines from the northwest, air cavalrymen from the south and other Leathernecks coming from the east along Highway 9.

Some Marines moved out from Khe Sanh to the hills on the west and engaged North Vietnamese. It was not known how many of the 16,000 enemy troops who had surrounded Khe Sanh remained in the area.

Helicopters blazed away with rockets and machine guns at the enemy trenches closely encircling Khe Sanh. Marines in Khe Sanh knew that some of the enemy were still out there. Eighty rounds of North Vietnamese artillery and rocket fire slammed into the base before nightfall.

This was a far cry from the early days of the siege, when 1,500 or more shells exploded on the sand-bagged bunkers and

Continued on Page 38, Column 6

FIRST CALL

Picking Pearson's Successor
Trudeau Builds Lead

OTTAWA (AP) — Justice Minister Pierre Elliott Trudeau, the acknowledged front-runner, continued to build up his lead Thursday as Canada's Liberal party opened its three-day session to choose a successor to Prime Minister Lester B. Pearson.

Other leading candidates refused, however, to concede that the apparent first-ballot strength of the 46-year-old Quebec intellectual would result in his election when the balloting takes place Saturday afternoon.

Foreign Minister Paul Martin, Transport Minister Paul Hellyer and former Trade Minister Robert Winters all expressed confidence they would emerge victors as weaker candidates released their delegates.

Rumors of a "Stop Trudeau" movement persisted, but Martin emphatically denied Thursday morning that he was involved in a reported deal with Hellyer.

One of the latest boosts to Trudeau came from Newfoundland's Premier Joey Smallwood, who threw his support to the justice minister along with an estimated 60 of his province's 84 votes.

500 - 700 Assured?

Some observers are predicting that Trudeau will get 500 to 700 votes on the first ballot. This would be far short of the more than 1,200 votes needed for election.

It was expected, however, that several of the eight leading candidates would withdraw after the first or second ballot. These include Health Minister Allen MacEachen, Agriculture Minister J. J. Greene and Eric Kierans, former health minister of Quebec Province.

The original field of 19 candidates was cut to 10 Thursday when four failed to qualify by the filing deadline.

Attention continued to focus on backroom talks which proceeded as the convention began its business in the gaily decorated auditorium of the Ottawa Civic Center at Lansdowne Park.

The principal business of the day was a series of workshop sessions at which all the candidates were given an opportunity to appear before groups of delegates to express their views on foreign and domestic policies.

The ev[illegible] session was set aside for [illegible] farewell tribute to Pearson, [illegible] is retiring at the age of 70 later this month.

PIERRE TRUDEAU

Inside The Call

Entered 2nd Class Matter Post Office, Allentown, Pa. 18105

Violence, Looting Erupt After Dr. King Slaying

Compiled From Wire Services

Shortly after the news of the slaying of Dr. Martin Luther King Jr. in Memphis, Tenn., Thursday, violence and looting flared in various major cities.

WASHINGTON (AP) — Crowds of Negroes gathered in a predominantly Negro shopping area Thursday night and looting broke out in an apparent angry reaction to the death of Dr. Martin Luther King.

Stores along a six-block section of 14th St. in the near Northwest were broken into. Glass littered the streets and Negroes clustered at the corners hooted and called "whitey" at passing whites in cars.

A spokesman at police headquarters said some youngsters had broken store windows along 14th street in a predominantly Negro section of the city. He added: "It is not what we call a major disturbance."

NEW YORK (AP) — Police rushed reinforcements to Harlem Thursday night as a small group of looters was reported ranging along 125th Street following the assassination of Dr. Martin Luther King in Memphis.

Bars shut down with patrons locked inside and stores which usually stay open late shuttered quickly.

Police sealed off 125th Street between Seventh and Eighth avenues.

The first report of looting came from Reid's Clothing Store on Harlem's main street. About 25 Negro youths were involved in the looting. There appeared to be the same number in other bands in the area.

At least 50 patrolmen were hurried to the area where horror had been the first reaction to the Memphis shooting.

BOSTON (AP) — Shortly after news was flashed of the fatal shooting of Dr. Martin Luther King Thursday night, a large crowd of Negroes stoned six police cruisers near a Negro housing project in the Roxbury section, police said.

One person was taken to Peter Bent Brigham Hospital with undetermined injuries after the outbreak.

Police said some persons in the crowd carried clubs and lengths off chain.

The crowd began throwing stones at the cruisers about 9 p.m.

Police sent reinforcements to the scene with orders for patrol cars not to use flashing roof lights.

Twenty minutes after the first disturbance police said, a second crowd gathered at an intersection a few blocks away.

Police said the crowd near the housing project dispersed gradually.

Cambridge police reported an orderly crowd of about 75 persons staged a sympathy march on a sidewalk near Harvard Square.

RALEIGH, N.C. (AP)—City police clashed with a group of about 30 young Negroes on Ra-

Continued on Page 6, Column 1

The Weather
Sunny and warm today and tomorrow.

CAMP OLYMPIC
Open House Sun., June 9

THE MORNING CALL

Lehigh Valley's Greatest Newspaper

NO. 25,325 ★ ALLENTOWN, PA., THURSDAY, JUNE 6, 1968 10c A Copy 48c Weekly Home Delivered

Worth Repeating
The young man who has not wept is a savage, and the old man who will not laugh is a fool. —George Santayana

Kennedy Keeps Weak Grip on Life

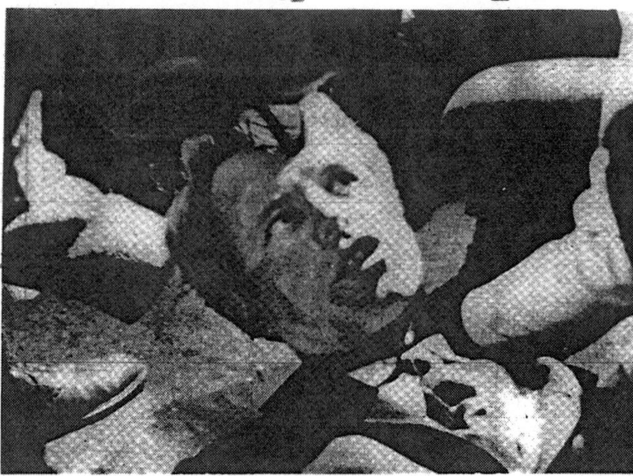

Sen. Robert F. Kennedy lies gravely wounded after he was shot during victory celebration. (Copyright, Los Angeles Times)

Police Hold Jordanian In Shooting

Anti-Semitism Called Motive

LOS ANGELES (AP) — Sirhan Bishara Sirhan, 24, is a Jordanian who hates Jews and who fell from a horse recently trying to become a jockey, those who knew him said Wednesday.

Sirhan was identified by Los Angeles police as the man who gunned down Sen. Robert F. Kennedy moments after the senator thanked supporters for his California primary election victory over Sen. Eugene J. McCarthy.

He "may have been inflamed" by a statement from Sen. Robert Kennedy during a televised campaign debate Saturday night, said a New York committee on American-Arab relations.

During the debate with McCarthy, Kennedy said the United States should supply jets to Israel.

Under maximum security guard in a hospital ward at the Los Angeles County Central Jail, Sirhan kept mum about the shooting. Police said he is the only suspect.

He was hospitalized with a broken index finger and sprained left ankle suffered in the melee of his capture, said an official at the jail.

"No! No!" sobbed Sirhan's mother, Mary, when she learned one of her five sons was arrested.

"All I know is he is a nice kid," said Said Sirhan in New York. He identified himself as a brother of the accused man.

"When there was trouble between Jordan and Israel, he would become inflamed," said John Shear, who worked with the prisoner at Hollywood Park race track.

"Since I wasn't interested in politics I would not discuss it," said Shear, an assistant trainer. "But he was violently pro-Jordan and anti-Israeli.

"During a number of lengthy conversations, Sirhan talked freely and with interest—until asked who he was and anything about Kennedy," said Los Angeles Police Chief Thomas Reddin.

Police said they found a note-

Continued on Page 8, Column 7

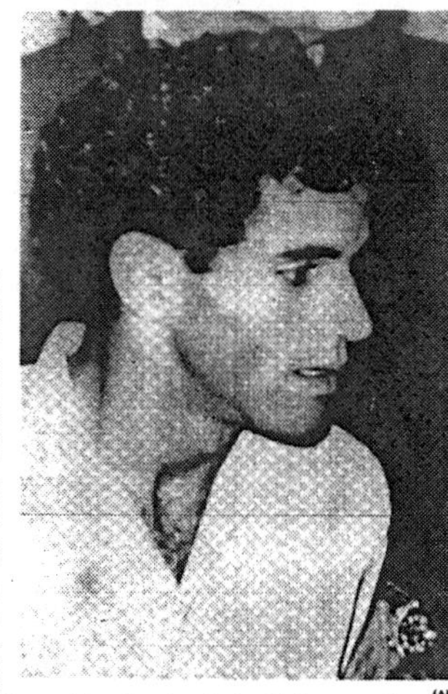

Suspect in shooting is hustled to arraignment. (AP)

Fears Grow As He Fails To Improve

Bullet Removed From His Brain

LOS ANGELES (AP) — Sen. Robert F. Kennedy showed no improvement and remained in extremely critical condition Wednesday night after surgeons removed from his brain most of

Related Stories, Photos On Pages 5, 8, 9, 18, 71

a bullet police said was fired by a mysterious young Jordanian.

"Senator Kennedy's condition is still described as extremely critical as to life," his press secretary, Frank Mankiewicz, told newsmen.

As newsmen kept vigil in Good Samaritan Hospital, Mankiewicz reported—12 hours after the delicate brain surgery on Kennedy — that "the team of physicians attending Sen. Robert Kennedy is concerned over his continuing failure to show improvement during the post operative period."

But the press aide, answering questions some 17 hours after Kennedy was cut down in a Los Angeles hotel, would not say Kennedy's condition is deteriorating.

"We felt it would be appropriate at this point," he said, "to stress that the critical condition related to survival during this period as well as to the period beyond."

Mankiewicz said although "there might have been some change," he thought Kennedy's life signs — pulse, breathing, blood pressure — were still good.

Earlier, Kennedy underwent a series of medical tests at Good Samaritan Hospital. Then, too, they showed no measurable improvement.

The man accused of the shooting was captured on the spot and identified hours later as Sirhan Bishara Sirhan, 24, a Jordanian native of Jerusalem, who has lived in nearby Pasadena, Calif., since boyhood.

A team of brain surgeons operated for 3 hours and 40 minutes, striving to save the life of the New York senator, brother of the assassinated President John F. Kennedy. Robert was gunned down at the moment of his greatest victory in the California primary as he campaigned for the White House.

His wife, Ethel, kept vigil in a hospital room near that in which her wounded 42-year-old husband was under intensive care at Good Samaritan Hospital.

The accused assailant was hospitalized, too. Police said he was under maximum security in a hospital ward at Los Angeles County Central Jail.

Sirhan was treated for a broken index finger and a sprained left ankle, suffered in the shooting melee at the Ambassador Hotel early Wednesday.

Police said his identity was traced through the .22 caliber pistol the assailant turned on Kennedy moments after the senator had thanked cheering supporters for his victory in the presidential primary.

Continued on Page 8, Column 1

House Moves Crime Bill For Passage

WASHINGTON (AP) — As Sen. Robert F. Kennedy lay gravely wounded by shots from a pistol, Congress continued to move Wednesday toward final passage of partial new restrictions on the sale of handguns.

The step came as the House voted 317 to 60 against sending to a conference the Senate-passed Omnibus Crime Bill, which includes a ban on mail order sale of handguns.

The House thus indicated its readiness to approve the bill and send it to President Johnson. The final vote is scheduled Thursday.

Although the measure also prohibits over-the-counter sale of handguns by nonresidents of a state, it doesn't restrict sale of rifles and shotguns as proposed by Johnson.

Chief sponsor of the stronger version was Kennedy's brother, Sen. Edward M. Kennedy, D-Mass.

And Robert Kennedy himself long had urged tougher restrictions. In a speech before the New York City Council last August, he said:

"If we act now, we can save hundreds of lives in this country and spare thousands of families all across this land the grief and heartbreak that may come from the loss of a husband, a son, a brother or a friend."

The Kennedys had suffered the loss of their other brother, President John F. Kennedy, who was slain with a mail order rifle in 1963.

The measure expected to be approved Thursday would not prohibit sale of rifles or shotguns through the mails, as proposed by Johnson and supported by Edward Kennedy and others.

At the White House, press secretary George Christian was asked if Johnson might now seek congressional approval of a stronger gun control bill.

"Let's just wait for developments on that," he said.

Angry Johnson Calls For End of Violence

(C) N. Y. Times News Service

WASHINGTON — For the second time in five years, Lyndon B. Johnson Wednesday undertook, in the midst of national shock and outrage, to offer prayer, comfort and assistance to his political rivals in the Kennedy family and then to try to heal the country's political and psychological wounds.

The President's first reaction to the shooting of Sen. Robert F. Kennedy Wednesday morning was that "there are no words equal to the horror of this tragedy."

But Wednesday night, in an emotional and at times even angry statement on television, the President pleaded with all Americans to end the violence in their midst once and for all, to tolerate neither hatred nor the preaching of violence and "for God's sake" to resolve to live under the law.

Johnson said he was appointing a commission of distinguished citizens to investigate both the circumstances and the causes of physical violence of all kinds in the United States in the hope that the nation would learn "how we can stop it" and profit even from its misfortunes.

To the commission, Johnson named Milton Eisenhower, the former president of Johns Hopkins University and the brother of former President Dwight D. Eisenhower; Archbishop Terrence Cooke of New York; Albert Jenner, Chicago attorney who worked for the commission that investigated the assassination of President Kennedy; former Ambassador Patricia Harris; Eric Hoffer, the longshoreman turned philosopher; Sens. Philip Hart, D-Mich., and Roman L. Hruska, R-Neb., Reps. Hale Boggs, D-La., the deputy majority leader in the House, and William M. McCulloch, R-Ohio, and Judge Leon Higginbotham.

The President described himself as shocked and dismayed and deeply disturbed as he knew all Americans were by this tragedy, which he described as the "latest spectacular example" of lawlessness and violence.

The President said he prayed to God that Kennedy's life would be spared and that he would be restored to full health and vigor both for his own sake and for the nation's and in the memory of his slain brother, and for the sake of the family which Johnson said had suffered "sorrow enough."

The entire nation was not to blame, Johnson said, because 200 million Americans did not strike down Robert Kennedy any more than they did John F. Kennedy or the Rev. Dr. Martin Luther King Jr.

Yet the President said it was "wrong to ignore" the connection between such crimes and the general climate of lawlessness, hatred and unreason in the country of which the nation has now had "ample warning." A nation that tolerates violence in any form, Johnson said, cannot expect to confine it to relatively minor incidents.

There was "never any justi-

Continued on Page 8, Column 5

Kennedy a Victim Of Modern World

By JAMES RESTON

(C) N. Y. Times News Service

NEW YORK — Robert Kennedy is only the latest victim of a modern world that has turned loose greater forces than it can control. The struggles between the nations, between the races, between the rich and the poor, between the individual and bewildering change have produced a plague of lawlessness and violence that is now sweeping the globe.

The pressures of all this are too much for weak and demented minds. The assassins of President John F. Kennedy, Rev. Martin Luther King Jr., and Lee Harvey Oswald, and the attacker of Senator Kennedy may merely be deranged demons, tormented by frustrations and intoxicated by fear or revenge. But there is something more to it than that.

This is not merely rejection of the view that life is essentially decent, rational and peaceful, or even a decline into individual moral insanity. There is something in the air of the modern world: a defiance of authority, a contagious irresponsibility, a kind of moral delinquency, no longer restrained by religious or ethical faith. And these things are now threatening not only personal serenity but public order in many parts of the world.

Evidence Abounds

Evidence of the use of force to achieve personal, group or national ends is all around us: in the war in Vietnam, in the Arab-Israeli war of last year, in the student revolts in the United States, France and Italy, in the massacres in Indonesia and in the political and racial assassinations of the last few years.

Rejection of traditional rules of personal and institutional conduct is now common, but this is not unprecedented and spectacular generalizations about this age are not very helpful. "At what point shall we expect the approach of danger?" Abraham Lincoln asked in 1837. "I answer, if it ever reach us, it must spring up amongst us.

"I hope I am not over wary; but if I am not, there is, even now, something of ill-omen amongst us. I mean the increasing disregard for law which pervades the country; the growing disposition to substitute the wild and furious passions . . . This disposition is awfully fearful in any community; and that it now exists in ours, though grating to our feelings to admit, it would be a viola-

Continued on Page 8, Column 3

Riot Fears Bring Alert Of Military

(C) N. Y. Times News Service

WASHINGTON — Several thousand Army and Marine Corps troops across the United States were placed on shortened alert early Wednesday morning in the event the shooting of Sen. Robert F. Kennedy should result in rioting that could not be handled by local and state authorities.

Precautionary moves throughout the military establishment were being taken lest the shooting of Senator Kennedy be followed by riots such as occurred after the assassination of Rev. Martin Luther King in April.

"We don't really expect trouble, but we want to be ready," commented a Pentagon official.

In Politics: Uncertainty

By TOM WICKER

(C) N. Y. Times News Service

WASHINGTON — The shooting of Sen. Robert F. Kennedy left the 1968 presidential campaign in a state of uncertainty Wednesday, with nothing certain but that it had been transformed.

The vital political question was the same as the source of the personal suspense at Good Samaritan Hospital in Los Angeles. Could Kennedy recover without permanent damage from so extensive an injury to the brain as he apparently suffered?

In the absence of any conclusive evidence on that point, all the presidential candidates immediately suspended political activity. Their motive was personal respect for Kennedy and his family; yet, their action reflected the fact that none could be sure how to proceed anyway.

Even if Kennedy were to make a complete recovery, for instance, there appeared to be great doubt Wednesday that it could be rapid enough for him to return to the 1968 campaign.

If he did recover so quickly, on the other hand, his whole personal and poltical situation would be something entirely different from what it was before the attempt on his life.

Third Shock Wave

Thus, for the third — and most harrowing —time, a shock wave of unexpected events has completely altered the shape of the 1968 campaign.

The first came on March 12 when Sen. Eugene McCarthy of Minnesota won 42 per cent of the Democratic vote in the New Hampshire primary, and Kennedy immediately thereafter became an active candidate.

The second transformation occurred on March 21, when President Johnson said he would neither seek nor accept renomination by the Democratic party. That led to the entry of Vice President Hubert H. Humphrey and his rapid progression to the front - runner's place among Democrats.

The mostly likely result of the critical wounding of Kennedy, as it appeared Wednesday, was that Humphrey's most formidable opponent for the nomination would be removed from the campaign.

This would leave only McCar-

Continued on Page 8, Column 3

Doubt Cast On Kennedy Recovery

By RALPH DIGHTON

LOS ANGELES (AP) — A grim possibility that Sen. Robert F. Kennedy might face an indefinite life of limited usefulness if he survives an assassin's bullet emerged Wednesday after first reports on the extent of brain damage.

Dr. John D. French, director of the Brain Research Institute at the University of California at Los Angeles, said in an interview that reports of injury to the central part of the brain raised grave doubts about Kennedy's recovery.

In New York, Dr. Lawrence Pool, Columbia Presbyterian Medical Center neurosurgeon, said Dr. Henry Cuneo, one of the men who operated on Kennedy, had authorized him to give this version of the injury:

"There was evidently serious damage to the cerebellum, the part of the brain on the extreme back of the head, on the right side; also to part of the right cerebral hemisphere, and also to the mid-brain, which is the main cable connecting the brain itself with all the rest of the body.

"This mid-brain deals with not only the function of motion in the arms and legs and sensation to the body but also with eye movements and even the life function itself, such as blood pressure, breathing, heart rate.

"So it's a very critical area, and this was injured, and this is why I fear—as Dr. Cuneo indicated—the outcome may be extremely tragic."

Dr. Pool said he was greatly fearful of the outcome, both in terms of Kennedy surviving and being in normal condition if he does survive.

Dr. French, also a neurosurgeon, said "if the central core, or brain stem, is damaged severely the outlook may be worse than if almost any other part of the brain were injured.

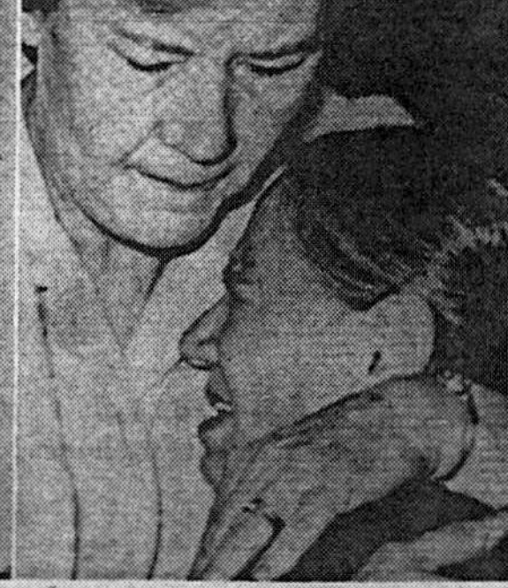

TWO SORROWING MOTHERS — Mrs. Rose Kennedy, lonely figure in St. Xavier Church, Hyannis, Mass. prays for her son Robert. Mrs. Mary Sirhan collapses in arms of friend at nursing home in Pasadena where she works, after hearing of son's arrest as suspect in senator's shooting. (AP)

Inside The Call

Entered 2nd Class Matter
Post Office, Allentown, Pa. 18105

Weather Showers Likely

SUNDAY CALL-CHRONICLE

25¢

NO. 2471 | Telephone 433-4241 | ALLENTOWN, PA., SUNDAY, JULY 20, 1969 | Entered 2nd Class Matter Post Office, Allentown, Pa. 18105 | SECTION A

Spacemen Check Out Moon Taxi

Aldrin (left) and Armstrong gather rocks in moon activity simulation. (AP)

Stage Is All Set For Lunar Walk

SPACE CENTER, Houston (AP) — The Apollo 11 astronauts tested their moon landing craft in lunar orbit Saturday and found it ready for a rendezvous with history Sunday.

Air Force Col. Edwin E. Aldrin Jr. crawled into the lunar module, nicknamed Eagle, and turned on all its systems for the first time since it was launched from Cape Kennedy four days and 250,000 miles ago.

"Everything looks super," ground control radioed afterward. "We're ready to go."

While commander Neil A. Armstrong and Air Force Lt. Col. Michael Collins waited in the command module, Aldrin checked his dozen of gauges and controls in the moon taxi.

Nothing was overlooked, for the landing module must work to perfection if Aldrin and Armstrong are to land on the moon and return safely to earth.

The test took more than two hours.

When it was over, Aldrin crawled back into the command module, the tunnel to the lunar machine was closed and the crew began getting ready for an eight-hour rest.

The crew's rest period — the shortest on their schedule since launch — was delayed for about

Related News, Photos
Pages A-2, A-3, A-4, A-6, B-1

half an hour when mission control reported difficulty in locking on the Apollo 11 radio signals.

Mission control sent signals to the craft to align its antennae automatically and asked the crew to monitor the procedure.

Apollo 11 rocketed into moon orbit at 1:22 p.m. EDT Saturday and almost immediately passed tantilizingly close to the spot where Armstrong and Aldrin will land Sunday.

The spacemen beamed the moon into the living rooms of the world via television during the second orbit and then conducted the moon machine tests during the next two orbits.

Collins conducted landmark tracking while Aldrin was checking the communications equipment that will carry the word and pictures to earth of man's first step on the moon.

That historic exploration is to

Continued on Page A-10, Col. 1

Five Seconds For Decision Of a Lifetime

SPACE CENTER, Houston (AP) — It is one more Sunday afternoon. You are one human being. Your name: Neil Armstrong.

Then at this one moment in all of man's existence, one number— 99—flashes on the instrument panel of one spacecraft. It is a code asking you a question.

Now, you must make one decision. Push one button, marked "PRO", meaning "proceed," and you commit yourself, your life, your nation's flag to the audacious attempt to land upon and walk the face of the moon.

5 Seconds to Decide

You have five seconds to decide.

Don't push the button, and you remain safe, relatively safe anyhow in lunar orbit, fairly well assured of making a safe return home.

The day is July 20, 1969. You are standing in the cramped cockpit of a moon ferry, the LM, which from the outside looks ridiculous, silly, even ugly.

Inside, standing on your right is Edwin Aldrin, occupation astronaut, age 39. Like you, he concentrates on the instrument panel which reflects the wizardry of computers, radar and the other fantastic mechanism brought together over a decade to function at this point in time.

For the next 12 minutes—if you decided to push the "PRO" button—Aldrin will be reading numbers and information from the instrument panel, while you, the pilot, make ever more critical decisions. . . .

99 . . . 99 . . . 99 . . . the panel light insists.

Flying Upside Down

You fly 50,000 feet above the surface of the moon, not quite 10 miles high. You are really flying face down, pointed feet first in space, travelling at 3,500 miles an hour. You are 245 miles from the pre-selected spot for a moon landing.

99 . . . 99 . . . 99 . . . the light insists.

If you don't push "PRO" you will hurtle past the moon, curve around it, and be able after two such orbits to rejoin the command ship piloted by Michael Collins. You know that your fragile moon ferry can't take you home. You know that if you do land, it must later rocket you up to rejoin the waiting Collins.

Five seconds now to make up your mind.

All instruments say everything looks okay. You hit the "PRO" button.

The computer, still working in p-63, program 63, begins putting on the brakes when the five seconds are up. The brakes are the descent rocket at the bottom of your spacecraft. Firing, it acts as a retro-rocket, to start taking you down.

Highlights Of Next Three Days

SPACE CENTER, Houston (AP) — Here are highlights of Apollo 11's fourth, fifth and sixth days in space, all times Eastern Daylight:

The day ahead (Sunday):

Astronauts Neil A. Armstrong, Edwin E. Aldrin Jr. and Michael Collins awake at 7:02 a.m. after a nine-hour rest period and eat breakfast.

Hatch separating lunar module (LM) landing craft and command ship is removed. Aldrin crawls into LM at 9:17 a.m. and switches on electrical power.

Armstrong follows at 10:16 a.m. He checks out LM communications and astronauts hook pressure suits into LM life support systems.

Landing Legs

LM landing legs deployed at 12:25 p.m.

Mission control gives go-no-go for undocking at 1 p.m., followed by a checkout of LM maneuvering jets.

Command ship piloted alone by Collins undocks with LM at

Continued on Page A-10, Col. 1

Sen. Kennedy Escapes Injury; Companion Killed in Crackup

MARY JO KOPECHNE

EDGARTOWN, Mass. (AP)— Sen. Edward M. Kennedy, D-Mass., escaped injury but a former secretary of his late brother, Robert, was killed when their car plunged into a tidal pond and sank about midnight Friday.

The accident went unreported for about eight hours. Police chief Domenic J. Arena said Saturday night that he will file a formal charge against the senator Monday charging him with leaving the scene of an accident. Kennedy would have 24 hours in which to answer the charge.

The incident occurred on Chappaquiddick Island at Martha's Vineyard, about 17 miles across the bay from the Kennedy compound in Hyannisport on Cape Cod.

It was the second time Kennedy was nearly killed. He suffered a broken back in a plane crash five years ago. All three of his older brothers met violent death.

Worked for Brother

Killed was Mary Jo Kopechne of Washington, a 29-year-old slim blonde who had worked as a secretary for Robert F. Kennedy, D-N.Y., and Sen. George Smathers, D-Fla. She was currently employed with Matt Reese & Associates, a Washington political consulting firm.

Kennedy was unharmed but

Related Photo Page A-10

said he was in a state of shock for several hours before reporting the accident to police about 9:30 a.m.

"I have no recollection of how I got out of the car," Kennedy said.

A medical examiner ruled Miss Kopechne drowned.

Kennedy said he dove several times attempting to rescue her from the car.

Police said her body was found in the back seat.

Kennedy told police he was driving back to Edgartown when he took a wrong turn on the unfamiliar road. He said his car went off the narrow, humpbacked bridge and plunged into the pond.

Police said the bridge, which has no railings, is used mainly by pedestrians and is in an isolated area.

Kennedy gave police this written statement regarding the accident:

"The car turned over and sank in the water and landed with the roof resting on the bottom. I attempted to open the door and window of the car but I have no recollection of how I got out of the car.

"I came to the surface and repeatedly dove down to see if the passenger was still in it. I was unsuccessful in the attempt.

In Shock

"I was exhausted and in a state of shock. I recall walking back to where my friends were eating. There was a car parked in front of the cottage and I climbed into the back seat. I then asked someone to bring me back to Edgartown.

"I remember walking around for a period of time and then going to my hotel room. When I fully realized what had happened this morning I immediately went to the police."

Medical Examiner Donald Mills quoted Dist. Atty. Edmund

Continued on Page A-10, Col. 7

Tragedies Haunt Kennedy Family

WASHINGTON (AP) — The involvement of Sen. Edward M. Kennedy, D-Mass., in an auto accident fatal to a former Kennedy secretary, is the latest in a series of tragedies for the Kennedy family.

The accident occurred early Saturday off Martha's Vineyard, an island in the Atlantic off the Massachusetts coast. Police said Kennedy was the driver of the car.

Police in Edgartown, Mass., identified the victim as Mary Jo Kopechne, about 29, a resident of Washington, D.C.

Police said she was a former secretary to the late Sen. Robert F. Kennedy.

Four of the nine children of Joseph P. and Rose Fitzgerald Kennedy have died violently.

Edward Kennedy suffered a broken back in a plane crash June 19, 1964.

Here is a listing of the tragedies that have befallen the Kennedy family.

Joseph P. Kennedy Jr.—born July 25, 1915, killed Aug. 12, 1944. A Navy pilot in World War II, he volunteered for a mission that involved parachuting from a bomber loaded with 10 tons of explosives before it hit a German V-2 rocket site. The bomber exploded prematurely from an unknown cause with him aboard.

John F. Kennedy—born May 29, 1917, assassinated by Lee Harvey Oswald in Dallas Nov. 22, 1963. The President and Mrs. Kennedy suffered the death of two children, a daughter stillborn and a son who died two days after birth from lung disease. In World War II, Kennedy a PT boat commander, suffered a severe back injury when his boat was rammed by a Japanese destroyer.

Rosemary Kennedy—born Sept. 13, 1919. In an institution

Continued on Page A-10, Col. 7

Luna 15 Is Still Circling the Moon

JODRELL BANK, England (AP) — Apollo 11 and Luna 15, American and Soviet ships in space, circled in lunar orbit Saturday as the Americans prepared to put the first man on the moon.

Luna 15, the unmanned probe with a purpose which the Russians have never revealed, was in its third day around the moon, after a slight midafternoon course change that lengthened its path just before the three Apollo astronauts went into moon orbit.

Officials at Jodrell Bank, the West's chief listening post on secretive Soviet space shots, and at Houston have scoffed at suggestions Luna 15 might interfere with the Americans.

Theory Advanced

In addition, American officials have said that there are only remote possibilities that the two vehicles could collide—much less come in sight of each other.

Luna's orbit change came during its 27th trip around the moon and Sir Bernard Lovell, director of Jodrell Bank Observatory, said his 250-foot-side electronic dish picked up Luna's signal again while it was halfway through its 28th orbit.

He said he could give no reason for the change and refused to speculate on what Luna 15 might do next.

"It could still do almost anything," he said.

Unofficial sources in Moscow had predicted all or part of Luna 15 would try a remote controlled moon landing to retrieve a soil sample—a task set for the Apollo astronauts during their moon walk.

Another theory was that Luna 15 was the first of a new series of Luna vehicles not meant to land until later and that it would be brought out of moon orbit back to earth—a feat Soviet space scientists have not yet performed.

Change Made

Lovell said he could not exclude the possibility that one new feature of Luna's performance, apparently continuous low-power radio transmissions behind the moon, indicated it might be communicating with a capsule already placed on the moon surface.

The length of the new orbit was given as 2 hours 3.5 minutes, an increase of three minutes. The maximum altitude was given as 137 miles and the minimum 59 miles. The previous orbiting time had been given as two hours and three seconds.

Networks List TV Moon Time

NEW YORK (AP) — Following is the television schedule of major networks for Apollo 11 coverage all times EDT:

Sunday: CBS and NBC, 11 a.m., beginning of 31 hours of continuous coverage. ABC, noon, beginning of 30 hours of continuous coverage.

Filipino Girl Is Named 'Miss Universe of 1969'

MISS UNIVERSE — Gloria Diaz, 18-year-old brunette from Parnaque, Rizal, Philippine Islands, is crowned Miss Universe of 1969 by outgoing titleholder Martha Vasconcellos of Brazil. The crowning topped the ceremonies at Miami Beach. (AP)

MIAMI BEACH, Fla. (UPI) — Pert Miss Philippines, Gloria Diaz, won the Miss Universe contest Saturday night, defeating 60 other girls for the global beauty title.

The 18-year-old blackhaired, blackeyed beauty, with vital measurements of 34½-23-34½, gasped as her victory was announced.

She said she had entered the beauty pageant to "make friends, meet people and foster better relationships with other countries."

First runnerup was Miss Finland, Harriett Eriksson. Second runnerup was Miss Australia, Joanne Bagrett, followed by Miss Israel, Hava Levy, and Miss Japan, Kkuyo Ohsuka.

A panel of 12 judges reviewed the girls on the edge of the runway. They included Broadway producer David Merrick, Belgian actress Monique Van Vooren, portrait photographer Yousuf Karsh, and a former Miss Universe, Norma Nolan of Argentina, who won the title in 1962.

In preliminary judging last Wednesday night 10 of the girls were chosen "best in swimsuit." Contest sponsors claimed that any of the other 51 entrants had as good a chance as the 10 bathing suit beauties to win, the beauty pageant.

Today's Index

Reading for Sunday

The civilized world is gripped by excitement and apprehension on the eve of the first man on the moon. For Lehigh Valley reaction see Page B-1.

And speaking of the moon, the idea of sending a man there isn't exactly new. In fact, an article published 79 years ago discusses the possibility. Page B-14.

Read the amazing story of how Allentown's GAC Corp. has grown from a second floor office to a $1.5 billion diversified business on Page D-1.

But all the news isn't good. As of last night it appears that the end of this week will mark the final curtain-falling of the struggling Allentown Summer Theater. Page B-1.

In one way or another the war in Vietnam has reached into almost every home. In the Lehigh Valley alone there have been more than 100 servicemen killed in the conflict. Page B-1.

The Weather
Partial clearing this afternoon. Fair tomorrow.

THE MORNING CALL

Lehigh Valley's Greatest Newspaper

NO. 25,914 ★ ALLENTOWN, PA., TUESDAY, MAY 5, 1970 10c a Copy 48c HOME DELIVERED Monday through Saturday

Dayan Offers 'Unlimited' Cease-Fire

Vows to Fight Any Aggressor

HAIFA, Israel (AP) — Defense Minister Moshe Dayan offered Egypt "an unconditional and unlimited cease-fire" Monday night.

"The government is ready to re-establish an unconditional and unlimited cease-fire, even if this will enable Egypt to reorganize and put up SAM-3 missile sites," he told a student rally.

"We are willing to accept this because we sincerely want a cease-fire, because it would end the war and open the corridor to some kind of an arrangement," he said.

At the same time, he vowed that if there was any attempt to push Israel from the Suez Canal cease-fire line by force, the country was "ready to fight physically to hold the lines even against Soviet aid."

But Dayan cautioned against getting into any fight in the air or on land with Soviet forces present in Egypt.

He also said he wished the United States would come out as "a real tiger, with biting teeth," in confronting the Soviets in the Middle East.

Dayan's call for a cease-fire, which came in reply to a question, was a surprise to observers in Israel.

The government has stated frequently that such a cease-fire would be useless because Egypt would only exploit it to rebuild its fortifications.

Israel claims the Egyptians are continually initiating fighting on the canal. It says this is a sign that Egypt does not want a cease-fire.

TRAGEDY ON CAMPUS — Kent State University students halt their massive demonstrating to stare at the body of a fellow student, who was fatally shot in the head. Helplessly kneeling at the youth's side is one of the Ohio university's coeds. (AP)

Pentagon Ends Bombings As Kosygin Raps New Raids On North, Cambodia Drive

By BOB HORTON

WASHINGTON (AP) — The Defense Department publicly called at least a temporary halt Monday to a series of recent heavy air attacks it said were directed against North Vietnamese missile and antiaircraft batteries and associated supply complexes.

The Pentagon announcement terminating the attacks—coupled with a warning they might be resumed—appeared designed to allay fears that the United States was resuming a major and general bombing campaign against the North.

The move came almost as Soviet Premier Kosygin deplored, in an unusual Moscow press conference, the raids over North

Related Stories on Pages 2, 12

Vietnam as well as U.S. offensive operations in Cambodia.

"By launching the war in Cambodia and resuming large-scale barbarous bombings of populated localities in North Vietnam, President Nixon actually nullifies the decision of his predecessor, President Johnson, on the termination from November 1968, of all air bombings and other actions involving the use of force against North Vietnam," Kosygin said.

Kosygin, as well as North Vietnam and Red China suggested the U.S. actions might undermine the Paris peace talks.

The Pentagon said air missions against three North Vietnamese areas were authorized in Washington as protective reaction measures to safeguard unarmed American reconnaissance planes flying over North Vietnam.

"These reconnaissance missions are essential to the safety and security of our forces in South Vietnam," Daniel Z. Henkin, the Pentagon's chief spokesman said. "This fact was made clear to the North Vietnamese at the time the bombing was halted in 1968."

One of the missions struck North Vietnamese installations near Barthelemy Pass above the 19th parallel and may have been the northernmost raid since March 1968 when Lyndon Johnson first limited U.S. bombing of the North to the country's southern panhandle.

Other sites hit were near BanKarai Pass, below the 19th parallel and another area just north of the Demilitarized Zone.

Henkin reporting that from 50 to over 100 planes were launched for each mission, called the strikes successful and said these were "all that were planned."

"We have no plans now for additional re-enforced protective reaction strikes," Henkin said, "but I want to tell you again that we are, of course, prepared as necessary to continue to protect our unarmed reconnaissance pilots."

Pentagon figures showed that of 10 aircraft lost over the North since the full bombing halt was instituted in 1968, only two have gone down this year including one last weekend.

Henkin contended, however,

Continued on Page 2, Column 1

Includes 500 Buildings

U. S. Spy Plane Sights Major Jungle Hideaway

SAIGON (AP) — U.S. reconnaissance aircraft sighted a jungle hideout with about 500 buildings Monday about two miles inside Cambodia where allied forces are searching for the headquarters of the supreme Communist command.

Pilots reported some of the buildings are two stories high and have what seem to be radio antennae strung between them.

Brig. Gen. Robert M. Shoemaker, head of the allied task force of about 8,800 Americans and 2,000 South Vietnamese troops, declined to speculate whether the complex might be part of the well dispersed headquarters of the enemy's Central Office for South Vietnam.

But, he told a news briefing, "it's definitely no village."

High-placed officials disclosed earlier that U.S. field commanders are planning intrustions of yet untouched enemy base camps along a 350-mile section of Cambodia's border with South Vietnam. At least one operation was reported in the final planning stages.

Defense Secreatry Melvin R. Laird said in Washington Saturday that all North Vietnamese and Viet Cong sanctuaries along the full length of the border would be attacked by the allies.

There are at least a half dozen enemy base camp areas in Cambodia from the western Mekong Delta to the area north of Saigon which are outside the areas attacked last week by upwards of 30,000 allied troops.

The two massive allied drives, one into an area known as the Parrot's Beak and the other into an area called the Fishhook, have accounted for 1,952 North Vietnamese and Viet Cong killed, according to headquarters and field reports late Monday. Some 466 enemy suspects have been detained.

American casualties stood at 14 dead and 47 wounded. South Vietnamese losses were put at 151 killed and 596 wounded.

The major aim of the twin allied offensives in Cambodia is to root out and destroy enemy base camps, storage areas and supplies. At last report more than 2,400 weapons had been seized or destroyed.

While pressing the search for enemy supplies, American forces rolled deeper into Cambodia on Monday to cut off any escape route for the estimated 7,000 North Vietnamese and Viet Cong troops who were believed inside the Fishhook before President Nixon sent in American ground troops.

In Cambodia's own war with the Vietnamese Communist command, Viet Cong and North Vietnamese forces who took a key ferry crossing on the Mekong River moved to within 30 miles of the Cambodian capital, Phnom Penh, on Monday.

Shots Kill 4 Kent State Students As Guardsmen Respond to Sniping

KENT, Ohio (AP) — Four students were shot to death and 11 other persons wounded, four seriously in a confrontation Monday with Ohio National Guardsmen and police at Kent State University. A state official said the shooting started when a rooftop sniper opened fire on the guardsmen.

The university, with an enrollment of 19,000, was closed and the town sealed off by police and guardsmen.

Gov. James A. Rhodes called on the FBI for help in probing the disorders.

The gunfire broke out as guardsmen dispersed an anti-war rally on the campus.

Adj. Gen. S. T. Del Corso said guardsmen were forced to open fire on their attackers.

"Regrettably but unavoidably, several individuals were killed and a number of others were wounded," he said in a statement.

The shooting came after guardsmen moved in with tear gas to disperse a rock-throwing crowd of 400 to 500 students in the Commons area near the football practice field.

"A lot of people felt their lives were in danger," said Brig. Gen. Robert Canterbury, who was on the scene, "which in fact was the case and the military man always has the option to fire if he feels his life is in danger.

"He has the right to protect himself."

"The guard expended its entire supply of tear gas and, when it did, the mob started to move forward to encircle the guardsmen," Del Corso said. "At the same time, a sniper opened fire against the guardsmen from a nearby rooftop. All guardsmen were hit by rocks and bricks.

"Guardsmen facing almost certain injury and death were forced to open fire on the attackers.

University President Robert I. White asked all students, faculty

Related Story on Page 7

and staff members to go home "as quickly as possible."

Twelve persons, including two guardsmen, were hospitalized in Ravenna and Akron. One guardsman was described as suffering from shock.

The university said the four persons killed—two girls and two boys—were students.

The dead were identified as Jeffrey Miller, 20, Plainview, N.Y., Allison Krause, 19, Pittsburgh, Pa.; Sandy Lee Scheuer, 20, Youngstown, Ohio, and William Schneider, no hometown given.

In Churchill, a Pittsburgh suburb, Arthur Krause confirmed that his daughter, a freshman student at Kent, was killed.

"I just can't talk about it," Krause said. "We just heard from the hospital."

"I don't know where the first shot was from," said Canterbury. He said he was with guardsmen but heard no order to fire.

"They started pelting everyone with bullets," said Mary Hagan, a student who witnessed the shooting. She said some students fell and others remained standing. They shouted that the shots were blanks, she said.

Miss Hagan said she heard one guardsmen issue a cease-fire order which halted the firing.

Of the violence, Rhodes said: "Today is the saddest day I have known as governor. There are no words adequate to express my personal dismay."

Officials at Robinson Memorial Hospital in Ravenna said a student identified as Ronald McKenzie, 21, of Richboro, Pa., was in serious condition with gunshot wounds in the neck and jaw. Three other students, identified only as Joe Lewis, John Cleary and Dean Mohler, were listed in critical condition with unspecified injuries at St. Thomas Hospital in Akron.

Miss Hagan said that after the shooting she heard students calling to National Guardsmen for help but that the guardsmen refused.

Continuing Wave

Many Campuses Hit By Antiwar Unrest

By the Associated Press

A continuing wave of antiwar demonstrations, focusing on U.S. involvement in Cambodia, swept many of the nation's colleges.

More than 1,000 police and National Guardsmen were sent into the College Park, Md., area on an alert basis in connection with University of Maryland disorders. Although the troops reportedly had not moved onto the campus, hundreds of police used riot gas to break up a crowd of about 1,000 antiwar protesters.

The administration of the university agreed to a one-day moratorium of classes Tuesday to allow a discussion of "developing national and international events."

National Guardsmen were put

Related Story on Page 5

on alert because of trouble at Case Western Reserve University in Cleveland, where dissidents have occupied the ROTC building.

The presidents of 30 colleges and universities signed a telegram urging the President to bring a rapid end to American military involvement in Southeast Asia and seeking an immediate meeting with him.

The telegram, drafted and released by James M. Hester, president of New York University, said in part, "We implore you to consider the incalculable dangers of an unprecedented alienation of America's youth and to take immediate action to demonstrate unequivocally your determination to end the war quickly."

Hundreds of students at other colleges boycotted classes and plans were announced for student-faculty strikes Tuesday and Wednesday.

It was school as usual, however, on a number of campuses. A sampling showed all was reported quiet at Arizona State, New Mexico's six biggest colleges, and schools in Utah, Idaho and North and South Dakota, among others around the country.

President Nixon's decision to

Continued on Page 2, Column 5

ON THE FIRING LINE — A Kent State University student waves a black flag as Ohio National Guard members take a firing position. The guardsmen moved, however, before the fatal volleys. (AP)

Cambodia Briefing Wanted, But Senators Score Nixon

WASHINGTON (AP) — The Senate Foreign Relations Committee Monday reluctantly accepted President Nixon's invitation to a White House briefing on Cambodia. Then it accused him of waging "a constitutionally unauthorized, presidential war in Indochina."

While the committee accepted Nixon's bid to a Tuesday White House session with the House Foreign Affairs Committee, Chairman J. W. Fulbright, D-Ark., said the panel is sticking to its original request for a private talk with the chief executive to discuss the U.S. move into Cambodia.

Fulbright said the Tuesday meeting would be only a briefing—to be attended by 53 persons if the full membership of both committees shows up—and he is skeptical of its value. He said Nixon has not yet replied to the Senate group's request for a private meeting—a suggestion which led the chief executive to set up the combined committee session.

Resolution Fought

Amid the dispute over consultation at the White House, the committee issued a report urging repeal of the Gulf of Tonkin resolution, adopted Aug. 10, 1964.

This approved U.S. military measures in Southeast Asia after reported Communist attacks on U.S. warships. It became the main executive department reliance for an expanding military role in Vietnam.

But the committee report said its repeal would not resolve the issue of congressional and presidential authority.

"In the committee's view ... the war in Indochina has been conducted from its outset without constitutional authorization," the report said. "The Gulf of Tonkin resolution ... is not a valid authorization for that war, providing only a frayed facade of constitutional legitimacy.

"Its removal would serve, at least, to clear the air of a legacy of confusion and illegitimacy. It would remain then for Congress to determine how the constitutional vacuum should be filled.

"Until it does, or until peace is made, the executive will be conducting a constitutionally unauthorized war in Indochina.

"The commitment without the consent or knowledge of Congress of at least 8,000 American soldiers to fight in Cambodia ... evidences a conviction by the executive that it is at liberty to ignore the national commitments resolution, and to take over both the war and treaty powers of the Congress when congressional authority in these areas becomes inconvenient," the Foreign Relations Committee said.

White House press secretary Ronald L. Ziegler was asked at his afternoon news briefing whether the President is conducting a constitutionally unauthorized war. He replied he thinks the answer is that the conflict is in relation to enemy-occupied territory and was undertaken against forces jeopardizing the U.S. position.

"He has taken action under the authority he has as chief executive to protect U.S. forces," Ziegler added.

Robber Called, Owner Did Not

MILWAUKEE, Wis. (AP) — A bandit made careful arrangements for his getaway Monday before robbing a suburban Shorewood restaurant of $3,030.

Police said the man, disguised as a telephone company employe, was allowed to enter the cafe about 10 minutes after it closed.

He took apart all the telephones in the place while five employes cleaned up.

When the telephones were dismantled, the robber pulled a gun from his tool box and demanded the money.

Then he fled, and the store manager had to run half a mile to the nearest police station because the telephones were inoperable.

Stock Market Reels to Biggest Loss Since John F. Kennedy Assassination

By JACK LEFLER

NEW YORK (AP) — The stock market reeled Monday to its biggest loss in more than six years as Soviet Russia and Red China denounced the United States for sending combat troops into Cambodia.

The drop all but crushed hopes that the market might soon be able to pull out of its long slump, Wall Street analysts said.

The Dow Jones average of 30 industrials plummeted 19.07 points, or 2.59 per cent, to 714.56, closing at its lowest level of the session. This was its biggest drop since falling 21.16 points on Nov. 22, 1963, the day President Kennedy was assassinated. The close was at the lowest level since that same date.

"The market is confronted with the question of whether the U.S. action in Cambodia will have ramifications beyond the driving of North Vietnam troops out," said Monte Gordon, research director for the brokerage firm of Bache & Co. "It also begins to raise the question of

Related Story on Page 32

whether inflation can be halted."

"The new developments have blunted the ability of the market to rally," he added. "The immediate outlook is that the market will work lower."

The market tumbled sharply in advance of Soviet Premier Alexei Kosygin's late-morning news conference on Cambodia.

After the contents of Kosygin's statement became generally known, early apprehension waned and the market tried to rally, slicing an early 16-point loss by the Dow industrials to about 8.

The decline resumed after Red China called the U.S. move in Cambodia provocative.

The setback ranged widely, with 1,228 issues falling and 188 rising among the 1,594 traded on the New York Stock Exchange.

Volume accelerated in late trading, but the day's total was only a moderately active 11.4 million shares.

Glamour stocks took the worst beating, with losses including Fairchild Camera $12.75 to $40.50, Memorex $11.25 to $68.25, IBM $13.75 to $283, Burroughs $6.75 to $122.25, and Polaroid $9.25 to $67.75.

Inside The Call

Today's Index

Entered 2nd Class Matter, Post Office, Allentown, Pa. 18105

Vietnam War Memorial

An 8-Page Review Of the Tragic Conflict

In Special Section Between E and F

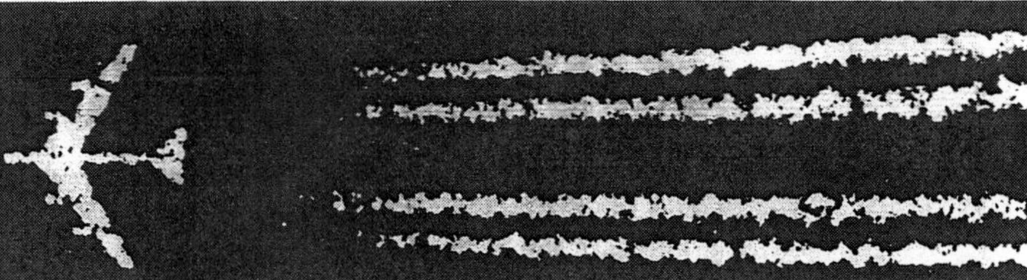

Weather Rain

SUNDAY CALL-CHRONICLE

25¢

NO. 2655 Telephone 433-4241 ALLENTOWN, PA., SUNDAY, JANUARY 28, 1973 Entered 2nd Class Matter Post Office, Allentown, Pa. 18105 SECTION A

War Officially Ends in Vietnam

Four warring delegations participate in signing ceremony of agreement to end war at Paris' Hotel Majestic. (AP)

Scattered Fighting Still Rages

SAIGON (AP) — Widespread fighting shattered the start of an official cease-fire in South Vietnam Sunday, with much of the fighting centered in the Saigon area.

Senior analysts said the fighting that extended beyond Sunday's 8 a.m. truce deadline was not a surprise. But they said they did not feel that Saigon's hold on the country was seriously threatened and it had not lost any significant territory.

Fears that the North Vietnamese would use tanks in last-minute attacks did not materialize.

The analysts said that it appeared the fighting would only die out gradually. This is because the South Vietnamese wanted to recapture territory lost in the past three days and the Communist side was trying to hold it.

Besides the Saigon area, fighting was reported in scattered parts of the central highlands and along central coast. Lt. Gen. Nguen Van Toan, commander of the 2nd military region, said about 15 incidents were reported after the 8 a.m. deadline.

In one of the incidents, two American helicopter crewmen were lightly wounded by ground fire near the An Khe pass on

Related News, Photos A-8, A-10

Highway 19. They were the first U.S. casualties reported after the cease-fire went into effect.

The U.S. Command said two American planes were shot down Saturday afternoon while supporting government marines in northeastern Quang Tri province, and listed four airmen as missing.

An American was killed in the last hours before the cease-fire, bringing to four the number of GIs killed since the agreement was announced last Wednesday. More than a score were wounded.

Fighting was reported continuing after the cease-fire hour in a corridor north of Saigon, as close as five miles to the downtown sector of the city.

Associated Press correspondent Mort Rosenblum reported from the field that major battle was under way beyond the 8 a.m. deadline along Highway 1 near the district town of

Continued on Page A-6, Col. 1

Bells Ring As Nation Ends War

By the Associated Press

Peace settled on the United States at 7 p.m. EST Saturday with the ringing of bells and the flying of flags as the nation turned to prayers, cheers, parades and silent contemplation to mark the end of the Vietnam War.

Church bells pealed and sirens sounded simultaneously across the country to usher in a 24-hour

Local Observance B-1

national day of prayer and thanksgiving as proclaimed by President Nixon.

The President, his wife, Pat, and daughter Julie attended special church services at the hour in Key Biscayne near the Florida White House.

Flame Ignited

Similar services were held in houses of worship throughout the nation as Americans bowed their heads in prayers of thanks at the 7 p.m. moment of cease fire. President Nixon had declared the time as a "national moment of prayer."

Continued on Page A-6, Col. 1

Cease-Fire Accords Are Signed At 2 Separate Paris Ceremonies

PARIS (AP) — The United States and North Vietnam formally called an end to their long undeclared war Saturday and their envoys drank a champagne toast to peace and friendship.

They were joined by the South Vietnamese and the Viet Cong in signing the documents that called for a cease-fire, the exchange of prisoners and a withdrawal of all U.S. forces from Vietnam.

The time for the cease-fire on Vietnam's battlefields was midnight Greenwich Mean Time — 7 p.m., EST. The exchange of prisoners and the withdrawal of U.S. troops is to take place within 60 days.

To get around the refusal of South Vietnam and the Viet Cong's provisional revolutionary government to recognize each other, Secretary of State William P. Rogers and North Vietnam's foreign minister, Nguyen Duy Trinh signed a separate set of documents later in the day.

The two ceremonies, the first lasting 18 minutes and the other 10 minutes, in the ornate gray-and-gold ballroom of the former Hotel Majestic, were followed by toasts with champagne provided by France, the host country.

Witnesses said all the envoys taking part clinked glasses, including Foreign Minister Tran Van Lam of South Vietnam and Mrs. Nguyen Thi Binh, the Viet Cong foreign minister.

All four ministers were silent during the signing ceremonies held under the floodlights of television cameras. But while Lam and the other South Vietnamese officials wore grim expressions throughout, Rogers and Hanoi's Trinh twice exchanged nods and a flicker of a smile.

Lam and Mrs. Binh attended only the first ceremony, which began and ended with a noisy "victory" celebration by several hundred Viet Cong and North Vietnamese sympathizers in front of the 700-room building near the Arc de Triomphe.

Lodges Protest

Lam later called on the French Foreign minister, Maurice Schumann, to lodge a formal protest that the demonstration was tolerated by French police. The demonstrators waved hundreds of Viet Cong and North Veitnamese flags and shouted slogans hostile to President Nguyen Van Thieu. South Vietnamese delegation sources said Schumann expressed his regrets.

As Rogers and Lam arrived for the ceremony, they were booed by the partisan crowd, while Trinh and Mrs. Binh were cheered. By the afternoon, police had broken up the demonstration and kept crowds several hundreds yards away.

Soon after the ceremonies, Rogers and Lam left Paris together for Washington. Rogers, who had been in Paris less than 24 hours, told newsmen, "It's a great day."

At Orly Airport, Rogers described the agreement as a "milestone" on the way to the generation of peace promised by President Nixon, and added: "I have every reason to expect that it will take hold and remain in effect."

The agreement bore immediate fruit in Paris, although the last-minute land-grab fighting continued in South Vietnam.

Commission Meets

Within an hour of the second signing ceremony, the Joint Military Commission held its first meeting in the same building. Some sources said the two sides exchanged the lists of their military prisoners of war.

Continued on Page A-6, Col. 1

Laird Says Draft Ended; Service Now Voluntary

WASHINGTON (AP) — Secretary of Defense Melvin R. Laird announced Saturday that "use of the draft has ended."

His action, placing the nation's armed forces on an all-volunteer footing for the first time in nearly 25 years, came five months ahead of President Nixon's goal.

In a message to senior defense officials, Laird said:

"With the signing of the peace agreement in Paris today, and after receiving a report from the secretary of the Army that he foresees no need for further inductions, I wish to inform you that the armed forces henceforth will depend exclusively on volunteer soldiers, sailors, airmen and Marines."

Laird's decision cancels plans to draft about 5,000 men before next June 30, when legal authority to induct young men into the armed forces will expire.

Pentagon manpower officials said that the flow of volunteers, spurred by a series of military pay raises and improved-fringe benefits, has encouraged them to believe these 5,000 men can be raised by recruiting.

Laird also issued a strong appeal for congressional approval of new bonuses and other legislation designed to make military service more attractive, partic-

Local Story B-1

ularly to National Guardsmen and reservists.

The Nixon administration has set a policy that, in any future war emergency, the roughly one-million National Guardsmen and reservists will be called before the country turns to the draft for the necessary military manpower.

Defense officials said there still is a possibility that a few doctors might be drafted. The Pentagon is pressing for passage of a bill that would give doctors extra pay, in hopes of attracting more medical professionals to a military career.

The special doctor draft has not been used since 1971, when the Pentagon asked for 1,600 physicians and osteopaths.

There are skeptics in the military services, and among some civilians, that the Pentagon can maintain an adequate military force entirely with volunteers, in the absence of the draft at least as a prod for recruitment.

Although the authority to draft young men into the military services will die June 30, the Selective Service law will remain on the books so that the standby machinery can be revived, if necessary. But to use that machinery, a president would have to go back to Congress and ask for restoration of the induction authority.

Young men will still be required to register for the draft at age 18.

Today's Index

Reds Issue POW Lists; First Group From Virginia

WASHINGTON (UPI) — The Defense Department notified the first family at 5:30 p.m. EST Saturday of the good news that a relative was alive in a prison camp in Indochina, and three hours later it made public the first names of known living POWs.

Military officers, in crisp Class A uniforms, visited the families personally to tell them that the name of their son, father or husband appeared on the list of living POWs given by the North Vietnamese and the Viet Cong to the United States Saturday morning in Paris.

The moving assignment went to casualty assistance officers at Air Force, Army, Marine Corps and Navy bases scattered across the land.

Navy Officers Included

Five in the first group were Navy officers with next of kin from Virginia Beach, Va., which is in an area with several large naval facilities.

The wife of Lt. Cmdr. Michael D. Christian in Virginia Beach "let out a big gush" of happy tears when an officer told her,

Story on Emmaus Air Force pilot B-1.

"Charlotte, it's official, his name is on the list."

Christian, a bombardier-navigator shot down April 24, 1967, had been listed among the missing in action.

Mrs. Jane Denton, also of Virginia Beach, confirmed that her husband, Navy Cmdr. Jeremiah A. Denton Jr., was on the list of living. She said simply she was "very happy."

Others on the first list and said to come from the Virginia Beach area were Capt. Allen C. Brady, Cmdr. Kenneth L. Coskey, and Lt. Cmdr. William M. Tschundy.

Pentagon officials said North Vietnam and the Viet Cong handed over "several lists" of prisoners in Paris, roughly six hours after signing of the Vietnam cease-fire agreement early Saturday.

The first word that the lists had been given to U.S. diplomats was flashed to the Pentagon at 2:13 p.m. EST in a telephone call from U.S. Air Force Brig. Gen. Russell Ogan, deputy director of the "Project Homecoming" prisoner return program, over a direct line from Paris.

Continued on Page A-6, Col. 8

AUGUST 9, 1974

President resigns, effective at noon, urging nation to rally behind Ford

Resignation coverage

WASHINGTON (AP) — President Nixon resigned Thursday night, saying he did so to heal the wounds of Watergate and to give America "a full-time President" in Gerald R. Ford.

He urged Americans to rally behind Ford, who will assume the powers of the presidency at noon Friday, the effective hour of Nixon's resignation.

Nixon said he would have preferred to fight the virtually certain impeachment that awaited him in Congress "no matter the personal agony that would have been involved."

But he said the interests of the nation demanded that he step down, to end the diversions of scandal that preoccupied the White House, and the impeachment process that kept Congress from other duties.

"America needs a full-time president and a full-time Congress, particularly at this time with the problems we face at home and abroad," Nixon said in a nationally televised and broadcast address.

Ford watched on television at his suburban Alexandria, Va., home, then stepped outside and pledged his best efforts for "what's good for America and what's good for the world."

He announced Henry A. Kissinger would remain as secretary of state and

Editorial on Page 14

said together they would work "in the pursuit of peace as we have achieved in the past."

Nixon said he hoped world peace would be a lasting monument to his 5½ years in the White House.

Ford said Nixon "made one of the great personal sacrifices for the country and one of the finest personal decisions on behalf of all of us as Americans."

America has many problems, Ford added, but "they can be resolved and will be resolved by the cooperation of the Congress, with the President and those that work with him."

Nixon noted that Watergate was implicit in much of what he said, but he acknowledged no misdeeds, saying only that some of his judgments had been wrong — and that he made them "in what I believed at the time to be in the best interests of the nation."

Nor did he present in his farewell address any defense against the charges he faced in Congress.

In fact, Nixon made no specific reference to the three articles of impeachment sent to the House of Representatives 10 days ago by the Judiciary Committee.

They charged Nixon with obstructing justice in the Watergate coverup, abusing the powers of his office and refusing to obey congressional demands for impeachment evidence.

Nixon said that throughout the Watergate scandals, he had felt it his duty to

See Page 3, Column 4

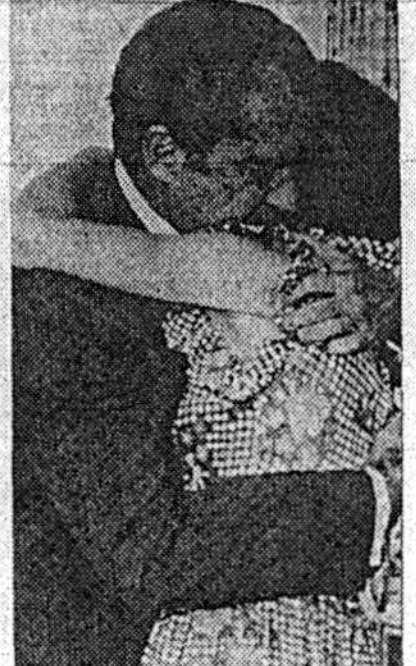

A tender moment

President Nixon embraces his daughter, Mrs. Julie Eisenhower after informing his family of his decision to resign.

THE MORNING CALL

Lehigh Valley's Greatest Newspaper

NO. 27,227 ★ ★ ALLENTOWN, PA., FRIDAY, AUGUST 9, 1974 15c 72c Home Delivered Mon. Through Sat.

Ford seen keeping current Cabinet intact

Associated Press Wirephoto

The nation's 37th President

WASHINGTON (AP) — As president, Gerald R. Ford will leave the current Cabinet intact and ask most top White House aides to stay on at least for the next few months, close associates of Ford said Thursday.

Although at least a dozen names are under consideration for vice president, a final choice is unlikely to be made for several days, the associates said.

One longtime friend of Ford's said the emphasis over the next few days would be placed completely upon a smooth transition of power within the White House.

"Jerry is by no means out to have any heads rolling," he said.

After a meeting with Secretary of State Henry A. Kissinger on Thursday afternoon, Ford warmly endorsed both Kissinger and the way U.S. foreign policy has been conducted by the secretary of state. Kissinger is expected to stay on.

Among potential vice presidents on a list drawn up by Ford's staff are former Atty. Gen. Elliot P. Richardson; former Secretary of Defense Melvin R. Laird; former New York Gov. Nelson A. Rockefeller; Sens. Robert A. Taft of Ohio, Mark Hatfield of Oregon, Edward W. Brooke of Massachusetts, Robert Stafford of Vermont, Charles Percy of Illinois, Bill Brock of Tennessee, Gov. Ronald Reagan of California, former New York Sen. Charles Goodell, and Reps. Albert H. Quie of Minnesota and John B. Anderson of Illinois.

The Ford associate said only a few among those on the staff list are under serious consideration by Ford and he predicted extensive investigations would be made into the smaller list over the next few days.

"After all, whoever it is might easily become president," he said.

The source said although a number of persons close to Ford have strongly urged that Rockefeller be the choice, Ford is unlikely to select the veteran millionaire politician.

Meanwhile, other sources close to Ford said he emphasized to top aides Thursday that a "smooth and orderly transition" to a new administration will take place.

They said Ford planned to watch President Nixon's televised address, but was unlikely to have any comment Thursday night.

But on Friday, Ford plans a television speech of his own, Ford aides said.

A final draft is now being edited and Ford will say, "No one in the country could be sadder than I, but the country must go forward," the associate said.

See Page 3, Column 1

Associated Press Wirephoto

The nation's 38th President

The reaction: *Congressional leaders urge an era of reconciliation under Ford*

WASHINGTON (AP) — Congressional leaders of both parties said Thursday night they hope President Nixon's resignation will lead the nation out of the agony of Watergate and into an era of national reconciliation under the presidency of Gerald R. Ford.

They universally praised Ford and pledged wholehearted support as he begins his new administration.

Many Republicans and some Democrats said Republican election chances have greatly improved in this fall's House and Senate races.

And some said the change of presidential leadership could lead to a GOP triumph — with Ford as the candidate — in the 1976 elections.

Senate Republican Leader Hugh Scott of Pennsylvania said Watergate had put the country on the "verge of a nervous breakdown" but that the way is now open to a "healing and mending" process under Ford's leadership.

"I have the greatest sympathy for the President and his family but no sympathy at all for the dreadful conduct of those associates who helped to bring him to this pass," Scott said.

Assistant Senate Democratic Leader Robert C. Byrd of West Virginia said Nixon's speech left many unanswered questions and "they may always be unanswered.

"You have a new man going in und I think the natural reaction of the people in both parties is going to be to join and support him in his efforts to unify the country," Byrd said. "I should think it would have a good impact on Republicans all over the country."

Assistant Senate Republican Leader Robert Griffin of Michigan, who called for Nixon to resign early in the week, called Nixon's decision both agonizing and courageous.

"If we unite now, behind our new President, giving him our help and our prayers, the republic will emerge from this wrenching experience, stronger than

The night of Watergate is over: the Constitution is safe, and America can become whole again," said Sen. Edward M. Kennedy, D-Mass.

House Speaker Carl Albert, who met

with Nixon just before his speech, quoted him as saying that "he couldn't be President and worry about Watergate too."

Here is further congressional and party comment on the change in leadership:

—George Bush, chairman of the Republican National Committee: "Now is the time for kindness ... Let us all try to restore to our society a climate of civility ... The battle is over."

—Democratic National Committee chairman Robert Strauss: "Democrats can take pride in the manner in which we have served the nation. We have been responsible and fair.... We Democrats hope to join with our new president in seeking common solutions to our nation's critical problems."

—Sen. Walter F. Mondale, D-Minn.: "The Congress has nothing to do with amnesty ... I think it just undermines and erodes the American respect and affection for the laws."

—John Gardner, chairman of Common Cause: "We don't want to sew up a wound with the infection still inside of it."

—Sen. Marlow Cook, R-Ky.: "It now becomes our primary duty and responsibility to the American people to unite in their support of Gerald Ford during this difficult period of transition. This must be a time when partisan interests are sacrificed."

—Sen. Charles H. Percy, R-Ill.: "It is important to remember that the Nixon presidency was brought down finally by the President's own words and actions."

Sen. Robert Dole, R-Kan., who was Republican national chairman during the 1972 elections, said he believes Ford's assumption of the presidency "will help us cast off this pall of the last few months" although a few people will remain forever bitter. He cited the late-night telephone calls this week from Kansas constituents who threatened to work against his reelection if Nixon resigns.

But if the Ford administration succeeds, Dole said, "I think a reservoir of good will be created and suddenly the Republican party becomes a force to reckon with again."

"There is a sadness over the [illegible] House

that such a thing happened in America," said House Democratic Leader Thomas P. O'Neill Jr. "Everybody is glad in a way that the climax is passed, but everybody is also sad."

House leaders went on record as saying impeachment proceedings against the President should be halted, unless Nixon announced he had done nothing wrong and was being hounded unjustly from office.

Many leaders of both House and Senate said that if the President chooses that path, impeachment should be voted and a Senate trial should commence as quickly as possible. But Albert said resignation is enough and that he favors stopping impeachment in any event.

Albert said any claim by Nixon to be entirely innocent of Watergate involvement or guilt would be partially answered by the final report of the House Judiciary Committee.

Sen. Edward Brooke, R-Mass., who last November called for Nixon to resign, said Ford has an opportunity to help solve the nation's problems and to lead the Republican party to thunderous success.

Inside

Weather

Cloudy, chance of rain. For details, see .... Page 5

Second Class Postage Paid at Allentown, Pa. 18105

MARCH 29, 1979

THE MORNING CALL

LEHIGH VALLEY'S GREATEST NEWSPAPER

ALLENTOWN, PA. 18105
THURSDAY, MARCH 29, 1979

NO. 28,528 ★

15¢

Index

Weather

Cloudy, breezy and milder today and tomorrow. For details, see........ Page D1

Associated Press

►Increases in radiation levels measurable 16 miles from site.
►No injuries reported; no evacuation planned.

Nuclear plant accident unleashes radioactivity

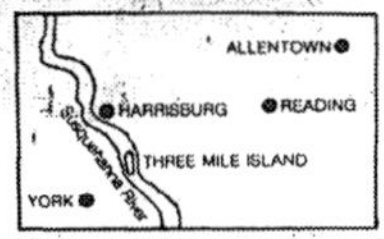

By BEN LIVINGOOD
Harrisburg Bureau Chief

HARRISBURG — An accident at Metropolitan Edison Co.'s Three Mile Island nuclear generating facility yesterday released radioactive elements into the atmosphere and sent radiation levels near the plant soaring high above normal levels.

There were no reported injuries as a result of the incident that forced the shutdown of the billion-dollar generating plant.

State officials, guided almost exclusively by information supplied by Met-Ed officials, said the amount of radiation released to the atmosphere was well below danger levels and no evacuation of the area was warranted.

Small increases in normal radiation levels were measurable as far as 16 miles from the site, officials said last night. A "serious" contamination problem remained at the plant site, officials said.

Radiation experts for the Department of Environmental Resources (DER), assisted by a team of investigators from the U.S. Department of Energy (DOE), continued to monitor the atmosphere in the area last night. State Civil Defense officials said they were standing by to activate evacuation procedures should the need arise.

The federal Nuclear Regulatory Commission (NRC) dispatched a team from its regional office at King of Prussia to conduct an investigation of the incident.

Two NRC probers at the scene reported late last night that while there remained "a serious contamination problem" at the plant site, radiation levels beyond the site were safe and falling.

They said some radioactive material was being released into the atmosphere, but that filters were helping to keep levels down.

They said most of the radioactivity remained on-site and that continuing air sampling analysis showed "no excessive radiation levels beyond the plant."

The matter first came to the attention of state officials when a plant supervisor notified Civil Defense authorities at 7 a.m. that "we have an emergency."

After conferring with DER and Met-Ed officials regarding the situation, Lt. Gov. William W. Scranton III, chairman of the Governor's Energy Council told a 10:45 a.m. press briefing

"Everything is under control. There is and was no danger to public health and safety. The incident occurred due to a malfunction in the turbine system. There was a small release of radiation to the environment. All safety equipment functioned properly."

But, by late afternoon, Scranton had altered his earlier assessment of the situation.

"This situation is more complex than the company first led us to believe," he told reporters at a 4:30 p.m. briefing. "Metropolitan Edison has given you and us conflicting information."

Please See NUCLEAR Page A15 ►

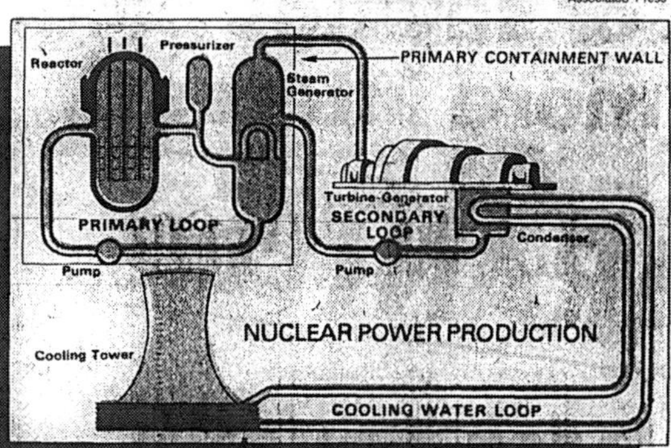

Diagram (above) shows steps of nuclear power generation operation while arrow in top photo pinpoints location of reactor where Met-Ed mishap occurred

How it happened

►Key questions, A3

By GARY SANBORN
Of The Morning Call

Yesterday's nuclear incident at Metropolitan Edison's Three Mile Island generating station began rather innocently in the plant's secondary system.

The secondary system, which includes the plant's steam generators, turbine generators and condensate piping, normally carries no radioactive contaminents.

Equipment malfunctions in the secondary system also are not usually the subject of great concern, because it is a system that comes in no direct contact with reactor coolant, the highly radioactive water that flows through the isolated primary system.

Here's how a secondary system problem led to a release of radioactive fission products to the central Pennsylvania countryside.

The sequence of events and their meaning was gathered in interviews with spokesmen for Met-Ed, the Nuclear Regulatory Commission (NRC) and industry experts.

At approximately 4 a.m., an air-operated valve in the plant's secondary feed water system closed, cutting off feed water to one of the plant's main feed pumps.

The feed pumps supply water to the plant's steam generators (sometimes called boilers), where the water is converted to steam by heat produced in the reactor core.

That steam is used to power the plant's turbine generators, which, in turn, produce electricity.

When feed water pressure was lost to one of the main feed pumps in yesterday's incident, the pump was automatically shut down, followed by the shutdown of the second feed pump.

The loss of the feed pumps, and the resultant loss of water to the steam generators, caused the automatic shutdown of the plant's turbine generators.

That caused an automatic reduction in the power level of the plant's nuclear reactor, operating at full power, to about 15 percent of full power.

However, the rapid heat transfer that had been occurring between the plant's primary and secondary systems, ceased, causing pressures and temperatures in the primary system to rise.

At some point, the plant's pressure forced an automatic full shutdown, but not before the pressure in the primary system was relieved through a pressure relief valve.

Highly radioactive primary coolant in the form of steam escaped into the reactor compartment, sealed off from the rest of the system by thick walls.

The coolant filled a drain tank in the reactor compartment, rupturing a disc designed to release excessive amounts of coolant to a second drain tank in the reactor building, outside the primary containment wall but still with very little danger of release to the atmosphere.

That tank also overflowed, sending radioactive coolant into a sump in the

Please See HOW Page A26 ►

U.S. embassy bomb death

►Brezhnev's illness raises speculation. A19.

MOSCOW (AP) — A young Soviet seaman — who said he "hated Brezhnev" and wanted to go to America, — holed up in the U.S. Embassy for eight hours yesterday, then killed himself by exploding a bomb strapped to his waist when Russian security men tried to force him out.

U.S. Ambassador Malcolm Toon, who gave the Russians permission for the operation, said the man was taken away in an ambulance and a spokesman at Moscow's Sklifosvsky Emergency Clinic said he was dead on arrival.

The 27-year-old seaman, who walked into the embassy at 2:30 p.m. (6:30 a.m. EST) and was interviewed by consular officials before disclosing that he had a bomb, described himself as a dissident who grew up in an orphanage and "hated Brezhnev," referring to Soviet President Leonid I. Brezhnev.

Toon said there was no breach of security and, "since he appeared in our view to represent a threat to the safety of American personnel and property, and since he was a Soviet citizen, we called upon the Soviet authorities for help." The ambassador said he believed it was unprecedented for American officials to give Soviets free rein to carry out an operation of this kind in the U.S. Embassy.

Toon said the Soviet officals entered the drama at 4:30 p.m. For approximately six hours a Soviet official tried to talk the man into surrender. Then four tear gas rounds were fired. A short time later there were two popping sounds Toon said might have been pistol shots. The explosion immediately followed.

The man reportedly detonated the small gray metal box attached to his body. It was a black powder device, Toon said, and burned nearly all the man's clothes off.

The drama began at 2:30 p.m. when the young Russian "was interviewed, as are most Soviet citizens applying for consular services, by one of our consular officers," Toon said. "It appeared very soon after the beginning of the interview that he was unbalanced."

$50-a-day deductions?

►Senate rejects limiting income. A4

WASHINGTON (AP) — Congress began work yesterday on legislation that would give members of the House and Senate a $50-a-day income tax deduction to help offset the cost of living in Washington.

Rep. Daniel Rostenkowski, D-Ill., chairman of a House Ways and Means subcommittee, conceded he was moving into a "sensitive" area. But he said he would push for swift subcommittee approval of the bill. A vote on the measure was expected at the next subcommittee meeting scheduled for April 4.

The bill would cost the government an estimated $2.5 million a year in lost income tax revenues. This figures out to an average tax reduction of more than $4,600 annually for the 535 members of the House of Representatives and the Senate.

The Senate was widely criticized when earlier this month it decided — without a roll call vote — to delay for four years imposing an $8,625 ceiling on how much outside income Senators can receive. The only current limit for Senators is a $25,000 annual ceiling on speech fees.

The Senate acted yesterday to reaffirm the earlier delaying action, but this time on a 54-44 roll call vote.

Two years ago, Congress came under attack when it voted its members

Please See CONGRESS Page A17 ►

Flynt convicted

ATLANTA (AP) — Hustler magazine owner Larry Flynt was convicted on 11 misdemeanor obscenity counts yesterday and ordered to pay a total of $27,500 in fines.

Fulton State Court Judge Nick Lambros also sentenced Flynt to 11 one-year jail terms, to be served consecutively. But Lambros said the jail terms would be suspended on payment of the fine and under the condition that Flynt not again violate the state obscenity laws.

Flynt's attorney, Herald Fahringer, said he would appeal the conviction. Flynt posted a $27,500 appeal bond and was released.

Flynt has been paralyzed in both legs from the mid-thigh down since he was shot a year ago during another obscenity trial in Lawrenceville, Ga. The charges in that case were dropped after the shooting. No one has been arrested for the shooting, and security was tight during Flynt's latest trial.

Flynt smiled as he was wheeled out of the courtroom when a spectator called out, "Bum rap, Larry."

Flynt was indicted after he came to Atlanta in 1977 and personally sold copies of his sexually explicit magazines Hustler and Chic. Flynt came here during of a crackdown on bookstall owners by Fulton County Solicitor Hinsgh McAuliffe. Flynt said McAuliffe's constant raids on stores selling adult magazines was a form of intimidation, and he dared the prosecutor to arrest him.

Flynt's attorney predicted that his client would not abide by the judge's order to keep his magazines out of Georgia. Flynt now is selling the magazines in Cincinnati, Ohio, where he was convicted in early 1977 on charges of pandering obscenity and organized crime.

After Flynt was shot, he named his wife as publisher of Hustler.

Cancer vaccine tested

DAYTONA BEACH, Fla. (AP) — An experimental anti-cancer vaccine that has helped some patients survive after lung surgery could one day be used to protect healthy people against the disease, a Canadian researcher said yesterday.

Dr. Thomas H.M. Stewart said he hoped to be ready within two years to seek funds and approval from the Canadian government for a trial with healthy volunteers who are at high risk of cancer, such as heavy smokers who work with asbestos or in uranium mines.

But Stewart emphasized at an American Cancer Society seminar here that the work is still highly experimental.

"If one is a complete optimist, one could hope by the turn of the century to offer immune protection for a number of solid tumors, but one must be realistic," said Stewart, professor of medicine at the University of Ottawa in Ontario.

In initial trials among 52 early-stage lung cancer patients in Canada, 81 percent of those who received the vaccine were alive four years after surgery as compared with only 49 percent of those with no vaccine.

The results were encouraging enough to spur a new trial with 300 patients now underway at 10 U.S. and Canadian medical centers.

In February, the head of the experiment at Roswell Park Memorial Institute in Buffalo, N.Y., Dr. Hiroshi Takita, said his early results were comparable to those obtained by Stewart in Ottawa.

But Stewart said the vaccine would have "limited use" in treating lung cancer because it was only valuable when the cancer was detected very early.

He said 90 percent of the 112,000 Americans expected to come down with lung cancer this year would be past that point where the vaccine would be of use. Lung cancer is the leading cancer killer, with 98,000 deaths expected this year.

Please See CANCER Page A17 ►

They can't get at this oil

WASHINGTON (AP) — The government has pumped some 74 million barrels of crude oil into Gulf Coast salt caverns for safe-keeping. Trouble is, there's no way to get it out, a congressional report said yesterday.

The General Accounting Office, an auditing branch of Congress, said the nation's growing Strategic Petroleum Reserve will be of little use in a national emergency like another Arab oil embargo until a withdrawal system is in place.

The General Accounting Office, an auditing branch of Congress, said the

Please See CAVERNS Page A17 ►

John Lennon as Beatle at 1966 press conference apologizing for remark "The Beatles are more popular than Jesus."

John Lennon shot to death

From Call news services

NEW YORK — Former Beatle John Lennon, who catapulted to stardom with the long-haired British rock group in the 1960s, was shot to death late last night outside his luxury apartment building on Manhattan's Upper West Side.

Police said Lennon, 40, was rushed in a police car to Roosevelt Hospital, where he was pronounced dead shortly after arriving. They said he had seven severe wounds of the chest, back and left arm.

Police said the shooting occurred outside the Dakota, the century-old luxury apartment house where Lennon and his wife, Yoko Ono, lived across the street from Central Park.

Police said they had a suspect and described him as "a local screwball" with no apparent motive for shooting Lennon.

Please See **LENNON** Page **A2**►

John Lennon in August of this year while recording latest album.
Associated Press

Index

NO. 28,963 (USPS 363-060)

THE MORNING CALL

LEHIGH VALLEY'S GREATEST NEWSPAPER

ALLENTOWN, PA. 18105, TUESDAY, DECEMBER 9, 1980

20¢

Weather

Periods of rain through tomorrow; a high temperature both days in the low 50s; a low tonight in the mid-30s. For details, see **Page B2**

Soviets tag Polish unions as counter-revolutionary

From Call news services

MOSCOW — The Soviet Union asserted explicitly for the first time yesterday that the independent trade unions in Poland were conducting a counter-revolutionary struggle against that country's Communist government.

Tass, the official news agency, said in a brief but pointed report from Warsaw that "counter-revolutionary groups, operating under the cover of branches of the 'Solidarity' union, have turned to open confrontation" with the Communist Party and the managements of factories and institutions.

The Tass story, which was broadcast by Moscow Radio and scheduled for prominent display in all the major Soviet newspapers, was by far the most ominous official comment from Moscow during the five months of the Polish crisis. Diplomats here were unanimous in declaring that it increased the possibility of armed Warsaw Pact intervention in Poland.

East Germany joined in the attack on Polish labor union activists, also charging that "counterrevolutionary groups" in Solidarity, the national organization for the independent unions, were threatening the Polish Communist Party and the government and were seeking "to destabilize still further" the situation in Poland.

Poland's Communist authorities joined with the independent trade union Solidarity in formally denying the Soviet report alleging "counterrevolutionary" disorders in the southern town of Kielce.

The allegation by Tass, the official Soviet news agency, is regarded here as the opening shot in a new propaganda campaign against Solidarity. It was denied by the union and a local branch described it as "a complete lie and falsification aimed at misleading Polish, Russian, and world opinion."

Western analysts here believe such allegations represent part of growing pressure tactics by the Kremlin and its East European allies against the Polish authorities and the new independent unions.

Meanwhile, U.S. concern about possible Soviet intervention in Poland has risen again because military preparations have continued since last week's Warsaw Pact summit meeting.

"We have detected military preparations in more than 30 Soviet and Warsaw Pact divisions over the past week," one senior Carter administration official said yesterday.

Meanwhile, the Pentagon ordered top U.S. military commanders in Europe to be on their toes because of the potential of war in Eastern Europe.

Pentagon officials stressed, however, that there was no alert of any U.S. troops in Western Germany.

Please See **POLAND** Page **A9**►

Associated Press

Soviet leader Brezhnev (center), poses with India Prime Minister Gandhi (right), and India President N. Sanjiva Reddy.

Brezhnev: West must forget about arms superiority

By STUART AUERBACH
Of The Washington Post

NEW DELHI, India — Soviet President Leonid Brezhnev signaled a willingness to reopen strategic arms limitation talks last night but warned the West that it must abandon any plans to achieve military superiority over Moscow.

The Soviet leader used a banquet toast on the opening day of his visit to India to send what diplomatic observers here saw as a clear message to Washington, without specifically mentioning the United States.

A remark by Brezhnev to U.S. Ambassador Robert Goheen in the airport receiving line underscored that Brezhnev was as interested in Moscow's superpower adversary in Washington as in his hosts in New Delhi.

"Give my regards to Mr. Reagan," Brezhnev told the ambassador, in one of the few comments he made to any diplomat.

Brezhnev's arrival was marred by minor demonstrations, and the Soviet leader's motorcade was rerouted for security reasons to avoid going through the center of New Delhi.

While Afghanistan is on the minds of many here and Poland preoccupies much of the Western world, Brezhnev placed much of the blame for what he called the "considerably colder" international climate at the doorstep of the United States and its allies.

"Influential politicians in the West have decided to whip up the arms race rather than limit it," he said, in what observers here saw as a reference to President Carter's decision not to try to push SALT II through a hostile Senate after last December's Soviet invasion of Afghanistan.

"They have made up their minds to achieve military supremacy rather than to maintain parity," he continued.

Carter, in his January 1980 State of the Union message, called for increased spending to match "the steady

Please See **BREZHNEV** Page **A9**►

Chrysler needs cash fast

By EDWARD COWAN
Of The New York Times

WASHINGTON — The Chrysler Corp told the government yesterday that it must have an additional $350 million of federal loan guarantees within the next 30 days if it is to keep operating.

The three-member Chrysler Loan Guarantee Board reacted cooly during a two-hour meeting with Chrysler executives, indicating reservations about enlarging the government's risk — $800 million of guarantees have been issued so far — but not refusing outright, according to government sources.

G. William Miller, chairman of the loan board and secretary of the Treasury, suggested that the company had to raise additional capital funds to sustain itself for the next two years or so.

"That's absolutely essential," a federal official said after the meeting.

Two methods of raising additional capital were discussed, informants said. One way would be for Chrysler to join forces with another company, either through a joint venture or by sale of a fractional interest, such as the American Motors Corp.'s agreement to sell a 46 percent interest to Renault of France.

Some officials speculated that Chrysler might be able to raise money from Mitsubishi, a Japanese auto maker, or Peugeot, the French auto company. Chrysler owns a minority interest in both.

A second way would be to persuade holders of Chrysler debt to exercise their option to convert the debt to equity — shares of ownership — for an additional cash payment. That, if done, would dilute the value of outstanding Chrysler common stock.

Lee A. Iacocca, Chrysler's chairman, and Gerald Greenwald, executive vice president for finance, outlined the company's deteriorating financial situation.

Iacocca and Greenwald told federal officials that the company's new line of K cars had been well received but that potential buyers were waiting for interest rates to decline so that their financing charges would be lower. One Chrysler source said the initial public reaction to last week's Chrysler announcement of interest-rate rebates was encouraging.

Owners of TMI sue government for $4 billion

WASHINGTON (AP) — The owners of the Three Mile Island nuclear plant filed a $4 billion damage claim against the federal government yesterday, alleging negligence by the Nuclear Regulatory Commission caused the TMI accident.

The claim, apparently the largest ever filed against the U.S. government, seeks to make taxpayers foot the bill for all losses sustained by General Public Utilities Corp. following the accident at TMI.

The utility charged the NRC with negligence in alerting power plant operators to an incident at a nuclear plant in Toledo, Ohio, which occurred 18 months before TMI and bore striking similarities to the TMI accident.

"If a proper warning had been given by the NRC, the TMI accident on March 28, 1979, would have been avoided," the damage claim said.

The incidents at the Davis-Besse reactor — also manufactured by Babcock & Wilcox — paralleled those at TMI. In both situations, a valve stuck open allowing vital cooling water to bleed out of the reactor. Neither of the reactors had indicator dials to tell operators whether the valve was open or not.

Unlike TMI, the Davis-Besse incident caused no damage to the reactor because it was only operating at 7 percent of capacity and the plant resumed operations soon afterwards.

The NRC conducted an investigation of the incident and implemented new operating procedures for the plant to guard against the valve being stuck in the open position, but GPU alleged other Babcock & Wilcox operators were not alerted to the problem.

NRC spokesman Joe Fouchard said the agency would have no immediate comment on the damage claim. The NRC has six months to accept or reject the claim, at which time GPU can file suit against the government in federal court.

GPU is facing severe financial problems as a result of the accident. Last month an NRC staff report suggested a Chrysler-style bailout by the government may be necessary to ward off bankruptcy and keep the utility from defaulting on the estimated $1 billion it is expected to take to clean up the damaged reactor.

The damage claim seeks to make the government pay the clean-up costs plus $430 million it estimates will be needed to repair or replace equipment damaged when the nuclear fuel core overheated.

It also asks for $1.59 billion to pay for higher costs it has incurred in purchasing replacement electricity from other utilities and $990 million in other revenue losses to the company. The claim against the government also held out the possibility that the company would seek an additional $800 million in damages if the sister unit to the damaged reactor is never allowed to operate again.

The utility said all its losses were calculated on the assumption that a sister reactor to the damaged one will be allowed to begin operating again in January 1982 and the damaged reactor can resume operation in 1988, a schedule many have called highly optimistic.

Iran says hostage crisis getting nearer to end

The New York Times

TEHRAN — The speaker of the Iranian Parliament said last night that the 13-month old crisis over the U.S. Embassy hostages "is now much closer to being solved."

As Iranian officials spent a fifth day considering the latest version of the U.S. reponse to its four demands for the freeing of the hostages, Hojatoleslam Rafsanjani said on the state television "the matter is much more clear now."

"The United States has, to an extent, clarified its position and it is now much closer to being solved," Rafsanjani said. "I think that if the United States has good will and if it truly wants to solve the matter, it will be solved."

Earlier in the day, Rafsanjani told a news conference that the new American response had "almost made it clear that it is ready to meet these demands."

The relatively straightforward and consistent statements made by the speaker — and the lack of the usual bombastic rhetoric — appeared to raise some hopes of the possibility of working out the release of the hostages, today in their 402nd day of captivity. Such hopes have repeatedly been dashed in the past, however.

A three-man Algerian delegation brought the latest U.S. message here Thursday, after meeting with Deputy Secretary of State Warren M. Christ-

Please See **HOSTAGES** Page **A9**►

Index

BRIDGE	D7	LETTERS	A11
CLASSIFIED	C7-11	LOTTERY	A2
COMICS	D8,9	MOVIES	D10
DEATHS	B8,C7	RESTAURANTS	C6
EDITORIAL	A10	SPORTS	C1-6
FINANCIAL	B9-12	TV	D4

THE MORNING CALL

NO. 29,489 (USPS 363-060) ★ ★ ★ ★

LEHIGH VALLEY'S GREATEST NEWSPAPER

ALLENTOWN, PA. 18105, TUESDAY, DECEMBER 28, 1982

25¢

Weather

Cloudy early today, rain likely later, high low 50s; rain tonight; cloudy, windy tomorrow. For details, see Page B2

Bethlehem Steel axing 10,000

A maintenance employee at the Lackawanna office seems dejected at news as she awaits ride home.

Associated Press

Lackawanna, Johnstown most affected

By PAUL WIRTH
Of The Morning Call

Bethlehem Steel Corp. will cut 10,000 workers and close much of its Lackawanna, N.Y., plant in a major reorganization plan aimed at improving profits.

The move will increase the company's fourth quarter loss by between $750 million and $850 million, making the total 1982 red ink more than $1 billion and possibly as high as $1.5 billion. That would be the largest annual loss in Bethlehem Steel's history.

The closings, coupled with the disposal of two West Coast steel plants, will reduce Bethlehem Steel's total steelmaking capacity by 19 percent. The company still will be the nation's second largest steelmaker, however, behind U.S. Steel Corp.

Many of the employees whose jobs are to be eliminated are already on layoff. Besides Lackawanna, permanent layoffs are also planned for portions of the Johnstown plant because of the reorganization.

The only immediate effect on the company's Lehigh Valley operations will be "some" home-office layoffs, but a company spokesman would not be more specific. Asked if similar closings are planned for other plants, the spokesman said all company operations continue to be reviewed "and we will take such actions as may be necessary."

The coke ovens, blast furnaces, basic oxygen furnace, hot strip mills and certain finishing mills at the Lackawanna Plant will be shut down by the end of 1983. Chairman Donald Trautlein said in a statement yesterday morning.

The changes will cause the elimination of 7,300 jobs at the plant, leaving only 1,300 at work. The plant's galvanizing line and bar mill, both modern facilities, will remain in operation.

At Johnstown, between 2,300 and 2,700 employees will be cut. The company says 2,600 to 3,000 will remain on the job. This does not include the rail freight car shop, not in operation now , which employs 1,900.

Trautlein says the company will reopen the freight-car shop "if costs can be made competitive," apparently referring to the company's belief that wage and benefit concessions must be won from the United Steelworkers union.

The chairman said the facilities are being closed because they are losing money and there are no "reasonable prospects" for them to make adequate profits in the future.

"This is not a bargaining ploy," insisted a company spokesman, who said the high cost of labor is only part of the reason for the closing. Other reasons include noncompetitive plants, changing markets and product mix, and continuing high import levels, he said.

Another reason, according to Trautlein, is that property taxes at the Lackawanna plant have been more than five times the average amount paid per ton of shipments at Bethlehem's five other major steel plants. The tax assessment of the Bethlehem plant was recently reduced, giving the company a $350,000 tax break in the Lehigh Valley area.

"We deeply regret having to take these actions," Trautlein said. He said company representatives will meet with union officials concerning the planned shutdowns.

"A joint and cooperative effort involving the United Steelworkers of America is a necessity" to ensure the success of the plan, Trautlein said. It was not immediately clear what the company would ask of the union.

A spokesman said there are no plans to ask the USW to negotiate separately with Bethlehem Steel. There has been speculation that some major steel companies might try to win lower wage and benefit agreements on their own, rather than relying on the traditional bargaining method of all major companies negotiating with the USW as a whole. Steelworkers have twice turned down industry requests for wage and benefit concessions, even though the union's leadership recommended them.

Officials of the steelworkers union in Johnstown and Lackawanna could not be reached for comment yesterday.

Steel observers have for some time believed the company would close the Lackawanna plant. "It has been common knowledge in the industry for years that the Lackawanna plant is in trouble," one analyst said yesterday.

Speculation intensified recently when the company, in announcing a major plant mod-

Please See STEEL Page A2 ▶

Watt drops wilderness candidates

By MARTIN CRUTSINGER
Of The Associated Press

WASHINGTON — Interior Secretary James Watt announced yesterday that he is withdrawing thousands of acres in 10 Western states from further consideration as protected wilderness areas.

The Interior Department said the action would affect more than 805,000 acres, but environmentalists predicted over 2 million acres would be dropped as possible candidates for wilderness protection.

Terry Sopher with the Wilderness Society said Watt's action "shows an astonishing degree of contempt for Congress" because he acted right after the lawmakers adjourned for the year and the decision will take effect immediately.

Watt's decision covers part of the 24 million acres of land being studied by the Bureau of Land Management for inclusion in the national wilderness system.

Specifically, Watt dropped from further consideration as wilderness: Study areas of less than 5,000 acres; areas where the federal government owns the land but not the mineral rights underneath, and areas that had

Please See WATT Page A2 ▶

Rain, snow storms lash much of U.S.

By DAVID L. LANGFORD
Of The Associated Press

Floods from more than a foot of rain poured through Dixie bayou country yesterday and hundreds fled in boats, while a blizzard virtually isolated some communities under 2 feet of snow in the Midwest.

Snow and ice stalled travelers on glazed highways from New Mexico to Nebraska.

At least 11 weather-related deaths have been reported since the holiday weekend began as a blizzard blasted Colorado and almost 15 inches of rain in two days sent rivers washing out of their banks in Louisiana, Texas and Mississippi. In addition, new snow in southern Colorado stalled a search for a postman missing since Christmas Eve.

A Greyhound bus skidded off icy Interstate 80 near Kearney, Neb., injuring 25 people, and snow, freezing rain, sleet and drizzle caused hundreds of accidents from El Paso, Texas, to Omaha, Neb.

"We've had just a tremendous number of accidents," said deputy police chief Gary Crinklaw in Omaha. "We're asking everybody to stay home unless they absolutely have to go out."

Please See STORMS Page A2 ▶

'Recession Rock' at Stabler

Singer brings 'Allentown' to the Valley

Lights beam down on singer Billy Joel (above) during concert at Stabler Arena; singer smiles at applause (far left); Allentown Mayor Joseph Daddona presents key to city to Joel, composer of the recession-rock hit 'Allentown.'

Morning Call photo
Joany Carlin

Ritter alleges campaign funds misappropriated by aide

ALLENTOWN, PA. 18105 •
NO. 34,091

Weather

Chance of snow 80 percent today, high around 20; mostly sunny tomorrow. Details B2.

Index

WEDNESDAY, JANUARY 29, 1986 • 30¢

Space shuttle explodes; teacher, 6 others dead

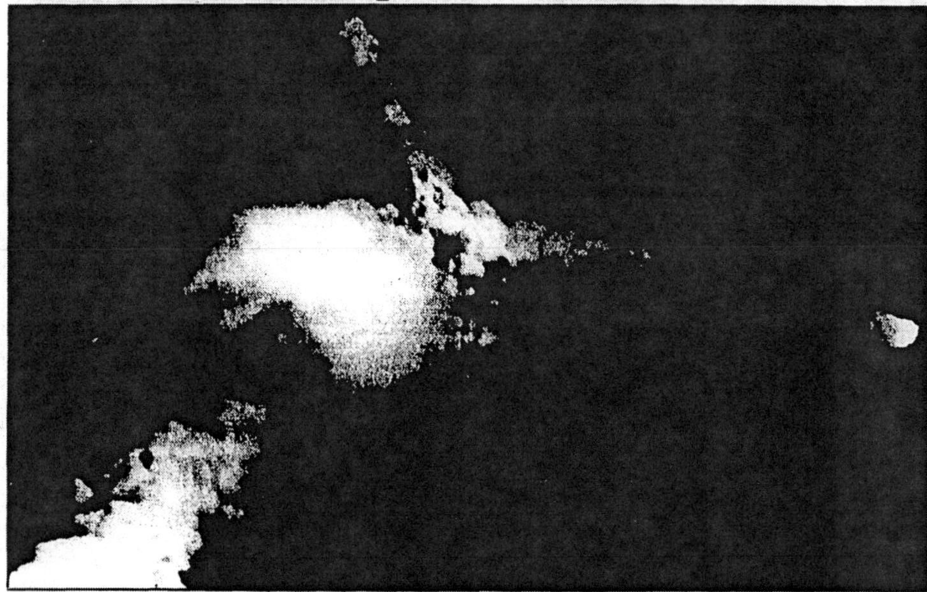

Contrails and huge ball of fire are all that can be seen of space shuttle Challenger after explosion shortly after liftoff yesterday. Associated Press

Video shows liquid fuel tank detonating

By HOWARD BENEDICT
Of The Associated Press

CAPE CANAVERAL, Fla. — A catastrophic explosion blew apart the space shuttle Challenger 74 seconds after liftoff yesterday, sending school teacher Christa McAuliffe and six NASA astronauts to a fiery death in the sky eight miles out from Kennedy Space Center.

"We mourn seven heroes," said President Reagan.

The accident defied quick explanation, though a slow-motion replay seemed to show an initial problem with one of two peel-away rocket boosters followed by the detonation of the shuttle's huge external fuel tank. The tank-turned-fireball destroyed Challenger high above the Atlantic while crew families and NASA officials watched in despair from the Cape.

> "Today's tragedy reminds us that danger awaits all who push back the frontier of space."
>
> Vice President George Bush

Other observers noted that the boosters continued to fly crazily through the sky after the explosion, indicating that the fatal explosion might have originated in the giant tank itself.

"We will not speculate as to the specific cause of the explosion based on that footage," said Jesse Moore, NASA's top shuttle administrator. National Aeronautics and Space Administration officials are organizing an investigat-

Please See SHUTTLE Page A2 ▶

CHALLENGER

Shuttle Orbitor

External fuel tank: 500,000 gallons

Solid rocket booster (2)

Main engines

1. Challenger lifts off at 11:38 a.m., delayed two hours over concern about ice on the launch pad.

Kennedy Space Center

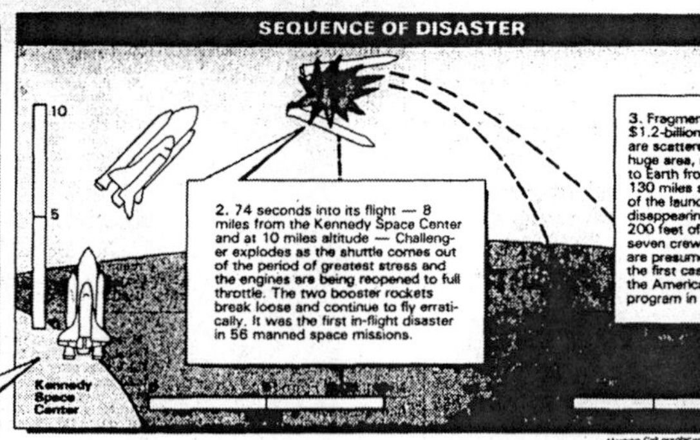

SEQUENCE OF DISASTER
10
5
2. 74 seconds into its flight — 8 miles from the Kennedy Space Center and at 10 miles altitude — Challenger explodes as the shuttle comes out of the period of greatest stress and the engines are being reopened to full throttle. The two booster rockets break loose and continue to fly erratically. It was the first in-flight disaster in 56 manned space missions.
3. Fragments of the $1.2-billion shuttle are scattered over a huge area, returning to Earth from 50 to 130 miles southeast of the launch site and disappearing in 70 to 200 feet of water. All seven crew members are presumed dead, the first casualties of the American space program in 19 years.

Morning Call graphic—Elaine Curler

Reagan honors shuttle heroes, delays speech

By MICHAEL PUTZEL
Of The Associated Press

WASHINGTON — President Reagan, stunned by America's first in-flight space disaster, abruptly postponed his State of the Union address yesterday to praise the lost Challenger astronauts as heroes and vow the nation's manned space flight program will continue.

"The future doesn't belong to the fainthearted," the president said. "It belongs to the brave."

In a nationally broadcast address less than an hour after NASA officially gave up hope that teacher Christa McAuliffe and the Challenger's six other crew members survived the explosion that destroyed their spacecraft, Reagan pledged never to forget them and promised their mission would not be America's last.

"I'd planned to speak to you tonight to report on the state of the union," Reagan said in a five-minute tribute from the Oval Office.

But he explained he was putting off for a week what aides had described as an upbeat, forward-looking speech because "today is a day for mourning and remembering."

"I've always had great faith in and respect for our space program," Reagan said, "and what happened today does nothing to diminish it. We'll continue our quest in space.

"There will be more shuttle flights and more shuttle crews and yes, more volunteers, more civilians, more teachers in space."

The Challenger Seven, Reagan said, "were daring and brave, and they had that special grace, that special spirit that says, 'Give me a challenge, and I'll meet it with joy.'"

Calling the disaster "a truly na-

Please See REAGAN Page A2 ▶

INSIDE

L.V. teacher's envy became despair

Walt Tremer
. . . Pa.'s candidate for NASA program

By TOM LOWRY
Of The Morning Call

Southern Lehigh school teacher Walt Tremer stood in an unusual chill at Cape Canaveral yesterday morning and watched with envy as the space shuttle Challenger lifted off with ease.

But moments later, Tremer's envy turned to despair as he witnessed his colleague Christa McAuliffe vanish in a dramatic, mid-air explosion. She was strapped in a seat Tremer had dreamed for months would be his.

Like the other candidates who weren't selected for the Teacher in Space Program, the 49-year-old robotics instructor said he always believed he would be aboard the shuttle Challenger in spirit, making yesterday's tragedy all the more difficult to bear.

Last night from O'Hare Airport in Chicago, waiting for an airplane home after being witness to the horrific consequences of space travel, a fatigued Tremer said if he had the chance to go up in the shuttle next week, he would.

> "There was an immediate horror. Everyone in our group began hugging and crying."
>
> Walt Tremer, Southern Lehigh teacher

"We all knew the risks," Tremer told The Morning Call from a phone booth. "As a pioneer, every one of the astronauts knows the risks. There's a cost to pay."

Tremer, director of Southern Lehigh's future technology center, was selected from a field of 578 applicants to become Pennsylvania's candidate for the NASA program. He had been invited by NASA to spend the week before the launch with the 113 other teacher-in-space candidates in Florida. The week of workshops and tours of the Kennedy Space Center was to be climaxed by the launch.

"We [the teacher candidates] are a pretty close group. This has been pretty devastating," said Tremer, waiting for a flight to Philadelphia.

The group of teachers arrived at the launch site at 7:15 a.m. yesterday, drinking hot chocolate and climbing back

Please See TREMER Page A2 ▶

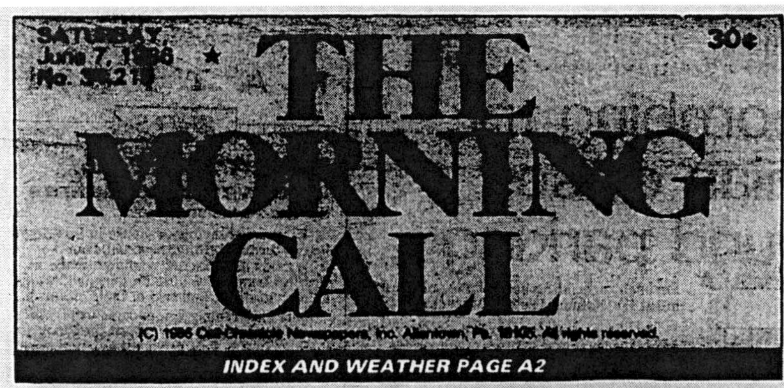

SATURDAY, June 7, 1986 ★ No. [illegible]

30¢

THE MORNING CALL

INDEX AND WEATHER PAGE A2

PULLOUT SECTION

3 employees slain in bank holdup

2 others wounded; 2 suspects held Page A3

INSIDE

Suspects Martin Daniel Appel (above, left) and Stanley Joseph Hertzog (above, right) are led to their arraignments.

Firefighters and rescue personnel load body of one of shooting victims into ambulance.

Morning Call photo—Andrea Mihalik

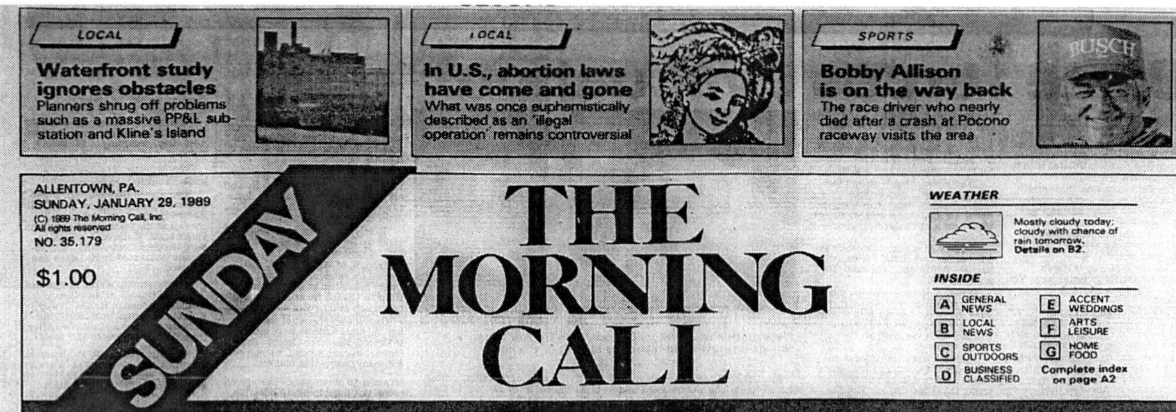

LOCAL

Waterfront study ignores obstacles

Planners shrug off problems such as a massive PP&L substation and Kline's Island

LOCAL

In U.S., abortion laws have come and gone

What was once euphemistically described as an 'illegal operation' remains controversial

SPORTS

Bobby Allison is on the way back

The race driver who nearly died after a crash at Pocono raceway visits the area

ALLENTOWN, PA.
SUNDAY, JANUARY 29, 1989
(C) 1989 The Morning Call, Inc.
All rights reserved
NO. 35,179
$1.00

SUNDAY

THE MORNING CALL

WEATHER

Mostly cloudy today; cloudy with chance of rain tomorrow. Details on B2.

INSIDE

Fire in Hotel Bethlehem leaves 3 dead, 14 injured

Guests generally kept calm

By ROSA SALTER
Of The Morning Call

Margaret Gidley was in the shower when she heard her roommates banging on the door saying the hotel was on fire.

In a matter of minutes, she and one roommate, Jeanne Moniz, found themselves on their hands and knees crawling down a hallway black with smoke.

"We put scarves around our faces. It was so black you couldn't see anything," said the Providence, R.I., woman. "I never prayed so much in all my life."

Gidley spent Friday night in Room 500 of Hotel Bethlehem, just a few doors away from the center of the fire that early yesterday morning killed three people and injured nine who were staying in the downtown Bethlehem landmark.

Yesterday morning, she found herself with about 50 occupants of the hotel — high-powered lawyers, aspiring young musicians and elderly residents relocated from a city high-rise — huddled together in blankets and nightgowns in the Colonial-era sanctuary of Central Moravian Church.

About 20 victims of the fire had been moved to the hotel from the Monocacy Tower apartments while it undergoes renovations, said Frank Loretti, executive director of the Bethlehem Housing Authority, which owns the apartments. Some apartment transferees had been in the hotel about 60 days.

Loretti went to the hotel with Clara

Please See RESCUE Page A2 ►

INSIDE

Firefighters battle blaze at the Hotel Bethlehem and look for guests in need of assistance, right. They take an elderly woman from the hotel by aerial ladder, far right.

TOM SCHROEDER / The Morning Call

By TIM REEVES
Of The Morning Call

Hotel Bethlehem Fire

W. Broad
W. Walnut
W. Market
Main St.
Monocacy Creek
378
North

A small but deadly fire that struck the Hotel Bethlehem yesterday morning killed three guests, injured 14 others and forced the evacuation of more than 100.

The landmark hotel was filled nearly to capacity when the fire struck shortly after 7 a.m. Two of the three people killed were residents of nearby apartments for the elderly. They were living in the hotel temporarily during repairs to their building.

Though it burned only two of the hotel's 126 rooms, the fire pushed searing black smoke quickly through the nine-story building.

One couple, trapped in their room by heavy smoke, tied two bedsheets together and climbed from their fifth-floor window to a rooftop below.

The cause of the fire was accidental, according to fire officials. Murial Brooks, of Westchester County, N.Y., said it started when she tried to plug her travel iron into a wall socket in Room 510. She was already dressed, and said she noticed a crease in her skirt.

Killed were Monique Forbes, 58, of Allentown, and John Kelly, 75, of Bethlehem, both by smoke inhalation. Forbes and Kelly were found inside Room 524, 40 feet from Room 510, according to Northampton County Coroner Joseph Reichel.

Also killed was Charles Knouse, 69, who was staying across the hall from Forbes and Kelly in Room 527. Knouse and Kelly lived in Monocacy Tower, the Bethlehem Housing Authority high-rise for elderly tenants.

They were staying in the hotel with 18 others while the 645 Main St. high-rise is under repair.

Knouse tried unsuccessfully to escape the fire. His body was found in the stairwell between the fourth and fifth floors, according to Lehigh County Coroner Wayne Snyder.

Three other Monocacy Tower residents were critically injured: Grace Eaton, 65, who is in St. Luke's Hospital being treated for burns, smoke inhalation and respiratory arrest, and Alma Evans, 79, and Joseph Glick, 83, who are at Muhlenberg Hospital Center.

Eleven others, including four firefighters and an emergency medical technician, were treated for less serious injuries. Three of the 11 were overnight patients. All were listed in stable condition.

Nine people escaped the hotel by fire department ladders. Others said they crawled to stairwells under the thick smoke. A few were carried out of the building by firefighters.

Please See BLAZE Page A2 ►

Congress' back door to raise upsets critics

By SCOTT J. HIGHAM
Call Washington Bureau

WASHINGTON — Daniel Webster may have been one of the first U.S. lawmakers to lose his seat for accepting a hefty pay raise, but today's congressmen are trying to make sure the New Hampshire legislator is among the last.

Webster was one of several congressmen booted from office 173 years ago because he voted to raise his salary from $6 per day to $1,500 per year, a raise that was later rescinded after an outpouring of public criticism.

Next week, congressional salaries are scheduled to rise again, but this time lawmakers are trying to avoid the wrath of their constituents by taking the $45,500 pay increase without touching their electronic voting cards.

"The process that's unfolding here is an absolute national scandal," said Patrick McGuigan, a senior scholar at the Free Congress Center for Law and Democracy, a conservative public policy group. "If they

Please See PAY Page A14 ►

Castro asked Khrushchev to fire nuclear rockets in '62, Soviet says

By DAN FISHER
Of The Los Angeles Times

MOSCOW — The world was even closer to the brink of nuclear war during the Cuban Missile Crisis of 1962 than has previously been thought, with warheads already on hand in Cuba for Soviet missiles targeted at Washington, New York, and other major U.S. cities, according to fresh details of the crisis that emerged at an unprecedented meeting of the participants here yesterday.

One of the most surprising disclosures emerged during a lunch break in the formal sessions. During lunch, one Soviet participant, a man described as having "definitive" knowledge on the subject, reportedly said that two days before the crisis peaked, Cuban leader Fidel Castro sent a message to the late Soviet leader Nikita S. Khrushchev, urging that the missiles be fired.

According to this account, that cable convinced Khrushchev that the confrontation had gone too far and the Soviet leader decided to agree to U.S. demands that the missiles be withdrawn.

The existence of such a cabled plea from Castro could not be corroborated from Soviet and Cuban participants attending the meeting. But three conference delegates confirmed that they had heard a knowledgeable Soviet participant give the account during a session break, and they said that the report clearly took the American side by surprise.

Reporters were barred from all but the opening and closing sessions of the extraordinary, two-day seminar, which was organ-

Please See CUBA Page A16 ►

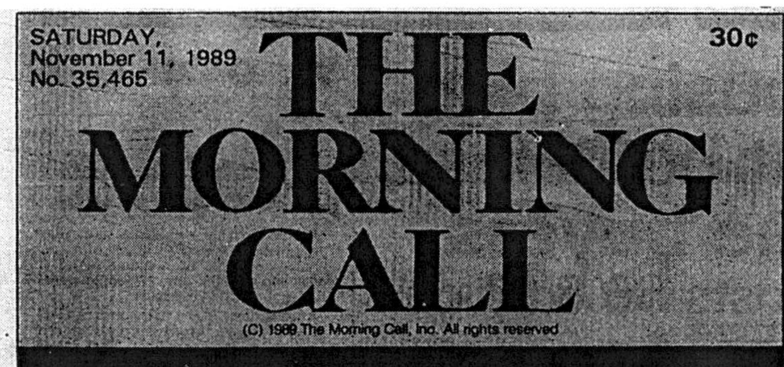

SATURDAY,
November 11, 1989
No. 35,465

30¢

THE MORNING CALL

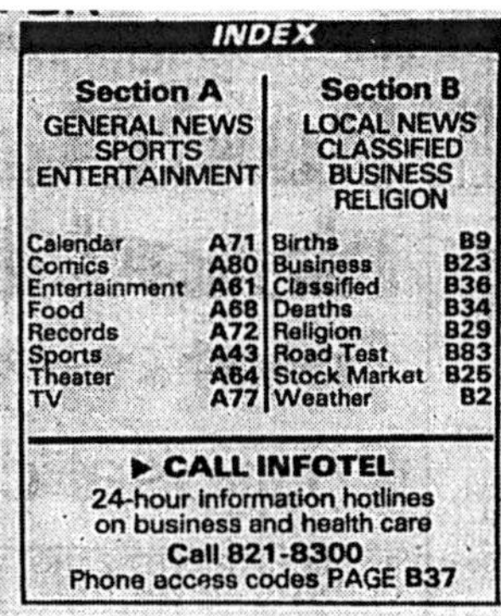

INDEX

▶ **CALL INFOTEL**
24-hour information hotlines
on business and health care
Call 821-8300
Phone access codes PAGE B37

PULLOUT SECTION

Local/Classified Pullout Section B Follows Page A42

WEATHER

Partly cloudy today, mostly sunny tomorrow; highs in the 50s, lows in the 30s. Details B2.

INSIDE TODAY

SPORTS

Liberty, Solehi win soccer matches

Liberty won 2-0 over Mechanicsburg in the opening state 3A soccer tournament yesterday while Southern Lehigh beat Octorara 4-0 in a 2A meet.
PAGE A43

LOCAL

Parkland cancer cases under study

The Parkland School District is investigating five cases of breast cancer in adult females working at the Kratzer School over the last five years, school officials said yesterday.
PAGE B1

BUSINESS

The Dow climbed 21.92 to 2,625.61, finishing the week with a loss of 3.90.
PAGE B25

Ford's Petersen ready to retire

Ford Motor Co. Chairman Donald Petersen, who shepherded the automaker to huge profits last year, said yesterday he would retire March 1.
PAGE B23

NATION

Bush unveils housing plan

President Bush yesterday unveiled a $6.8 billion housing proposal built around government grants, tax credits and a proposal made a year ago by Gov. Michael Dukakis
PAGE A2

Hole punched in Berlin Wall

Krenz makes free travel permanent

Page **A3**

Associated Press

East German border guards watch as a hydraulic crane begins razing a portion of the Berlin Wall. A new border crossing was opened in the wall at Bernauer Strasse.

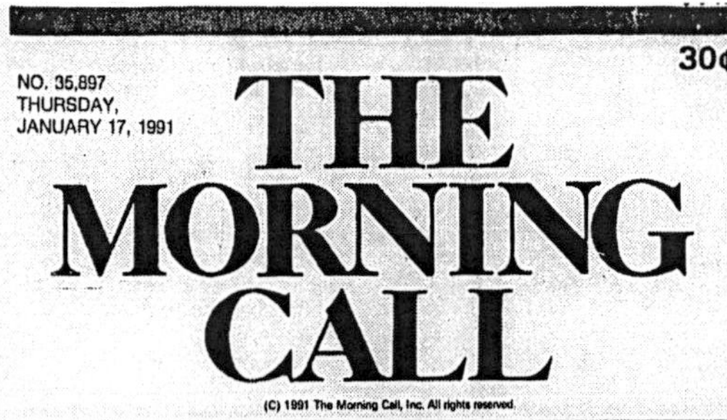

30¢
NO. 35,897
THURSDAY,
JANUARY 17, 1991
THE
MORNING
CALL
(C) 1991 The Morning Call, Inc. All rights reserved.

GULF COVERAGE

- ▶ Lawmakers rally around the president's decision **A3**
- ▶ Scene was 'awesome' as jets left to bomb Iraq **A3**
- ▶ Local reservists' families watch, pray and listen **A4**
- ▶ Organized terrorism unlikely to hit Lehigh Valley **A5**
- ▶ Allentown woman leaves Israel to avoid the war **B6**
- ▶ Bush frees oil stra.egic reserves as prices soar **B10**

Stories a·e on pages A3-6, A10-12, A20, B6, B10

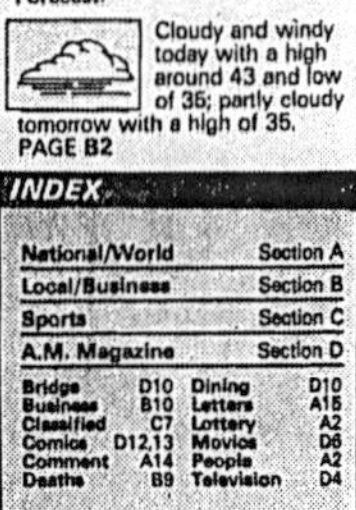

WEATHER
Forecast:
Cloudy and windy today with a high around 43 and low of 35; partly cloudy tomorrow with a high of 35.
PAGE B2
INDEX
National/World Section A
Local/Business Section B
Sports Section C
A.M. Magazine Section D
Bridge D10 Dining D10
Business B10 Letters A15
Classified C7 Lottery A2
Comics D12,13 Movies D6
Comment A14 People A2
Deaths B9 Television D4

ALLIES POUND IRAQ, KUWAIT

F-15E Eagle
McDonnell Douglas
F-15
single-seat fighter
version shown

Type

F-15E is a two-seat, air-superiority fighter-bomber, capable of carrying a heavy payload of bombs and missiles into enemy territory.

Specifications

Weight (empty)	31,700 lbs
Max weapon load	23,500 lbs
Max takeoff weight	81,000 lbs

Source: *Jane's All The World's Aircraft* AP/Ross Toro, Karl Tate

"The liberation of Kuwait has begun."
President Bush

Desert Storm launched with predawn air strikes

By EDITH M. LEDERER
Of The Associated Press

CENTRAL SAUDI ARABIA — The United States and its allies hurled a mighty air armada against Iraq early today to crush that Arab nation's military power and drive it from conquered Kuwait.

"The liberation of Kuwait has begun," President Bush declared in Washington.

Wave after wave of warplanes, in hundreds of sorties on a starlit night, streaked north from Saudi Arabian bases to punish Iraq for its five-month defiance of the rest of the world.

In Baghdad, reporters said bomb explosions shook the ground of the Iraqi capital. An oil refinery 10 miles away was in flames, and flashes of light brightened the night sky, apparent anti-aircraft fire, they said.

"Operation Desert Shield" became "Operation Desert Storm" around 12:50 a.m. (4:50 p.m. EST) as F-15E fighter-bombers took off from the largest U.S air base in central Saudi Arabia. "This is history in the making," said Col. Ray Davies, the base's chief maintenance officer.

The air offensive, aimed at troops and other strategic sites in both Iraq and Kuwait, included U.S. Air Force planes, British Tornado fighter-bombers, 150 Saudi Arabian F-15s and Tornados, and aircraft of Kuwait's exiled military, allied officials said.

First reports indicated Iraqi resistance was limited, U.S. defense officials said. Early word on U.S. casualties was "very, very encouraging," said Defense Secretary Dick Cheney. Bush, on U.S. national television, said no ground assault was launched immediately against the dug-in Iraqi army in Kuwait.

There was no immediate word from Iraq on damage and casualties there or in Kuwait. Nor was there any immediate sign of an Iraqi missile attack on Israel, as Baghdad had threatened.

"We've been waiting here for five months now. Now we finally got to do what we were sent here to do."
Col. Ray Davies
chief maintenance officer at Saudi air base

Rumors flew through the Persian Gulf that Iraq launched Scud ground-to-ground missiles against Saudi Arabia, but Cheney called those reports false. An Israeli military

Please See DESERT Page A18 ▶

Valley residents react to war with fear, pride

By TIM DARRAGH
And DAVID HERZOG
Of The Morning Call

At the American Legion in Fountain Hill, George Laughlin joined his friends in silence as they stopped their bingo games to hear President Bush address the country.

Not far away, Kathy McHale watched television alone, clutching a rosary, her husband at a classified site in the Middle East.

Some students at a Moravian College lounge gathered quietly around a television. Others played pool and video games.

For the Lehigh Valley, life went on — normally for some, in turmoil for others — the night the United States of America went to war against Iraq.

Like others around the world, numbed Valley residents congregated wherever a television set was available, their reactions reflecting the nation's ambivalence toward the seemingly irreconcilable notions of projecting strength and avoiding war.

At Stahley's Cellarette in Allentown, Dennis Andreas had no doubt about what had to be done last night. "In my opinion, the United States got backed down too many times," said Andreas, describing himself as an Army veteran of the Vietnam war who was wounded in combat.

"If I could be over there, I would be," he said, seated at the bar. "I'm not a warmonger, don't get me wrong . . . But if the president says you're supposed to do it, you do it."

Please See REACTION Page A9 ▶

Pentagon hotline

The Department of Defense plans on opening toll-free hotlines for families of military personnel in the Persian Gulf but had not established the lines as of press time.

Please See CALL Page A18 ▶

HARRY FISHER / The Morning Call

Muhlenberg College students Brad Bonn and Heather Stamm hold candles at a peace vigil held last night at the campus chapel.

'Battle has been joined,' Bush declares

By TOM RAUM
Of The Associated Press

WASHINGTON — President Bush summoned American and allied forces to war with Iraq yesterday night, declaring solemnly that "the battle has been joined" to free Kuwait. Operation Desert Storm began with an aerial assault that met little resistance, military officials said.

"We will not fail," Bush vowed as F-15E and other fighter bombers were locking onto strategic military targets across Iraq and Kuwait. Hostilities were well under way when the president spoke to the nation at 9 p.m.

The president expressed hope "this fighting will not go on for long, and that casualties will be held to an absolute minimum." He later moved to stabilize the oil markets by opening up sales from the nation's reserve.

Congressional leaders swiftly pledged their support. Sen. Sam Nunn, who led the opposition to war authority, said, "Our servicemen and women will be given all the resources to do the job. I believe we will prevail in a matter of days or weeks."

An anti-war protest outside the White House grew to more than 1,000 demonstrators as word spread of the president's decision, and mounted police were called for crowd control. "Shame, shame," the demonstrators shouted.

The president marshalled a potent international alliance to challenge Iraq's occupation of the oil-rich kingdom of Kuwait and issued his war order less than 24 hours after the expiration of a United Nations deadline. Some 425,000 Americans were deployed in the Gulf region, backed by the Pentagon's most sophisticated aircraft and weaponry.

Bush tells the nation about the launching of Desert Storm.

Defense Secretary Richard Cheney told reporters that the first foray was conducted by hundreds of American, British, Saudi and Kuwaiti aircraft. "So far there has been no air resistance" from the Iraqis, Cheney said.

He provided no details on casualties, but said reports were "very encouraging." He said the battle plan was designed to "focus on military targets, to minimize U.S.

Please See BUSH Page A8 ▶

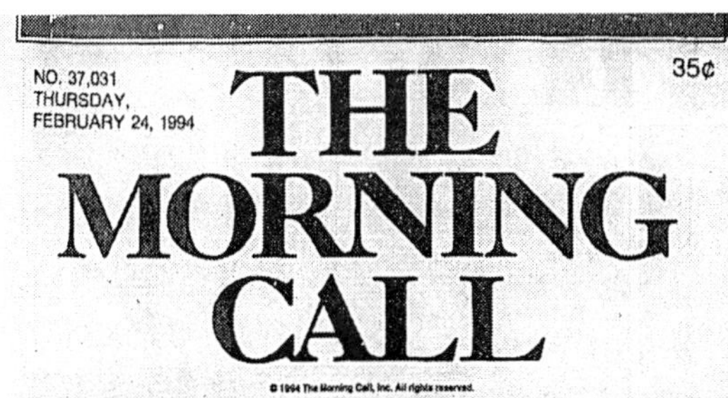
NO. 37,031
THURSDAY,
FEBRUARY 24, 1994

35¢

THE MORNING CALL

BUCKS, BERKS AND MONTGOMERY COUNTIES

Blair wins gold, enters history books
◄ PAGE C1

Kerrigan splendid, Harding bungles
PAGE C1

Sinkhole buckles building in downtown Allentown

This view from the ninth floor of the Hamilton Financial Center shows the sagging facade of Corporate Plaza in Allentown and the sinkhole in which a water main erupted.

LISA A. JOHNSTON / The Morning Call

Corporate Plaza damage forces area evacuations

Morning Call staff writers Kristin Casler, Rosa Salter, Martin Pflieger and Dan Fricker contributed to this story.

A geyser from a broken water main shot 25 feet into the air yesterday as a monster sinkhole opened in N. 7th Street and nearly swallowed Allentown's seven-story Corporate Plaza.

Giant shards of glass and bricks tumbled to the pavement into the evening as the building just north of Center Square verged on collapse.

Residents and businesses in a two-block area were evacuated before dawn because of danger to their buildings from the sinkhole and potential debris from a collapse. No one was injured.

Officials debated yesterday whether the sinkhole or water main break came first. Insurance adjusters and attorneys will have the final say.

The buckling street caused structural damage and sealed the fate of four buildings on the east side of the street owned by city-affiliated agencies. They will be razed within days, Mayor William Heydt said.

"This is completely catastrophic. Downtown Allentown has seen one of its saddest days today," said Robin Turner, executive director of the Allentown Downtown Improvement District Authority.

Corporate Plaza, built in 1986 and appraised at $9.5 million, was a key to downtown revitalization. Owner Mark Mendelson had little comment for the media. But his attorney Bill Harvey, who has an office in Corporate Plaza, said "It's pretty distressing."

Mendelson and his crew of engineers, attorneys and insurance people will meet this morning with de-

Please See **SINKHOLE** Page A4 ►

Rebuilding records task facing tenants

By ELLIOT GROSSMAN
And DEBBIE GARLICKI
Of The Morning Call

For attorney William Platt, the partial collapse of Corporate Plaza seemed like deja vu. But this time, Platt was prepared.

It was in 1975 that Platt's law firm experienced a serious interruption in its operations. A fire in its offices at the Commonwealth Building on Hamilton Street in Allentown destroyed clients' records.

"We lost everything," Platt said. "I reconstructed files and accounts from ashes."

Platt, the former Lehigh County district attorney, has since changed firms and moved to Corporate Plaza.

And though the loss of his current offices pose major problems, this time Platt's firm will be able to reconstruct information in its computer system.

The firm stores magnetic computer tapes in a bank vault to back up its regular computer files.

But other businesses in Corporate Plaza were not so lucky. Some, such as Beyer-Barber Co., kept their active computer records and their backup records in the building.

"Hopefully, the clients will work with us and be patient with us until we get up to full strength," said Donald Guman, the firm's president. "Nobody anticipated losing all the records."

Corporate Plaza's tenants spent yesterday trying to find other office space to use — at least temporarily.

"It's been a scramble for everybody," said Robin Turner, executive director of the Allentown Downtown Improvement District. "They're looking for the best space available."

Please See **TENANTS** Page A7 ►

INSIDE

INDEX

WEATHER

Forecast:

Rain this morning, ending later in the day, mostly cloudy tomorrow; daytime high temperatures in the mid 40s, overnight lows 25.
PAGE B2

STATE

Election officials certify Marks' win

Republican Bruce Marks, who won a federal court ruling to oust Democratic state Sen. William Stinson, was certified by city and state election officials yesterday as winner of a Nov. 2 election.
PAGE A3

Abortion Control Act takes effect March 19

Lawyers for abortion providers and the state yesterday reached an agreement permitting Pennsylvania's Abortion Control Act to take effect at midnight March 19.
PAGE B1

BUSINESS

The Dow Jones average closed down 19.98 at 3,891.68.
PAGE B16

Bell Atlantic, TCI drop $12 billion merger
PAGE B16

READERSHIP POLL

You Call It!

Tell us how you feel about a current news story.
With the ***You Call It!*** telephone survey, you can tell the Lehigh Valley your opinion. See page **A2** for today's question and check tomorrow's Morning Call to see how area residents responded.

NOVEMBER 18, 1995

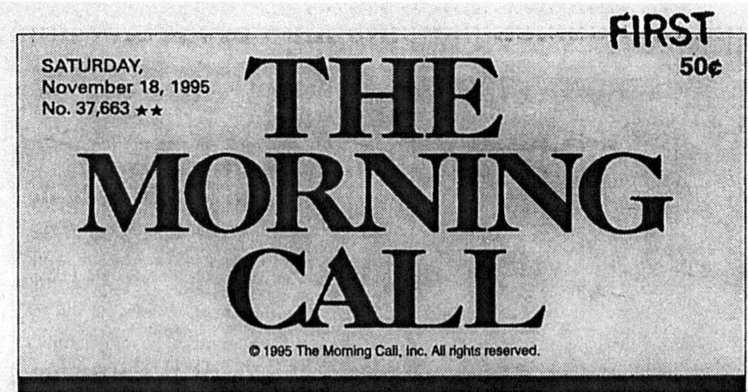

FIRST

SATURDAY,
November 18, 1995
No. 37,663 ★★

50¢

THE MORNING CALL

INDEX

Section A		Section B	
GENERAL NEWS SPORTS ENTERTAINMENT		LOCAL NEWS CLASSIFIED BUSINESS RELIGION	
Calendar	A58	Births	B11
Comic	A64	Business	B25
Comment	A41	Classified	B41
Disc Review	A61	Deaths	B38
Entertainment	A43	Religion	B33
Food	A49	Road Test	B83
People	A47	Stock Market	B26
Sports	A68	Weather	B2
Theater	A45		
TV	A62		

▶ CALL INFO-TEL
24-hour information hotlines
(610) 821-8300
Full category listing
now in TV Channel Choices

PULLOUT SECTION

Local/Classified
Pullout Section B
Follows Page A42

WEATHER

Today Tomorrow

Light snow, rain today; cloudy then clearing tomorrow. Highs, low 40s; lows, mid-30s. Details

Steelmaking will end today in Bethlehem

THE LONG GOODBYE

P A G E B 1

DAN DeLONG / The Morning Cal

Three steel workers head into Bethlehem Steel's basic oxygen furnaces (left), which will close today.

Some progress reported in private budget talks, Page A3

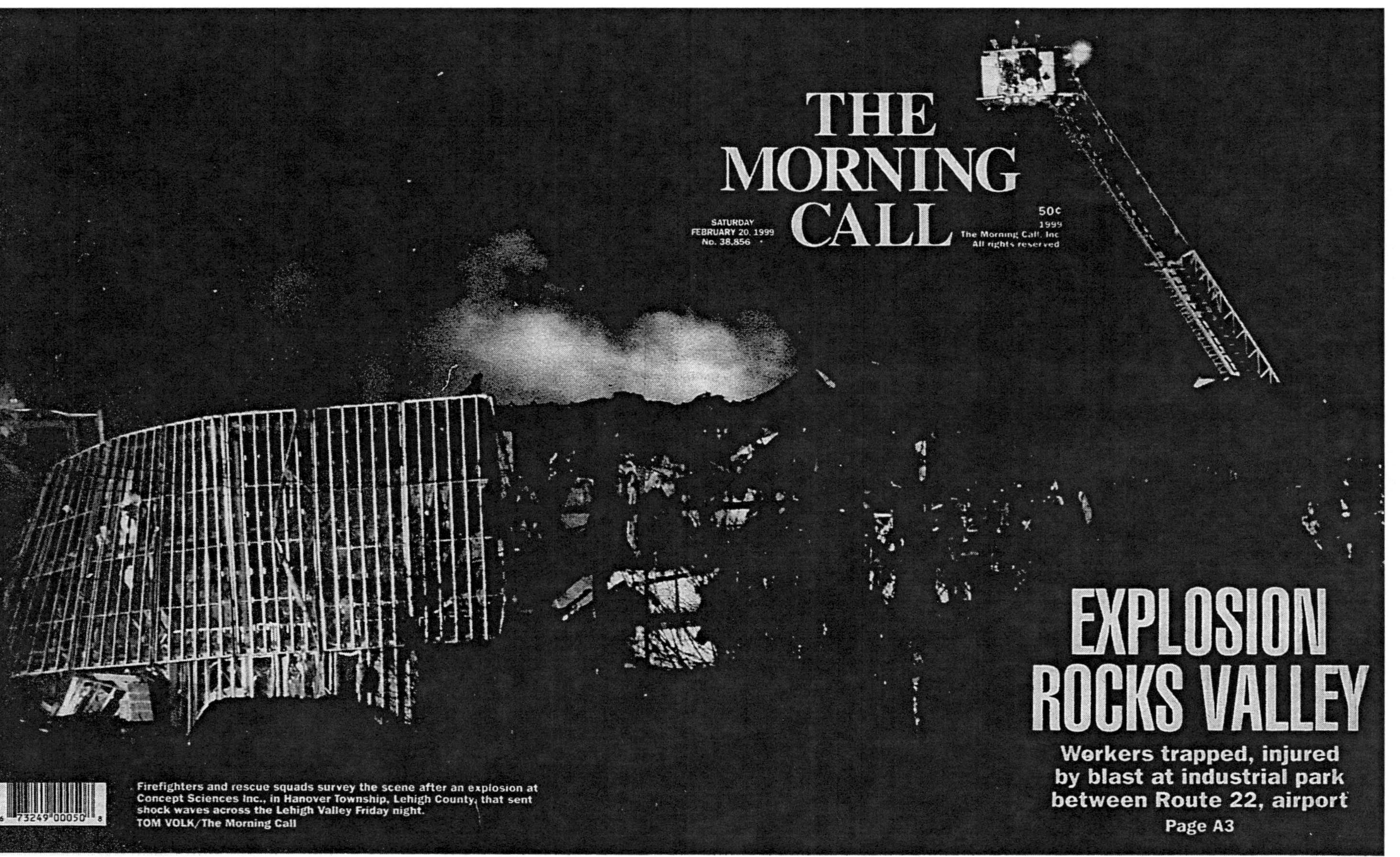

THE MORNING CALL

SATURDAY
FEBRUARY 20, 1999
No. 38,856

50¢

EXPLOSION ROCKS VALLEY

Workers trapped, injured by blast at industrial park between Route 22, airport

Page A3

Firefighters and rescue squads survey the scene after an explosion at Concept Sciences Inc., in Hanover Township, Lehigh County, that sent shock waves across the Lehigh Valley Friday night.
TOM VOLK/The Morning Call

SEPTEMBER, 12, 2001

THE MORNING CALL

Sunny

78° / 55°

Forecast, B16

mcall.com

The Morning Call's online source.

http://www.mcall.com

WEDNESDAY

SEPTEMBER 12, 2001 •

NO. 39,792

Complete coverage of the attack on America

Index on A2

50¢

TARGET: AMERICA

DEATH TOLL CATASTROPHIC

Bush: Lives lost in 'evil, despicable acts of terror'

Planes hit towers, Pentagon

Page A3

Bin Laden viewed as prime suspect

Page A26

Hijacked jet slams into west Pa. field

Page A5

Sorrow, anger envelop the Valley

Page A3

President promises retaliation

Page A7

SHAWN BALDWIN / Associated Press

A shell of what was once part of the facade of the World Trade Center's twin towers rises above the rubble that remains after Tuesday's terrorist attack.

APRIL, 10, 2003

Photos show day of conflict, celebration. A4, A5

ALLENTOWN, LEHIGH, BERKS EDITION

THE MORNING CALL

THURSDAY, APRIL 10, 2003 • www.mcall.com 50¢

SYMBOLIC of the fall of Baghdad, a noose is placed around the neck of large statue of Saddam Hussein, far left. After being pulled by a U.S. vehicle, the statue starts to fall and touches the ground to the cheers of watching Iraqis.

Associated Press

BAGHDAD FALLS

Iraqis celebrate as they topple Saddam's statue

'War is not over,' White House cautions

INSIDE

- U.S. hawks take noticeably aggressive stance toward Iraq's neighbor, Syria. **A2**
- U.S. troops in Baghdad sense war's end is near amid cheering, looting. **A3**
- Valley viewers react with different concerns to the fall of Baghdad and the toppling of Saddam's regime. **A6**
- Veterans differ on Saddam's escape in '91 Gulf War, but are confident he'll be out this time. **A6**
- Fall of Baghdad resonates with area members of Congress. **A8**
- Local families watch the troops in Baghdad while thinking of and worrying about their kin serving in Iraq. **A9**
- Joyous Kurds pour into the streets as U.S. troops take over Baghdad. **A10**
- Saddam's fall sparks mixed emotions among Arabs; some are glad he's gone but worried about America's role. **A11**
- White House urges no gloating over progress of war in Iraq. **A12**
- As Iraqi regime falls, families of missing hope for their relatives' return. **A13**
- Iraq war is a factor in International Monetary Fund's slower forecast for the global economy. **D1**

Carolyn Cole Los Angeles Times

LANCE CPL. SHAWN HICKS gets a warm welcome — and a kiss — from Iraqis celebrating the arrival of American troops in central Baghdad and the apparent end of the Saddam Hussein regime. Iraq's ambassador to the United Nations admitted that U.S. troops had overrun his country Wednesday, saying, 'The game is over.'

INDEX

For home delivery, call 610-820-6601 or 800-666-5492

THE MORNING CALL (ISSN 0884-5957) is published daily by The Morning Call Inc., 101 N. 6th St., Allentown, Pa. 18101. Periodicals postage paid at Allentown, Pa. POSTMASTER: Send address changes to THE MORNING CALL, P.O. Box 1260, Allentown, Pa. 18105-1260

By Craig Gordon and Thomas Frank

Special to The Morning Call

BAGHDAD, Iraq | The heart of Iraq's capital city fell to advancing American troops Wednesday along with a quarter-century of iron rule by Saddam Hussein, whose end was marked by the symbolism of jubilant Iraqis helping to pull his 20-foot-tall likeness to the ground.

Inside the city, a top U.S. commander declared the Iraqi military effectively defeated after 21 days of war.

"There is no government left to speak of," said Maj. Gen. Buford Blount, head of the Army's 3rd Infantry Division. "By securing Baghdad, we set the conditions to ensure the regime is no longer functioning."

But Blount, in a message echoed by Vice President Dick Cheney and others

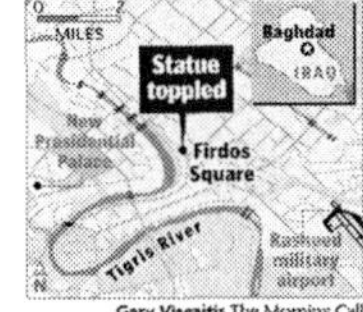

Gary Visgaitis The Morning Call

throughout the U.S. government, stopped short of declaring victory despite clear signs that Saddam's grip on the nation had been broken, with the Iraqi military in tatters and its leaders far from sight.

"The war is not over," said White House spokesman Ari Fleischer, who also deflected questions over when and how President Bush might declare victory.

Pentagon officials warned that tough days of fighting might lie ahead. Military commanders turned their attention to the northern city of Tikrit, Saddam's ancestral homeland and a place where many believe his most loyal followers will mount a do-or-die last stand.

A leading Kurdish opposition group claimed Saddam already had fled there. U.S. officials acknowledged they didn't know Saddam's whereabouts — or whether he is dead or alive — after a bombing strike in Baghdad on Monday they had hoped would kill him and his two sons.

Despite Washington's attempts to use words of caution to counter pictures of Iraqis dancing in the streets, it was clear Wednesday that the bulk of the war is now behind American troops.

Even Iraq's ambassador to

WAR PAGE **A3**

Up next: U.S. to slam Saddam's power base

By Stephen J. Hedges

Special to The Morning Call

WASHINGTON | With objectives falling at a pace that is stunning in military terms, the U.S. invasion force in Iraq is shifting its sights and firepower to the north central city of Tikrit, the hometown and political power base of Saddam Hussein.

Saddam's whereabouts and fate remain unknown, and the ability of his loyalists to regroup and mount a defensive stand north of Baghdad is questionable. But several thousand Republican Guards remain in Tikrit, Pentagon officials said, and additional Iraqi regular forces still guard the northern Kurdish cities of Kirkuk and Mosul.

Those last fingerholds on power for Saddam's regime could dissolve when a battle is joined, repeating the experience of Iraqi forces charged with defending Baghdad. Or they could put up a stiffer fight, making the price that U.S. and British forces pay for the regime's final removal that much higher.

"The regime has been run out of a number of Iraqi cities and towns," Defense Secretary Donald Rumsfeld said Wednesday. "But other Iraqi cities are still being contested, and there will still be

STRATEGY PAGE **A2**

DECEMBER 30, 2006

SADDAM HANGED

U.S. judge rejects appeal; execution filmed

By Christopher Torchia and Qassim Abdul-Zahra
Of The Associated Press

BAGHDAD, Iraq | Saddam Hussein, the shotgun-waving dictator who ruled Iraq with a remorseless brutality for a quarter-century and was driven from power by a U.S.-led war that left his country in shambles, was taken to the gallows and executed around 10 p.m. EST Friday, Iraqi state-run television reported.

It was a grim end for the 69-year-old leader who had vexed three U.S. presidents. Despite his ouster, Washington, its allies and the new Iraqi leaders remain mired in a fight to quell a stubborn insurgency by Saddam loyalists and a vicious sectarian conflict.

Also hanged were Saddam's half-brother Barzan Ibrahim and Awad Hamed al-Bandar, the former chief justice of the Revolutionary Court. A state-run Iraqiya television news announcer said "criminal Saddam was hanged to death and the execution started with criminal Saddam then Barzan then Awad al-Bandar."

Mariam al-Rayes, a legal expert and a former member of the Shiite bloc in parliament, told Iraqiya television that the execution "was filmed and God willing it will be shown. There was one camera present, and a doctor was also present there."

Al-Rayes, an ally of Prime Minister Nouri al-Maliki, did not attend the execution. She said Al-Maliki did not attend but was represented by an aide.

The station earlier was airing national songs after the first announcement and had a tag on the screen that read "Saddam's execution marks the end of a dark period of Iraq's history."

The execution came 56 days after a court convicted Saddam and sentenced

SADDAM PAGE A13

MORE COVERAGE INSIDE: Complete obituary, analysis on ex-dictator's downfall A13

THE MORNING CALL

SATURDAY, DECEMBER 30, 2006 • www.mcall.com 50¢ 2

Partly cloudy
50° | 26°
Forecast, B8

INSIDE

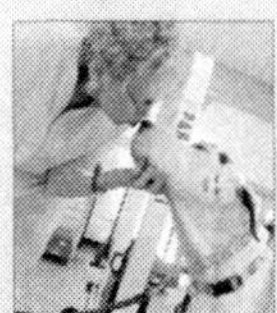

Since Bailey, life's looking up

Multiple sclerosis blurred Dale Allen's vision and weakened her right leg. Depression followed. Then came a service dog that changed her life. **B1**

ABOUT $10,500 HAS BEEN RECEIVED by the Salvation Army of Bethlehem in memory of Kevin Muzila, gunned down at 15. Funds will aid his family. **B1**

NEWS TO USE

KID-FREE ZONES

Is it rude to exclude children from a wedding reception? Advice Goddess Amy Alkon tackles this prickly question. **D16**

PARTY MUSIC

What are you going to do after you've sung "Auld Lang Syne?" Bring some variety to your New Year's Eve party with these new musical video games. **D16**

LOCAL FAVORITE

The Hellertown Bike Park is a great place to get lost or be found, says writer Geoff Gehman. Discover the charms of this rough sanctuary, centered on a steel slag dump. **D3**

FIRE KILLS FIVE IN ALLENTOWN

Doug Kilpatrick Special to The Morning Call

ALLENTOWN FIREFIGHTERS bring out one of the bodies of the five fire victims at 624½ Park St. on Friday morning.

Community activist, others died from smoke.

By Melanie A. Hughes, Romy Varghese, Manuel Gamiz Jr. and Kirk Beldon Jackson
Of The Morning Call

An electrical malfunction near Christmas decorations in a row home sparked a morning fire Friday that killed five and injured eight in Allentown's deadliest blaze since 1974, the year arson claimed nine lives at the Caboose bar.

MORE INSIDE
■ Photographs of the fire scene.
PAGE **A6**

Flames quickly spread inside 624½ Park St., then to the front porch and on to neighboring porches in the Stevens Park neighborhood, Fire Capt. Bob Scheirer said. The 6:33 a.m. two-alarm fire was under control within a half-hour, but it left at least 10 people homeless heading into the holiday weekend.

A mother and daughter and three of their friends were killed by smoke inhalation, apparently while sleeping, Lehigh County Coroner Scott Grim said. Two were found in a second-floor bedroom, and the others on the third floor. The house had no

FIRE PAGE A2

'They were all friends, just one big happy family'

By Romy Varghese, Manuel Gamiz Jr. and Kirk Beldon Jackson
Of The Morning Call

Barbara Houx sold flowers on holidays at the same Allentown corner and dressed up in a clown costume for community events.

Her daughter Casundra Miller was four months pregnant.

Friends and family who flocked to the scene of Friday's fatal house fire in Allentown were shocked at the loss of Houx, 52; her daughter, 28; her daughter's boyfriend, Randy Keding, 27, and ex-boyfriend Shawn Sandt, 22; and Houx's friend Allen Lindenmuth, 48.

Most neighbors of the row home, near Sixth and Tilghman streets, knew of Houx. For more than a decade she had sold flowers on Fridays and Saturdays at Seventh and Tilghman streets. In the last couple of years she cut back to selling flowers just on holidays — except Christmas "because she sang in the choir," said Catherine Grubbs of the Starr Flower Co. in Bath.

Houx was also active in the community. She was vice president of the Stevens Park Safe Neighborhood Association and a member of the Target Area Leadership, or TALL team, of Weed and Seed, a revitalization program, according to her friend Everett Bickford, president of the neighborhood association.

Others said Houx's involvement with the neighborhood association led to threats.

VICTIMS PAGE A3

Randy Keding

Barbara Houx

Casundra Miller

Shawn Sandt

Allen Lindenmuth

AT A GLANCE

- **What:** House fire kills five adults.
- **How:** Electrical source near Christmas decorations suspected.
- **When:** Firefighters arrive at 6:36 a.m.
- **Where:** Steven's Park neighborhood, Allentown

NATION WORLD | MOURNING FOR FORD BEGINS; BROWN EULOGIZED | SNOWSTORM WALLOPS WEST; BUSH HEEDS TWISTER WARNING | MICHAEL JORDAN, WIFE GRANTED DIVORCE | A12

6 73249 00050 8

MARCH 31, 2008

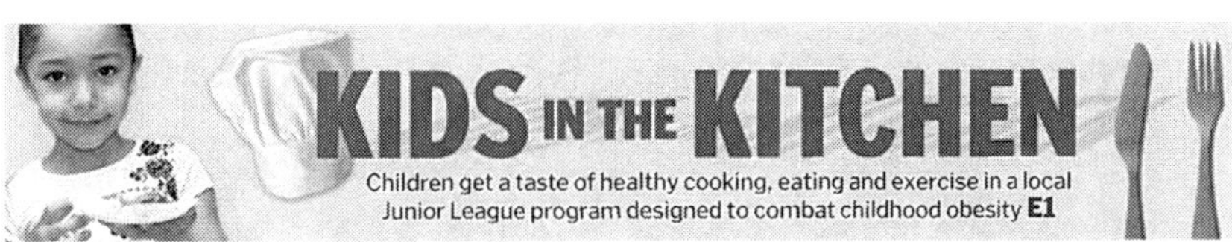

KIDS IN THE KITCHEN
Children get a taste of healthy cooking, eating and exercise in a local Junior League program designed to combat childhood obesity E1

THE MORNING CALL

MONDAY, MARCH 31, 2008 • themorningcall.com 75¢ 1

Rain likely
46° | 45°
Forecast, B8

INSIDE

Late St. Pat's parade attracts big crowd

Allentown's St. Patrick's Day Parade attracted its largest crowd of spectators in at least 12 years, thanks to shifting the route to the city's residential West End and perfect spring weather. **B1**

A "SUSPICIOUS" EXPLOSION at a strip mall that rocked homes nearly a mile away set off a fire that gutted five businesses in Nockamixon Township, officials said. **B1**

COLONIAL REGIONAL POLICE moved from Bath into new headquarters in Hanover Township, Northampton County, after two years of conflict over the move. **B1**

GOODWILL KEYSTONE AREA, known for its thrift stores, also provides a host of business services such as janitorial and mailing work in the region. **A16**

NEWS TO USE

HOW IS INFLATION MEASURED? Is renter's insurance worth it? The Motley Fool answers those questions and talks about Hewlett-Packard's hat trick. **A16**

A READER WONDERS with all the earth-moving going on at the Sands BethWorks project in South Bethlehem if the support columns for the Minsi Trail Bridge have been compromised. **Road Warrior, B1**

NATION WORLD

MUQTADA AL-SADR ordered his Shiite militiamen off the streets but called on the Iraqi government to stop its raids against his followers. **A4**

LEADING DOCTORS urged a return to older, tried-and-true treatments for high cholesterol after hearing full results of a failed trial of Vytorin. **A4**

CHINESE SPECTATORS cheered as Greece handed off the Olympic flame for its journey to Beijing but pro-Tibet protesters stole the limelight. **A6**

Home delivery: 610-820-6601

6 73249 00050 8

COCA-COLA PARK DEBUT  IRONPIGS VS. PHILLIES

BASEBALL IS BACK

10,188 people christen new stadium in Allentown at exhibition game won by the major leaguers

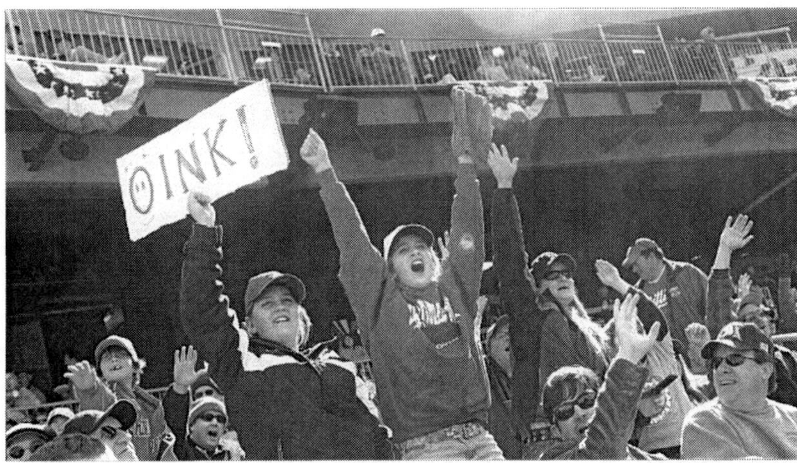

Emily Robson Special to The Morning Call

JESSICA STUMP of Allentown (holding sign), Celina Danish of Allentown (center) and April Kummerer of Emmaus (right) cheer on the IronPigs at the first game at Coca-Cola Park in Allentown. It's been nearly 50 years since a major league-affiliated team has played in the Lehigh Valley.

By Darryl R. Isherwood and Paul Muschick
Of The Morning Call

Some came early to grill burgers and dogs. Others headed straight for the fence at the first-base line, hoping to score an autograph or two.

A sellout crowd streamed into the new Coca-Cola Park on Allentown's east side Sunday to celebrate the first major league-affiliated baseball game in the Lehigh Valley in nearly 50 years.

The exhibition game between the Triple-A Lehigh Valley IronPigs and their parent team, the Phillies, was played under sunny skies, though a chill was in the air. The Phillies won, 5-3.

"The Philadelphia Phillies playing on Allentown soil, this is historic stuff," said fan Mark Vresk, who, to ensure he got tickets for the game, got in line at 4:30 a.m. the day the tickets went on sale.

Fans were impressed with the stadium and its attractions, though some complained about traffic, parking and long lines at food stands.

The stadium's opening boosts the Lehigh Valley's profile and solidifies its

IRONPIGS PAGE A10

Rob Kandel The Morning Call

THE IRONPIGS' John Ennis delivers a pitch in the eighth inning.

Old-timers remember Valley's ghosts of baseball past

By Daniel Patrick Sheehan
The Morning Call

More than one fan at Sunday's first-ever Lehigh Valley IronPigs game gazed on the fresh-from-the-wrapper confines of Coca-Cola Park and saw ghosts springing out of the emerald grass of a long-gone baseball childhood.

None of the old-timers who watched games at Breadon Field in the 1940s and '50s ever expected those ghosts to turn again into flesh-and-blood players, but there they were, big as life in IronPigs white and Phillies red, stretching and swatting batting practice pitches cut toward the Coca-Cola scoreboard.

"I was a batboy there for a couple of games," said Earl Kistler of Allentown, a 72-year-old Phillies fan looking back

OLD-TIMERS PAGE A10

MORE INSIDE

■ Resident baseball geek Bill White gives the lowdown on Coca-Cola Park.
PAGE A10

ONLINE extra
themorningcall.com/ironpigs

HISTORY MAKING DAY
Multimedia slide show, photo gallery and The Hog Blog look back on Sunday's events.

INTERNATIONAL LEAGUE PRIMER
Meet the 13 other teams the IronPigs will face this year in the International League.

COMPLETE COVERAGE, including columns by Gordie Jones and Keith Groller, begins on C1

ELECTION 2008
PICKING THE PRESIDENT

On the road ... with Barack Obama

Six-day bus tour across Pennsylvania is filled with as many small, telling moments as main events.

By John L. Micek
Call Harrisburg Bureau

STATE COLLEGE | First, it's a rally in front of 22,000 screaming supporters at Penn State University. More than an hour later, it's a more intimate stop at a sports bar off Route 322 in rural Mifflin County.

Such are the extremes of Democratic presidential candidate Barack Obama's first barnstorming tour across Pennsylvania.

The six-day bus excursion that the Illinois senator hopes will help him close the double-digit polling gap that separates him from U.S. Sen. Hillary Clinton, D-N.Y., started Friday in the towns of western Pennsylvania that are believed to Clinton strongholds.

MORE INSIDE

■ Obama will make his first visit to the Valley today.
PAGE A3

Then it looped through the vast rural middle of the state, stopping in Johnstown and Altoona, before continuing on to eastern Pennsylvania and concluding in the Philadelphia suburbs that Obama campaign hopes will propel him to victory in the state's April 22 primary.

"I think he can make a lot of progress. I don't know if I want to make predictions about whether he can win," U.S. Sen. Bob Casey, D-Pa., tells reporters after a town meeting at Greater

TOUR PAGE A2

OBAMA'S ALLENTOWN VISIT

Barack Obama will be at Muhlenberg College in Allentown today as part of his bid for the Democratic nomination for president.

Tickets are no longer available. Here are the details:

■ Sen. Obama is expected to arrive around 5:50 p.m. at Memorial Hall, located on Liberty Street between 23rd and 24th streets.

■ Doors will open at 3:50 p.m. Participants will file through metal detectors.

■ No backpacks, bags, food, water or signs are permitted.

BARACK OBAMA addresses the crowd at Penn State.

OCTOBER 30, 2008

BETHLEHEM CASINO: Sands putting its chips on an early opening, **A2**

PENNSYLVANIA POLL: Many want 1-party rule for White House, Congress, **A3**

Use it for life.

THE MORNING CALL

• 5 **THURSDAY,** OCTOBER 30, 2008 | 75¢ themorningcall.com

>> SO YOU KNOW

KidsPeace's Autumn Ball on Saturday will raise money to help autistic children and their families. MORE TO KNOW: **A10**

MOSTLY SUNNY **49°** | **27°** FORECAST **B10**

PHILADELPHIA PHILLIES: 2008 WORLD SERIES CHAMPIONS

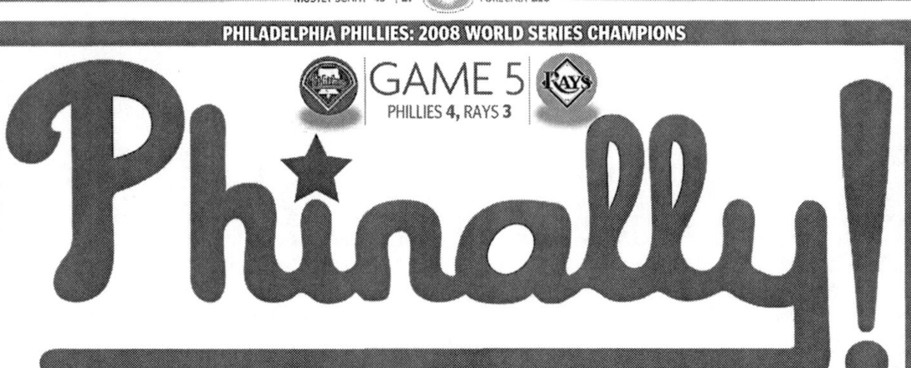

GAME 5

PHILLIES **4**, RAYS **3**

Phinally!

- **Phillies fans go wild celebrating city's first major pro sports title since '83**
- **Brad Lidge closes out Rays after Pedro Feliz's game-winning hit**
- **Winning it all is 'something you live for,' says Series MVP Cole Hamels**

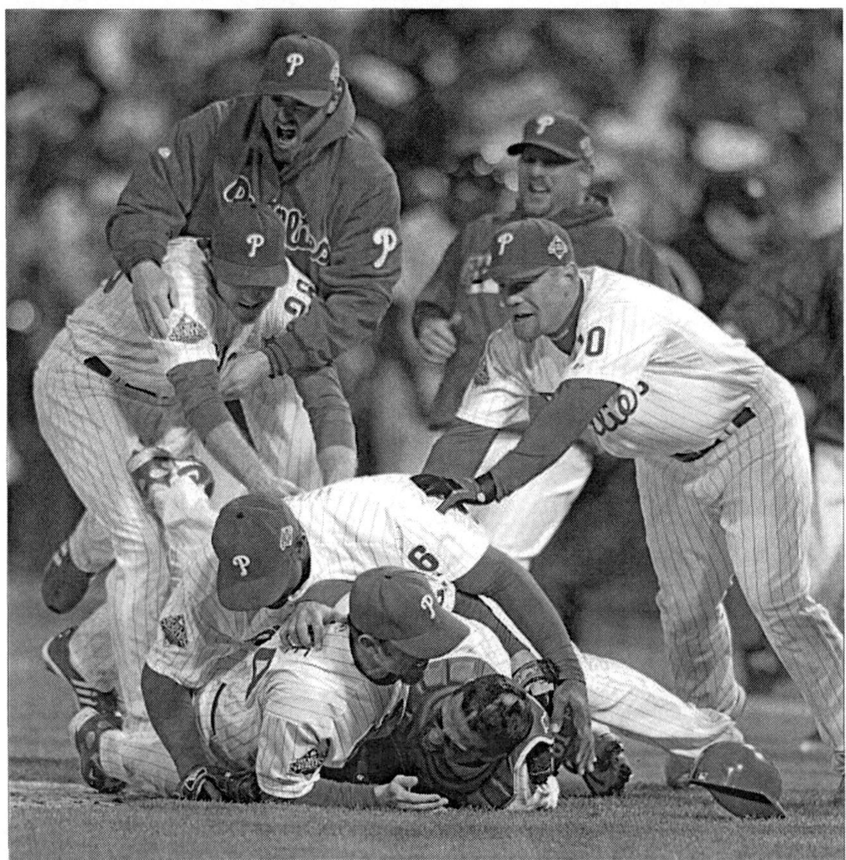

Michael Kubel The Morning Call

PHILLIES RELIEVER BRAD LIDGE is mobbed by teammates after he sealed Philadelphia's first World Series title in 28 years. Lidge capped off a perfect season, going 41 for 41 in save chances in the regular season and seven for seven in the postseason. A parade down Broad Street is set for Friday. Game story, parade details, **C1**

COVERAGE INSIDE

- Lasting images from the championship run, **A4**
- Dying 90-year-old Valley woman's wish granted, **B1**
- Miller: Phils' entire roster showed skill, grit, **C1**
- Groller: Fairy tales come true sometimes, **C1**

COMING FRIDAY

CELEBRATE the Phillies' victory with an eight-page special section marking the team's rise to the top of the baseball world.

NOVEMBER 5, 2008

★ELECTION RESULTS★

15TH DISTRICT: Republican incumbent Dent easily tops Bennett, **A13**

11TH DISTRICT: Kanjorski survives close contest with Hazleton's Barletta, **A13**

Use it for life.

THE MORNING CALL

• 4 WEDNESDAY, NOVEMBER 5, 2008 | themorningcall.com | 75¢

» SO YOU KNOW
Big Brothers Big Sisters Lehigh Valley will honor program efforts with its Bigs and Littles of the Year.
MORE TO KNOW: **A16**

SCATTERED RAIN 63° | 48° FORECAST B12

BARACK OBAMA was elected the nation's 44th president on Tuesday, becoming the first black American to occupy the nation's highest office. On his way to victory, Obama, 47, shattered fundraising records and, many Americans believe, his ascendancy will help lighten the nation's centuries-old burden of racism. Serving just half his six-year Senate term before launching his White House bid, Obama attracted record crowds along the campaign trail, drawn in part by his formidable skills as an orator. He will face the challenge of unifying a nation in financial crisis and orchestrating the U.S. role at a pivotal moment on the world stage.

Morry Gash Associated Press

PRESIDENT-ELECT BARACK OBAMA waves to supporters as he takes the stage at his Election Night party at Grant Park in Chicago. He'll become the nation's 44th president in January.

With sweetest victory, blacks' joy is unbounded

By William J. Ford and Tim Darragh
Of The Morning Call

Clyde Bosket Sr. was in Washington, D.C., on that hot August day in 1963 when Martin Luther King Jr. revealed his dream to the world, speaking memorably about blacks "languishing in the corners of American society."

"This sweltering summer of the Negro's legitimate discontent will not pass," King intoned from the steps of the Lincoln Memorial, "until there is an invigorating autumn of freedom and equality."

Now, on a sweet autumn day 45 years and 68 days later, Bosket watched as Barack Obama, son of a Kenyan father and American mother, became the president-elect of the United States of America.

Bosket and his wife, Mattie, could hardly contain themselves around 11 p.m. as the television networks declared Obama the winner.

"Oh boy, this is beautiful," Mattie said, beaming.

The couple laughed and hugged, and the 79-year-old semi-retired barber even lifted his wife off the floor as they watched the returns from their

HISTORIC PAGE A7

Obama first black president — in electoral landslide

By Scott Kraus
Of The Morning Call

Batting away John McCain's furious last-minute push to take Pennsylvania, Barack Obama built an insurmountable lead Tuesday night to become the nation's first black president.

Obama also picked up vital victories in Ohio and Virginia, critical swing states captured in 2004 by George Bush on his way to re-election. No Republican has captured the White House without Ohio's 20 electoral votes. Virginia hasn't picked a Democratic president since 1964.

McCain had pinned his hopes on Pennsylvania, but a two-week blitz of visits and campaign ads failed to close an Obama lead that had swelled to double digits in October as the economy faltered.

Obama fared well in Philadelphia and its suburbs, as well as in western Pennsylvania. He also held leads in Lehigh, Northampton and surrounding counties. McCain won only the central and northern regions of the state.

Obama also swept through territory typically friendly to Democrats in the East and Midwest of the nation.

OBAMA PAGE A5

MAY 23, 2009

STATE CHAMPION: Allen High's Amber Troxell wins javelin title, SPORTS 1

Use it for life.

THE MORNING CALL

SATURDAY

• 1 75¢ themorningcall.com

MAY 23, 2009

Isolated t-storms 80° | 58° FORECAST SPORTS 8

SPORTS 1
STECKEL RETURNS: Ex-NFL coach draws big crowd at book-signing

LIFE 1
THOMAS TO PULL INTO PHILLIPSBURG: Will visit Delaware River Railroad

SANDS CASINO RESORT BETHLEHEM GRAND OPENING

'HERE WE GO, SANDS, HERE WE GO!'

Gamblers line up hours early to be among first to try their luck

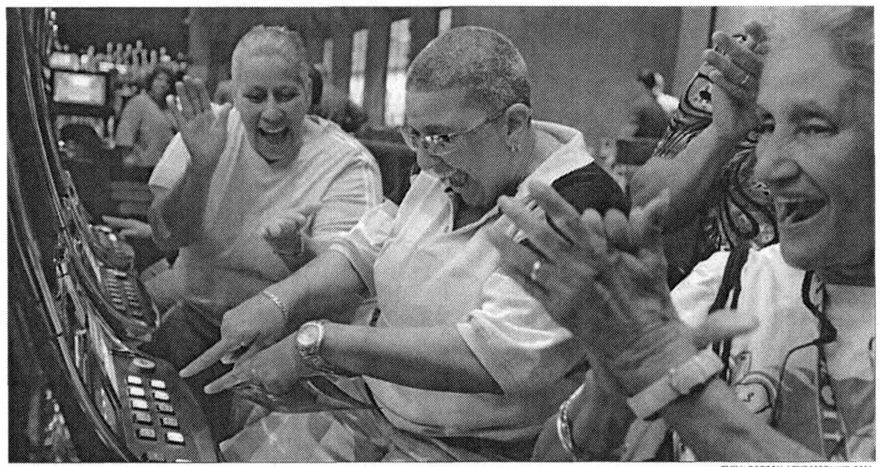

EMILY ROBSON / THE MORNING CALL

Lucia Carambot (center) of Bethlehem is excited to have won in the first five minutes of playing slots at the Sands Casino Resort Bethlehem. Milagros Vasquez (left) of Bethlehem and her mother, Bernarda Santiago (right) of Philadelphia, celebrate Carambot's win.

By Matt Assad, Christopher Baxter and Nicole Radzievich
OF THE MORNING CALL

At the head of a surging crowd, the would-be gamblers in the front row all had a strategy to be the first to drop money into the slot machines — and the first to strike it rich — at Friday's opening of the Sands Casino Resort Bethlehem.

Roe Christian of Easton arrived four hours before the 9 a.m. scheduled opening and grabbed the pole position, while Milagros Vasquez of Bethlehem eyed a Monopoly machine just a few paces away.

Thomas Blair of Bethlehem arrived at 3:30 a.m., and when he found the parking garage hadn't opened yet, he parked nearly a mile away and walked back to the casino to be the first person to arrive.

"This is history," said Blair, a retired iron worker who recalled fondly how, as a boy, he watched Bethlehem Steel cranes move ore from the pit where the casino now stands. "There's a new business in town. I wanted to be part of it. Plus, I really like to gamble."

As the crowd chanted, "Here we go, Sands, here we go," casino officials opened the $748 million gambling hall 20 minutes early, and in gushed four years of pent-up anticipation for gambling in Bethlehem. Blair may have been first in line, but when the dam broke, his 64-year-old legs couldn't keep up with the gaggle of mostly women who ran around him.

"This feels a lot like Black Friday at work," said Cheryl Peych, a Wal-Mart worker from Emmaus, looking over her shoulder at the crowd. "As employees, we know to get out of the way and let it go, because when a crowd like this gets going, there's no stopping it."

Some of the decidedly senior crowd said

Please see CASINO **NEWS 2**

A crowd waits behind the ropes for officials to let them onto the casino floor on Friday.

EMILY ROBSON / THE MORNING CALL

"Hey, it's something to do. I'm retired, and I don't really like gardening."

— Donald Boylan, Long Island, N.Y.

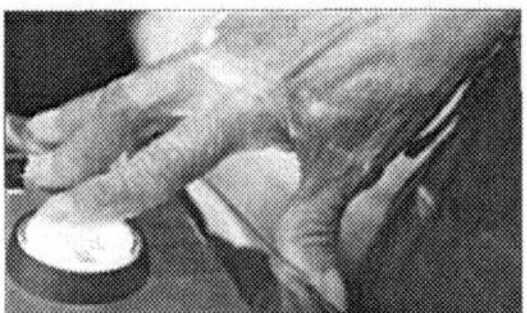

"Gonna be here a lot. Could be trouble. Could be lots of trouble."

— Milagros Vasquez, Bethlehem

Price of electricity becomes 'a jobs issue'

Businesses say electric rate hikes will put many in Valley out of work.

By Spencer Soper
OF THE MORNING CALL

When electric rates spike for PPL customers next year, it could force some companies out of business or encourage them to move to states where power is cheaper, a group of large power users told state lawmakers Friday.

If lawmakers don't act to curb the rate hikes expected in January, more Pennsylvanians will lose their jobs at a time when unemployment is at its highest rate in more than 20 years, the group contends.

The cost increase is estimated to be 20 percent to 40 percent for small to midsize businesses. The increase for large industrial electric users, which includes most manufacturing operations, is not yet known. But some industrial users expect their electric bills could double.

"The price we pay for electricity is a jobs issue," said Terry Bennett, who manages Lafarge North

Please see DEREGULATION **NEWS 4**

INSIDE NEWS

Interim U.S. Attorney Laurie Magid is out as the top federal prosecutor in eastern Pennsylvania. She's being replaced temporarily by Assistant U.S. Attorney Michael Levy. **News 12**

Allentown police have tracked leads and investigated possible sightings but have been unable to find a mentally challenged teen who ran away from her foster home Sunday. **News 6**

Economy has us grillin' and chillin' at home

AAA estimates a 3.4% drop in travel for mid-Atlantic region.

By Brian Callaway
OF THE MORNING CALL

Recession-battered families around the region are settling for a backyard barbecue sort of Memorial Day weekend, ignoring hotel getaway bargains and gas prices that remain far lower than last year's.

AAA, the travelers' advocacy group, estimates that the number of vacationers in the mid-Atlantic region will dip 3.4 percent this year — the steepest decline of any part of country.

Travel nationwide is expected to increase slightly this year. But in Pennsylvania and neighboring states more people seem to be sticking close to home and saving their money as the summer vacation season begins.

"We usually go away to the beach," said Kristine Horn, a special education teacher in the Allentown School District, where a software glitch earlier this month

Please see TRAVEL **NEWS 12**

EGYPTIAN UNREST: Fears of a coup after Mubarak refuses to leave, **News 18**

LEHIGH VALLEY'S NEWSPAPER

THE MORNING CALL

themorningcall.com

• 5 $1.00 FEBRUARY 11, 2011 **FRIDAY** SUNSHINE 34° | 19° FORECAST **SPORTS 10**

ALLENTOWN DISASTER

BLAST KILLS FIVE; NEIGHBORHOOD IN RUINS

ROB KANDEL/THE MORNING CALL

The remains of eight houses in the 500 block of N. 13th Street after an explosion at 544 N. 13th late Wednesday night. The five dead were found in the rubble of two homes.

Tragedy stokes fear of city's aging gas lines

By Daniel Patrick Sheehan, Arlene Martinez, Matt Assad and Manuel Gamiz Jr.
OF THE MORNING CALL

As Thursday dawned, the extent of the explosion and fire in central Allentown became starkly visible: half a block reduced to cinders by a catastrophe that killed five people, displaced scores from their homes and raised fears about the soundness of the aged gas pipelines beneath the city.

The victims of the blast were identified by family members as William Hall, 79, and his wife Beatrice, 74, of 544 N. 13th St.; and three members of the Cruz family at 542 N. 13th St., including a 4-month-old boy.

About a dozen other people were injured and more than 350 were forced to evacuate

Please see BLAST ***NEWS 10***

MONICA CABRERA /THE MORNING CALL

Firefighters battle the flames in the 500 block of N. 13th Street in Allentown.

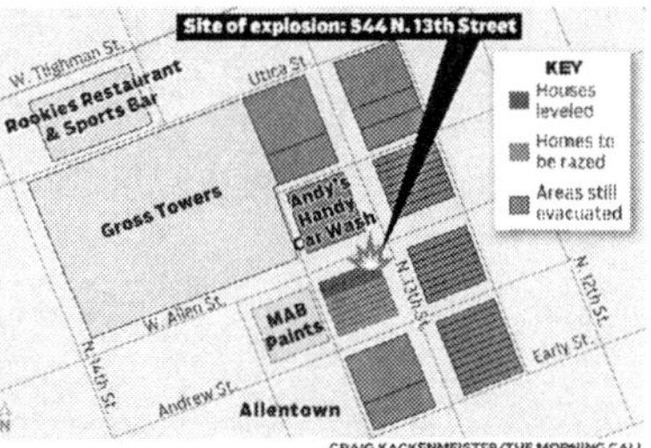

CRAIG KACKENMEISTER/THE MORNING CALL

MORE COVERAGE

ON THE WEB:
- Videos and photo galleries
- Timeline and historic photos of other explosions

themorningcall.com

MORE INSIDE
- Neighbors share harrowing tale
- How to help blast victims
- Evacuees should be home today

NEWS 10, 11, 12, 15

TWO TALES OF LOSS

One family had deep roots; other new to neighborhood

Halls had lived in their home since 1962; Cruzes moved next door in 2009.

By Devon Lash, Arlene Martinez and Adam Clark
OF THE MORNING CALL

Every first and third Saturday of the month, Bill and Bea — as just about everyone called them — helped out at the food bank in the basement of their church.

It wasn't out of character for the couple, who had spent 52 years of marriage living lives of quiet devotion to their family, church, community and country.

CONTRIBUTED PHOTO

William and Beatrice Hall were described as giving, selfless people.

They campaigned for their local politicians and voted in every election. He served in the Army during the Korean War as a combat engineer.

She sang in the church choir and loved to share her favorite meatloaf recipe.

William Hall, 79, and his wife, Beatrice, 74, were two of the five people who died in the thunderous blast that shook the city of Allentown late Wednesday night.

The Halls' home at 544 N. 13th St., where they had lived since 1962, was the site of an apparent gas explosion and fire that gutted a row of homes on the block's western side, left dozens injured and forced hundreds to evacuate the surrounding blocks.

Three members of the next-door Cruz family — 69-year-old grandmother Ofelia Ben, her 16-year-old granddaughter Catherine Cruz, and

Please see VICTIMS ***NEWS 11***

NOVEMBER 2, 2011

REVERSAL: BANK OF AMERICA SCRAPS DEBIT CARD FEE, NEWS 19

LEHIGH VALLEY'S NEWSPAPER
THE MORNING CALL
themorningcall.com
FIRE IN A BOTTLE
LIFE/FOOD
Easton Salsa shares recipe for hot sauce

• 5 $1.00 NOVEMBER 2, 2011 WEDNESDAY FOG THEN SUN 56° | 34° FORECAST SPORTS 8

ALLENTOWN'S HOCKEY ARENA PROJECT

A FIRST LOOK

Mayor unveils plans for $100 million complex that includes four-level arena, sports bar, restaurant, retail shops

WHAT TO EXPECT:
4 LEVELS IN THE ARENA
30 CORPORATE CLUB BOXES
8,500 SEATING FOR A HOCKEY GAME
10,000 SEATING FOR A CONCERT
200+ VIP PARKING ON SITE
3 RESTAURANT/SHOPS: SPORTS BAR, CLUB RESTAURANT AND TEAM STORE OPEN YEAR-ROUND LOCATED ON HAMILTON STREET
"The vision is to revitalize the downtown by really activating the site 365 days a year."
— Allentown Mayor Ed Pawlowski
ALLENTOWN ARENA

CONTRIBUTED ARTIST'S RENDERING

A sketch of the proposed $100 million hockey arena complex that's on track to open in 2013. The arena is to have a glass and steel, two-story entrance at Seventh and Hamilton.

By Matt Assad and Scott Kraus
Of The Morning Call

When Allentown Mayor Ed Pawlowski looks down Hamilton Street, he envisions thousands of hockey fans pouring out of a $100 million arena and into a downtown entertainment district of sports bars, restaurants and retail shops.

While it may take imagination to visualize such a scene in Allentown's struggling downtown now, Pawlowski on Tuesday brought some clarity to how the city plans to get there when he released the first designs for the arena, which alone is projected to draw 500,000 people downtown each year.

The first architectural renderings show a glass and steel, two-story entrance at Hamilton and Seventh streets, transitioning into a row of new places to eat, drink and shop extending down the 700 block of Hamilton Street. For Pawlowski, the shiny new arena, on track to open in 2013, is a first step toward a much larger development he's counting on to create a new Allentown.

"The vision is for an entertainment district to create one of, I think, America's most dynamic urban revitalization projects centered around this multi-anchored development, which is the arena," Pawlowski said. "The vision is to revitalize the downtown by really activating the site 365 days a year."

After promising new details on the proposed 8,500-seat arena for months, Pawlowski on Tuesday released a 25-page slide show that paints a picture of a new Hamilton Street landscape, highlighted by an arena that will host concerts, community events, and be home to the minor league Phantoms, the Philadelphia Flyers' top affiliate, in time for the 2013 hockey season.

The arena is to include a sports bar and restaurant, a merchandise shop and a handful of Hamilton Street retail shops. Those businesses will be open daily, regardless of whether the arena is hosting a hockey game or other event.

"During non-event nights, you will have this great sports bar that will be fronted on Hamilton," Pawlowski said. "During event nights it will be closed off to the general public and it will become the premium seating and the club-level seats."

Pawlowski said when there isn't a hockey game, the venue can hold 10,000 people for the kind of concerts current Lehigh Valley facilities are too small to attract.

"If Elton John or Sting plays Philadelphia," Pawlowski said, "you're going to see them up here, too."

Please see ALLENTOWN **NEWS 15**

INSIDE NEWS

Lehigh County authorities are investigating the suspicious death of a man whose body was found Tuesday morning in a remote section of South Whitehall Township. **News 6**

The Lehigh Valley added 1,200 jobs in September, pushing the unemployment rate down to 8.9 percent, according to figures released Tuesday by the state. **News 18**

SNOWSTORM'S AFTERMATH

PPL tree trimmers out in full force

Mother Nature — not utililty's vegetation policy — to blame for outages, company says.

By Peter Hall and Sam Kennedy
Of The Morning Call

PPL tree trimmers swarmed through a wooded enclave of South Mountain homes off S. Pike Avenue in Salisbury Township, bringing bucket trucks and chain saws to clear the way for power line repairs.

Like thousands throughout the Lehigh Valley, residents of Tupelo Street and Black Gum Drive have been without electricity since Saturday, when an unprecedented October snowstorm felled thousands of trees still wearing their autumn foliage.

"Basically there's nothing that can prevent it," said Mike McGill, a PPL contractor from Lock Haven, Clinton County. "If the leaves weren't

Please see TREES **NEWS 4**

Travis Austin, a worker for a PPL contractor in Madisonville, Ky., works to restore power on Tupelo Street in Salisbury Township on Tuesday.

MICHAEL KUBEL/ THE MORNING CALL

MORE INSIDE

■ Tips on how to deal with damaged trees.
■ Storm debris collection sites.
NEWS 2

FOR HOME DELIVERY CALL 1-800-666-5492 OR VISIT themorningcall.com

NOVEMBER, 10, 2011

PRECINCT-BY-PRECINCT ELECTION RESULTS, NEWS 24, 25

LEHIGH VALLEY'S NEWSPAPER

THE MORNING CALL

themorningcall.com

• 3 $1.00 NOVEMBER 10, 2011 THURSDAY CLOUDY, RAIN & COOLER 56° | 38° FORECAST SPORTS 8

'I WISH I HAD DONE MORE'

PATERNO OUSTED

Trustees fire legend; Bradley named interim coach | Spanier also out in wake of Sandusky scandal | Fans shocked, saddened over what led to Paterno's exit

MICHAEL KUBEL/MORNING CALL FILE PHOTO

Joe Paterno has coached his last game at Penn State. After 46 years at the helm, Paterno was fired Wednesday night by the school's board of trustees and replaced on an interim basis by assistant coach Tom Bradley.

BY MARK WOGENRICH
Of The Morning Call

Joe Paterno is no longer Penn State head football coach and Graham Spanier is out as university president, the university's board of trustees announced Wednesday night in its response to the child sex scandal that has overwhelmed the university and shocked the nation.

Paterno, who had coached 46 years at Penn State, was replaced on an interim basis by his assistant football coach Tom Bradley. Spanier's duties will be assumed temporarily by Rodney Erickson, Penn State provost.

The moves were made "in the best long-term interests of the university," said John P. Surma, vice chairman of the trustees.

Spanier's resignation had been widely expected, but Paterno's immediate removal came as a surprise to many in the university. Earlier in the day, Paterno said he would finish the season and then retire. Students were gathering late Wednesday in the Beaver Canyon in State College to protest Paterno's firing.

"This is a tragedy. It is one of the great sorrows of my life. With the benefit of hindsight, I wish I had done more."

— Joe Paterno, in a statement to the media Wednesday morning

Two national championships. The envied graduation rate of his players. The rigid focus on academics. All of that will be remembered, but the legacy of the man behind Happy Valley forever will be linked to the role Paterno played in the sex scandal.

Paterno built his legendary coaching career, a football program considered pristine and a university in central Pennsylvania from an initial desire to raise tuition for law school. On Wednesday, that career reached a stunning conclusion amid one of the most sordid legal and moral scandals in college sports history.

The Hall of Fame football coach who built the Penn State program on the principle of "Success with Honor" announced his retirement, four days after his former assistant Jerry Sandusky was charged with 40 counts of sexual abuse of children.

Paterno, who will turn 85 in December, said in a statement Wednesday night: "Right now, I'm not the football coach, and that's something I have to get used to."

He had intended to coach Saturday's game against Nebraska, but the trustees scuttled that plan. Paterno's dismissal concludes one of the swiftest and most important falls in sport.

Less than two weeks ago, Penn State defeated Illinois for Paterno's 409th career victory, a record among NCAA Division I football coaches. Following the game, Paterno accepted a plaque commemorating the moment from Spanier and then-athletic director Tim Curley.

Now Paterno is gone and Spanier is gone. And Curley has been on administrative leave since being charged with perjury in the Sandusky case.

Kevin Harley, a spokesman for Gov. Tom Corbett, said late Wednesday that the governor was not surprised by the university's action.

"The governor said [earlier Wednesday] that he wanted the Board of Trustees to act

Please see PATERNO NEWS 8

INSIDE NEWS

Ron Angle's strong support for selling Gracedale turned out to be his "Waterloo." An analysis of Angle's defeat in Tuesday's election, **News 5**

Herman Cain defended his character during Wednesday night's Republican presidential debate and again called sexual harassment accusations "false." **News 15**

Gov. Tom Corbett on Wednesday signed a bill that bans text-messaging and emailing while driving, **News 17**

'Unconditional support' undermined PSU president

Graham Spanier had backed pair of charged university administrators.

BY ANDREW MCGILL, MATT ASSAD AND DANIEL PATRICK SHEEHAN
Of The Morning Call

Bowing under the weight of an escalating child sex scandal that has engulfed Penn State, university President Graham Spanier stepped down late Wednesday.

Spanier's departure ends his 15-year stint at the helm of one of the nation's largest universities, and came hand-in-hand with the Penn State board of trustees' decision to sack Joe Paterno just hours after he announced his own retirement.

In a news conference with nearly the full board in attendance, trustee John P. Surma said his colleagues unanimously decided it was in the best long-term interests of the university to change leadership.

Spanier

"We handled it the best way we could," he said.

Spanier will be terminated on the terms of his contract, which Surma said will likely include some settlement agreement.

Executive Vice President and Provost Rodney Erickson will take over as interim president.

Unlike Paterno, who garnered the support of the student body, Spanier's exit seemed inevitable almost from the time it was learned that he was told about a 2002 incident in which former assistant football Jerry Sandusky sexually assaulted a 10-year-old box in a university locker room shower.

Spanier quickly offered "unconditional support" to two Penn State officials, athletic director Timothy Curley and Senior Vice President for Business and Finance Gary Schultz, who were charged with perjury and failure to report the alleged child

Please see SPANIER NEWS 11

MORE COVERAGE INSIDE

- Penn State fans, players shocked and saddened, **News 8**
- College football analysts Matt Millen and Kirk Herbstreit weigh in on Paterno's firing, **News 8**
- Keith Groller: Paterno's punishment has already been inflicted, **News 9**
- A timeline of Joe Paterno's career, **News 9**
- Public relations experts say Penn State had to clean house, **News 11**

CPSIA information can be obtained at www.ICGtesting.com
Printed in the USA
BVOW052218260812

298681BV00004B/1/P